Confederates from Canada

Confederates from Canada

*John Yates Beall and the Rebel Raids
on the Great Lakes*

RALPH LINDEMAN

McFarland & Company, Inc., Publishers
Jefferson, North Carolina

All maps were created by Christianna Kretschmann.

LIBRARY OF CONGRESS CATALOGUING-IN-PUBLICATION DATA

Names: Lindeman, Ralph, 1949– author.
Title: Confederates from Canada : John Yates Beall and the rebel raids on the Great Lakes /
Ralph Lindeman.
Other titles: John Yates Beall and the rebel raids on the Great Lakes
Description: Jefferson, North Carolina : McFarland & Company, Inc., 2023. | Includes bibliographical
references and index.
Identifiers: LCCN 2023039263 | ISBN 9781476692784 (paperback : acid free paper) ∞
ISBN 9781476651132 (ebook)
Subjects: LCSH: Beall, John Y. (John Yates), 1835–1865. | United States—History—Civil War, 1861–
1865—Underground movements. | United States—History—Civil War, 1861–1865—Commando
operations. | Johnson Island Prison. | Confederate States of America. Secret Service—Biography. |
Soldiers—Confederate States of America—Biography. | United States—History—Civil War, 1861–1865—
Great Lakes Region (North America) | Privateering—Confederate States of America.
Classification: LCC E470.95 .L563 2023 | DDC 973.7/36—dc23/eng/20230905
LC record available at https://lccn.loc.gov/2023039263

BRITISH LIBRARY CATALOGUING DATA ARE AVAILABLE

ISBN (print) 978-1-4766-9278-4
ISBN (ebook) 978-1-4766-5113-2

Front cover images: top Johnson's Island Military Prison (Alabama Department of Archives and
History); left ship Passenger ferry Philo Parsons (Historical Collections of the Great Lakes, Bowling
Green State University); right ship USS Michigan (Library of Congress, Prints & Photographs
Division,LC-DIG-det-4a05316); center image John Yates Beall (West Virginia and Regional History
Center, WVU Libraries); background Lake Erie Islands map by Christianna Kretschmann.

Printed in the United States of America

McFarland & Company, Inc., Publishers
Box 611, Jefferson, North Carolina 28640
www.mcfarlandpub.com

For my mother,
who instilled in me
at an early age
a love and respect
for writing, reading and learning,
and for my wife, Nancy,
who set a deadline

Table of Contents

Acknowledgments		ix
Preface		1
1.	The Prisoner	5
2.	The Island	10
3.	The Prison	18
4.	First Arrivals	24
5.	Rebels on the Island	28
6.	A Plan Emerges in Canada	34
7.	A Meeting in Richmond	40
8.	"Fire in the Rear"	44
9.	Pirates on Chesapeake Bay	52
10.	Life on the Island	62
11.	The Northwest Conspiracy Takes Shape	69
12.	Confederate Commissioners Head to Canada	77
13.	Battle Plans and Diplomacy	85
14.	A Gathering in Chicago	95
15.	Hard Times on the Island	102
16.	"I Seize This Boat and Take You as Prisoner"	109
17.	A Confederate Flag Flies on Lake Erie	117
18.	A Telegram from Detroit	122
19.	Chase and Escape	128
20.	Aftermath	134
21.	A Visitor to Montreal	141
22.	The Ill-Fated Voyage of the CSS *Georgian*	151
23.	A Train from Sandusky	159
24.	Behind Bars on Mulberry Street	166
25.	The Trial	169

Table of Contents

26. Cries for Mercy 179

27. The Execution 184

Epilogue 187
Chapter Notes 203
Bibliography 221
Index 227

Acknowledgments

While writing a book is most often a solitary pursuit, the process leading up to the actual writing and the period following the writing usually involve the help of many other people. I owe all those who helped me before and after the writing a heartfelt thank you.

My research could not have gotten underway without the help of Nan Card at the Rutherford B. Hayes Presidential Library in Fremont, Ohio. She located the files and rolled out carts piled high with the many boxes of materials the library had amassed about Johnson's Island and its time as a Civil War prison camp. Ron Davidson at the Sandusky Library was also helpful in providing historical information and newspaper files the library had collected about Johnson's Island. The late David Bush—a professor and the director of the Johnson's Island archeology project at Heidelberg University in Tiffin, Ohio—cheerfully showed me around his "dig" at the former prison site and opened his files to me at the university.

I also owe a debt of thanks to the staffs at the National Archives and Records Administration and the Library of Congress who aided me as I immersed myself in Civil War military records and other books, journals and newspapers of the period. Along these lines, I also want to thank the Internet Archive and Project Gutenberg for the work they have done in digitizing and placing on the web books, journals and other materials that are long out of print.

Several people also helped me by reading and commenting on my book—some as I pounded out each new chapter and others after I had a completed manuscript. From the start, my friend and former editor at Bloomberg/BNA, Toby McIntosh, provided invaluable assistance with his specific comments on my draft chapters and his broader visions about the book project overall. Another friend, Russell Canan, offered helpful comments on the chapters and also gave me advice based on his personal experience with books he has published. Barry Sheehy and Edward Steers, Jr., two distinguished authors of books that covered aspects of the Confederates in Canada, were kind enough to read my manuscript and offer valuable comments and insights. I also want to thank my other "reader-reviewers"—Tom Jernigan, Louise Jung, Pamela Martin and Lynne Franco.

I owe a big thank you to Jana Belsky who worked tirelessly to track down photographs of many of the book's main characters as well as the ships and boats that played major roles. And many thanks to my niece Christianna Kretschmann, who lent her excellent cartographic skills to the project, providing helpful maps.

I also want to thank the following friends and colleagues for their interest in the project and encouragement along the way: Carl Bogus, John Burgess and David Summers, as well as many others whose gentle but persistent queries of "how's the book going?" helped keep me focused.

Finally, I want to thank my wife Nancy Miller who gave me her loving support and encouragement—and patience—over the years I spent researching and writing about people and events of the nineteenth century. Her eyes were the first to see each new chapter after my own and she proposed worthwhile edits and other suggestions for the manuscript. She shared my joys and frustrations along the way and it is a better book because of her.

Preface

The American Civil War has been the subject of thousands of books covering various aspects of the conflict. And yet, I have found that many people—even some of those well-versed in the general history of the war—are surprised to learn that there were Confederate agents in Canada, scheming to launch attacks in several northern states, with the goal of changing the course of the war. This book tells the story of an effort by Confederate agents to initiate commando-style attacks around the Great Lakes states, including Ohio, Illinois, New York, and other northern states with the goal of inflaming already-growing anti-war sentiment and defeating Lincoln in the 1864 presidential election. Their hope was that by replacing Abraham Lincoln with a Democrat in the White House, the North would be willing to enter settlement negotiations with the South. A key part of this clandestine effort was a raid by Confederate agents from Canada in September 1864 to free rebels held in a Union Army prison located in Ohio on a small island in Lake Erie.

Although I have had a longtime interest in the Civil War, I only came upon information about this Confederate raid in recent years. During my youth, our extended Lindeman family gathered for reunions, staying at summer cottages in a small community named Lakeside on the shores of Lake Erie near Sandusky, Ohio. Lakeside is located only a few miles from Johnson's Island, the site of the prison camp that held captured Confederate officers. I remember visiting Johnson's Island as a child and seeing the tall statue of a Confederate soldier standing in front of a cemetery containing the graves of Confederates who had died at the prison. The prison structures had long since been dismantled. It was only many years later that I learned more about Johnson's Island and its connection to the Confederate raids from Canada.

I had often thought of writing a history of Johnson's Island, focusing on its time as a Civil War prison camp. As I approached retirement, I spent several long afternoons at the Library of Congress looking over books and journals with information about the history of the island. In the materials I reviewed, there were a few references to an attempted raid on the island by Confederates in 1864. But the information was not detailed or well-documented. The few accounts of the raid I did find failed to provide much context or explain how it fit into the overall objectives of the Confederacy in the war. I decided to make this raid the subject of my book. As

I began my research, there were many questions that remained unanswered. Who conducted the raid? Why did it originate in Canada? What was the raid's objective? Why did it fall short of success? And how did it relate to the South's overall goals in the war? Finding answers to these and other questions became my challenge as I began my research for the book.

As I pursued information about particular aspects of the raid, I often would come across other historical threads that became important parts of the story. For example, in addition to releasing Confederate prisoners of war, I discovered there were tactical reasons why Confederate officials wanted to attack the Johnson's Island prison camp. The state of Ohio was a hotbed of anti-war sentiment in late 1864 when the raid took place. After three years of war, citizens in Ohio and other northern states were frustrated with the Lincoln administration's lack of progress in bringing the conflict to an end. Opposition to the war had grown so strong that leaders of the Confederacy believed that, by expanding the war into northern states with violent raids and attacks, citizens in those states would respond by voting for peace at the ballot box in the 1864 election, leading to Lincoln's defeat.

I began digging into the history and background of those opposing the war, who were led by a group of anti-war Democrats known as Copperheads. Confederate leaders expected—or at least hoped—that their raids also would spark a militant response by a "citizens' army" of Copperheads residing in several northern states which would rise up and unseat local governmental officials. How was it that Confederate officials in Canada and Richmond came to hold such exaggerated expectations about their ability to foment insurrection in the northern states?

I also discovered that the attempted raid on Johnson's Island was only a part of a broader Confederate plan. That plan originally targeted the political convention of the Democratic party in Chicago, which was held in August 1864, as the starting point for a widespread uprising of Copperheads in the northern states. Why the Chicago attack failed and how the Johnson's Island raid became the fallback plan also became an important part of the story.

I also learned the Confederate activities originating in Canada had an impact on diplomatic relations between the United States and Great Britain, which was officially neutral during the Civil War. As frustration grew among Union Army commanders over the series of Confederate raids and raid attempts, my research showed they came close to sending Union troops in pursuit of the raiders across the border into Canada, a British territory at the time. How these diplomatic tensions between the U.S. and Great Britain played out became another key part of the story.

The raid on Johnson's Island was led by a wealthy Confederate soldier-turned-agent from Virginia named John Yates Beall, whose activities during the war serve as a narrative thread to connect the larger issues and subjects covered in the book. What motivated this young, plantation-born Virginian to become such a committed rebel agent, even after a serious injury early in the war cut short his service in the Confederate Army? While writings and other records from Beall himself are sparse, I used excerpts from a diary Beall kept—sporadically—as well as first-hand accounts of other rebel agents who worked with Beall to piece together what I believe is a reasonably accurate portrayal of the Confederate leader and the convictions that inspired him.

As I pursued information about Beall, I also came across tantalizing hints of a connection between Beall and Lincoln's assassin, John Wilkes Booth. They likely first encountered each other as militia members just before the Civil War began in 1859 at the hanging of John Brown, the abolitionist who led the raid at Harpers Ferry. And the record shows Beall and Booth were in Canada at around the same time in the fall of 1864 when the initial plots against Lincoln began. Was there any real connection between the two men? And, most importantly, how accurate were the rumors that arose immediately after the assassination—that Booth's killing of Lincoln was motivated in part by Lincoln's refusal to commute Beall's death sentence after he was convicted as a spy?

Using contemporary newspaper accounts, diaries, records from the Union and Confederate armies and navies and trial transcripts, I have attempted to present a factual, thoroughly-sourced—and rollicking—tale of the Confederate raiders from Canada. The story presented in this book is my best effort to put together the first comprehensive account of the Beall raid on Lake Erie and the major issues and events that surrounded it during the Civil War.

CHAPTER 1

The Prisoner

New York Harbor—February 24, 1865

A reporter for *The New York Times* stood near Battery Park on lower Manhattan as a fresh breeze swept across the waters of New York Harbor. He looked south over the channel to Governors Island about a half mile away, the site of a Union Army fort.

Fort Columbus, the largest military fortification in New York City, had served as a granite and brick sentinel guarding the harbor since 1796. The fort sat on the northern end of Governors Island, a 172-acre, tree-covered site, which in 1623 had been the location of the first Dutch settlement in New York.[1]

On the southern side of the massive fort, the reporter noted new construction. The dark outline of a wooden gallows was clearly visible against the bright blue sky, with its "dangling rope, swaying in the fresh sea breeze."[2]

Shortly after the Civil War broke out in April 1861, the Union Army had converted most of the fort's barracks into prison cells to house captured Confederate military. Unlike other Union prisons holding captured Confederates, Fort Columbus held relatively few at any one time. In September 1864, 301 prisoners were imprisoned at Fort Columbus. But by February 1865, just two months before Confederate General Robert E. Lee would surrender at Appomattox, the population of the barracks had dropped to 152 inmates.[3]

One of those inmates was a thirty-year-old Virginian named John Yates Beall, who sat in a double-walled cell located in the basement of the east barrack. In his dark chamber lit by a single oil lamp, Beall had spent hours in recent days reading a Bible given to him by one of the prison guards.

A military commission had heard Beall's case a few weeks earlier and had recently issued its verdict. The commission had convicted Beall as a "spy and guerrilla" for aiding the Confederacy. He was sentenced "to be hanged by the neck until dead."[4]

Of medium height, with piercing hazel eyes, brown hair and a mustache with goatee, Beall was an unlikely "spy and guerrilla." He was born in 1835 to wealthy, plantation-owning parents near Charles Town, Virginia (later to become West Virginia). The family plantation, Walnut Grove, was located just outside Charles Town.

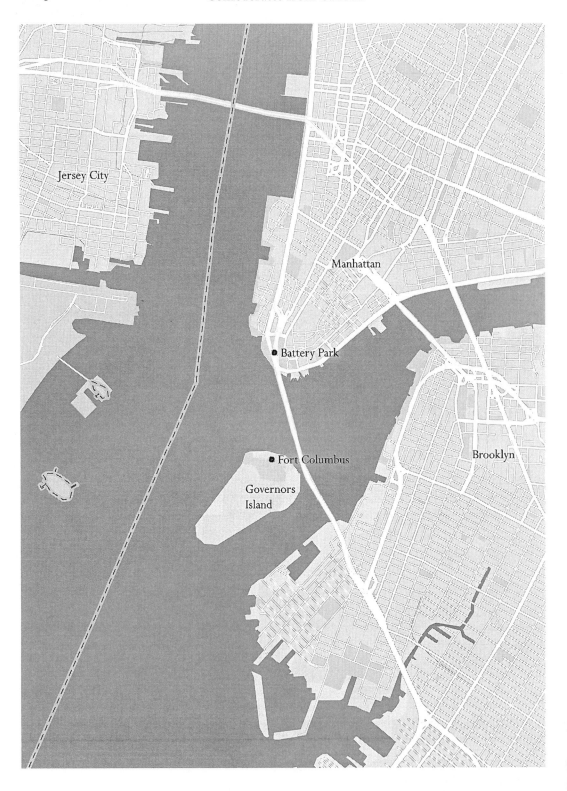

New York Harbor.

Governors Island, Fort Columbus, New York Harbor (Library of Congress, Prints & Photographs Division, HABS NY-4-6).

Like most other Virginia plantations, it had a group of slaves which ranged in number from about fifty to twenty by the time the war began.[5]

Growing up in a family of nine, Beall had an older brother and a younger brother, along with four sisters. The Beall family had deep roots in Jefferson County. Hezekiah Beall, John Yates Beall's paternal grandfather, was one of the earliest settlers in the valley.[6]

Indeed, the Beall family had taken root in America before the nation's founding. A Beall ancestor, the Scottish-born Ninian Beall, arrived in America in 1650 after being captured and then exiled by Oliver Cromwell's army during the English civil wars. He settled in what was then Maryland and at one time held title to some 25,000 acres, including what later became much of Georgetown, now part of Washington, D.C.[7]

On his mother's side, Beall's maternal grandfather, John Yates, emigrated to Jefferson County from England in 1792 when he was thirteen, coming to live with an uncle, Charles Yates, who was one of the area's largest landholders. Beall became close to his grandfather who, as he approached the end of his life in 1851, decided to return to England to visit relatives. He requested that his grandson John, then just sixteen, accompany him on the trip, giving the teenaged Beall an early perspective on the world beyond Jefferson County, Virginia.[8]

Beall attended the University of Virginia and studied law. While Beall "was entirely unambitious of college distinctions," he "was profoundly interested in law and political economy," according to his college roommate and boyhood friend, Daniel Lucas, who later wrote a "memoir" of Beall's life. Within the narrow circle of his intimate friends, Lucas wrote, Beall "was much beloved, and recognized as a character as generous and fearless as he was modest, reticent, and retiring."[9]

While he had studied law, Beall never practiced. As Lucas wrote, "nor is it certain that he ever valued his legal attainments in any other light than as the proper accomplishment of every gentleman and scholar—an essential part of liberal and polite education."[10]

Beall had started the war as a volunteer in the Confederate infantry but, after a bullet from a Union rifle nearly killed him, he left active service and continued to aid the Confederate cause in other ways. Still in his twenties, Beall possessed a calm determination and assurance that won the admiration of the men he led. "John Y. Beall was a most extraordinary man," wrote one of his associates. "He was well educated, manly, brave and had the faculty of at once commanding the respect and confidence of all of any age who came in contact with him."[11]

The events on Lake Erie five months earlier, in September 1864, were now just a memory for Beall as he remained behind bars. His capture of the passenger ferry *Philo Parsons* had been the first act in a planned commando-like operation targeting a prison for Confederate officers located on a small island in Lake Erie.

The raid and the chaos that was to follow in cities along the shores of the Great Lakes—Buffalo, Cleveland, Detroit, Chicago and Milwaukee—were intended to inflame the growing anti-war passions in the northern states at the time. Confederate officials hoped the resulting uproar might lead to Lincoln's defeat in the November 1864 election, potentially changing the course of the war.

If the Democratic candidate, former Union General George B. McClellan, were to win the White House, it was widely believed that anti-war Democrats would force a cease-fire and enter into settlement negotiations with the Confederacy. Or at least that was the hope among Confederate officials in Richmond, Virginia.

In convicting Beall as a spy and guerrilla, the six-member Union Army military commission focused on the fact that Beall—and the twenty other similarly-dressed raiders who were with him—were not in military uniform when they commandeered the *Philo Parsons* and another passenger ferry. The military tribunal gave little weight to the fact that in 1863 the Confederate Navy had commissioned Beall as an Acting Master, equivalent to a lieutenant in the modern Navy.

But that was all in the past and, on this Friday, February 24, 1865, guards would come in a few hours to escort Beall to his death. Beall's calm demeanor made an impression on those who saw him in his final hours. A minister described him "as much at ease as if he were in his own parlour…. There was no bravado, no strained heroism, no excitement in his words or manner, but a quiet trust in God, and a composure in view of death, such as I had read of, but never beheld to the same degree before."[12]

He added, "[Beall] introduced the subject of his approaching end himself, saying that, while he did not pretend to be indifferent to life, the mode in which he was to leave it had no terror or ignominy for him, he could go to heaven … as well from the gallows as from the battlefield, or his own bed."[13]

John Yates Beall (West Virginia and Regional History Center, WVU Libraries).

Along with reading the Bible, in the days before his execution, Beall—sitting at a small wooden table—had penned farewell letters to his friends and relatives.

"Remember me kindly to my friends," he wrote to his younger brother Will. "Say to them I am not aware of committing any crime against society. I die for my country. No thirst for blood or lucre animated me in my course; for I had refused, when solicited, to engage in enterprises which I deemed destructive, but illegitimate."[14]

In the hours before his death, Beall sat in his cell with James McClure and Albert Ritchie, two old friends from the University of Virginia who had been allowed to visit. "This time was spent in calm, quiet, pleasant conversation," Ritchie, a Baltimore lawyer, later wrote. "Old friends were inquired after … old scenes recalled."[15]

Beall spoke of his approaching death and gave directions for the disposition of his body, which he asked not to be returned to Charles Town until after the war ended. He also dictated his epitaph: "[He] died in defense of his country."[16] He also arranged for his diaries and prayer book to be sent to his betrothed, Martha O'Bryan, a twenty-nine-year-old schoolteacher Beall had met three years earlier. "This will surprise my mother because she does not know I am engaged," Beall said.[17]

Beall had one more task to attend to. He expressed a desire to have his photograph taken. The resulting image shows Beall dressed in a dark linen suit, a vest, and a black silk cravat tied beneath a white shirt collar. His gaze is directly into the camera, a look of calm determination on his face.

At twelve noon, guards delivered Beall's last meal. The platter came out a short while later almost untouched. At half past twelve, a military detail arrived at Beall's cell. They found him alone, sitting quietly in his chair, gazing toward the floor, apparently deep in thought. They did not have to explain why they were there. He addressed them with a smile, saying, "I am ready, gentlemen."[18]

CHAPTER 2

The Island

Sandusky, Ohio—First Week in October 1861

A tall man with a long, graying beard made his way down the dock to the passenger steamer *Island Queen*, about to set sail from Sandusky, Ohio, for a pleasure cruise around the Lake Erie Islands.

He was William Hoffman, a fifty-four-year-old Lieutenant Colonel in the Union Army. Hoffman was no ordinary tourist. Unlike the thirty other passengers aboard the *Island Queen*, Hoffman had a mission. He was looking for an island suitable to establish a military prison for Confederate soldiers.

Hoffman had recently been named the Union Army's Commissary-General of Prisoners and would be responsible for the care and treatment of Confederate prisoners of war. A graduate of the West Point class of 1829, Hoffman was a veteran of the Mexican-American War as well as the Indian Wars in Illinois and Florida.

Just nine months earlier, before the war began, Hoffman had had his own brief experience as a military prisoner. Stationed in San Antonio, Texas, when that state joined the Confederacy in February 1861, he was taken prisoner when the Union Army commander in San Antonio surrendered federal property to Texas authorities.[1]

But Hoffman was soon paroled and sent back to the Union Army in a prisoner exchange. The terms of his release said that he would no longer be able to take up arms against the South, which likely played a part in his being appointed Commissary-General of Prisoners, a position that would keep him far from the battlefield.[2]

The war was now a little more than six months old. Troops on both sides were still being recruited and trained. In July, Union Army and Confederate forces had clashed in the first major battle of the war at Bull Run, Virginia (also known as Manassas), about thirty miles south of Washington, D.C. Smaller battles and skirmishes had flared in Missouri, North Carolina, and Western Virginia since then.

Already, however, there were increasing signs that the war would be bloodier and more protracted than originally anticipated by either side. A longer war would mean more casualties—and prisoners.

Hoffman was in Sandusky on orders from Montgomery C. Meigs, another

General William Hoffman (Library of Congress, Prints & Photographs Division, DIG-cwpb-03953).

career military officer who, as Quartermaster-General of the Union Army, was the senior official responsible for logistics and supplies.

Meigs, known for his consummate planning abilities, had already determined that the Union Army would need one or more new facilities specifically designed to confine prisoners of war. On July 12, he wrote to Secretary of War Simon Cameron, "It is to be expected that the United States will have to take care of large numbers of prisoners of war."[3]

At this early point in the conflict, neither side yet had a coherent policy or method for incarcerating captured prisoners. In Richmond, the Confederates were holding captured Union Army prisoners in a converted tobacco warehouse that later became known as Libby Prison.[4]

In the North, the Union Army had been making do with a few makeshift military prisons at military installations such as Camp Chase in Columbus, Ohio; the Rock Island Arsenal in Illinois and Fort Columbus in New York. In St. Louis, a mix of Confederate soldiers and citizens accused of disloyalty to the Union were held in a converted medical college and a deserted slave pen. Other captured Confederates were being held in local jails and penitentiaries.[5]

Meigs, a Georgia-born West Point graduate, already had an idea of where to construct the new military prison. Earlier in his military career, he had spent time in Detroit, Michigan, as an officer with the Army Corps of Engineers.

During the 1840s, Meigs had supervised the construction of Fort Wayne on the Detroit River, one of several fortifications on the nation's northern tier intended to thwart a potential British invasion from Canada which, in the 1840s, was still deemed a threat. During this time, Meigs likely became familiar with the four sparsely-populated islands located on Lake Erie, clustered about fifty miles southeast of Detroit. Far from the scenes of battle and located within Ohio's borders, the islands were flanked by three other stalwart Union states—Michigan, Pennsylvania, and New York. To the north was Canada.

In July, Meigs had recommended to War Secretary Cameron that one of the Lake Erie islands be considered "as a depot and place of confinement for prisoners of war."[6]

By early October, Meigs had received Cameron's approval and ordered Hoffman to travel to Sandusky, a port town on the shores of Lake Erie, which was only a short boat ride away from the islands. Located on a bay about halfway between Cleveland and Toledo, Sandusky in 1861 was a city of about 8,000 residents. Because of its location on the lake, the city had become a railroad and shipping hub.

The city possessed what was considered to be the best natural harbor on Lake Erie. Indeed, until the 1820s, it was widely expected that Sandusky was destined to become Ohio's leading port city, overshadowing Toledo and Cleveland. The city's residents were still angry over a decision by the Ohio legislature—said to be well-greased by kickbacks—that diverted a planned canal north from the Ohio river to Cleveland instead of Sandusky. The corrupt bargain led to Cleveland's development as Ohio's leading Lake Erie port, inhibiting Sandusky's future growth.[7]

At this early point in the war, Sandusky displayed few tangible signs of the conflict. Even so, news of the battles made its way into the pages of the city's newspaper, the *Daily Commercial Register.*

During the week that Hoffman arrived in town, the newspaper's front page contained an appeal titled "To Arms, Ye Brave," asking for recruits to join the 55th Regiment of Ohio, headquartered in nearby Norwalk. Privates in the regiment were promised thirteen dollars a month, along with "abundant and wholesome food, and ample clothing." Those serving for at least two years would also receive a one hundred dollar bounty, with "the prospect" of receiving 160 acres of land.[8]

Also appearing in the *Daily Commercial Register*'s pages was a request for blankets for the Third Cavalry Regiment in Monroeville, a town about twenty-four miles to the south. "Will not the good people of Sandusky send an avalanche [of blankets] down upon them tonight?" the notice asked.[9]

Brick and stone commercial buildings lined Sandusky's Water Street, so named because it fronted on the lake. The town's commercial docks were located a few steps away, at the foot of Columbus Avenue, which ran perpendicular to Water Street. It was from these docks that the *Island Queen* would sail and take Hoffman to four islands—North Bass, Middle Bass, South Bass and Kelleys. The islands—each several miles across, mostly forested, with a few farms and rocky shorelines—were located just north of Sandusky and south of the Canadian border, which bisected the lake.

Trips on the *Island Queen*, a 110-foot side-wheel steamer, were a popular diversion for tourists and church groups from Toledo and Cleveland. The boat left the Columbus Avenue dock at 3 p.m. daily and ferried passengers and freight between Sandusky and the islands.[10]

Aboard the *Island Queen*, Hoffman had a chance to examine North Bass and Middle Bass islands, spending the night at South Bass island. The next day, he rejoined the lake steamer and proceeded to Kelleys Island where he spent another day.

After two days, Hoffman returned to Sandusky having made little progress with respect to his military mission. He had concluded that none of the four islands he had visited were well-suited for a military prison camp.

North Bass, the northernmost of the four islands, had "sufficient cleared ground," Hoffman found, but he determined that its location—a little more than a mile from Canadian waters—could encourage escape attempts over the ice in winter.[11]

Moreover, the island's inhabitants were not willing "to give up their farms for any reasonable rent … as they have made their homes there," Hoffman wrote in his report to the Army's senior command.[12]

Middle Bass Island had many of the same drawbacks as North Bass, Hoffman concluded, along with a lack of cleared ground.

Hoffman had spent a night on South Bass Island, which contained the sheltered

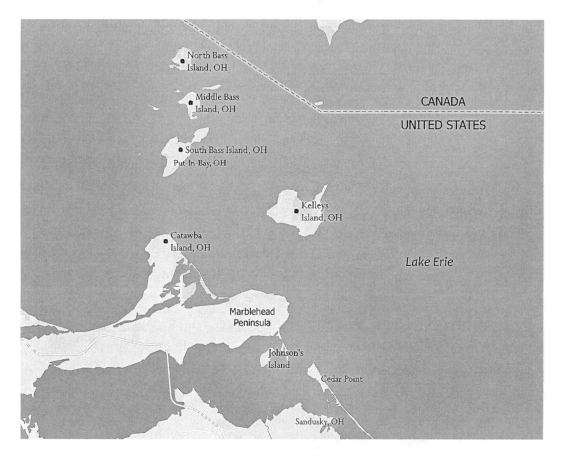

Lake Erie Islands.

port town of Put-in-Bay. The island was near the location on Lake Erie where Commodore Oliver Hazard Perry had defeated the British Navy nearly fifty years earlier during the War of 1812. While South Bass Island had several possible sites for a
prison, its location—about twenty miles northwest of Sandusky—made it "too far
distant," Hoffman reported.[13]

In particular, Hoffman was concerned there would not be enough time to build
a prison before the snow and ice of winter arrived, citing the likelihood that much of
the lake would be frozen by the first week in December.

Hoffman also spent a day on Kelleys Island, the largest of the four islands on the
Island Queen's itinerary. He ruled out this island as well, but for a different reason.
Supporting about a hundred families, Kelleys Island contained several vineyards
along with a "brandy establishment" which, Hoffman figured, "would be too great a
temptation" for the guards at the prison.[14]

There was one other island that Hoffman surveyed during his Ohio visit. It
was easily seen from the Sandusky harbor and Hoffman had passed it at least twice
during his trip on the *Island Queen*. It was called Johnson's Island, named after its
current owner, Leonard B. Johnson.

Island Queen (Historical Collections of the Great Lakes, Bowling Green State University).

The island was located not in the open waters of Lake Erie but in sheltered San-dusky Bay, about three miles north of the town and just short of a mile south of the Marblehead Peninsula, which helped form the bay. About a mile long and a half-mile wide, the three-hundred-acre island was undeveloped and mostly forested.[15]

Johnson's Island had several advantages that, taken together, made it "decid-edly the best location for a depot that I have seen," Hoffman reported in his recom-mendation to Meigs, sent on October 22.[16] The island's proximity to Sandusky would facilitate construction of the prison and aid in supplying it, Hoffman noted. More-over, if prisoners escaped, "the neighborhood could be put on the lookout for them by the discharging of a cannon and their recapture would be almost certain," Hoff-man wrote.[17]

Leonard Johnson was willing to lease half the island to the Union Army for five hundred dollars a year, Hoffman reported, adding that fallen timber on the other half of the island could be used as fuel. By leasing half the island, Union officials would be able to assert effective control over the entire island, Hoffman wrote, guar-anteeing that "no person would be permitted to land on it except by permission."[18]

Union officials lost little time in approving Hoffman's recommendation. On October 26, 1861, Quartermaster-General Meigs notified Hoffman that he should "proceed at once" to construct a prison on Johnson's Island.[19]

* * * * *

Also, during that same week in October, a twenty-six-year-old John Yates Beall was back in Charles Town, Virginia, on leave from his service as a private in the Confederate Army.

Two years before the war began, Beall had joined a local militia unit in Charles Town. During that time, Beall's most significant duty as a private in the militia had been maintaining order at a public hanging.

On December 2, 1859, Beall's militia unit, known as the "Botts Greys" (with Lawson Botts commanding), had been one of two militia units on special guard duty when the radical abolitionist John Brown was hanged at Charles Town's county jail.

In October 1859, Brown and eighteen supporters had temporarily seized control of the federal armory at Harpers Ferry, Virginia (now West Virginia), in an unsuccessful attempt to provoke an insurrection among slaves in Virginia. After Brown's capture by U.S. Army troops under the command of then–Colonel Robert E. Lee, he was convicted of treason and sentenced to death.

Another militia unit on guard duty in Harpers Ferry at the time of Brown's hanging was known as the "Richmond Grays." Its members had come to Charles Town by train two weeks earlier. Joining the unit just before it left Richmond was a twenty-one-year-old civilian, wearing borrowed military clothing, named John Wilkes Booth. The young man had pleaded with privates on one of the train cars to allow him onboard, saying that it was important to him to attend the hanging of the abolitionist Brown.[20]

Beall and Booth likely encountered each other that day, according to a biography by a Beall relative, as Beall spent part of his time selling produce from his family's plantation to militia members. It is also possible Beall and Booth had a chance to "rub elbows" at the home of Beall's aunt Louisa, who offered her home as a place to stay for some of the Richmond Grays.[21]

Shortly after the war began, Beall's unit, the Botts Greys, was merged into the Confederate Army regiments that became known as the Stonewall Brigade following the battle of Bull Run (known as First Manassas in the South) in July 1861.

Beall had missed the battle of Bull Run much "to his regret and embarrassment," according to Beall's biographer.[22] Beall had been home on an earlier furlough at the time. The battle was an early Confederate victory over poorly trained Union troops. It was also the battle in which Confederate General Thomas Jackson earned the nickname of "Stonewall," after turning back a charge by Union troops.

Now, while Hoffman sailed around the Lake Erie islands on the *Island Queen*, Beall was furloughed a second time so he could accompany an ailing member of his unit back to Charles Town.

On October 16, 1861, news spread through the town that several hundred Union troops were attempting to cross from Maryland into Virginia near Harpers Ferry on the Potomac River just a few miles away. The Union troops' objective was to capture a flour mill and wheat storehouse kept by the Confederates near Bolivar Heights, a plateau overlooking Harpers Ferry.

That area of Virginia was under the command of Lieutenant Colonel Turner Ashby in the 7th Virginia Cavalry, who was responsible for guarding the state's northern border, an area stretching from Harpers Ferry on the west to Point of Rocks, Maryland, on the east.

Beall was determined not to miss action a second time and, although it was not his assigned unit, he rushed to join the Confederate force under Ashby's command. Ashby's troops were hardly a well-trained fighting force. Comprised of a couple hundred raw recruits, they also included "a motley crowd of farmers, mechanics, cowboys and other civilians" who were "not remarkably well drilled."[23]

Arriving at the scene of battle, Beall quickly volunteered to lead a charge against a handful of Union troops who were firing from inside a deserted brick house. As he advanced, a Union bullet ripped into his chest, broke three ribs, and pierced his right lung.[24]

In what became known as the Battle of Bolivar Heights, Union troops ultimately forced the poorly-trained Confederates to withdraw. One of Beall's Charles Town neighbors, Dr. Andrew Hunter, had taken his wagon out to watch the battle and serve as an ambulance driver, if needed.[25]

After the battle ended, Hunter saw the wounded Beall lying in a heap on the ground and transported him back to his family home in Charles Town a few miles away. Beall's wounds from the battle and his prolonged recovery, would play a key role in the actions he took on behalf of the Confederacy for the rest of the war.

CHAPTER 3

The Prison

Sandusky, Ohio—November 1861–March 1862

After senior Union Army officials had approved his recommendation for the Johnson's Island prison, William Hoffman, the Commissary-General, faced a challenge: No one in the United States had ever designed a prison specifically to house prisoners of war. The prison on Johnson's Island would be the first and, as it turned out, the only newly-constructed prisoner of war camp during the Civil War.[1]

As Hoffman began the task of planning the prison, he drew on his past. He had grown up in a military family, moving across the country and living in Army garrisons for most of his youth as his father, also a lieutenant colonel, took new assignments at Army posts on the nation's western frontier.

Moreover, in his thirty years as a commissioned officer, Hoffman had spent years living in military garrisons and had experience building military outposts, including one in Florida during the Seminole War, a fort in Kansas on the Santa Fe Trail, and Fort Bridger in Wyoming.[2]

When it came time to design a prison for Johnson's Island, it was no surprise that Hoffman modeled the prison on a military fort. In this case, however, the building's security features were essentially reversed from those of a fort. They were aimed inward to prevent prisoners from escaping instead of outward to fend off external attacks. For example, elevated walkways for guards would be placed on the outside of the stockade fence surrounding the prison.[3]

In a dispatch to Montgomery Meigs, the Quartermaster General, Hoffman estimated that the prison complex could be built for about $26,000[4] (equivalent to about $660,000 today).

The prison site was on forty acres of already-cleared ground on the south side of the island facing the city of Sandusky, three miles away across the bay.[5] The city's docks, commercial buildings, and church steeples were visible through the trees and brush near the Johnson's Island prison site.

Hoffman's original design called for a prison to accommodate Confederate prisoners, including both officers and enlisted men. They would be housed inside a stockade fence fifteen feet high. Four blockhouses, each two stories, would be constructed near the main gate for officers. Four more blockhouses, further inside the

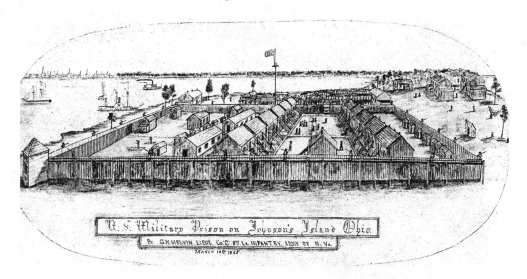

Johnson's Island Military Prison (Alabama Department of Archives and History).

stockade, would house enlisted men.[6] Each of the blockhouses for officers, which included twenty-two separate rooms, could hold about 256 men.[7] The four block-houses for enlisted men, with only three large rooms per floor, could house over three hundred prisoners each.[8] Eventually, the prison would be expanded to include five more blockhouses for enlisted men.[9]

Each prisoner blockhouse contained at least two large mess rooms, with cooking and heating stoves. Bunk beds, tables and benches were also provided.[10] More than forty buildings stood outside the stockade, including two more blockhouses for prison guards, a hospital, storehouse, bakery, barber shop, carpenter shop, horse stable and hay barn.[11]

Hoffman's overall prison design reflected the view that captured soldiers were not criminals.[12] The prison complex would provide for incarceration in open barracks, allowing prisoners to converse easily and interact. In addition, a large prison yard would provide space for prisoners to engage in outdoor activities during the day. There would be no constant surveillance of their activities.

By mid–November, a construction contract had been awarded to local builders William T. West and Philander Gregg.[13] West, a prominent Sandusky figure, was also a co-owner of the West House Hotel, one of the largest hotels in the state of Ohio.[14] The hotel, located on Water Street across from the Sandusky docks, would play a role in the events involving Confederate raiders that took place three years later.

With winter closing in, preparations were made to haul most of the building materials across Sandusky Bay onto Johnson's Island as soon as possible. Much of the island was heavily wooded, reducing the amount of lumber that needed to be transported across the bay. Hoffman had initially hoped to have construction completed by the end of 1861. But with uncertainties about the winter weather, he set a completion date of February 1, 1862.[15]

Although as Commissary-General Hoffman was responsible for Confederate prisoners throughout the Union, his attention during the winter of 1861–1862 seems to have been focused almost entirely on construction of the Johnson's Island prison complex.

Hoffman's attention to detail was well-known throughout the military ranks. According to one authority: "He was a stern disciplinarian, who seemed to have memorized the Army Regulations. Concerned with the most minute formalities of military conduct and proper protocol, he expected precision and perfection in the reports, returns, records, and rolls of his subalterns."[16]

This aspect of his character, while valued among his superior officers, was considered to be excessive among many of the enlisted men under his command. They commonly referred to him as "Old Huffy."[17]

These traits came through in many of his Army dispatches during this period. On November 10, "Old Huffy" wrote to the commander of the Union Army Arsenal at Allegheny, Pennsylvania, notifying him that, as part of the construction of the Johnson's Island prison, he intended to position a short-barreled cannon at each of the blockhouses used as guard quarters.

The cannons would be mounted on carriages, allowing for easier movement, Hoffman explained in the dispatch. "Will you be kind enough to give me the dimensions of such a carriage with a little plan of it, if it is not too much trouble?" he asked the arsenal commander, in an attempt to ensure that his design for the blockhouses could accommodate the cannon carriages.[18]

Meanwhile, as Hoffman focused on construction and design details, the attention of his superiors turned to staffing. On October 29, Secretary of War Cameron wrote to Ohio Governor William Dennison, asking him to raise "a select company of volunteers" for guard duty at the prison.[19] Dennison replied, saying he would "cheerfully comply" with Cameron's request and recommended that the new guard corps be named the "Hoffman Battalion."[20]

On December 28, Hoffman appointed William S. Pierson to be commander of what was then known as the Johnson's Island Prison Depot.[21] Pierson, a thirty-six-year-old Sandusky native, was a local businessman who had once served as mayor of the city. A Yale graduate, he had also practiced law briefly in New York City.[22]

With no military experience, Pierson's main qualification seemed to be his availability.[23] Hoffman was resigned to taking on Pierson as the prison commander, largely because more qualified candidates who had military experience were needed on the fields of battle.[24]

On January 1, 1862, an advertisement appeared in the Sandusky *Daily Commercial Register,* announcing that men who enlisted for service in the Hoffman Battalion would receive a $100 bounty. "Men enlisted to garrison [duty] … on Johnson's Island receive the above bounty in addition to good pay, excellent quarters and abundant rations," the ad stated. Enlistees were also required to "be of good height, and between the ages of twenty and forty."[25]

By late January, construction of the prison buildings was complete, meeting Hoffman's deadline. The on-time completion was due, in part, to the "unusually favorable" weather during the winter of 1861–1862, according to William T. West, the project's lead contractor.[26]

Although construction was completed, a few more details needed to be addressed before the prison was ready to open its gates to prisoners. On February 24, Hoffman wrote to Meigs, the Quartermaster-General, telling him that the prison's guard force, then numbering only a few dozen, was still in need of training.[27]

In addition, Hoffman noted that the revolvers he had ordered for guards had not yet arrived. Moreover, the winter's accumulation of ice in Sandusky Bay was just starting to break up. Once the ice cleared, Hoffman wrote, the prison would be able to receive "a limited number of prisoners, say 500 to 600."[28]

By the time Hoffman sent this dispatch to Meigs, however, events on the battlefield had already "rendered the depot at Johnson's Island obsolete," as one historian put it.[29]

The events on the battlefield took place near the Tennessee-Kentucky border on February 15, 1862, when—after three days of battle—a newly-appointed Brigadier General in the Union Army demanded that Confederates surrender Fort Donelson on the banks of the Cumberland River in Tennessee. The general, Ulysses S. Grant, told the Confederates he would accept nothing less than "unconditional and immediate surrender."[30]

A day later, Confederate General Simon B. Buckner accepted what he called the "ungenerous and unchivalrous" surrender terms delivered by Grant and surrendered more than 12,000 Confederate troops to the Union Army.[31] At this point, the prison on Johnson's Island was designed to hold about 1,280 prisoners.[32]

* * * * *

During the period that the Johnson's Island prisoner depot was under construction, Beall spent several weeks recuperating at his family's home near Charles Town, Virginia, following his injury in the battle of Bolivar Heights in October 1861. At that point in the war, both Union and Confederate troops were crisscrossing the landscape near Charles Town and Harpers Ferry almost constantly. Between August 1861 and February 1862, control of Harpers Ferry shifted between Union and Confederate forces four times.[33]

Beall's family physician recommended he travel south—far below the battle lines in Virginia—to minimize the possibility of being caught up in army skirmishes and to find warmer temperatures where he could improve his chances of recovery.[34]

In late November 1861 Beall—still weak but with his condition improved enough to travel—journeyed by horse and rail to Tallahassee, Florida. There he met Robert Williams, a wealthy owner of a cotton plantation near the Georgia-Florida border.[35]

Williams, a lawyer and one of the early settlers of Tallahassee, also owned a second plantation near Pascagoula Island, a barrier island off the coast of Louisiana. Williams and his wife Susan soon developed a strong attachment to Beall, and they invited him to accompany them on a visit to their Louisiana property. It was there that Beall first met the woman he intended to marry.[36]

Martha O'Bryan, a cousin of Susan Williams, was a twenty-six-year-old school-teacher from Nashville. About medium height, with a penetrating gaze, she wore her brown hair pulled back in a bun. Martha and her older sister, Fannie, had fled their home in Nashville as Federal troops marched into central Tennessee late in 1861. Invited by Susan and Robert Williams to stay at their estate on Pascagoula Island, the two sisters were already comfortably settled there when Beall arrived.[37]

Beall and Martha O'Bryan spent long days in each other's company on the barrier island, enjoying their mutual respite from the war. Beall eventually asked Martha to marry him. She accepted but told him they would have to wait until the war was over for their wedding, noting that the war made things too unsettled in both of their lives.[38]

By March 1862, Beall decided he had gained enough strength to return to Virginia where he hoped to rejoin his army unit. Promising they would stay in touch by writing, he and Martha said their farewells.[39]

When Beall arrived back in his home state, however, he found that Charles Town was occupied by Union troops. Union General Nathanial P. Banks was using the area as his base of operations to fight Stonewall Jackson in the Shenandoah Valley Campaign.[40] Beall then decided to abandon his thoughts of returning to active military service.

Among the few writings of Beall—chiefly letters and sporadic diary entries—there is surprisingly little said about his views on the war, slavery or the reasons for his own participation in the conflict. As the war progressed, the Beall "memoir" written by his friend Daniel Lucas—which includes entries from a Beall diary—shows that Beall followed events on the battlefield closely by reading accounts in newspapers. While his diary entries include favorable comments when the South prevailed in battles, Beall reveals scant information about any deeper feelings he may have had about the war.

As a born and bred Virginian brought up in a wealthy family living on a plantation with slaves, Beall would seem to be the quintessential supporter of the Confederacy. Lucas attributes Beall's support for the Southern "cause" to beliefs he learned from his father, George, who was a strong advocate of states' rights, which Lucas refers to as the "Virginia School."

"The teaching of his father ... indoctrinated him into the Virginia School; and the ardour of his devotion to States rights, as understood by Jefferson, embodied in the famous Kentucky Resolutions of 1799, or taught by Madison and set forth in the still more celebrated Virginia Resolutions of 1798–1799," Lucas wrote. The Kentucky and Virginia resolutions asserted that the Alien and Sedition Act enacted by a

Federalist Congress overstepped federal authority. The resolutions are often considered the founding documents of the states' rights movement.[41]

Beall's support for the Confederacy was "both natural and logical," Lucas noted, describing it as a matter of honor. "Devoted to honour, he could not submit to the degradation of assisting in the subjugation of the Cotton States," Lucas wrote, "because, in the exercise of their undoubted right, they had decided to sever the connection between themselves and the other States of the Federal Union." In short, according to Lucas, "John Beall, nurtured, reared, and educated under the teachings of the Virginia School, saw in the contest in which he offered up his life, a high and sacred political principle worthy of the sacrifice."[42]

With his plans to rejoin his military unit blocked by the presence of Union troops, Beall had a new idea for his service on behalf of the Confederacy, one that would eventually take him to Canada.

CHAPTER 4

First Arrivals

Sandusky, Ohio—April–June 1862

On April 10, 1862, a special train of the Sandusky, Dayton and Cincinnati rail line pulled into Sandusky late in the afternoon.[1] The passengers on board included two hundred Confederate prisoners—most of them captured after the surrender of Fort Donelson in Tennessee—who had initially been held at Camp Chase, a military prison and Union Army training site, near Columbus. They would be the first prisoners of war to be incarcerated at Johnson's Island.

Flanked by fifty Union troops acting as guards, the parade of prisoners walked the ten blocks from the train depot to the city's docks while shopkeepers and passersby looked on. A reporter for Sandusky's *Daily Commercial Register* wrote:

> They were clad variously. Some had the characteristic butternut color, and some did not. Some wore blue coats with brass buttons; others had on coats of no particular color.... Some wore hats and some had on caps ...Some had the "don't care a dime" swagger ... some were sullen in appearance, while others seemed to forget themselves in their curiosity to see the sights.... An average of their features would be marked with a case-hardened sort of expression, shaded with a malicious frown.[2]

The lake steamer *Island Queen* was waiting for the prisoners at the Water Street dock and would transport them, in several trips, over the short distance to the island. The boat's captain, George Orr, had hoisted the Union flag for the occasion, prompting one rebel to spit on it and wind it around the boat's flagstaff as he boarded. Orr immediately reprimanded him, but also spoke a "few consoling words," that appeared to calm the soldier who then unwrapped the flag.[3]

Sandusky residents were quickly having to adjust to the new set of neighbors who would live just offshore. A day after the prisoners arrived, the *Daily Commercial Register* ran a notice:

> Fishermen, yachtmen and others need now to be careful not to land on Johnson's Island, especially near the lower end and near the fence. The guards carry loaded pieces and have orders which might make it very uncomfortable, to say the least, to attempt a landing with any sort of a boat on the island. The island is under Uncle Sam's jurisdiction, and he will have it well watched.[4]

Hoffman, the Commissary-General, had already taken steps to expand the prison complex to accommodate additional prisoners and guards. In March, he had notified Meigs, the Quartermaster-General in Washington, that he had arranged for the contractors, West and Gregg, to build ten more prisoner barracks, which were to be completed by May.

Together with the barracks already standing, Hoffman told Meigs, the addition of the new quarters would enable the Johnson's Island prison depot to hold up to five thousand men—"by crowding."[5] A second company of guards had also been recruited, with additional barracks planned to house them.[6]

On April 13, just two days after the first group of prisoners arrived, Edwin M. Stanton, the new Secretary of War who had replaced Simon Cameron in January, sent a dispatch to Hoffman telling him that Johnson's Island would "hereafter be held as a prison for officers alone."[7]

No explanation was given for Stanton's decision, but one possibility might have been to reduce the chances of insurrection among the Confederate captives by sequestering their leaders.[8] The additional security provided by the island's isolated location could have been another factor in confining officers there.[9]

The first prisoners to arrive at the new prison facility generally gave it good reviews. Confederate Captain John Henry Guy, a member of the Goochland, Virginia Light Artillery, had been among the rebel soldiers captured at Fort Donelson who were initially imprisoned at Camp Chase near Columbus. He was transferred to Johnson's Island on April 24.

Comparing his new quarters with Camp Chase in Columbus, Captain Guy wrote in his diary: "When we consider the increased extent & the beauty of our prison grounds, the improved water, the fine breezes, the fine prospect around us, & the healthiness of this place, we are satisfied with the change."[10]

At the same time, Stanton's decision to use the prison exclusively for Confederate officers led to some grumbling from officers who found themselves living in quarters built for enlisted men.

Along with his praise of the prison's location, Captain Guy expressed these sentiments: "Strangers from all parts of the country are huddled promiscuously together and many of them are very far from being pleasant companions although officers." He added, "Those who were first brought on from Camp Chase filled the officers' quarters and we who happened to come last find ourselves in miserable buildings."[11]

At around the same time, however, Hoffman was starting to have some second thoughts about his selection of William Pierson as the prison depot's commanding officer. In March, even before the first prisoners set foot in the prison yard, Pierson had taken it upon himself to issue a set of rules governing prisoner behavior, which would come to be known as "Pierson's Ten Commandments." The first nine rules dealt with the hours of the day that prisoners could be outside of their barracks, what time prisoners needed to be in their bunks, and similar requirements.

The tenth rule stated that prisoners who violated any of the rules would be subject to being shot. "Guards and sentinels will be required to fire upon all who violate the above orders," Pierson's final directive stated. "Prisoners will, therefore, bear them carefully in mind, and be governed by them, to forget under such circumstances is inexcusable, and may prove fatal."[12]

Hoffman's doubts about Pierson were revealed in an April 25 letter to Ohio's Governor David Tod (who had succeeded Dennison) in which Hoffman expressed his disappointment that a more experienced officer was not available to take command. He described Pierson as "very gentlemanly and courteous ... industrious and attentive," but bemoaned "his want of experience in military matters," noting that "cases requiring prompt and decisive action may arise when he would be quite at a loss to know what to do."[13] Pierson remained at his post, however, and would continue to do so until January 1864.

Two months after his letter to Governor Tod, Hoffman received a telegram from Pierson that described a fledging effort among the prisoners to organize themselves. The Johnson's Island commander said he had learned "the prisoners have a military organization; that they have a general and adjutant and other officers; that they are to obey orders; that they are to revolt...."[14]

Pierson's telegram also contained a warning. "A scheme is reported to be [afoot] in Canada by Southern sympathizers to release the prisoners on the island," he wrote.[15] It was the first of several warnings Union officials would receive during the war citing the threat posed by Confederates in Canada, including an expanding group of ex-Confederate soldiers, agents, and Great Lakes privateers who were gathering in Canada within reach of the Johnson's Island prison.

* * * * *

By May 1862, Beall had given up trying to locate and rejoin his Confederate militia unit near his home in Charles Town, Virginia. The area was still overrun with Union troops, drawn there in response to Confederate General Stonewall Jackson's campaign in the Shenandoah Valley. Beall decided to set out for Iowa where his older brother, Hezekiah, worked in a flour mill.

Traveling by horseback, stagecoach, wagon and rail, Beall arrived a few weeks later in the small town of Cascade, Iowa, about twenty-seven miles southwest of Dubuque.[16] Along with Hezekiah, Beall knew that old family friends, the Chew family, also lived in Cascade.

Thomas and Margaret Chew ran a flour mill in Cascade where Hezekiah was employed. They lived on a knoll overlooking the Maquoketa River in what was then the largest house in town. Thomas Chew had built the stone house with a gabled roof for his new bride, Margaret, in 1861.[17]

Shortly after his arrival in Cascade in June, Beall looked up the Chews, partly because Margaret's family in Maryland had been friends with Beall's parents. The Chews offered Beall an upstairs room in their home as a place to stay.

Beall would spend a little more than three months in Cascade. As an erstwhile Confederate soldier in a northern state, he decided to keep a low-profile, rarely venturing into town and staying close to the Chew property where he could also see his brother at the mill. Beall occasionally helped out at the flour mill, although his injuries still prevented him from engaging in strenuous work. Margaret, who had acquired some nursing training, was able to treat and comfort Beall when his wounds flared up.

Margaret also gave Beall support in another way. She was what was known as a "Copperhead," a southern sympathizer in the North who opposed the Union war effort.[18] Already at that point in the conflict, war weariness was a growing sentiment in several northern states. For months, Union forces had been bogged down outside Richmond where Union General George B. McClellan seemed unwilling to mount an offensive and instead sent repeated requests back to Washington for more troops. In Virginia, Confederate General Stonewall Jackson had marched up and down the Shenandoah Valley, tying up Union troops that far outnumbered Jackson's small army. Union Army enlistments were also falling.

The growing anti-war sentiment was particularly acute in the upper Midwest. In Illinois, conservative Democrats in the state legislature had attempted—but ultimately failed—to draft a new state constitution that would have stripped the governor of powers over the state militia.[19]

In neighboring Iowa, one of the most strident voices against the war was that of Dennis A. Mahoney, editor of Dubuque's leading newspaper, *The Dubuque Herald*, who blamed the war on "Northern fanaticism."[20] Secret societies were sprouting in the state to oppose the war and abolitionists.

In a late-August entry in his diary, Beall noted that federal authorities had arrested Mahoney and suggested the *Herald* had been shut down. "Here in the west, they have arrested old Mahony [sic] and scared some of the leading secessionists.... My papers have ceased, the *Herald's* subscription has run out, and the news has been suppressed—no cause assigned, save that it does not support the Administration," Beall wrote.[21]

By late September, Beall decided that his time in Cascade should come to an end. Margaret Chew and his brother Hezekiah had warned him that he was at risk of being exposed as a rebel soldier in hiding. Under the cover of darkness, Beall left Cascade and headed north.

CHAPTER 5

Rebels on the Island

Johnson's Island—Summer 1862

Sandusky residents had watched for months as newly-constructed barracks and stockades replaced trees on Johnson's Island. As spring turned to summer in 1862, the citizens of Sandusky had little contact with the rebel prisoners now living just offshore. Yet they remained curious about their new neighbors. The number of prisoners on the island now exceeded 1,000.[1]

Tour boats began offering excursions from the Sandusky docks to Johnson's Island, allowing passengers the chance to view the prisoners. On June 26, the *Daily Commercial Register* ran a front-page ad, announcing a "Grand Excursion & Pic Nic" aboard the steamer *Island Queen* to Put-in-Bay and Kelleys Island on the Fourth of July.

The trip would provide an opportunity "to get a near view of the Prisoners' Quarters and other Government Buildings on Johnson's Island." The boat would leave at 9:30 a.m. and return at 5:30 p.m. A round trip ticket cost fifty cents. Music would be provided by the Union Brass Band.[2]

Prisoners on the island watched as the excursion boats sailed by their quarters. Edward Drummond, a native of Maine who had moved to Georgia and joined the Confederate Army, observed that on one occasion a band aboard the *Island Queen* had played "Dixie" to the enjoyment of the prisoners, noting "such a tremendous shout never went up as went from this pen."[3]

Another prisoner, however, was outraged when a boat carrying newly-freed slaves as passengers passed by the island. "O! how the black Bucks & wentches [sic] laugh at us," William Speer wrote in his diary.[4]

By now, daily life among the prisoners had settled into a routine. At 6 a.m. breakfast was served in the barracks, consisting of coffee, bread, and beef, either fried or boiled. Roll call was at 7:30 a.m. in the prison yard where names were called, and a count was taken.[5]

Later in the morning, usually around 10 a.m., newspapers and mail arrived, both of which were eagerly seized on by the prisoners.[6] The papers included the daily Sandusky *Daily Commercial Register*, *The New York Herald* (usually several days old), and *The Cincinnati Enquirer,* a publication later banned by prison authorities because of its pro-secessionist leanings. With the exception of the *Enquirer*, prisoners were allowed to subscribe to any newspaper they wanted for most of the war, making Johnson's Island unique among northern prisons.[7]

To save money, several prisoners would pitch in to pay for a single newspaper subscription. When the latest edition arrived, the prisoner most skilled at reading out loud would stand on the top step of one of the barracks and read the news to the group gathered in the prison yard.[8]

Prisoners were eager to learn about the most recent developments on the battlefield. On June 30, the *Daily Commercial Register* reported on Union General George McClellan's stalled campaign on the Virginia Peninsula outside Richmond. In the first major series of battles in the east, McClellan's efforts to advance on Richmond, the Confederate capital, were repulsed by a newly-appointed commander of the Confederate troops, General Robert E. Lee. News that the Confederate lines were holding was read aloud and a series of cheers went up in the prison yard that were "immense," according to one diarist.[9]

The prison's commander, William Pierson, was not pleased. The next morning at roll call he informed the prisoners that their conduct a day earlier was "unbecoming" and that it would be difficult "to restrain the sentinels from firing under such circumstances."[10]

Dinner was served around noon. The food rations given to prisoners were generally the same as those offered to the prison guards, consisting of fresh beef, pork, baker's bread, sugar, coffee, beans, and hominy.[11]

Prisoners could supplement these items with food packages sent by relatives or purchases from the prison store run by a private businessman, known as a "sutler," who was permitted to sell merchandise to the prisoners.

In the afternoon, the prisoners were free to spend time as they wished, conversing, playing cards, reading, or sleeping.[12] Many prisoners spent their free time making small trinkets from gutta percha, a hard, rubberlike resin. The rubber, patented in 1851, was used to make everyday items such as buttons and combs. Prisoners would carve new items from the hard rubber, fashioning rings and watch chains among other things.[13]

Supper was served just before sunset and, afterwards, prisoners were confined to their quarters. At 9:30 p.m. taps were played, and lamps were to be extinguished.[14]

The warm weather, along with the newly-constructed prison complex, generated positive reviews from most of the prisoners who arrived that first summer of the prison's operation. Johnson's Island was "the least disagreeable prison I ever saw or heard of," one prisoner wrote, adding, "It is a salubrious, pleasant place." Another inmate was awed by the beauty of the surrounding lake, noting the "rolling waves," "deep blue waters" and "small schooners with their white sails floating about near and far."[15]

With the lake at their doorstep, swimming was a popular activity among the prisoners, when permitted. In groups of about a hundred at a time, prisoners were taken the short distance from the prison to the lake shore two or three times a week and allowed to spend about twenty minutes in the water.[16]

The few complaints from prisoners about these activities centered on a lack of privacy. Prisoner Edward Drummond expressed disgust when he saw a group of women at the rail of a passing excursion boat using opera glasses to view the bathing Confederates.[17]

Baseball was another favorite activity, which was surprising since the game—also known at the time as base ball or bat ball—had been popularized in New York and Massachusetts, among other northern states, in the years before the war. Several amateur teams were playing in northeastern states with game scores reported in newspapers. Soldiers took up the game during the Civil War, helping to spread its popularity as the national pastime.[18]

The prisoners on Johnson's Island played on two teams: the Southerns—made up of officers below the rank of captain—and the Confederates—comprised of officers of higher rank. The games were well-attended, attracting spectators from Sandusky and other nearby towns. By 1864, the games would gain such popularity that a championship playoff was attended by a crowd of 3,000, including prisoners, guards, and citizens from the surrounding area.[19]

One of the most unusual activities engaged in by any prisoner on the island was photography. Prisoner G.B. Smith, a Confederate lieutenant from Tennessee, held on to a camera lens he owned after he was captured and brought it to Johnson's Island. On his arrival at one of the prison blockhouses, he built a rudimentary darkroom and studio in the attic of the building. Prisoners wanting a photographic record of their incarceration would climb a ladder to the upper floor, then crawl across rafters to Smith's "studio" where they would pose for portraits by the prisoner-photographer. He mounted his lens in a tobacco box to create a crude camera. He would bribe guards to obtain chemicals for his darkroom and used tin from old oyster cans as his photographic plates. Most prisoners seemed pleased with the results. After receiving a tintype with his image memorialized by Smith's camera, prisoner Virgil Murphey wrote in his diary that he was "very well satisfied."[20]

* * * * *

As the prisoners were settling into their new routines and adjusting to life on the island, decisions were being made at the highest levels of the U.S. government and the Confederacy that would impact the number of prisoners who would be kept on Johnson's Island and in other prison camps across the country.

Since the war began, there had been no formal policy for exchange of prisoners between the North and the South. This was intentional, at least on the part of the Lincoln administration, which did not want to take steps that could be interpreted as recognizing the Confederate States of America as a legitimate government, separate from the United States. As a result, under the laws of war, the Confederacy had no legal standing to exchange prisoners.[21]

As a practical matter, however, prisoners were being exchanged. For most of 1861 and during the first half of 1862, there were informal, or "special," prisoner exchanges, carried out on an ad hoc basis.

They occurred sporadically on the battlefield, handled by the field commanders, or between prisons in the North and South to prevent extreme overcrowding. The prisoners selected for release were usually those who were feeble and infirm, or those who had families to support. The goal was to avoid replenishing the fighting forces of the opposing side.[22]

As the war continued and number of captured troops increased, pressure to change the policy began to build. One reason was simply the administrative burdens of keeping track of the prisoners, along with the costs associated with their incarceration. In addition, reports of poor conditions in Confederate prisons and mistreatment of Union prisoners began filtering into the North.[23] As early as December 1861, Congress passed a joint resolution calling upon the Lincoln administration to "inaugurate systematic measures for the exchange of prisoners in the present rebellion."[24]

When Lincoln named Edwin M. Stanton to replace Simon Cameron as Secretary of War in January 1862, one of Stanton's first official statements declared that it was the duty of his department to care for the prisoners of the South.[25]

The capture of Fort Donelson in Tennessee by Union General Ulysses Grant in February 1862—when the North suddenly found itself with over 12,000 captured rebel soldiers—demonstrated the inadequacy of the informal exchange policy. Until then, the South held more prisoners than the North. Now, both sides had strong incentives to pursue a formal exchange policy.[26]

Negotiators for the Union Army and Confederacy began preliminary talks in February 1862, but the talks proceeded slowly, frustrating both sides. Public pressure for change continued.

In July, *The New York Times*, a generally pro–Lincoln administration publication, expressed frustration over the lack of a formal exchange policy. Invoking humanitarianism as a reason for an official policy, the editors wrote, "Our captives pine, our wounded men die of grief, loneliness, and neglect, while the hearts of family and friends are breaking in the distant North to have them at home to nurse and tend."[27]

On July 12, Stanton ordered General John A. Dix, the Union Army commander at Fort Monroe, Virginia, to meet with his counterpart in the Confederacy, General D.H. Hill, to negotiate a formal policy—or "cartel"—to govern prisoner exchanges.[28]

Dix was a former U.S. Senator from New York who had also served as Treasury Secretary in the Buchanan administration. In January 1861, just before the Lincoln administration took office and four months before the war began, Dix had gained notoriety for a directive he sent to Treasury agents in New Orleans: "If anyone attempts to haul down the American flag, shoot him on the spot."[29]

Dix joined the Union Army in May 1861 as a Major-General. At age sixty-four, he was considered too old for a battlefield command and was assigned to head the

Union Army's Department of Virginia, an administrative district, based at Fort Monroe near Hampton, Virginia, on the Chesapeake Bay. The Department comprised areas of the South that were controlled by Union troops.

On the Confederate side was D.H. (Daniel Harvey) Hill, a Major General and division commander in the Army of Northern Virginia, who had fought in the Peninsula Campaign around Richmond. He was an 1842 graduate of West Point who resigned his commission following the Mexican-American War to become a math professor at Washington College (now Washington & Lee University). He had authored an algebra textbook used throughout the South, which included problems for students to solve that were deemed to be "anti–Yankee." An example: "Two Indiana volunteers ran away from the field of battle at the same time; one ran half a mile per hour faster than the other, and reached Saltillo, Mexico, which was 6 1/2 miles from the field of battle, 5 minutes and 54 seconds sooner than the other. What was their respective speed of travel?"[30]

On July 22, following a series of meetings, the two generals reached an agreement on a prisoner exchange cartel. The cartel established an agreed "scale of equivalents" to manage the exchange of officers and enlisted personnel. For example, a general could be exchanged for another general or sixty privates or common seamen; a Navy captain or an Army Colonel could be exchanged for officers of equal rank or for fifteen common seamen or privates.[31]

The cartel also allowed for the exchange of non-combatants, including citizens accused of disloyalty and civilian employees of the military. It designated two locations for the exchanges to take place, one on the James River in Virginia for prisoners in the East, and another at Vicksburg, Mississippi, for prisoners in the West.[32]

On Johnson's Island, even before the cartel was signed, rumors of an impending release swept across the prison camp. "We have some news about an immediate exchange but no confidence in anything," Edward William Drummond wrote in his diary on June 24. Three days later, Drummond wrote about a rumored telegram from the War Department that was supposed to announce an immediate exchange. He also reported a rumor that officials at Johnson's Island had stopped all orders to supply the commissary.[33]

There was truth to the rumors. The new cartel quickly led to a reduction in the prison population on the Island. After peaking at 1,462 prisoners in August 1862, the number of prisoners declined to 822 by the end of September. It was in September that Drummond finally received his own release.[34]

The Dix-Hill Cartel would remain in effect for only about a year, however. A series of disputes over how to handle certain categories of prisoners brought the exchanges to a halt. As a result, the number of prisoners on Johnson's Island would soon begin to increase once again.

Two months after the cartel was signed, General D.H. Hill and his division, as part of the Army of Northern Virginia, followed Confederate General Robert E. Lee into Maryland where Hill fought in the Battle of Antietam.

One year later, General Dix was promoted to head the Union Army's administrative district for the Eastern United States, based in New York, which covered New York and most of New England. In that position, more than two years later, Dix would eventually take a leading role in deciding the fate of a Confederate prisoner held at a military prison in New York harbor. The prisoner's name was John Yates Beall.

CHAPTER 6

A Plan Emerges in Canada

Canada West—November 1862

After leaving the Chew household in Iowa, Beall traveled east, making his way across Illinois and Michigan until he reached Canada in mid–November 1862. He checked in to Riley's Hotel near Hamilton, Canada West (now Ontario), about fifty miles southwest of Toronto.[1] The hotel, three stories tall with sixteen bedrooms, was the largest inn west of Toronto.

By 1862, Canada's eastern provinces—which included the cities of Toronto and Montreal—were home to hundreds of escaped Confederate soldiers, couriers, spies, raiders, blockade runners, and soldiers of fortune.[2]

It is likely that during his stay in Iowa—which had already become a hotbed of anti-war sentiment—Beall became aware of the growing cohort of Confederate agents in Canada. With his battle injury making it unlikely that he would be able to return to full-time military service, Beall decided he could serve the Confederacy in an alternative capacity as part of a slowly-developing Confederate clandestine force based in Canada.

At the time of the Civil War, Canada did not yet exist as a nation. The territory—held by Great Britain and known as British North America—consisted of five provinces extending from Lake Superior east to the Atlantic Ocean, two colonies on the Pacific coast, and an immense unsettled area in between.[3]

Entry into Canada was relatively easy for Confederates traveling north from the southern states. Taking what was becoming a well-traveled sea route, Confederate agents would board fast-moving blockade runners, sail to Nassau or Bermuda, then north to Halifax, Nova Scotia and down the St. Lawrence River to Montreal.

Others willing to venture by land through the northern states traveled from ports in New York state across Lake Ontario, often as passengers on grain boats, arriving at Toronto or Hamilton.[4]

Traveling east from Iowa, Beall likely crossed the border near Detroit, where the Detroit River separates the U.S. from Windsor in Canada. Crossings at border towns such as Windsor and Niagara Falls were common in the war's earlier years. As the war progressed, however, the U.S. and Canada strengthened a fledgling passport control system, first introduced in the U.S. during the summer of 1861, making surreptitious crossings at those border towns more difficult.[5]

Exactly where in Canada Beall traveled during the two months he was across the border is unclear. Beall's "memoir," written by his boyhood friend Daniel Lucas, contains only one sentence about his visit to Canada at this time, including a reference to his stay at Riley's Hotel.[6]

Both Montreal and Toronto were centers of Confederate activity and Beall could have made his way to one or both cities. Montreal, on the Saint Lawrence River, was then the largest city in Canada with a population of about 100,000. It was a banking and business center as well as an inland port. The Confederate exile community in Montreal was estimated to number about three hundred to five hundred.[7]

As Montreal historian Barry Sheehy put it:

> From 1861 until the end of the war in 1865, clandestine activities in Montreal closely resembled what occurred in places such as spy-riddled Casablanca, Lisbon or Geneva during the Second World War. The city was alive with refugees, soldiers of fortune, blockade runners, US army recruiters, and spies; all of them afloat on a sea of illicit money flowing from Confederate bank accounts, cotton trading, blockade running, and the sale of arms, food, and equipment to Richmond.[8]

John F. Potter, the U.S. Consul in Montreal, described the congregation of Confederates as "enemies of the United States, scoundrels [who are] too cowardly to stay at home and fight, too indolent to labor."[9]

The chief Confederate gathering place in Montreal was a hotel on St. James Street named St. Lawrence Hall. Built in 1851, "The Hall," as it was known, was patronized "by an upper class of people, and by stopping there you become identified with the best social element," as one of the establishment's advertisements put it.[10]

In the early 1860s, recent guests of note included Charles Dickens and the Prince of Wales. Another guest whose name would appear on the hotel's register before the end of the war was John Wilkes Booth.

Toronto, the largest port on Lake Ontario, was another city in Canada where Confederates gathered. Confederate agents stayed at the Queen's Hotel, centrally located near the city's main railway station. By 1862, the newly-refurbished hotel offered over 210 rooms, seventeen private parlors, a fine restaurant and private gardens. On its main floor was a telegraph office that offered instant communication with Confederate allies in the South. The hotel also carried the latest American newspapers.[11]

While details are sparse, it is likely that during his stay in Canada from November 1862 to January 1863, Beall mingled with many of the Confederates then in the lower Canadian provinces, whether located in Hamilton, Toronto, or Montreal. Far from the battlefields of the war, in a neutral country, Beall had found an ideal location to begin formulating plans for a future military mission against the Union.

* * * * *

In the years leading up to the Civil War, diplomatic relations between the United States and Canada, as well as Great Britain, had remained stable, if not particularly close. A reciprocal trade treaty in 1854 had helped promote economic ties between the U.S. and Canada and with Britain itself.[12]

From the earliest days of the war, the Lincoln administration's primary objective was to make sure European powers, especially Great Britain and France, did not intervene on behalf of the South. If Britain were to join the war on behalf of the South, it would quickly tip the military balance in favor of the Confederacy and destroy any chance the Union might have of ending the rebellion.

The Confederacy's goal was precisely the opposite—to bring Britain into the conflict as its ally. Confederate President Jefferson Davis and his administration in Richmond held out hope that Britain's need for ready access to the South's cotton for its textile mills would cause it to intervene. The Union Navy's blockade of the South constrained cotton shipments to Europe and drove up the price of cotton, leading to the layoff of tens of thousands of British mill workers.[13]

For its part, Great Britain's sympathies were divided with respect to the Union and Confederacy. On the issue of slavery, Britain tilted decidedly toward the North because of its opposition to the practice, which Great Britain had outlawed in all of its colonies by 1833.[14] However, when the Lincoln administration made clear early in the war that emancipation of the slaves was not an overriding objective, public opinion among some segments of the population in Great Britain and Canada became uneasy, at least until Lincoln issued the Emancipation Proclamation in late 1862.[15]

At the same time, Britain maintained trade and commerce with the South. Along with the cotton trade between Britain and the Confederacy, British banks provided loans to the Confederate government and British shipyards built warships for the Confederacy.

Despite Britain's support for the South on issues of trade, it maintained a policy of strict neutrality in the war, refusing to recognize the Confederacy as a separate nation. By taking a neutral stance, Great Britain provided assurance to the northern states that any overt aid to the South would not come from the Canadian provinces. Great Britain's neutrality also provided a degree of diplomatic protection for the Canadian provinces.

The border between the northern states and Canada was undefended. By late 1862, the Union Army was the largest standing army in the world. While the U.S. and Great Britain had been at peace since the end of the War of 1812, fear in Britain of an invasion of Canada by the Union Army was not unfounded.[16] William Seward, Lincoln's Secretary of State, was well-known for his desire to annex the eastern Canadian provinces north of New England. He believed it was out of the question that Great Britain would go to war to preserve its faraway provincial holdings in lower Canada.[17]

Joining in the support for annexation were leading New York newspapers such as the *Herald* and *Times*. They advocated the idea of absorbing the eastern Canadian provinces as "compensation" for loss of the South—replacing the poor, agricultural Southern states with provinces that were more compatible with the North both geographically and culturally.[18]

Apart from abstract geopolitical concerns, ongoing activities at sea early in the war had the potential to spark conflict between U.S. and Great Britain. The Union Navy's blockade of the southern coast gave rise to a new type of ship traffic: blockade runners—fast-moving, often privately-owned steamers that would slip through the blockade, usually at night, carrying cargoes to and from neutral ports such as Nassau and Havana. From those locations, British merchant ships would transport goods to and from England or other locations in Europe.

And it was on the high seas that Great Britain and the Union Navy had a clash in late 1861 that brought the two nations dangerously close to war. Captain Charles Wilkes, commanding the USS *San Jacinto*, was assigned to search for seagoing Confederate raiders—ships that attacked U.S. merchant vessels in the coastal waters off the Southern states.

In a departure from his assigned naval duties, in early November 1861, Wilkes ordered his crew to intercept the RMS *Trent*, a British Royal Mail paddle steamer, in international waters off the coast of Cuba.[19]

Wilkes's mission in the intercept—which he undertook on his own without orders from any superior officer—was to seize two Confederate envoys aboard the *Trent*, James Mason and John Slidell. Wilkes had learned they were headed for England and France to seek diplomatic recognition of the Confederacy.

After the Union ship intercepted the *Trent*, Wilkes took Mason and Slidell into custody. He then sailed the USS *San Jacinto* to Boston where Mason and Slidell were confined in Fort Warren, a Union military prison, while the *Trent* continued on to England.

Wilkes, at age sixty-three, had already had a long maritime career, which included leading the civilian U.S. Exploring Expedition in 1838–42. The expedition, the first of its kind, circled the globe, surveying the oceans and collecting specimens. The expedition was also the first to identify Antarctica as a separate continent.

Wilkes had the reputation of being something of a trouble-maker and poor manager. On his return from the exploring expedition, Wilkes was court-martialed for mistreating his sailors and losing one of the expedition's ships off the coast of what is now Washington state.[20]

When news of the Confederate diplomats' capture spread, Wilkes was greeted with acclaim by citizens in the North, who at that early point in the war had received little encouraging news from the battlefield. Though short of a military victory, Wilkes's seizure of the Confederate diplomats gave Northerners something worth cheering about.

The Lincoln administration was willing to let the celebrations continue—until it appeared that Great Britain was preparing for war. As the world's leading naval power, Britain was unwilling to permit a clear violation of its sovereignty go unanswered. Preserving the neutrality of non-belligerent ships in international waters was, after all, the very principle that had sparked the War of 1812 between the U.S. and Britain.

By December 1861 Britain had dispatched troops to Canada and fortified its garrisons along the border. British Foreign Secretary Lord John Russell issued an ultimatum demanding that the Lincoln administration release the Confederate diplomats or face war.

Meeting with his cabinet, Lincoln quickly concluded that there was simply no way the Union could conduct war against both the Confederacy and Great Britain. The British Navy could easily knock out the Union's limited maritime forces, destroying trade and likely bankrupting the U.S. Treasury. Moreover, a fortified British military presence north of the border could easily open up another front, dividing the Union Army and exposing Washington, D.C., to attack. "One war at a time gentlemen, one war at a time," the President was reported to have said after agreeing to Britain's demand.[21]

The envoys, Mason and Slidell, were released and placed on a vessel bound for England. What became known as the "Trent Affair" was successfully defused.

* * * * *

By late January 1863, Beall had formulated a plan. In his discussions with the growing band of Confederate agents and escaped rebel soldiers, Beall came to appreciate that southern Canada offered the perfect location from which to launch a military raid against the North—across the Great Lakes, which were virtually undefended.

The Rush-Bagot Treaty of 1817 between the U.S. and Great Britain had essentially demilitarized the Great Lakes following the War of 1812. By the time of the Civil War, there was only one warship on the Great Lakes, the USS *Michigan*, which was used primarily as a recruiting vessel for the Union Navy at ports on Lake Erie. The Welland Canal—which allowed ships to sail between Lake Ontario and Lake Erie, bypassing Niagara Falls—was undefended.[22]

The Confederates assembled in Canada also were aware that the new prison housing Confederate officers on Johnson's Island was not heavily defended, beyond the detachment of prison guards on the island. Indeed, some of the rebels in Canada at that time were escapees from the prison. With over a thousand Confederate officers confined on the island, it made a tempting target.

These were among the facts that Beall considered as he worked through the details of his plan. The operation he had in mind would not be a simple raid, however. Because the Great Lakes and Canada were involved, it had an international dimension. And, although Beall did not know it yet, his operation—by the time it was executed—would become an important cog in a larger plan put in motion by the Confederacy that had the potential to alter the course of the war.

CHAPTER 7

A Meeting in Richmond

Richmond, Virginia—February 1863

After nearly two years of war, Richmond, Virginia, was overcrowded, crime-ridden and smelly. By February 1863, the population of Richmond had swollen to over 100,000 residents, an increase of almost 200 percent since the war began. The Confederate capital was a magnet for laborers, bureaucrats, army recruits, gamblers, speculators, vagabonds and vamps.

The population boom had overwhelmed the city's small police force, spawning a crime wave that hit all parts of the city. Juvenile toughs roamed through the town, threatening local residents from the shaded streets on the West End to the cobblestoned alleyways in the Shockoe district. Gambling dens and houses of prostitution proliferated.

The occasional fresh breezes from the James River, which flowed along the city's southern edge, could not disperse soot and fumes from Richmond's massive Tredegar Ironworks, the largest iron manufacturer in the Confederacy. Spread out along the river's banks, Tredegar's red-brick furnace buildings produced everything from heavy ordnance and iron cladding for the Confederate Navy to cannons, bullets and buttons for the Confederate Army.[1]

It had taken Beall nearly three weeks to make his way from Canada to Richmond where he hoped to persuade Confederate officials to adopt his plan for the raid on the Johnson's Island prison camp. Traveling mostly by rail, he rode from Detroit to Cincinnati, then on to Baltimore where he boarded a small two-masted schooner, known as a "pungy," and sailed across Chesapeake Bay into Virginia, successfully evading the Union Navy's blockade.[2]

After he arrived in Richmond in early February 1863, Beall's first stop was on Main Street at the law office of his old friend Daniel Lucas, also from Charles Town. The two had known each other since childhood and shared a room while attending the University of Virginia.[3]

Of slight build, with brown hair and a thin mustache, Lucas—like Beall—came from a wealthy family and grew up in a large mansion known as Rion Hall. A spinal injury, acquired as a child when his nurse dropped him on the floor, became a permanent disability and limited Lucas's participation in the war.

At the beginning of the war, Lucas had served briefly as an aide to Confederate General Henry Wise. But now, no longer in the military, Lucas had become comfortably ensconced in a successful law practice in Richmond where he was able to make the most of his proximity to and contacts with Confederate officials.

Entering Lucas's office, Beall noticed another man seated near Lucas. It was Edwin Gray Lee.[4] A member of the Lee family in Virginia, Lee's grandfather was the brother of American Revolutionary War General Light Horse Harry Lee. Edwin Lee was also a second cousin of Robert E. Lee. Beall knew Edwin Lee well. Lee was a cousin of Beall's friend Daniel Lucas and Beall and Lee had known each other since childhood. Lee's family home was in Shepherdstown, Virginia (now West Virginia), just up the road from Charles Town where Beall's family lived. A graduate of the College of William and Mary, Lee—like Lucas—had studied at the Lexington (Virginia) Law School (now Washington & Lee University), finishing three years behind Lucas.

Lee was tall and strikingly handsome, clean-shaven, with light brown hair. He had started the war as an aide to Stonewall Jackson, serving with Jackson's "Stonewall Brigade" from the First Battle of Bull Run to the battles outside Richmond and the campaign through the Shenandoah Valley. The brigade was the same one Beall had served in before he was injured.

Lee was now sitting in his cousin's Richmond law office because he had just taken medical leave from the Confederate Army. Lee suffered from pains in his chest and had experienced coughing fits for weeks. Lee did not know it yet but he was showing the first signs of tuberculosis, a disease that would eventually kill him.

Despite not having seen Lucas or Lee since early in the war, Beall spent little time on pleasantries and quickly got to the point. He needed to meet with the Confederate high command, including President Jefferson Davis himself, if that could be arranged. He wanted to present his plan for a raid from Canada on northern cities along the Great Lakes and the release of Confederate prisoners from Johnson's Island on Lake Erie.[5]

* * * * *

The home of Jefferson Davis, known as the Confederate White House, was located at 12th and Clay Streets in Richmond's Court End neighborhood, not far from the State Capitol and the Governor's Mansion. The Confederate White House was actually colored light gray, the color derived from the off-white stucco that covered the exterior walls. The two-story neo-classical mansion had been built in 1818 by John Brockenbrough, a Richmond banker. Davis, his wife Varina, and their three young children had lived in the house since August 1861.

Davis was not a well man. For most of the war, he was afflicted by repeated bouts of malaria, stabbing pain in his facial nerves, and a legacy of wounds from his service in the Mexican War during the 1850s. These maladies kept him from venturing far from his home and, as a result, he often conducted official business from a small office on the second floor of the Confederate White House.[6]

Arriving for their appointment with Davis, Beall and Lee—who had arranged the meeting—ascended the granite steps to the front door of the White House. They entered the oval foyer area and were escorted up the stairs to Davis's office which was dark, lit only by gaslights and wood burning in the fireplace.

Davis greeted the men and listened as Beall outlined his proposal for a Confederate raid from British North America onto the Great Lakes. A key element of the plan would involve the capture of the USS *Michigan*, the Union Navy's first iron-hulled ship. As the only Union warship on the Great Lakes, the *Michigan*—with its fourteen guns—was docked at Erie, Pennsylvania, its home port.[7]

According to Beall's plan, Confederate raiders would commandeer the *Michigan* and attack the Johnson's Island prison camp, allowing the prisoners to escape. The *Michigan,* under rebel control, would then cruise along the Great Lakes shoreline, bombarding cities such as Buffalo, Cleveland, Detroit, Chicago and Milwaukee.

Beall tried to impress upon Davis the importance of bringing the war to the people of the North, a population that so far had escaped any serious deprivation or property damage as a result of the war. While making clear that the Great Lakes raid was his preferred plan of action, Beall also presented Davis with a second option, an alternative commando-type operation, that would take place on the Chesapeake Bay. Under this proposal, Beall and a small group of hand-picked volunteers would use small craft to disrupt Union shipping on the Bay.

Privateering, or the practice of using private vessels to attack a more powerful enemy's merchant ships, was a well-worn tactic used by weaker forces in war. The colonies employed it during the Revolutionary War and the American Navy used it against Great Britain during the War of 1812. Since the beginning of the Civil War, the South had used privateering to overcome its lack of the financial and manufacturing resources to build a navy.

In fact, shortly after the Confederate firing on Fort Sumter in April 1861, Jefferson Davis issued a declaration inviting "all those who may desire, by service in private armed vessels on the high seas, to aid this Government in resisting so wanton and wicked an aggression, to make application for commissions or letters of marque and reprisal to be issued under the seal of these Confederate States."[8]

By 1863, however, privateering was dying off, in part because the Union Navy's increasingly successful blockade of the South's coastal waters left privateers with no sure access to Southern ports. In addition, Davis had been persuaded by Confederate Naval Secretary Stephen Mallory to rely more on larger vessels, which could be manufactured in England and operate more successfully against similar-sized Union merchant ships on the high seas.[9]

Davis sat quietly as Beall made his case. It was clear that Beall wanted him to give his approval for the raid across Lake Erie and the subsequent attacks on Johnson's Island and cities along the Great Lakes rather than the privateering option.[10]

The Confederate leader was not prepared to make any decision immediately, however. He instructed Beall that he should have another meeting, this time with Mallory, the Confederate Navy Secretary, and describe for him the two options.[11]

Stephen Mallory had been one of Davis's first choices to join his cabinet after the war began. Born in Trinidad and raised in Key West, Mallory had studied and practiced law in Florida and was a recognized authority on maritime law. Before the war, he had represented Florida in the U.S. Senate where he chaired the Committee on Naval Affairs. Of medium height, with a full face and tousled brown hair, Mallory had a thin line of beard that stretched from ear to ear under his clean-shaven chin, making him appear as if he was wearing a fur collar.

After hearing Beall's proposals, Mallory told Beall he supported the plan for the Great Lakes attacks and, with the backing of Davis, got the Confederate cabinet to approve it and authorize $100,000 to carry it out.[12]

Days later, however, before Beall had taken any steps to begin implementing the plan, Davis started to have doubts. He was concerned that using British Canada as a base for Confederate operations against the North could disturb British officials to the point where they could alter their position of neutrality and favor the North.[13]

Because of that risk, Beall was told not to initiate the raid across Lake Erie. That left Beall with his second option—to assemble a team and carry out privateering operations against Union shipping on the Chesapeake Bay. On March 5, 1863, Beall received a formal medical discharge from the Confederate Army and was commissioned an Acting Master in the Confederate Navy. Edwin Lee also received a medical discharge from the Army and was commissioned a Captain in the Navy.[14] The raid on Lake Erie would have to wait—at least for a while.

CHAPTER 8

"Fire in the Rear"

U.S. Capitol, Washington, D.C.—January 14, 1863

On January 14, 1863, a tall man with dark brown hair strode to the front of the House chamber in the U.S. Capitol and took his place at the lectern. He was about to deliver a farewell address to the packed chamber. Forty-three-year-old Clement Vallandigham, a two-term Democrat from Ohio, had lost his seat the previous fall in the 1862 election after Ohio Republicans had gerrymandered his Dayton area district to favor Republican voters.

A leading opponent of the war, Vallandigham voiced his frustration: "Twenty months have elapsed, but the rebellion is not crushed out; its military power has not been broken; the insurgents have not dispersed. The Union is not restored; nor the Constitution maintained; nor the laws enforced."

He continued, "Six hundred days have passed; a thousand millions been expended; and three hundred thousand lives lost or bodies mangled; and today the Confederate flag is still near the Potomac and the Ohio, and the Confederate Government stronger, many times, than at the beginning."[1]

The Ohio Congressman, known as a "Peace Democrat," spoke in the closing days of the 37th Congress, which had convened at the start of the war in 1861 and would close in March 1863.

Vallandigham was the leader of the anti-war Democrats in Congress. By early 1863, the time of Vallandigham's farewell address, a strong anti-war sentiment had grown in the states of Ohio, Indiana, Illinois, and Iowa, which in the 1860s were known as the "Northwest," an area principally covering the northern states between the Appalachians and the Rockies.

This anti-war sentiment would create a growing distraction for the Lincoln administration and its conduct of the war, even threatening Lincoln's re-election in 1864. Confederate officials in Richmond, including Confederate President Jefferson Davis, were also becoming aware of the deteriorating support for the war in the North. Within a year, they would enlist a team of Confederate agents in Canada and in states in the Northwest—including John Yates Beall—to take advantage of it.

Continuing his address, Vallandigham denounced Lincoln's infringement of civil liberties, including the suspension of the writ of habeas corpus, closures of opposition newspapers, and arrests of politicians and editors sharply critical of the war. The Lincoln administration had produced "one of the worst despotisms on earth," he said, adding "The war had brought nothing but 'defeat, debt, taxation,' and 'sepulchers.' These are your trophies."

Vallandigham was born in 1820 in Lisbon, Ohio, near Youngstown, the son of a Presbyterian minister. Educated at home, by age two, he knew the alphabet and by the time he was twelve spoke Greek and Latin fluently. By age twenty, after attending Jefferson College in Philadelphia, he began making speeches for the Democratic party and practicing law. A few years later, he became editor of the *Empire*, an influential Democratic newspaper in Dayton, Ohio.[2]

Edwin M. Stanton, Lincoln's Secretary of War, had been a close friend of Vallandigham before the war, lending him $500 to begin his law practice.[3] However, their opposing views on slavery—with Stanton a staunch abolitionist and Vallandigham an anti-abolitionist—ended their friendship.

In his farewell address, Vallandigham reserved his strongest condemnation for what he viewed as a major shift in the North's war objectives. With the introduction of the Emancipation Proclamation in the fall of 1862, the Lincoln administration had subordinated the goal of preserving the Union—which had strong support in the North—to ending slavery, Vallandigham asserted. "The war for the Union was abandoned, while 'the war for the Negro [was] openly begun.'"

Also in the speech, which lasted nearly ninety minutes, Vallandigham criticized the Eastern financial interests, which were profiting from the war. "And let not Wall Street, or any other great interest, mercantile, manufacturing, or commercial, imagine that it shall have power enough or wealth enough to stand in the way of reunion though peace," he stated.

He raised the specter that states within the Union could

Clement Vallandigham (Library of Congress, Prints & Photographs Division, LC-DIG-ppmsca-49766).

break away and join the Confederacy. "If you of the East, who have found this war against the South, and for the negro, gratifying to your hate, or profitable to your purse, will continue it," be prepared for "eternal divorce between the West and the East."

At the close of the speech, Vallandigham's colleague, Democrat Daniel Wolsey Vorhees of Indiana, said the outgoing Ohio congressman "had held the House spellbound with one of the ablest arguments" he had ever heard.[4]

Republicans referred to Vallandigham and his supporters as "Copperheads," meant as a term of derision, likening them to the poisonous snake that can strike without warning. The Peace Democrats, for their part, attempted to turn the label in their favor. As a protest against the curtailment of civil liberties, they wore so-called Liberty pins made to resemble copper pennies of the time which displayed the head of an American Indian with "Liberty" written on his headband.[5]

Another commonly-used term for the anti-war Democrats was "Butternuts," a contemptuous reference to the color of the basic, home-dyed clothing often worn by rural southerners.[6]

Geography and composition of the population in the states of Iowa, Illinois, Indiana, and Ohio played a part in this growing anti-war sentiment. Before the war, there was considerable contact and trade between residents of states in the Northwest and the South. The southern borders of Iowa, Illinois, Indiana, and Ohio touched states in the Confederacy or border states. The southern tip of Illinois reached further south than much of Kentucky or Virginia.[7]

Moreover, a significant number of citizens then living in the Northwest states were southerners by birth. Between 10 and 12 percent of the residents living in Indiana and Illinois were born in the South. Eight percent of Iowa's population came from a Southern state. And nearly 6 percent of people in Ohio came from the South.[8]

These Northwest states also had large numbers of German and Irish immigrants, many of them Catholics, who did not consider the war their fight and, as a result, were less inclined to support the war than native-born northerners.[9]

Lincoln and his cabinet were well aware of the declining support for the war in the Northwest. In early 1863, the president confided to Republican Senator Charles Sumner of Massachusetts that he was more worried about "the fire in the rear"—meaning anti-war Democrats in the North—than about "our military chances."[10]

By late 1862 and early 1863, a series of events occurred that stirred up more anti-war sentiment in the Northwest. These included

- issuance of the Emancipation Proclamation, which Lincoln announced in September 1862 and took effect on January 1, 1863;
- accelerated conscription efforts by the Lincoln administration, including imposition of a formal draft, to fortify Union troop strength; and
- military setbacks on the battlefield—most recently with the ignominious defeat of the Union Army at Fredericksburg in December 1862.

By July 1862, it had become increasingly clear to the Lincoln administration that the continued existence of slavery in the South was serving to support the Confederate war effort. Slaves who had not already fled to the North worked farms in the Confederate states and provided manpower for other activities, including manufacturing, which assisted the rebel army.[11]

Recognizing the link between slavery and the war fortunes of the Confederacy, in the summer of 1862 Lincoln decided to draft a proclamation announcing the Union's intent to emancipate the slaves. Freeing slaves would strike at the heart of the rebellion, Lincoln concluded.[12]

In order to avoid the perception that issuing the proclamation was an act of desperation, however, Lincoln's war cabinet advised him to delay his announcement until the next Union Army victory on the battlefield. This came on September 17, 1862, with the Battle of Antietam near the town of Sharpsburg, Maryland, the bloodiest single day battle in American history. The combined number of casualties among Union and Confederate troops came to 22,719, with over 3,600 killed.[13]

In reality, the battle was effectively a draw, with Robert E. Lee's Confederate Army escaping across the Potomac River and heading back to the South. Afterward, Lincoln was critical of the Union Commander, General George B. McClellan, believing he was overly cautious and had failed—when he had the chance—to deliver a crippling blow to the Confederate forces. Moreover, Lincoln was incensed that, following the battle, McClellan had not pursued Lee across the Potomac, missing a chance to attack Lee's Army in retreat.

But Antietam came close enough to a Union Army victory that Lincoln went ahead and released the proclamation. Along with promoting the North's strategic objectives in the war, the Emancipation Proclamation had the additional benefit of fortifying the antislavery movement in Britain, which helped defuse any sentiment across the Atlantic to recognize Confederate independence, an issue that had been in play since the war began.[14]

Before the proclamation, Britain's ruling classes were intent on continuing the cotton trade with the South, while the rest of the population was indifferent. But Lincoln's announcement helped to revive the British antislavery movement and what enthusiasm there was in Britain to recognize the Confederacy subsided.[15]

By the time of Vallandigham's farewell speech in the House of Representatives in January 1863, anger and opposition to the Emancipation Proclamation was pervasive in the North, particularly in the Northwest. Citizens in Ohio, Indiana, Illinois, and Iowa were under a growing impression that "they have been deliberately deceived into this war … under the pretense that the war was to be for the Union and the Constitution, when, in fact, it was to be an armed crusade for the abolition of slavery," complained George H. Pendleton, a Democratic congressman from Ohio.[16]

The indignation over this perceived shift in war aims was accompanied by a fear of freed Blacks coming North. Another Democratic congressman from Ohio, Samuel S. Cox, voiced fear that a flood of former slaves would invade the state. "Is there a member here who dare say that Ohio troops will fight successfully or fight at all, if the result shall be the flight and movement of the black race by millions northward to their own State?" he asked.[17] Efforts were underway in both the Ohio and Illinois legislatures to prohibit the immigration of Blacks from Southern states.[18]

Many workers in the Northwest feared the possibility that newly-freed Blacks would accept lower wages and take their jobs. This fear was particularly acute among small farmers who were concerned that large-scale agricultural operations, similar to plantations in the South, would take root in the Northwest, using former slaves to work the farms.[19] In a related incident, riots erupted in Toledo, Ohio, when grain operators attempted to bring newly-freed Black laborers into their workforce.[20]

Another development that created resentment in the North—and helped boost the ranks of the Copperheads—was the Lincoln administration's formal imposition of a military draft in early 1863. The first step toward a military draft had taken place nine months earlier, in July 1862, when Congress passed the Militia Act, which allowed Lincoln to call up state militias for nine months of service.[21] While falling short of a compulsory draft, it required all men between the ages of 18 and 45 to register for the draft. It also allowed Blacks in the North to enroll in the Army.

To help enforce the Militia Act, Secretary of War Stanton issued a series of orders that exacerbated concerns of citizens in the Northwest already fearful of heavy-handed government actions. Each state governor was required to appoint a state provost marshal with power to arrest Army deserters. The provost marshals were, in effect, the Union's military police. They sought out and arrested deserters, spies, and civilians suspected of disloyalty; confined prisoners; maintained records of paroles and oaths of allegiance; and controlled the passage of civilians in military zones As historian Jennifer L. Weber put it:

> [The provost marshals] gave state governments, and the federal government by extension, a reach into local communities they had never before had. Now the federal government had a network of agents that reached into every nook and cranny of the country. These men could report on antiwar activities and, with the state provost marshal, crack down more effectively on transgressors.[22]

Stanton's orders also authorized U.S. Marshals and state law enforcement officials "to arrest and imprison any person or persons who may be engaged, by act, speech, or writing, in discouraging volunteer enlistments, or in any way giving aid and comfort to the enemy, or in any other disloyal practice against the United States."[23] Persons arrested under the orders were to be tried before military commissions.

Arrests of so-called dissidents increased immediately. Local officials interpreted the vague offense of "giving aid and comfort to the enemy" inconsistently across jurisdictions, further embittering anti-war advocates who considered their rights to be infringed upon. In Canandaigua, New York, officials ordered the arrest and imprisonment without trial of a man who cut down a flagpole bearing the American flag.[24]

Numerous newspaper editors were arrested under Stanton's sweeping orders. Among them was Dennis A. Mahoney, the prominent Copperhead editor of *The Dubuque Herald,* whose anti-war screeds were likely read by Beall during his stay at his brother's home in Cascade, Iowa.[25]

Mahoney was an Irish immigrant who had come to the U.S. in 1830 as a child with his parents. He studied and practiced law and served as a state legislator before he began editing *The Dubuque Herald.* A radical opponent of the war, Mahoney's writings aroused a storm of indignation among Union supporters. On the night of August 14, 1862, he was arrested in his home by the local U.S. Marshal. He was taken to Washington, D.C., and incarcerated in the old Capitol prison.[26]

While he was imprisoned, Mahoney was nominated to serve in Congress by Iowa Democrats in the district that included Dubuque. Although he was defeated in the primary election, he carried Dubuque County by a majority of 1,457 votes.

Mahoney was released after about three months and was never tried. When he returned to Iowa, he discovered that the *Herald* had been sold in his absence. He then was elected sheriff. After four years, he returned to newspapering and became editor of the St. Louis *Daily Times* in 1869.

By March 1863, the "nine-month men" who had enrolled in the Union Army the previous summer were about to end their enlistments, as were the "two-year men" who had signed up at the beginning of the war. At the same time, desertions were increasing at an alarming rate, accelerated in part by objections to the Emancipation Proclamation as well as discouragement over the military outlook.[27]

The confluence of these events led Congress to pass and Lincoln to sign a more comprehensive draft law, the Enrollment Act, also known as the Civil War Military Draft Act. The controversial measure, enacted in March 1863, required the enrollment of every male citizen between the ages of twenty and forty-five, including immigrants who had filed for citizenship.

Before the Enrollment Act, states had been responsible for raising troops. With enactment of the new law, conscription was now a national effort run by the federal government.[28] Moreover, the act established a corps of federal provost marshals and a board of military enrollment in each congressional district, further entrenching federal presence in local communities. This, in turn, intensified tensions between the federal government and opponents of the war.

One more factor contributing to the rise of anti-war sentiment in the Northwest states was the stalemate on the battlefield. As the war approached its two-year mark, the Army of the Potomac now had its third commander. Major General Joseph J. Hooker had been appointed by Lincoln following the defeat of Union troops at the battle of Fredericksburg, Virginia, in December 1862 under the previous commander, Major General Ambrose Burnside.

In mid–November 1862, Burnside—with 120,000 troops—had planned to cross the Rappahannock River at Fredericksburg and quickly move on to Richmond ahead of Lee's Confederate troops. His plans were frustrated by bureaucratic delays that prevented makeshift pontoon bridges—to aid in the river crossing—from reach-ing Burnside's Army outside Fredericksburg. Instead, Confederate troops arrived in time to take the high ground above the river before Burnside attempted the crossing on December 11.

The result was a bloodbath. Confederate artillery positioned along the ridge at Marye's Heights mowed down Union soldiers making their way uphill from the river. The Union Army suffered more than twice as many casualties as the Confed-erate Army, with Burnside's troops listing 12,653 casualties against the Confederate Army's 5,377.

Burnside offered his resignation, but Lincoln declined to accept it, keeping him on in the Union Army, although with a demotion. In March 1863, Burnside was assigned to be the military commander of an area well outside the field of battle. He was to take command of the Department of the Ohio, a military administrative dis-trict that encompassed the states of Ohio, Indiana, Kentucky, and Illinois—an area that happened to be near the epicenter of Copperhead activity.

* * * * *

In April 1863, less than a month after assuming his new position, Burnside issued a controversial order that would inflame Copperhead sentiment in Ohio and surrounding states. It would also result in the arrest of the Copperhead leader, Clement Vallandigham. Burnside's Order No. 38 decreed that "persons found within our lines who commit acts for the benefit of the enemies of our country will be tried as spies or traitors, and, if convicted, will suffer death." The order continued, say-ing that those "declaring sympathies for the enemy will no longer be tolerated," nor would "treason, expressed or implied."[29]

Peace Democrats, including Copperheads, in Ohio condemned the order as a violation of civil liberties, particularly with respect to freedom of speech. On May 1, 1863, as the public hostility mounted, Vallandigham appeared at a rally in Mount Vernon, Ohio, a small town northeast of Columbus. Before a crowd estimated at between 15,000 and 20,000 people, Vallandigham assailed Order No. 38 as a "base usurpation of arbitrary authority," and criticized the Lincoln administration as con-ducting "a war for the freedom of the blacks and the enslavement of the whites."[30]

Informed of Vallandigham's remarks, Burnside ordered Union soldiers to arrest him. On the night of May 5, at two-thirty in the morning, sixty-seven soldiers sur-rounded Vallandigham's home in Dayton, Ohio. When Vallandigham refused to surrender, they broke down the front door of his house, seized the Copperhead leader in his bedroom and transported him by train to Cincinnati where he was placed in prison.[31]

The next day, May 6, Dayton was calm but that night, in response to Vallan-digham's arrest and capture, a mob of Copperhead supporters ransacked and burned down the office of the Dayton *Journal*, a Republican newspaper that supported Lin-coln. Sporadic rioting continued to occur and over two hundred Union troops were called in to restore order. Demonstrations also took place in other cities across the northern states, in another sign of the growing anti-war sentiment.[32]

Vallandigham was charged with violating Order No. 38 by, among other infractions, "publicly expressing sympathy for those in arms against the government of the United States." In a trial before a five-man military commission, Vallandigham's defense lawyers argued that, as a civilian, he was entitled to be tried in a civil court and that his Mount Vernon remarks were protected speech. After a two-day trial, the military commission rejected Vallandigham's defenses, finding him guilty on all charges and sentencing him to prison at Fort Warren in Boston until the end of the war.[33]

President Lincoln had been "surprised and embarrassed" by Burnside's arrest of Vallandigham and could foresee that the Democratic leader's incarceration would make him a martyr to Democrats opposing the war and further inflame anti-war sentiment.[34] In response to the arrest, groups in Ohio had begun attacking Union officers attempting to enroll new recruits, weakening the Army's recruitment efforts.[35]

Seeking to defuse the situation, Lincoln ordered that Vallandigham's punishment be modified. Instead of being imprisoned in a Union Army fort for the duration of the war, Vallandigham would be banished from the northern states and sent to the Confederacy.[36]

On May 25, a Union Army cavalry escort took Vallandigham to Shelbyville in Middle Tennessee, which was still under Confederate control, and released him.[37] Neither Vallandigham, nor the Confederacy, was content with the Copperhead leader's new domicile, however, in part because Vallandigham still considered himself to be a loyal citizen of the Union.[38] Within a few weeks, Vallandigham boarded a sea-going blockade runner and made his way to Canada where, by the second week of June, he was in Windsor, Canada West.[39]

From his new residence in Windsor, directly across the border from Detroit, Vallandigham's political fortunes took a strange turn. The Ohio Democratic party, at its convention in June, nominated Vallandigham to be its candidate for governor, running on an anti-war platform.[40] Despite attempting to run a spirited campaign, *in absentia*, Vallandigham lost to Republican John Brough who won overwhelmingly in the October general election.[41] Within a year, the Vallandigham would be back in the United States and deeply enmeshed in efforts by the National Democratic Party to oust Lincoln from the White House in the 1864 election.

CHAPTER 9

Pirates on Chesapeake Bay

On the Chesapeake Bay, Mathews County, Virginia—April–November 1863

Early in April 1863, John Yates Beall, as a newly-appointed Acting Master in the Confederate Navy, began organizing his Confederate commando force on the Chesapeake Bay. The Bay, nearly two hundred miles long north to south, was the largest water body on the east coast. With 11,684 miles of shoreline, the Bay's coastal areas provided an ideal base of operations for Beall's privateers. They could attack Union commercial vessels at will on the open waters of the Bay and then make a quick escape into any of the small, isolated inlets lining the shore.

Union forts guarded the Chesapeake Bay on all sides. In the north, Fort McHenry dominated the harbor of Baltimore where shipyards built and repaired Union ships throughout the war. Baltimore was also the nearest seaport to Washington, D.C.

At the Bay's southern end—where the Bay narrows and meets the Atlantic Ocean—the Union Army maintained Fort Monroe near Newport News, Virginia. The Union Army also stationed a garrison on the west side of the Bay at Yorktown, Virginia, on the York River. Since early in 1862, the Union Army had also effectively taken control of the Eastern Shore, the narrow peninsula on the east between the east side of the Bay and the Atlantic. The northern part of the peninsula was part of Maryland, a border state that remained in the Union, while the peninsula's southern end was in Virginia.

That the Union was able to maintain control of Virginia's coastal areas was partly a result of the North's blockade of the Confederate coastline which began early in the war on the Atlantic coast and eventually extended to the Gulf of Mexico and the mouth of the Mississippi River at New Orleans.

To further augment control of the Chesapeake region, in late April 1861, the Union's Navy Secretary Gideon Welles also established a "federal flotilla" of as many as twenty-five Navy gunboats to patrol the Bay and protect vessels transporting troops and supplies to battlefronts in Virginia and other points south.[1]

Rather than being intimidated by the forceful Union presence on the Bay, Beall saw it as an opportunity. His model, he said, would be the notorious Confederate raider John Singleton Mosby who led "Mosby's Rangers," a cavalry unit known for its lightning-quick attacks inside Union lines in Northern Virginia. After the attacks, Mosby and his men always managed to elude capture, blending in with local farmers and townsfolk.[2] Beall aimed to do the same on the Bay.

With his focus on the Chesapeake, Beall was following in the footsteps of another Confederate raider, John Taylor Wood, whose attacks on the Bay in 1862 had caused severe disruption of Union shipping. Wood, a graduate of the U.S. Naval Academy who aligned with the Confederacy, had by 1863 been promoted to serve as an aide to Confederate President Jefferson Davis, leaving the Chesapeake waters open for another Confederate raider.[3]

Beall established his base on the peninsula between the Rappahannock River and the York River just above Mobjack Bay on the Chesapeake. A rural, sparsely-populated peninsula with a few farmers and fishermen, this area in Mathews County, Virginia, contained mostly small inlets, hidden coves and forest which provided a secluded sanctuary for his small band of commandos. Beall made his camp near the village of Mathews Courthouse in the small county with nearly 217 miles of coastline, the most of any county in the state.

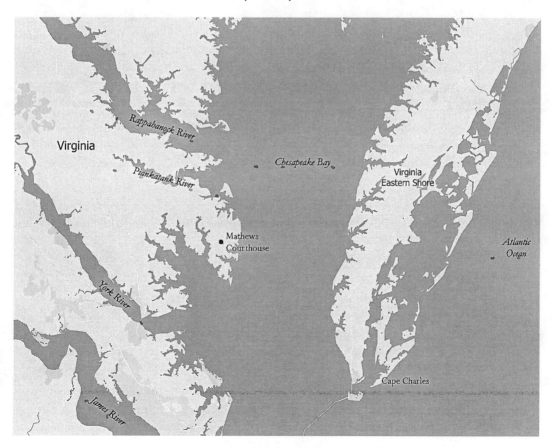

Chesapeake Bay Region.

Beall lost little time in assembling his team. For a variety of reasons, it was a small one—starting with about ten men at most. By the fall of 1863, the group would expand to between fourteen and eighteen men. Beall's recruitment task was complicated by the fact that, at the time, the Confederacy was rigorously enforcing its conscription law that mandated all able-bodied men enroll in the military.[4] Members of Beall's force would not be considered active or official military, they would receive no pay, no uniforms or official recognition of any kind. But they would be entitled to divide any captured booty among themselves.[5]

One handicap for Beall was that he had little actual experience with boats, let alone experience navigating or operating vessels on a water body as large as the Chesapeake Bay. Despite that shortcoming, it seemed to be of no great concern either to Beall or the Confederate officials in Richmond who authorized the venture.

Beall did make an effort to find men who had such experience, however, and that included Edward McGuire, who had served as an Acting Master in the U.S. Navy but resigned when the war started to join the Confederacy.[6] Among Beall's men, McGuire soon acquired the title of "Lieutenant"—or second-in-command—while Beall adopted the title of "Captain."[7]

Another recruit with naval experience was Roy McDonald. Most of the others were men looking to aid the Confederate cause but who—for reasons of health, military discharge, or random circumstance—were not already part of the Confederate military.

Beall's team also included three men who were newspapermen. George C. Stedman and William W. Baker worked on the staff of the *Richmond Enquirer,* Stedman as an editor and Baker as a printer's apprentice. Thomas McFarland, came from the *Richmond Whig.*[8] Baker later wrote, "Seeing all my young friends joining the army, I became anxious to again become a soldier and talked the matter over with Mr. Stedman, who stated to me that he was also contemplating leaving the *Enquirer* and joining some arm of the service."[9]

Soon thereafter, Baker and Stedman joined what Baker called the "Volunteer Confederate Navy," signing on with Beall's commandos.[10] Details are sketchy on exactly how the two became connected with Beall's group. It also is not clear why Baker, who was about twenty years old, had not already been required to join the military under the Confederacy's conscription law.

Also accompanying Beall during the beginning of his time on the Chesapeake was Edwin Gray Lee, a longtime friend of Beall, who—with Daniel Lucas, another Beall friend—had assisted in Beall's initial meeting in early 1863 with Jefferson Davis in Richmond. Lee would soon leave Beall's team, however, because of health reasons.

The recruit with perhaps the most unusual background was Bennet G. Burley, a young Scotsman from Glasgow. Burley, twenty-two years old, had read about the American Civil War and sailed across the Atlantic to play some role in the conflict, looking more for adventure than caring about which side he ended up on. As Beall's boyhood friend and biographer, Daniel Lucas, later wrote, Burley "strayed into the Confederacy."[11]

Barrel-chested, stout, of medium height, with brown hair and blue eyes, Burley arrived in New York with another Scotsman, John Maxwell, who had sailed with him from Scotland. The two traveled south to Richmond where Burley attracted the attention of Confederate Navy officials. Burley had brought from Scotland a design for a type of torpedo, an invention of his father who was a master mechanic.[12]

The Confederate officials who first encountered Burley did not quite know what to make of this Scotsman who had appeared before them claiming he wanted to join their ranks. Rather than look into how they might make use of Burley's torpedo device, they put him in prison—Richmond's notorious Castle Thunder, a former

Bennet Burley (by permission of Graeden Greaves).

tobacco warehouse that housed civilian prisoners.

After a time, however, word of Burley and his device spread among officials at the Confederate Navy's office in Richmond. Burley was taken to the office of John Brooke, Chief of the Confederate Navy's Bureau of Ordnance and Hydrography. An 1847 graduate of the U.S. Naval Academy at Annapolis, Brooke had resigned from the U.S. Navy in 1861 and joined the Confederacy.[13]

Brooke had some familiarity with inventions. While still with the U.S. Navy before the war, he had worked with Samuel Morse to develop and lay the first transatlantic cable, connecting the U.S. and England by telegraph. After joining the Confederate Navy, Brooke was instrumental in converting the frigate USS *Merrimack* into the ironclad vessel, renamed the CSS *Virginia*. In perhaps the most famous naval battle of the Civil War, the CSS *Virginia* fought the Union ironclad USS *Monitor* in the Battle of Hampton Roads in March 1862 off the coast of Virginia. Although the battle itself was indecisive, it heralded a new age in naval ship construction, with ironclad vessels replacing vessels with wooden hulls.

Brooke offered Burley and Maxwell the chance to leave prison and demonstrate their torpedo invention. He suggested they journey to New York City and deploy the weapon against a Union Navy vessel anchored in New York Harbor. Burley and Maxwell accepted the offer and headed north.

One drawback with respect to Burley's torpedo was that, rather than being launched from another ship, it had to be physically carried and attached with screws to the target vessel. A long fuse on the torpedo was then lit by a match.

One night during that spring of 1863, Burley and Maxwell rowed a small boat into the middle of New York harbor. Maxwell slid into the water, swam to a Union warship, attached the torpedo, lit the fuse and swam away. The fuse failed to ignite the torpedo. Shortly thereafter, a lookout on the ship spotted the rowboat and called out but the two would-be saboteurs made a quick escape into the night.[14]

Despite the unsuccessful torpedo launch, upon their return to Richmond, Burley and Maxwell learned of Beall's plans for raids on Chesapeake Bay and were encouraged by Brooke and other Confederate Navy officials to join Beall's group.

*　*　*　*　*

In April 1863, Beall and his newly-formed commando force such as it was—about ten men at the time—began surveying the surroundings around the Bay and nearby peninsulas. Confederate General John Winder, commander of the area around Richmond, gave Beall and his men clearance to pass through Confederate lines into areas held by the Union Army.[15] This area included the so-called "Virginia Peninsula," southeast of Richmond, bounded by the York River on the north and James River on the south. The cities of Hampton and Newport News were located on the southeastern end of the peninsula where the rivers met the Bay.

Also in April, Beall's group had its first encounter with an opposing force when the men surprised a camp of Union "contrabands," freed slaves who had escaped to the North and were now members of the Union Army. The contrabands were armed, and Beall's force attacked, killing one contraband and capturing another. Though the remaining contrabands ran off, Beall's group now had acquired an additional cache of weapons.[16]

Since Lincoln's Emancipation Proclamation took effect in January, the Union Army had been actively recruiting African-Americans, enrolling them in regiments of the United States Colored Troops, a newly-formed branch of the Army. By the end of the war, some 180,000 Blacks would serve in the Union Army, a number comprising over one-fifth of the adult male Black population younger than age forty-five. As the Union Army took control of more territory in the South, the contraband military units provided labor to construct fortifications and guard supply lines.[17] Contrabands tended to camp near established Union Army outposts and the contraband camp Beall found was on Virginia's Back River, about ten miles north of Fort Monroe, the major Union fort on the Bay at the eastern tip of the peninsula.

In late June, twenty-seven Union troops, searching for rebels, landed on the peninsula where Beall had established his base camp. Beall's men shot and killed a Union officer and an enlisted man. In retaliation for the shootings, the Union troops set fire to eight houses of area residents who had provided food and shelter to Beall's men.[18]

In July 1863, Beall's commandos conducted their first real attack against the

Union. They severed the underwater telegraph cable linking Washington, D.C., and Fort Monroe. The cable line—which ran from Fort Monroe to Virginia's eastern shore—had been completed in May 1862.[19] In a report sent to Stephen Mallory, the Confederate Navy Secretary, Beall—in an uncharacteristic act of bravado— enclosed a small section of the cable as evidence of how easy it was to disrupt Union communications.[20]

In August, Beall and his team crossed the Bay and attacked Cape Charles Light, one of the key lighthouses on the Bay near the southern tip of Virginia's eastern shore. The team destroyed most of the lighthouse equipment—including the lamps and reflectors—and made off with the lighthouse keeper's small sailboat.[21] They also took the lighthouse's supply of three hundred gallons of whale oil, which—after it was brought to Richmond and sold—helped bolster the team's finances.

In these early months, Beall's team had largely conducted raids on stationary, land-based targets. By September, however, Beall's commando team had amassed sufficient supplies, weapons and men to begin attacks on Union shipping in and around the Bay. The team was now operating with about eighteen men and had a fleet of two sailboats—one painted black named the "Raven" and the other painted white named the "Swan."[22] These two-masted boats, or yawls, suited the needs of Beall and his team almost perfectly. They were fast on the water, easy to maneuver and hard to spot from larger vessels that had decks high above the water line.

On September 19, 1863, in their first foray on the Chesapeake's open waters, the team captured the Yankee sloop *Mary Anne* and two smaller fishing boats. The commandos made use of the fishing tackle they had confiscated and "spent the day fishing in the sand shoals," according to William W. Baker, the former printer's apprentice with the *Richmond Whig* who had recently joined the group. They later "enjoyed one of the most elaborate fish suppers that I ever remember," Baker wrote.[23]

Over the next five days, Beall and his team ventured into the open ocean, sailing on the Atlantic side of the Chesapeake Bay's eastern shore. Beall and his men captured four more Union-flagged ships. Among these was the large merchant schooner, the *Alliance,* which had sailed out of Philadelphia with a valuable cargo of supplies bound for Union troops in South Carolina. At the time, federal forces had laid siege to Charleston in an attempt to retake Fort Sumter.

After stripping the other three vessels of valuables, Beall and his team put the crews ashore and scuttled the ships, sending them adrift into the Atlantic. Beall and a few men stayed aboard the *Alliance* and ordered the ship's captain and mate, at gunpoint, to sail around the southern tip of Virginia's eastern shore into the Bay. They planned to take the *Alliance* into one of the hidden inlets near Beall's camp in Mathews County. There they would unload the ship's cargo of supplies and send the supplies on to Richmond where they were badly needed.[24]

The *Alliance* entered the Bay and sailed northwest as far as the Piankatank River near the northern end of the peninsula where Beall's camp was located. It missed the channel and ran aground. The grounded sloop was quickly spotted by a federal gunboat, the USS *Thomas Freeborn*, part of the Federal Flotilla. Beall's men unloaded as much of the *Alliance*'s cargo as they could before federal troops approached. After setting the *Alliance* on fire, the commandos escaped into the forest.[25]

The attacks on Union shipping by Beall and his team had come in rapid succession, targeting at least five separate vessels in different locations around the Bay. Federal authorities did not immediately realize that just one group was responsible for the maritime mayhem. But the crews from the scuttled ships, including the *Alliance*, soon found their way to Union outposts along the Virginia shore and told their stories.[26]

The Union Army and Navy quickly made plans to combat Beall's commandos, which the Union military authorities were now calling the "Confederate Volunteer Coast Guard." The Union Army leader assigned to lead the land-based military units, Brigadier General Isaac J. Wistar, commanded the garrison at Yorktown. He was convinced the Confederate Volunteer Coast Guard group he was pursuing numbered from forty to one hundred men.[27]

Within days, Wistar had assembled a strike force of nearly 1,000 men, made up of one full infantry regiment (the 4th U.S. Colored Infantry), two cavalry regiments (the 11th Pennsylvania Cavalry and 1st New York Mounted Rifles) and one artillery battalion. The Navy force included as many as ten gunboats positioned at points surrounding the narrow peninsula where Beall made his camp.[28]

Wistar's strike force left Yorktown on October 5, 1863, and quickly sealed off the Middle Peninsula between the Rappahannock and Yorktown Rivers where Beall's commandos were located. They blockaded waterways and positioned troops across land passages. The cavalry units embarked on a three-day sweep of the peninsula "to beat the bush and flush the game," according to the *Richmond Enquirer*.[29]

Aware of the approaching federal force, Beall and his team tried to conceal the *Raven* and *Swan*. They filled the two boats with sand, sinking them in the shallow waters just off the property of one of the local residents, Sand Smith. By now, after living on the Middle Peninsula for about six months, Beall and his men had made the acquaintance of most of the residents living in the vicinity. Many of the residents, loyal to the Confederacy, treated Beall's team as family and would often share meals with them.[30]

Beall and some of his men were having dinner at the home of a local resident, Thomas Smith, when they learned that federal troops were less than a quarter mile away. William Baker, one of Beall's men, suddenly found the sweet potatoes on his plate "hard to swallow."[31]

Beall and his men made a quick escape, heading north, picking their way in the darkness through miles of forest and scrub brush. They managed to elude the federal troops positioned on roads and pathways across the peninsula, sometimes only a few yards away from Beall and his men. The escaping commandoes were aided by Thomas McFarland, a member of Beall's team who, curiously, had apparently spent time as an Indian scout before he went into the newspaper business at the *Richmond Whig.*[32]

By daybreak, Beall, McFarland and the handful of men who had accompanied them had made their way about twenty miles north of Mathews Courthouse into an area known as the Dragon Swamp. They hid there for several more days.[33]

Three other members of Beall's team were not so lucky. Thomas McGuire, Beall's second-in-command, and two other commandoes were captured by Union troops.

Meanwhile, Beall and Bennet Burley, the Scot, returned to Richmond, where they planned to wait until the federal force on the peninsula dispersed. Burley, in one of the actions that would contribute to his reputation as a bon vivant, took advantage of the respite from raids on the Chesapeake—to appear in a play.

He played a part in a production, appropriately titled "The Guerilla," put on by Richard D'Orsay Ogden, the British-born manager of the Richmond Theater.[34] As it would turn out, Burley's time with Beall during the Civil War was but a prelude to an illustrious career Burley would have after the war when he returned to Britain and became a correspondent for the London *Daily Telegraph*. He would win fame as a war correspondent in the late 1800s for his widely-read dispatches from Egypt, Sudan and South Africa.[35]

After several more days, with his manhunt showing meager results, Wistar, the Union General, was "greatly incensed" by, among other things, the lack of assistance the military effort was receiving from the local population.[36] A group of soldiers from the 11th Pennsylvania cavalry approached the home of Sand Smith, a close relative of Thomas Smith who had shared dinner with Beall's commandos just before the Union raid. Having been harassed by Union troops on an earlier occasion, this time Smith loaded his shotgun and fired at the soldiers as they approached, killing one.[37]

The Union troops rushed Smith, tackled him, tied his hands behind his back and put him on a horse. As his daughters watched, the soldiers put a rope around his neck and tied the other end of the rope to a nearby persimmon tree. The horse was then driven off and Smith fell to the ground, still alive. Smith and his daughters begged for mercy, but the soldiers took aim and fired five shots into Smith, killing him instantly.[38]

In early November, Beall returned to the peninsula and reassembled his remaining team which had spread out across the countryside since the federal raids began. He also recovered the *Raven* and the *Swan*. Told of Sand Smith's murder at the hands of Union troops, Beall vowed "to do all the injury that was possible to the Federals," Baker wrote.[39]

Beall chose as his next target a federal gunboat lying at anchor on the east side of the Bay near the Tangier Inlet. Beall's team first captured a schooner that had entered the area. Beall and a few men remained with the schooner and ordered two other men to hide the *Raven* and *Swan,* fearing that the boats would attract unwanted attention because they were so much larger than the tenders, or dinghies, that typically accompanied schooners.[40]

This decision to split the team proved to be the undoing of Beall's commando force. On November 14, two of the men, Baker and another member of the team, known simply as "Fitzgerald," were sent to conceal the *Raven* and *Swan*. Following that, they fell asleep on the shore. They were soon spotted by fishermen who alerted a nearby federal gunboat. Beall's men awoke to the call of "surrender!" from a Union lieutenant. As they arose and gazed toward the water, Baker and Fitzgerald saw two barges filled with Union soldiers holding guns pointed directly at them.[41]

Under questioning, the men admitted they were part of Beall's commando force. As many as five hundred Union soldiers then stormed through the area and quickly rounded up the remaining members of Beall's team. Beall, who had remained aboard the schooner, was the last to be captured a short time later. While it is possible that Beall could have escaped the roundup, Baker later wrote, he had waited too long to find out what happened to the men sent to hide the *Raven* and *Swan*. The federal troops soon found Beall and took him into custody.[42]

On November 16, Beall and the other members of the raiding crew were taken to Drummondtown (now Accomac), a town on Virginia's Eastern Shore, and placed in the town jail where they remained for the next two days. On the morning of November 19, Union troops ordered Beall and his team out of their cells and escorted them onto a transport ship, the *General Meigs*, bound for Fort McHenry in Baltimore harbor.[43] The fort had gained fame after its attack by the British during the War of 1812, which inspired Francis Scott Key to write the "Star Spangled Banner." During the Civil War, the fort served as a Union prison for Southern sympathizers and Confederate prisoners of war.

Aboard the *General Meigs*, Beall and his team were confined in a hold below deck that had been used for transporting livestock. The weather on Chesapeake Bay was freezing, with wind howling through every crack of the ship's hull, causing the men to "shiver with cold." On the third day of their captivity, the ship's captain sent down "a few hard crackers," the only food the men had been given since their capture.[44]

In the afternoon of November 19, Beall and the other captives arrived at Fort McHenry where they were separated and placed in rooms with a mix of Confederate prisoners, Yankee prisoners (chiefly Army deserters) and "a lot of spies paid to stay in confinement and watch the movements of the prisoners and report their conversations," according to one of Beall's men.[45]

Breakfast on the first morning of their incarceration consisted of hard tack "hard as hickory wood," and coffee, which after a careful analysis turned out to be "a concoction of dandelion root, sweetened with burnt molasses."[46]

A day or two later, on orders from the fort's commander, Beall and his men were put in irons—heavy shackles for some of the men and a ball and chain weighing up to forty-two pounds for others.[47]

News of the capture and incarceration of Beall and his team was greeted with joy and relief among the Union military on the Chesapeake. Brigadier General Henry H. Lockwood, in charge of Union Army troops in the Chesapeake region, declared that he expected Beall's capture "will put an end to these depredations." He noted Beall and his team were not in military uniform and recommended they be tried by either a military commission or civil authorities:

> They are unable to show anything which, in my judgment, would entitle them to be considered or treated as prisoners of war…. They are without orders and many of them without uniform…. [T]hey are but partisans, receiving no pay from the so-called Confederate States, and trusting entirely for remuneration for their services to the possession of such property, public or private, as they may chance to capture…. I would respectfully suggest that they be tried either by military commission or that they be sent back here [Drummondtown] for trial by the civil authorities.[48]

It would not be the only time that Beall's appearance as a "partisan"—without uniform designating him as a member of the Confederate military—would be noted and acted upon by Union Army officials.

CHAPTER 10

Life on the Island

Johnson's Island Prison Camp, Ohio—
July 1863–January 1864

In July 1863, nearly a year and a half since the Johnson's Island prison camp opened, life on the island had taken on a boring sense of monotony for the 1,710 Confederate officers held there.[1] The same rhythms and routines marked each day: reveille at 6 a.m., followed by breakfast, then roll call on the prison grounds at 7:30 a.m., a mid-morning visit by the "sutler"—an appointed civilian who sold provisions to the prisoners, mail call, a mid-day meal they called dinner, then hours of idleness on their own until an evening supper, confinement in quarters at sundown and lights out after taps sounded at 9:30 p.m. until the next dawn.[2]

"Prison life is nearly the same day by day, with little variety or change," prisoner J.L. Stockdale, wrote in his diary. Another inmate, Thomas Gibbes Morgan complained of "this horrid life of inactivity and uselessness," in a letter to his brother.[3]

It was during that same summer of 1863 when prison life on the island began to change—and take a turn for the worse. For the first time, overcrowding became a problem. After the prisoner exchanges went into effect under the cartel in July 1862, the prisoner population on the island had steadily dropped. From a high of nearly 2,000 prisoners in September 1862, the population dropped to 366 by March 1863. Two months later in May, the number of Confederate officers on the island bottomed out at just seventy-two.[4]

But in June and July the numbers began to rise and by August 1863 there were again more than 2,000 prisoners on the island. This time the prison population would not stay at that number for only a month and then decline, as it had the previous September. The prison population would remain over 2,000 for the rest of the war, reaching a high of 3,231 in December 1864.[5]

The bulging prison population that began in 1863 was partly a result of the Union Army's success on the battlefield. After the Union Army victory at Gettysburg in July, 13,621 captured Confederate soldiers were in Union hands and many of those in custody were sent to Johnson's Island.[6]

Unlike the pattern after most battles, however, there was no exchange of prisoners after Gettysburg. This was because by July 1863—a little more than a year since the cartel was signed—the system for prisoner exchanges had effectively collapsed.

There were multiple reasons for the cartel's demise. One major factor was a new policy put into effect by the Confederacy. On May 1, 1863, the Confederate Congress in Richmond took action in response to Lincoln's Emancipation Proclamation which, along with the 1862 Militia Act—an early draft law—enabled African-Americans to enlist and serve in the Union Army.

The Confederate response came in the form of a legislative resolution declaring that Union officers leading Black soldiers were "inciting servile insurrection." Captured Union officers with Black troops under their command were to be put to death, according to the resolution. The Black troops, if captured, would be sent back to their states of origin and likely returned to slavery.[7]

Succumbing to the growing public clamor for retaliation, in July Lincoln signed an order stating that for every Union soldier killed under the Confederate resolution regarding Black soldiers a rebel soldier would also be executed. Furthermore, the order stated that for every Black soldier sold or returned into slavery, a rebel soldier would be placed under hard labor.[8] As it turned out, there would be little implementation of the policies regarding treatment of Black prisoners on either side, largely because the fog of war did not often allow for such orderly reciprocal responses. At the same time, the practical effect of the policies was to end prisoner exchanges under the cartel.

Also by the summer and fall of 1863, news started to reach the North about poor conditions for the Union troops held in Richmond's three prisons—Libby, Belle Island and Castle Thunder.[9] William Hoffman, the Union Army's Commissary General of Prisoners, noted that Union prisoners in the South, "have been stripped of all their outer garments and then crowded into prisons inconceivably filthy, so much so that it would be shocking to humanity to confine in such a place even the most abandoned criminals."[10]

Apart from retaliatory motives to discontinue prisoner exchanges, there was also the plain fact, cited by Union General Ulysses Grant and others, that by releasing Confederate soldiers and returning them to the South, the Union was simply helping to replenish Confederate ranks.[11]

Among aspects of prison life on Johnson's Island that deteriorated at this time were sutler privileges, or the ability to buy things at the prison store by those prisoners fortunate enough to receive spending money from friends or relatives. The sutler store at the prison offered a way for prisoners to supplement limited government rations with fresh fruit, vegetables, butter, milk and delicacies.[12] Other products available included writing paper, postage stamps, clothing, towels, tobacco, pipes, glassware, shaving equipment and other personal items.[13]

Leonard B. Johnson, the island's owner, served as the prison sutler for most of the war. Despite his offerings, he was not a particularly popular figure. The prisoners considered him a cheat. This concern came to a head in February 1864 when

Johnson attempted to require his customers to pay three dollars for a lithograph of the prison and the City of Sandusky before he would accept money for any other purchases.[14] This triggered a boycott by the prisoners and ultimately prison officials ordered Johnson to discontinue the practice and provide refunds.[15]

In late July 1863, the officer in charge of Union Army prisons,Commissary-General William Hoffman, made a retaliatory move of his own, ordering that no longer could prisoners buy extra clothing at the sutler store. Prisoners on Johnson's Island would be limited to one set of outer garments and one set of underclothing. "If they buy either coats or pants, they must be a gray cloth … with plain buttons, without trimmings," Hoffman wrote. Prisoners already having that amount of clothing would not be permitted to buy or obtain more. Shoes were to be of "poor quality" and under no circumstances would prisoners be allowed to buy boots "of any kind."[16]

The prison's commanding officer, Lieutenant Colonel William Pierson, sent a reply to Hoffman, noting that prisoners sometimes received clothing sent through the mail by relatives or friends. Hoffman responded, saying prisoners would not be permitted to receive any clothing beyond the basic items listed in his directive. Any other clothing items would be returned to the sender.[17]

In September, as the weather began to turn colder, Hoffman relented somewhat on his clothing policy. He wrote to Pierson, telling him he could allow prisoners to purchase additional clothing when "it is absolutely necessary." For prisoners without the means to purchase clothing, Hoffman said Pierson could make requisitions to provide extra clothing "if recommended by the medical officer."[18]

Along with crowding and restrictions on sutler privileges, hygiene on the island was becoming a problem. The latrines were clogged and overflowing. The island's substrata of hard limestone made it impossible to dig deeply enough to build efficient latrines or dependable wells for drinking water. Seepage from the latrines into the wells was causing widespread dysentery and diarrhea among the prisoners.[19]

* * * * *

On October 28, 1863, a huge ship entered Sandusky Bay, approached Johnson's Island and docked just offshore.[20] It was the USS *Michigan*, the only Union warship sailing on the Great Lakes at the time. Launched in 1843, the *Michigan* had eighty-eight officers and crew. More than fifty yards long, it was the first iron-hulled ship built for the U.S. Navy. The ship was armed with eight large cannons, or "parrott rifles," and six smaller cannons known as "boat howitzers" or Dahlgren guns. It was powered by both steam and wind, with a black smokestack poking above the top deck, along with three tall masts. Large paddlewheels flanked both sides of its hull.[21]

The *Michigan* was repositioned from its home port of Erie, Pennsylvania, to Johnson's Island on the orders of Secretary of the Navy Gideon Welles, who was responding to reports of a planned Confederate raid on the island from Canada.[22] In fact, officials of the Confederate Navy in Richmond, with the approval of

USS *Michigan* (Library of Congress, Prints & Photographs Division, LC-DIG-det-4a05316).

Confederate President Jefferson Davis, had decided to move ahead with the plan proposed by John Yates Beall several months earlier. Beall would not be involved in the plan's execution, however. At the time, in October 1863, Beall was still raiding Union shipping on the Chesapeake Bay and attempting to avoid being captured by Union troops.

On October 7, 1863, twenty-two Confederate Navy officers—who would comprise part of a raiding team headed for Johnson's Island—sailed from North Carolina into the Atlantic aboard the blockade runner CSN *R.E. Lee* on their way to Halifax, Nova Scotia. The ship was under the command of a forty-one-year-old Navy Lieutenant, John Wilkinson, an experienced blockade runner whose success in piercing the Union blockade brought him to the attention of senior officials in the Confederate Navy. Along with its crew, the *R.E. Lee* carried $35,000 in gold and a supply of cotton that could be sold in Halifax for as much as $76,000. With these funds, Wilkinson planned to reach Montreal and buy weapons and supplies for a raid on Johnson's Island.[23]

On October 16, the *R.E. Lee* and its Confederate crew reached Halifax and five days later the men arrived in Montreal where the raiding team expanded to fifty-four members, with the addition of thirty-two Confederates in Montreal who had escaped from Union prison camps.[24] As Wilkinson and the raiding team purchased weapons and supplies in Montreal, they placed coded messages in the personal columns of *The New York Herald* to alert leaders of the Confederate prisoners on Johnson's Island that a raid was imminent.[25]

On October 22, the Secretary of the Union Navy, Gideon Welles, ordered the USS *Michigan* to reposition from Erie, Pennsylvania, to Johnson's Island.[26] At this point, Welles' order appears to have been largely precautionary, based solely on rumors of a possible raid.

Around the first or second week in November, the raiding team arrived in St. Catherines, a town in Canada on Lake Ontario near the northern end of the Welland Canal. Built in the 1820s, the canal allowed ships to transit between Lake Erie and Lake Ontario, bypassing Niagara Falls. Wilkinson and his men planned to sign on and take passage as crew members aboard one of the many lake steamers carrying grain between Chicago and New York. Their weapons cache would be carried as freight in boxes labeled "Machinery, Chicago."[27]

At some point during their cruise through Lake Erie on the way to Chicago, the team planned to seize control of the grain steamer and head for Johnson's Island. Once they reached the prison camp, they would fire on the prison camp's guard stations, allowing the prisoners to escape. It is unclear whether capturing the *Michigan* at its home port of Erie, Pennsylvania, was part of the original plan. But when the gunboat arrived at Johnson's Island on the Navy Secretary's orders, it became an even more tempting target because, if seized by the Confederates, the vessel's guns could be used to fire on northern cities along the Great Lakes.

Shortly after the raiding team had assembled in St. Catherines, however, an informer revealed the plans to officials in Canada. On November 11, the Canadian Governor General, Lord Charles Monck, sent a telegram to the British ambassador to the United States, Richard Lyons, notifying him of "a serious and mischievous plot" by people "hostile to the United States." Monck ordered Canadian authorities to closely monitor all shipping through the Welland Canal, looking for suspicious activity. Lyons, in turn, notified Secretary of State William Seward of a planned attack on Johnson's Island, information which was quickly passed on to Secretary of War Edwin Stanton.[28] Stanton sent telegrams to governors and mayors in cities along the shores of Lake Erie, alerting them to a possible attack.[29] Navy Secretary Welles sent a telegram to Captain John C. Carter aboard the *Michigan* ordering him "to use the utmost vigilance" and "take every precaution to avoid a surprise."[30] Army officials dispatched several hundred additional troops to Sandusky to fortify the guard force on Johnson's Island.[31] With their operation severely compromised, Wilkinson and the raiding team abandoned their plan, split up and made their way back, by sea, to their North Carolina starting point.

By December, the threat of an attack on Johnson's Island had faded. Many of the additional Union troops sent to Sandusky were withdrawn, in part because they were staying in tents that would not provide adequate shelter in winter.[32] The USS *Michigan* returned to its home port of Erie, Pennsylvania.[33] Within the next year, however, the vessel would have a chance to play a more active role at Johnson's Island.

* * * * *

A potential raid by Confederates from Canada was only one of the matters that punctuated the otherwise dreary routines of the rebels on Johnson's Island. Prisoners on the island, like those confined at other prison camps in the North and South, saw the occasional shooting of prisoners by guards and escape attempts.

Inside the prison yard, an area extending thirty feet from the exterior wall of the prison was known as the "deadline," beyond which prisoners were forbidden to enter. It was marked by a line of stakes in the ground about twenty-five feet apart. Guards were under orders to shoot without warning any prisoner who crossed the line. "Its use was to prevent prisoners crowding against the fence, and I do not remember that we regarded it in any other light than a very necessary precaution," prisoner Horace Carpenter wrote.[34] Carpenter noted that, for the most part, prisoners had discretion whether to cross the line and, as a result, "such trifles as deadlines worried us but little."[35]

More often, shots were fired at prisoners for being out of their quarters after dark. The one documented death caused by a Johnson's Island prison guard occurred a few months after the prison opened. In August 1862, prisoner Elijah Gibson was shot and killed as he crossed the prison yard at night. Gibson, who was visiting another prisoner in a different prison block from his own, apparently forgot about the nighttime curfew. As he exited the prison block and started across the yard, a guard yelled for him to return to the block. When Gibson failed to turn around, the guard fired a fatal shot into his chest.[36]

Guards also fired into the block houses when prisoners burned lights after dark, which was prohibited. "They know they are too strong for us now & these infamous home guards, Hoffman's Bat., are getting large & shooting at everybody—shot several times last night," Robert Bingham wrote in his diary in January 1864. On another occasion, a guard fired shots into a block house after ordering lights to be extinguished. The prisoners inside attempted to explain there were no lights burning and the guard was seeing reflected light from another building occupied by guards. The guard ignored the pleas and fired a round that injured two prisoners inside.[37]

The location of Johnson's Island three miles from shore made escape seem almost impossible without the aid of a boat, which added to the complexity of any breakout scheme. Prisoners soon learned that another escape route—trying to dig tunnels under the prison walls—was a fruitless effort because of the hard limestone a few inches under the soil on the island. Escape attempts that succeeded usually occurred in the dead of winter when thick ice on the lake made it possible to walk across it and reach the mainland. But even then, escapees would have to withstand bitter cold and biting winds.

According to Union Army records, only twelve Confederate prisoners escaped from the island during the war, although reports in prisoner diaries cast some doubt that the number of escapes was really that limited.[38]

For example, while prison records show no escapes in 1863, prisoner John Dooley wrote in his diary on October 1, 1863, that a prisoner had hidden under straw on a supply boat docked on the island and made his way to the mainland. After his escape, the former prisoner wrote to friends on the island, confirming that he had returned to the South.[39]

A few months later, in early January 1864, cold weather assisted five prisoners in their escape. With temperatures well below zero, prison guards were reluctant to venture far from their sheltered sentry posts, limiting their usual patrol. This allowed the escapees to improvise a ladder and scramble over the wall at a location not easily seen by the guards. At roll call the next day, other prisoners answered for the escapees who, by that time, were on their way north to Detroit and then across the Detroit River to Canada.[40]

The frigid winters on Lake Erie were a new experience for the Southern prisoners, most of whom had never seen snow. The winter of 1863–64 was particularly severe. The ice on the lake was so thick that prisoners watched as several hundred newly-hired prison guards marched three miles across the frozen lake from Sandusky to Johnson's Island.[41]

Prisoner Henry E. Shepherd wrote that there was one stove in the block house he shared with seventy other prisoners. "The fuel given us was frequently insufficient," he wrote. "And in our desperation, we burned every available chair or box and even parts of our bunks found their way into the stove. During this time of horrors, some of us maintained life by forming a circle and dancing with the energy of despair."[42]

Temperatures plunged to more than twenty degrees below zero on the night of January 1, 1864, a memorable weather event remarked upon in several prisoner diaries. The cold was so intense that guards did not patrol and were allowed to stay inside their quarters. "The big gate could have been left open and few of the prisoners would have taken the chance of escape in view of almost certain death," wrote prisoner Horace Carpenter.[43]

The ice on block house windows was a half inch thick, prisoner Robert Bingham noted. With two other prisoners, he was allowed to go outside the gates for extra firewood. When they returned, all had frostbitten fingers.[44]

Two weeks after the sub-zero temperatures in early January, many prisoners on the island were suffering from pneumonia or the flu, with three or four inmates dying a day, according to prisoner J.L. Stockdale.[45] In all, twenty prisoners died on Johnson's Island during January 1864. Another seventeen died in February.[46]

While prisoners were shivering and dying on Johnson's Island during the winter of 1863–64, in Richmond, Confederate President Jefferson Davis was becoming even more focused on launching an attack on the North from Canadian soil. Despite his ongoing concerns about antagonizing Great Britain, he was coming to the realization that such an attack might represent the Confederacy's last, best hope of reversing its losing momentum in the war.

CHAPTER 11

The Northwest Conspiracy
Takes Shape

Richmond, Virginia—January–March 1864

On January 5, 1864, a Confederate officer walked into Richmond's main market on 17th Street accompanied by an aide. He headed for the fresh cuts of meat set out on wooden stands. As he pointed out the beef, poultry and pork cuts he wanted, a clerk wrapped them and handed them to the aide who placed them on a cart. A small crowd gathered as the officer handed some bills to the clerk and walked off, with the aide pushing the cart now piled high with some seventy pounds of meat for Confederate troops.

The meat purchase caught the attention of the Richmond *Daily Dispatch* which reported "a scene of no little excitement" at the market the previous day. "Surely, the government does not intend to come into the city markets to get supplies at a time like this," the editors of the *Daily Dispatch* wrote. "If its agents do not furnish meats with all the railroads and other public highways at their command, how is it possible for the butchers in the city markets to supply them?"[1]

That military officers now had to scrounge in local markets for food to feed their troops was but one example of the hardships facing the Confederacy as 1864 began. In the previous six months, the Confederate military had suffered reverses on all fronts. In July 1863, Lee's Army had retreated from Pennsylvania, returning to the South after the defeat at Gettysburg. Vicksburg, the Confederacy's last stronghold on the Mississippi River, had fallen within days of the Gettysburg battle, after a forty-day siege by Grant's army. Union forces now held control of the Mississippi from St. Louis in the north to New Orleans at the Gulf of Mexico, effectively splitting the Confederate states in half. Missouri, Arkansas, Louisiana, and Texas—states on the western side of the river—"were almost as completely severed from their sister Confederate states east of the great stream as if they had been removed to the other side of the Pacific Ocean," a Southern author wrote years later.[2]

Resources to sustain the Confederate military, including supplies as basic as food, were being rapidly depleted. Many areas of the South, now occupied by Union forces, had suspended farming. And even those areas free of hostile occupation could not gain access to transportation routes to deliver crops to markets. The

South's rail system, barely adequate in the best of times, had been decimated by the war. Moreover, with the cessation of prisoner exchanges, there were thousands of Union prisoners held by the Confederacy to be fed.[3]

Skyrocketing inflation had devalued Confederate currency. A pound of tea cost twenty-two dollars, coffee twelve dollars, brown sugar ten dollars, and a quart of milk was four dollars.[4]

The Union Army of the Potomac was now stationed at its winter camp at Brandy Station, Virginia, about seventy miles southwest of Washington, D.C. In March, Lincoln would promote Ulysses Grant to Lieutenant General; he would lead Union troops in the Virginia campaign aimed at destroying Lee's Army.

Around this time, Jefferson Davis shed some of his resistance to the risks associated with conducting operations out of Canada, in part because of the Confederacy's deteriorating military position. Abandoning his earlier caution about provoking a neutral Britain, in a message to the Confederate Congress in December 1863, Davis asserted that the Confederacy was no longer bound by treaties between the United States and other nations that were signed before the war.[5] This presumably included the Rush-Bagot Treaty ratified in 1818 which effectively demilitarized the Great Lakes after the War of 1812. As historian Robin W. Winks put it, "The door was open to lighting a 'fire in the rear' of the North."[6]

Jefferson Davis and his administration turned their attention to the antiwar sentiment in the North. Reports from Ohio, Indiana, and Illinois told of growing support for the Copperhead movement and surging membership in secret societies opposed to the war, such as the Order of American Knights (later called the Sons of Liberty). Much of the anti-war feelings centered on actions of the Lincoln administration that infringed on individual liberties, such as the suspension of the writ of habeas corpus. Provided for in the Constitution, the doctrine allows any person to file a writ asking a court to determine the legality of an arrest that results in someone being held in custody by authorities. The Constitution allows a president to suspend habeas corpus during a rebellion or invasion. In April 1861, Lincoln ordered the suspension of habeas corpus for anyone "discouraging volunteer enlistments, resisting militia draft, or guilty of any disloyal practice affording aid and comfort to the rebels."[7] The order initially covered Washington, D.C., Philadelphia and New York. As the war went on, the order's reach was expanded and by 1863 Congress passed a law codifying Lincoln's order, imposing the suspension across the entire country.

During the war, more than 13,000 citizens were arrested because of their anti-war views, some for acts as minor as shouting: "Hurrah for Jeff Davis." An Episcopal priest was arrested for failing to include a prayer for Lincoln in the Sunday service.[8] Newspapers the administration deemed anti-war were shuttered.

These unprecedented responses by the U.S. government served to further inflame anti-war sentiment, particularly in the Northwest states. Some reports, perhaps exaggerated, even hinted that the antiwar sentiment in these states was so intense that the states might secede from the Union and form an alliance with the Confederacy.[9]

Was there a way the Confederacy could take advantage of the antiwar sentiment, including the Copperhead movement, in the Northwest states to open another front against the North? If so, what sort of attacks could be made, where would they originate, where would they occur and who would lead them? The planning and plots that took place in Richmond to answer these questions came to be called the "Northwest Conspiracy," a last-ditch attempt on the part of the Confederacy to reverse the course of the war.

As one historian wrote:

> [The] plans of a Copperhead uprising as they were understood in Richmond, seemed attractive indeed. Even if the [up]rising failed to bring about the creation of a Northwest Confederacy, a widespread insurrection in the heartland of the Union and the withdrawal from the field of the military forces needed to deal with it, would paralyze the Northern war effort and would render impossible the prosecution of the war for months and perhaps forever; at the very least, the Confederacy would gain a desperately needed breathing space. Moreover, any such insurrection, even if ultimately unsuccessful, would dishearten and demoralize the troops from the northwestern states, the only component of the Union armies that the South believed had done any real fighting in the war. And if there were a second secession, one which did not carry the stigma of being based on a desire to perpetuate slavery, the moral advantage which the North enjoyed in the eyes of the world would be utterly destroyed. The greatly wished-for recognition of the Confederacy by the European powers and the irretrievable collapse of the Northern effort to reconstitute the Union by force of arms would then inevitably follow.[10]

The push to use dissension in the northern states to the South's advantage had begun soon after the Union held off-year elections in the fall of 1863. Herschel V. Johnson, a senator in the Confederate Congress and a former governor of Georgia, wrote to Jefferson Davis, pointing out that more than a million votes were cast against Republicans collectively in the elections held in the North.[11]

"Is this not evidence of a very strong hostility to Lincoln?" he wrote. "It is true, I have no doubt that they profess to be for the war and a restoration of the Union. But I am well satisfied that if Lincoln could be defeated—or the candidate of his party—in the next presidential election, it would end the war and lead to peace." He urged Davis to send an agent to Canada and, from there, begin to organize Peace Democrats in the North against Lincoln, an effort he said would lead to a negotiated settlement of the war.[12]

Also during the fall of 1863, George P. Kane, a Confederate sympathizer and former Baltimore police marshal living in Montreal, wrote to Davis, proposing a plan to launch attacks against cities along the Great Lakes and release the prisoners on Johnson's Island.[13]

Reclaiming the manpower of Confederate troops held in Union prisons was also receiving increased attention in Richmond. The South had little ability to replenish troops lost in battle after prisoner exchanges had ceased with the collapse of the cartel governing the exchanges in July 1863. Moreover, actions such as expanding the military draft were not options because there were few able-bodied men not already serving in the Confederate military.[14] Indeed, there were reports reaching Richmond that estimated the number of Confederate troops held in Union prisons were "well-nigh equal to the efficient numerical strength of Lee's army."[15] Thus, attacks on cities along the northern border with Canada and release of Confederate prisoners of war formed the central elements of the plans underway in Richmond in early 1864.

In February 1864, Davis and the Confederate Congress took the first concrete steps to execute a plan to foment insurrection in the North, appropriating five million dollars to establish a Confederate Secret Service to conduct covert activities in the Union states and Canada. Nearly one million dollars were specifically earmarked for use in Canada.[16]

* * * * *

Meanwhile, Beall and his Chesapeake crewmen—chained in their cells since mid–November 1863 at Fort McHenry—were part of a prison population at the Baltimore fort that had swelled to nearly seven thousand. In the months following the Battle of Gettysburg, a large number of the Confederate soldiers captured in the fighting were sent to Fort McHenry, now known in Confederate circles as the "The Baltimore Bastille."[17]

Guards would sometimes offer to remove the prisoners' chains for short periods of time. While others took advantage of the brief respite, Beall refused. "No! Let them alone until your government sees fit to remove them!" he said.[18]

Beall's time at Fort McHenry happened to coincide with a brief stop by President Lincoln in Baltimore. On November 18, 1863, the president's special Baltimore & Ohio train pulled into Baltimore's Camden station—about three miles from the fort—on its way to Gettysburg where Lincoln would deliver his address commemorating the battlefield.[19]

At Fort McHenry, prison officials permitted Beall to write a letter to Confederate authorities in Richmond, detailing the conditions of his confinement along with that of the other eighteen men captured with him. After receiving the letter, Confederate officers in Charleston, South Carolina, retaliated by placing nineteen prisoners from the Union Navy in irons. One of those chained was the nephew of the commander at Fort McHenry. The Confederacy's retaliatory action had its desired effect. In late December 1863, prison officials at Fort McHenry ordered the shackles permanently removed from Beall and the other eighteen Confederates. In all, Beall had remained in chains for forty-two days.[20]

* * * * *

With funding secured to take advantage of antiwar sentiment in the North, all Jefferson Davis lacked was a commander to lead the effort. He had a man in mind: Captain Thomas H. Hines, a twenty-five-year-old Kentuckian. Hines was tall, thin, with a drooping mustache and a "sleepy-eyed appearance that belied his quick mind."[21]

Hines had already spent two years as an officer with Confederate General John Hunt Morgan's cavalry regiment based in Kentucky. During his time with Morgan, Hines had gained experience—and notoriety—as a covert agent slipping in and out of enemy territory where he was "able to elude apprehension with almost fictional ease."[22] He met with Copperhead leaders in Ohio and Indiana and came to serve as Richmond's liaison with several anti-war groups in the North.

In the summer of 1863, Hines had taken part in a raid by Morgan—widely celebrated in the South—into Ohio and Indiana. The raid was originally intended to divert the Union Army

Thomas H. Hines (House Divided Project at Dickenson College).

away from Confederate forces in Tennessee. Morgan went beyond his orders, however, working with Hines to test the level of Southern support in Ohio and Indiana, well outside their planned area of activity.

On July 8, 1863, Morgan and a cavalry force of 1,400 men crossed the Ohio River from Kentucky into southern Indiana where they obtained supplies and horses from southern sympathizers in the state. On July 13, Morgan's raiders entered Ohio twenty miles northeast of Cincinnati. Heading east across the state, then north, they battled and skirmished with Union forces for nearly two weeks, plundering shops and farms and robbing banks. But there was no general uprising in the state. Many Ohio townsmen, in fact, fought against Morgan and his men as they terrorized local communities. It was one of the first signs that the level of support for the Confederacy in the northwest states might not meet the expectations of officials in Richmond.[23]

On July 26, Morgan's raid came to an end when Union troops captured him and his remaining force of about 364 men in the northeast corner of the state, a few miles south of Youngstown.[24] More than half of Morgan's men had been captured a week earlier as they attempted to ford the Ohio River and escape into West Virginia. Many were sent to Camp Douglas, a prisoner of war camp near Chicago.

Morgan's action near Youngstown marked the northernmost point reached by any Confederate military force in the war, surpassing even the so-called "high water mark" reached by Lee's Army in Pennsylvania at Gettysburg. The men, including Morgan, captured following the Youngstown raid were sent to the massive Ohio

Penitentiary near Columbus. The penitentiary at that time was used chiefly to house common criminals rather than prisoners of war. However, Major General Ambrose Burnside, in charge of the Union Army's District of Ohio, believed there was not an existing military prison in the country that could hold Morgan and his men. Reinforcing that view, Ohio Governor David Tod prohibited the newly-arrived Confederate prisoners from working in the penitentiary shops, convinced that if they were allowed into the shops, they would soon find the means to take over the prison.[25]

Hines, singled out for special attention, was sent to Johnson's Island where he spent several weeks with other imprisoned Confederate officers strategizing about escape plans and attacks against the North from Canada.

As a biographer of Hines wrote: "Canada lay across the lake and plans were made every day to cross the waters on makeshift rafts, start an army across the border and come down on the Yankees' back. It was a favorite thought of Hines. As they sat in the shade of the prison barracks, he would draw maps with a pointed stick in the dust and show his fellow prisoners how it could be done."[26]

Before long, Hines had organized an escape plan that involved about two hundred other Confederate officers on the island. They would overpower the guards and steal boats to cross Lake Erie into Canada. But their planning went for naught after an informer revealed the plot to prison authorities, including Major William Pierson, who had served as the prison commander since it opened in April 1862. As punishment, Hines and several other members of Morgan's regiment held at Johnson's Island were transferred to the Ohio Penitentiary where they joined Morgan and other captured raiders.[27] It would prove to be an auspicious reunion.

The records are unclear on exactly when Hines entered the Ohio Penitentiary, but a detailed account suggests it was around September 1863.[28] Hines, reunited with Morgan and about sixty-nine other members of the cavalry regiment, soon began planning another escape.

Hines had noticed that the floor in his section of the penitentiary lacked mold even though sunlight never reached it. He guessed, correctly, that there was an air shaft beneath his and other neighboring cells. After conferring with Morgan, Hines and two other men began digging into the concrete floor with knives stolen from the penitentiary kitchen. Making slow progress, they disposed of much of the excavation debris by hiding it inside Hines's mattress after he had removed its straw filling.[29] Hines was to later recall that his rock-filled bed eventually came to feel "like a Hindu torture platform."[30]

After three weeks, they had managed to cut a hole eighteen inches square that led to the air shaft. The shaft, barely wide enough for a body even as thin as Hines's, ran horizontally under the flooring to an opening onto the prison yard, still several yards short of the prison's outer wall.

On the night of November 26, hours before dawn, Hines, Morgan and five other men slipped down into the air shaft and made their way to the penitentiary yard. They exited into a driving rain. While sentries took shelter from the downpour, Morgan and his men were able to elude detection and made their way to the outer wall and, using homemade grappling hooks, climbed up and over the twenty-five-foot wall.[31]

They followed railroad tracks that ran past the penitentiary and soon arrived at a train depot where—using money smuggled into the prison inside a Bible given to Morgan by his sister—they bought tickets for the night express train to Cincinnati. Morgan and Hines hopped off the train outside Cincinnati and hired a boat to take them across the Ohio River. Two of the other five men were captured a few days later but the three remaining men were never found.[32]

Morgan eventually made his way through Kentucky and into Virginia. Hines took a more circuitous route into Tennessee where he was recaptured. Sentenced to hang by Union authorities, Hines exercised his skills both as a raconteur and as an escape artist. He first put his captors at ease by telling stories for hours, then—when they let their guard down—he quickly disarmed them and disappeared into the night. Hines was caught again and escaped one more time before he arrived in Richmond in February 1863.[33]

Once in Richmond, Hines went to the Confederate White House on 12th and Clay Streets where he met with three top Confederate officials—Jefferson Davis, Secretary of War James Seddon, and Secretary of State Judah Benjamin. In their discussions, Hines emphasized that, by his estimates, between thirty thousand and fifty thousand Confederate troops were confined in Union prison camps in Illinois, Indiana, and Ohio—precisely those states where the Copperheads and antiwar sentiment were the strongest. Hines proposed to organize a force to release the prisoners, using the several hundred Confederate soldiers and officers who had already escaped from Union capture, fled north and sought sanctuary in neutral Canada. Many of them were former members of Morgan's cavalry whom Hines already knew.[34]

Under his plan, these soldiers would form the vanguard of a force that would join with Southern sympathizers in the northwestern states, including members of the Sons of Liberty and other secret societies. They would seize arms from Union depots and arsenals and mount a revolt against the northwestern state governments. They could also march south, creating as much damage and havoc as possible, on their way back to the Confederate states.[35]

Davis, Seddon, and Benjamin were already aware of reports from other Confederate agents in the North that Copperheads were planning an armed insurrection to overthrow the governments of Ohio, Indiana, Illinois, and Missouri. The plan was to have the new governments secede from the Union and withdraw from the war. Other states, including Michigan, Wisconsin, Minnesota, Iowa, and Kansas, would be expected to follow.[36]

Just a year earlier, Confederate leaders had listened as John Yates Beall appealed for their support to launch an attack from Canada on northern cities and release the prisoners on Johnson's island. Davis had refrained from acting then, citing the risk of violating British Canada's neutrality to the point where Britain might throw its support to the North.

By February 1864, however, officials in Richmond faced a much more dire situation on the battlefield, one that posed an existential threat to the Confederacy. The potential rewards of Hines's proposed plan—even more grandiose than Beall's—were great compared with the risks of not trying.

After a couple more weeks of deliberation, Davis decided to move ahead on Hines's plan. He was impressed with Hines's experience, particularly his escapes, which could be used on a larger scale to free the rebels held in Union prisons.

On March 16, Davis directed Secretary of War Seddon to issue a formal order to Hines. The order read:

> You are detailed for special service to proceed to Canada, passing through the United States under such character and in such mode as you may deem most safe, for the purpose of collecting there, the men of General Morgan's command who may have escaped, and others of the citizens of the Confederate States willing to return and enter the military service of the Confederacy, and arranging for their return either through the United States or by sea.[37]

Hines immediately set out for Canada where he would eventually meet up with John Yates Beall.

CHAPTER 12

Confederate Commissioners Head to Canada

Richmond and City Point, Virginia—April–May 1864

Snowflakes fell in Richmond in early April 1864 but by the middle of the month the days had turned warm, the sun shined brightly, and the cherry trees were in bloom across the city.[1] Jefferson Davis knew spring would also bring renewed fighting. The Confederate Army would soon face a newly-promoted Ulysses Grant. His victories in the Western theater of the war, chiefly the battles of Vicksburg and Chattanooga, convinced Lincoln he was a general who could truly fight. In March, Lincoln had elevated Grant to the rank of Lieutenant General and, in that role, he would serve as General-in-Chief of the Armies of the United States. In the coming months, Grant and Confederate General Robert E. Lee would face off in battles that would rage across Virginia and likely determine the fate of the Confederacy.

Also approaching was the election. In November, voters across the Union would cast their ballots for president and determine whether Lincoln would win a second term. Davis recognized that, at this point in the war, ballots could be as effective as bullets in achieving the goals of the Confederacy. So long as Lincoln remained in the White House, there was no hope for any compromise that would allow Southern independence and preserve the institution of slavery.

On the other hand, if a Democrat replaced Lincoln in the White House—after running on a platform opposing Lincoln's conduct of the war—many possibilities opened up, including a cessation of the fighting and possibly the start of negotiations between the North and South toward a settlement of the war.[2]

If there ever was to be a time to explore the possibilities of a negotiated settlement—and at the same time attempt to gain leverage by intensifying the anti-war sentiment in the North—it was now, Davis concluded. Davis's idea was to use agents in Canada to stir up anti-war sentiment in the North and to incite insurrection in the Northwest states to the extent possible. Davis had picked the Kentuckian Tom Hines, the former raider with Morgan's Confederate cavalry, to lead insurrection activities. However, he still needed men to coordinate political actions that could lead to a negotiated settlement, actions that should begin well before the election to take advantage of any Lincoln defeat.

Rather than attempt to negotiate directly with Washington, which he considered a waste of time, Davis decided to appoint emissaries representing the Confederacy to seek out leading opponents of the Lincoln administration and peace advocates generally. Like Hines, they would also be based in Canada.

As Davis wrote in his memoirs:

> A commission of three persons, eminent in position and intelligence was accordingly appointed to visit Canada with a view to negotiate with such persons in the North as might be relied on to aid the attainment of peace. The commission was designed to facilitate such preliminary conditions as might lead to formal negotiations between the two governments, and they were expected to make judicious use of any political opportunity that might be presented.[3]

By the end of April 1864, Davis had found the three men who would form his team.

* * * * *

On May 6, 1864, a sleek, narrow 154-foot side-wheel steamer named the *Thistle* sailed slowly down the Cape Fear River in North Carolina, having left Wilmington the night before. The *Thistle* was heading for the open waters of the Atlantic. Built in 1854 in the shipyards of Clyde, Scotland, the ship was a fast-moving blockade runner, part of the fleet of privately-owned vessels operating on behalf of the Confederacy to evade the Union blockade.

Blockade running was a risky but profitable activity during the Civil War. By 1864, the value of cotton in European markets had skyrocketed nearly 1000 percent since the war started, with a bale of cotton selling for between five hundred and six hundred dollars or more.[4] At the same time, food in the Confederacy was at a premium and imported food from the North or even Europe could command extremely high prices. As a result, owners of fast-sailing schooners and other vessels turned to running the blockade as a way to make huge profits by trading goods—and sometimes ferrying people—to and from the Southern states.

Aboard the *Thistle* were two of the three men who would serve as Confederate commissioners in Canada. The lead commissioner, Jacob Thompson, was a fifty-four-year-old lawyer from Mississippi. Thompson and Confederate President Davis, fellow members of Mississippi's aristocratic planter class, had known each other for nearly half a century. Tall, with brown hair, a goatee and a long face, Thompson had also spent twelve years representing Mississippi in the U.S. House of Representatives from 1839 to 1851.[5]

Thompson ran a losing campaign for the Senate in 1856.[6] As compensation for his loss, Thompson was rewarded with a cabinet post, serving as Secretary of the Interior in the Buchanan administration. When the war started, he joined the Confederacy and served as an aide to Confederate commanders in the western theater. After Vicksburg fell in 1863, he was elected to the Mississippi state legislature, which was where Davis found him in April 1864.[7]

Well-read and highly intelligent, Thompson was fluent in Italian and French.[8]

He was supportive and loyal to his friends and family but was often seen as humorless. Years after their association during the war, Hines would describe Thompson as inclined "to trust too many men, doubt too little and suspect less."[9] Indeed, Thompson was known to hand out money to just about anyone who could convince him they had a viable scheme—real or not—that could advance Confederate goals.[10]

In early April, Davis summoned Thompson to Richmond, asking him, "If your engagements will permit you to accept service abroad for the next six months, please come here immediately."[11] They met in Richmond at a meeting that went on into the early morning hours.

Jacob Thompson (Library of Congress, Prints & Photographs Division, LC-DIG- cwpbh-02849).

Davis outlined his plan for the Canada assignment. Thompson was to focus on fanning the anti-war sentiment of the Copperheads and other opponents of the war in the North—through raids and other attacks—to bring the fighting to an end. Inside Canada itself, Davis instructed Thompson to mobilize the population of former Confederate prisoners of war and other Confederate agents, using them as a guerrilla force for the attacks.[12]

The second commissioner on the *Thistle* was Clement Claiborne Clay of Alabama. Like Thompson, Clay was a lawyer and plantation owner. During the 1840s, he had served in the Alabama state legislature and later in the U.S. Senate, resigning when the war started. He was then elected to the Senate of the Confederacy.

Clay, forty-eight-years-old, came from a political family; his father served as Alabama's governor and then a U.S. Senator from the state. Clay was the third cousin of Henry Clay, the Kentucky legislator and statesman who had tried to defuse sectional conflict decades earlier as the "Great Compromiser." With curly brown hair, a full beard, and sad, languid eyes, Clay was frail and sickly, afflicted with asthma and other ailments that made him "peevish, irritable and suspicious," qualities that did not auger well for harmonious relations with his fellow commissioners.[13]

Clay was defeated for reelection to the Confederate Senate in 1863 and had hoped for appointment to a high-level foreign post or a position in Davis's cabinet. Neither was forthcoming, however, and when Davis offered Clay the Canada mission he accepted it, with some misgivings because the posting would be in Canada instead of Europe.[14]

Thompson and Clay were bound for Canada. Their plan was for the *Thistle* to take them as far as Bermuda, eight hundred miles due east of the North Carolina coast.

Clement C. Clay (Library of Congress, Prints & Photographs Division, LC-DIG-ppmsca-26708).

This was a common transit point for Confederate agents making their way to Canada by sea after running the blockade.

In Bermuda, they would transfer to a British steamer that would take them as far as Halifax, Nova Scotia. From there, the two commissioners would make their way overland through New Brunswick to the St. Lawrence River where they would venture by rail or sail to their ultimate destinations of Montreal and Toronto.

Near nightfall on the Cape Fear River, as the *Thistle* approached the river's mouth on the coast, the ship's crewmen could make out in the distance a blockading squadron of thirteen Union ships. The ship's captain warned that the real danger would come in the morning when the *Thistle* would no longer be cloaked by darkness.[15]

In order not to attract the attention of enemy vessels during its runs through the blockade, the *Thistle* was kept in excellent operating condition. "All the parts of the machinery were kept well oiled, so that they worked noiselessly," wrote another *Thistle* passenger, William W. Cleary, who served as secretary to Thompson and Clay.[16] Every light on board was extinguished. The ship's engine burned anthracite coal which emitted little or no smoke. And "a sort of a hood was put over the furnace to prevent any reflection of its fires being seen," Cleary added.[17]

At about 7 a.m. the next day, the *Thistle's* lookout sighted a Union ship sailing directly toward them at a rapid speed, with black smoke pouring from its stacks. To distract the approaching vessel, the Confederate ironclad CSS *Raleigh* attempted to engage it while the *Thistle* ran north. But that diversion only worked for a short time. Over the next five hours, the *Thistle* and its Union pursuer played cat and mouse off the North Carolina coast.[18]

Ultimately, the *Thistle's* efforts at evasion failed as the Union vessel, now identified as the USS *Connecticut*—one of the swiftest ships in the Union Navy—came closer, just short of its guns' firing range. Expecting capture or worse, Thompson and Clay began burning papers and notes they had brought aboard. As they did so, the Confederate team fortified themselves with "Dutch Courage"* from the captain's shelves, Cleary wrote later. "We all agreed afterward that we were very cool and calm—that is, each man said he was—and that we would have tried with patriotic integrity to escape a fate not provided for in our instructions."[19]

As the *Thistle's* passengers continued to scuttle their possessions, the *Connecticut* suddenly seemed to stall, an apparent mechanical problem halting its pursuit. "At any rate, we got away and in a short time were out of sight of that ominous black smoke," Cleary wrote.[20]

Safely beyond the range of the Union's coastal squadron, the *Thistle* continued to Bermuda. Upon its arrival in St. George, a Union Jack flying in the harbor saluted the *Thistle*, now with a Confederate flag flying at its stern. After a few more days, the Confederate party sailed from St. George aboard the British mail steamer *Alpha* and arrived at Halifax, Nova Scotia on May 19.[21]

Two days after they arrived in Halifax, Thompson and Cleary boarded a boat and sailed across the Bay of Fundy to St. John, New Brunswick. From there, they went by carriage to Riviere du Loup on the St. Lawrence River and then to Montreal by rail.[22] Clay stayed in Halifax for several more days before rejoining Thompson in Montreal, arriving the first week of June.[23]

The third commissioner, James Holcombe, was already in Canada. Holcombe, a law professor at the University of Virginia, had initially been sent by Davis to Halifax three months earlier to investigate a possible legal claim for the Confederacy. A Union ship, the USS *Chesapeake,* had been captured and brought to Canada by pirates who claimed to be acting for the Confederacy. Davis wanted Holcombe to determine whether the Confederacy had any right to the ship and its cargo. When Holcombe learned that the men were British subjects instead of Confederates, he advised Davis not to pursue a claim.[24]

Holcombe had been born in Virginia but moved to Indiana as a child when his parents decided they wanted to raise their family in a free state. He attended Yale as an undergraduate and received a law degree from the University of Virginia Law School. After practicing law in Ohio for a few years, in 1851 Holcombe joined the law

---

*"Dutch Courage" refers to liquor. The phrase, intended to be derisive, was often used by the British in the 17th and 18th centuries when speaking of the Dutch, who were frequent rivals on the high seas.

faculty at the University of Virginia. At the law school, Holcombe authored several legal treatises and became an outspoken supporter of slavery.[25]

With Holcombe already in Canada, Davis asked him to take on a second assignment: locate Confederate soldiers who had escaped from prison camps in the North and arrange passage back to the Confederacy for those who wished to return to their military units. Holcombe soon learned, however, that the number of such men was nowhere near as large as officials in Richmond had expected, or hoped—probably not more than a hundred. Davis then asked Holcombe to serve as a commissioner and remain in Halifax to assist Thompson and Clay when they arrived.[26]

* * * * *

On May 5, 1864, the day before Thompson and Clay started their voyage down the Cape Fear River, John Yates Beall became a free man. Shortly after his chains were removed in December 1863, he and the other members of his team were transferred from Fort McHenry to Fort Monroe, the Union garrison on the coast near Hampton Roads, Virginia, where the Chesapeake Bay meets the Atlantic Ocean. After two months, they were transferred again, this time to Point Lookout, another Union prison in Maryland on the Chesapeake Bay south of Baltimore. After about two more months, in late April or early May, Beall and his men were taken to City Point, Virginia.[27]

City Point was a rail hub located at the junction of the James and Appomattox Rivers about twenty miles south of Richmond. City Point had earlier been the site of prisoner exchanges until the end of the prisoner exchange cartel in 1863. At the time of Beall's release, it was being fortified to become the Union Army's field headquarters for the siege of Petersburg, nine miles further south. Petersburg, where five rail lines converged, was a vital rail center that provided supplies to Richmond. Grant knew that if he severed the supply lines between Richmond and Petersburg, the Confederacy could not survive.

The siege, which lasted from June 1864 to April 1865, involved a series of assaults, probes, skirmishes and battles. During the siege, Grant's troops would build over thirty miles of trenches that extended from Petersburg to the outskirts of Richmond, in a precursor to the type of trench warfare that followed fifty years later during World War I. The siege was successful in cutting off Richmond from Petersburg and ultimately led to Lee's surrender at Appomattox.

In late December 1863, with the formal prisoner exchange cartel still sidelined, Major General Benjamin F. Butler was ordered to "take charge" of Confederate prisoner exchanges at several Union prisons.[28] Butler, formerly the commander at Fort McHenry, was now the head of the Union Army's Department of Virginia at Fort Monroe. With more reports about the poor treatment of Union prisoners held by the Confederacy, Butler's appointment "was a concession to the demand of the people of the North that something should be done to obtain the release of the prisoners in the South," according to historian William Hesseltine. Butler had pressed Lincoln officials to address the prisoner treatment issue, even sending vaccines to Robert Ould, the Confederate official in charge of Union prisoners held by the South.[29]

Any exchanges had to be "man for man" and "officer for officer of equal rank," according to the order from Major General Ethan Allen Hitchcock, the Army's Commissioner for Prisoner Exchanges.[30] Butler then sent 505 sick and injured Confederate prisoners to City Point for exchange with the South. Robert Ould, the agent of exchange for the Confederate Army, sent an equivalent number of Union troops for exchange.[31] It appears that Beall and several of his men were included as part of this prisoner exchange, although none of them at the time were sick or injured.

After his release, Beall went to Richmond, spending a few days visiting friends. He also met again with Confederate officials, including Davis and Navy Secretary Mallory, volunteering for new assignments. They referred him to Secretary of War James A. Seddon who tried to convince Beall to join the Confederacy's newly-created Secret Service. Beall rejected the offer, telling Seddon he did not want to be under the command of superiors he did not know and where "obedience might have demanded a sacrifice of his own moral convictions."[32]

Instead, before Beall left Richmond, he took advantage of an opportunity to once again take up arms against the Union Army, if only for a few days. He joined Confederate ranks as a combatant to defend Richmond from advancing Union forces.

Grant's spring campaign in the spring of 1864, known as the Virginia Overland Campaign, had begun. After crossing the Rapidan River in early May, Grant fought General Robert E. Lee's Army of Virginia in the Battle of the Wilderness, the first major battle in the campaign which took place about seventeen miles east of Fredericksburg.

The Wilderness was an area of dense pine forest and scraggly undergrowth, too thick to allow the use of heavy artillery. Soldiers fired half blindly toward the other side, with the shots of hot lead igniting kindling of dried pine branches and needles that set the forest ablaze. As many men were killed by flames as by gunshots in the two days of battle. More than 17,000 Union troops were killed, injured or missing, while Lee's forces suffered more than 7,500 casualties.[33] Neither side won any significant advantage. Unlike his Union Army general predecessors, however, Grant did not withdraw after the setback but proceeded with his offensive, going south, attempting to position his Army between Lee and Richmond.

On May 8, the Union's Army of the Potomac under Major Gen. George Meade moved south toward Spotsylvania where the next major battle would take place. Major General Phillip Sheridan, the Army of the Potomac's cavalry commander, appealed to Meade, asking him to use the cavalry offensively to attack rather than the more traditional cavalry roles of screening and reconnaissance. Specifically, Sheridan told Meade that if he were permitted to break off and operate as a separate offensive unit, he could defeat his cavalry counterpart on the Confederate side, Major General J.E.B. Stuart.

Meade went to Grant, the senior commander, telling Grant that Sheridan wanted to "be left alone" to go after "Jeb" Stuart and the Confederate cavalry. Grant knew Sheridan. Sheridan's cavalry had assisted Grant in the Western theater earlier in the war. "Did Sheridan say that?" Grant queried. "Well, he generally knows what he's talking about," he told Meade. "Let him start right out and do it."[34]

The next day, Sheridan's ten thousand cavalrymen began moving south toward Richmond to engage Stuart's cavalry. Church bells in Richmond clanged in alarm as citizens learned of the Yankee cavalry's approach. The city was thinly defended, with a ragtag force of only a few thousand local troops, mostly made up of boys and recovering rebel soldiers just released from hospitals.[35]

Skirmishes between the two cavalries went on for several days, centering on an area six miles north of Richmond. On May 11, even though Stuart was outnumbered nearly two to one, he brought his full force of 4,500 cavalry to battle Sheridan. In what later became known as the Battle of Yellow Tavern, Stuart was shot by a Union sniper, mortally wounding the Confederate general.

It was at this point that Beall joined the fighting, attaching himself to a rebel engineering unit fighting along Mechanicsburg Road north of Richmond. His military escapade did not last long, however. After a few days, the fighting subsided. Sheridan realized that, although he may have been able to pierce Richmond's defenses and take the city, he lacked the forces and staying power to withstand any counterattack.[36] As the fighting subsided, Beall lost patience with the lack of attention being given to his unit by Confederate officers. With the unit he was with essentially stranded and on its own, Beall left the battlefield.[37] Sheridan turned east, then north and soon rejoined Grant's main force. Sheridan's raid had little lasting impact on the war, other than the death of Stuart, one of the South's best generals.

During this period following his release,[38] Beall also headed south to Columbus, Georgia, where he would have what he later called "the happiest two weeks of my life." He spent the two weeks with his fiancé Martha O'Bryan who was staying in Columbus with relatives until the war subsided in her permanent home of Nashville. They had not seen each other for two years.[39]

Beall tried to convince O'Bryan to marry him then, not waiting until the end of the war. They would then go to England where he had relatives. Martha could stay with Beall's relatives while he returned to leading commando attacks against Union shipping on behalf of the Confederacy—this time on the other side of the Atlantic. O'Bryan turned down the invitation, telling Beall she thought it would be unpatriotic to leave her family and friends in the midst of a war while she lived in safety. It was a decision she later said she would regret for the rest of her life.[40]

Beall returned once again to Richmond, but this time he did not stay long. He headed north. By June, he had gone as far as his old privateering base on the Chesapeake Bay near Mathews Courthouse, Virginia. He continued north through Baltimore, then to New York. In August, he would arrive in Canada where he would meet Jacob Thompson and Thomas Hines.[41]

CHAPTER 13

Battle Plans and Diplomacy

Canada West—Summer 1864

The Queen's Hotel in Toronto was widely considered to be one of the preeminent hotels in all of British North America. Built in 1844, the four-story hotel had 210 rooms, seventeen parlors, a fine restaurant, a private garden, an elevator and running water in all its rooms. It was located directly across from the railroad station and had a commanding view of Lake Ontario.[1]

By 1864, the hotel had acquired another feature of note. It was the central gathering place for southerners who had come to Toronto, with a clientele that included aristocratic former plantation owners, Confederate agents and fugitive rebel soldiers, many of whom had escaped from Union prison camps.

Historian James D. Horan described the scene:

> There was no mistaking the escaped Rebel prisoners. They hung around the lobby and bar of the Queen's, trying to appear respectable in torn gray coats and cracked jackboots or in cast-off clothes they had robbed from some clothesline after climbing the board fences of Camps Chase, Morton, or Johnson's Island. They were gaunt, hollow-eyed men, with faces lined and tanned the color of old leather by the relentless sun which had scorched the treeless prison yards that rainless summer.[2]

As of early June 1864, the hotel's guest list included one more émigré from the Confederacy: Jacob Thompson, the lead Confederate commissioner appointed by Jefferson Davis. Thompson had come to Toronto after a brief stay in Montreal. He and his fellow commissioner, Clement Clay, had arrived in Montreal in late May. Thomas Hines had arrived in Toronto in late April. He had taken a room in a boarding house near the Queen's Hotel, in part to maintain some distance from Thompson, at least publicly.[3]

The stylish hotel met the standards Thompson looked for in his accommodations, providing comfortable rooms, fine cuisine and an extensive collection of wine. It also had a telegraph office on the main floor that provided quick communication with Richmond. Guests could follow the day's news thanks to easy access to several U.S. newspapers that arrived each day in the hotel lobby.[4]

While Thompson and Clay traveled to Canada using the sea route through Bermuda, Hines had come by land. He left Richmond in early April and headed north, crossing the Potomac River at night and entering Washington, D.C. Hines had no particular need to stop in the Union capital but, according to Hines family lore, he did so to win a bet. The night before he departed Richmond, a group of fellow Confederate officers feted him at a banquet. Over champagne, Hines wagered with another officer that he would pass through Washington on his way to Canada and shake hands with President Lincoln.[5]

After the war, according to Hines's son, Hines reunited with his betting partner and collected on the bet. It is unclear exactly what Hines offered as proof of his rendezvous with the president but at this stage of the war Washington was awash with Rebel agents who could have vouched for his claim. There is even speculation that Hines may have been able to obtain an audience with Lincoln because of his strong resemblance to John Wilkes Booth, Lincoln's favorite actor.[6]

From Washington, Hines traveled to Cincinnati, then on to Detroit where he took the ferry across the Detroit River to Windsor in Canada. He arrived in Toronto the week of April 20.[7] After Thompson's arrival in early June, Confederate officials in Richmond revised Hines's earlier orders to make it clear that his role would be subordinate to Thompson and the other commissioners.[8]

Later in June, Thompson remained in Toronto while Clay and James Holcombe established their base of operations on the southern side of Lake Ontario. Clay went to St. Catherines, a resort town on Lake Ontario a few miles from Niagara Falls. Here Clay, who remained afflicted with various ailments, could take advantage of "pleasant curative baths" while keeping in touch with Copperhead groups on the other side of the border.[9]

St. Catherines was located next to the Welland Canal—first built in the 1820s— which allowed ships to transit between Lake Erie and Lake Ontario, bypassing Niagara Falls. Railroad lines near Niagara Falls ran west, south and east across the United States, permitting Clay to meet with visitors from the Union and the Confederacy.[10]

Holcombe took up residence on the Canadian side of Niagara Falls at the Clifton House, a three-story, sixty-room hotel, with a full-on view of the Horseshoe Falls. Holcombe and Clay also met with a steady stream of prominent Democrats, many of them strong anti-war Democrats, who crossed the suspension bridge to the Canadian side of Niagara Falls to meet at the Clifton House.

Clay and Holcombe were joined by George Sanders, another Confederate who spent time in both Montreal and Niagara Falls. Sanders became so involved with the activities of Thompson, Clay and Holcombe that historians of this period often refer to him as an unofficial, fourth commissioner.[11]

Sanders was the former editor of New York's *Democratic Review,* a political organ of the Democratic party. Before the war, he had also worked as a navy purchasing agent and later had arranged arms purchases for the Confederacy. Jefferson Davis asked Sanders to help Thompson create support for Copperhead peace efforts.[12] Sanders and Thompson met with northern Democrats, trying to find a peace candidate to run against Lincoln in the 1864 election.[13]

Sanders had little respect for Canadian neutrality and tried to convince

Thompson that launching robberies of Buffalo banks from Canada was a legitimate act of war by the Confederacy.[14] Sanders also advocated the assassination of leaders he considered to be tyrants, including Lincoln.[15]

Thompson, Clay, Holcombe and Sanders were hardly the ideal team to develop and execute high-level clandestine plots for the Confederacy against the Union. As individuals, each of the men lacked the necessary experience and judgment to perform the duties Davis had assigned them. As a group, they bickered and lacked trust in each other. John B. Castleman, a close friend of Hines and

George N. Sanders (McCord Stewart Museum [I-13580.1]).

a former member of Morgan's raiders, had first-hand experience working with Hines and the commissioners in Canada. In his memoir, Castleman describes Thompson as "always a gentleman but ... not a diplomat." He adds, Thompson was "disqualified for the duties of commissioner by being unable to realize that many men were not as honorable as he."[16]

Of Clay, Castleman wrote, "He was not a practical man, he lacked judgment and he was in ill health, was peevish, irritable and suspicious. He distrusted his colleague, Thompson, and he relied on those who were often unworthy."[17]

Holcombe, while recognized as an accomplished legal scholar, had "neither experience nor tact nor knowledge of men, all of which were requisites to deal with the serious questions presented to the Confederate commissioners," Castleman wrote.[18]

Sanders had such a strong personality that he "controlled Mr. Clay" and "dominated" Holcombe, according to Castleman. Although Sanders "had no influence" with Thompson or Hines, "he was a constant menace to the interests for which the Confederate commissioners were made responsible," Castleman wrote.[19]

One of the first duties Thompson needed to take care of after his arrival in

Canada was depositing nearly one million dollars in Canadian banks. The bills of exchange in gold and hard currencies that Thompson brought from Richmond were deposited in the Bank of Montreal and the Ontario Bank. Another $100,000 was deposited in the Niagara and District Bank in St. Catharines. According to Montreal historian Barry Sheehy, "Given the capital ratios for banks at the time, the money deposited in the Ontario Bank (Montreal) and Niagara and District Bank (St. Catherines) gave the Confederates enormous influence, if not effective control, over these institutions."[20]

On June 9, Hines traveled west to Windsor in Canada-West, just across the river from Detroit, to meet with Clement Vallandigham, the anti-war Democrat who was now living in exile. Vallandigham was now the leader of the Sons of Liberty, the successor organization to the Order of American Knights. It was the largest and most well-known of the organized anti-war societies. Despite his domicile in Canada, Vallandigham was in communication with Copperhead groups and other Sons of Liberty chapters across the northwest states. Hines's meeting with Vallandigham was a "preliminary interview" to sound out Vallandigham about his support for activities to foment insurrection in the northwestern states.[21]

Vallandigham's response was encouraging and on June 11 Hines met with Vallandigham a second time, now joined by Thompson and officers of the Sons of Liberty. At this meeting, Vallandigham made much of the strength of the Copperhead movement, telling Thompson and Hines that there were as many as three hundred thousand Copperheads in Illinois, Indiana, and Ohio whose strength they could call on. Many of the Copperheads had military training, having served in the Union Army, Vallandigham said. All of them were ready to join an armed uprising and take over their state governments, he added. All they lacked was funding.[22]

Thompson offered Vallandigham money to buy arms but Vallandigham refused, saying he did not want to be directly involved. Instead, he turned to James J. Barrett, a Sons of Liberty member with the title of Adjutant-General, and told Thompson to turn over the money to him.[23] Ultimately, Thompson committed nearly $500,000 to the plot to foment insurrection in the northwestern states, an amount that, adjusted for inflation, would come to about $9.4 million in 2022.[24]

Also present at the meeting was Charles Walsh, the Brigadier General of the Sons of Liberty who was also a Democratic political boss in Chicago. Walsh pointed out that the Democratic party was scheduled to hold its convention to nominate a presidential candidate in Chicago beginning on July Fourth. Camp Douglas, a large prisoner of war facility, was located in Chicago two hundred yards from Lake Michigan and about three miles from the heart of the city.[25] It was named after Stephen A. Douglas, the Illinois Democrat who ran against Lincoln in the 1860 presidential election, who had died of typhoid in 1861. The camp was initially used to train soldiers early in the war. With the capture of thousands of Confederates after Grant's 1862 victory at Fort Donelson in Tennessee, it was transformed into a prisoner of war camp. By August 1864, the prison held more than 7,600 Confederate prisoners who were housed in crude, clapboard shacks.[26]

The discussion turned to the feasibility of using the crowds and clamor of the convention as cover for an ambitious three-pronged attack on Camp Douglas. Hines would lead a squad of former Confederates from Canada. They would be joined in Chicago by a force of thousands of armed Copperheads and Sons of Liberty members who would overwhelm the guards at Camp Douglas and release the prisoners. The freed prisoners would seize arms from local arsenals and—together with the Copperheads, other disaffected citizens and Hines's force from Canada—"move as small armies," in the words of historian John C. Waugh.[27] As they moved through northern states, they would release prisoners at other prison camps in Indiana (Camp Morton) and Ohio (Johnson's Island, Camp Chase). They would march south, sever telegraph lines, seize the railroads, storm state capitals and take control.[28] In a coded report to Confederate Secretary of War James Seddon, Hines estimated the force could number as many as fifty thousand men.[29] Even if the effort failed, it would create enough havoc to force Union Army leaders to divert Union troops away from the Virginia battlefields to the northern states to quell the insurrection.[30]

There are some accounts, not necessarily substantiated, that Confederate General Jubal Early's raid on Washington in July 1864 was also part of the plot. "General Early was to lay siege to Washington, and thus make it impossible for the federal government to send troops to the points to be attacked [by the released prisoners and Confederate sympathizers]," according to an article in *Confederate Veteran* magazine published in July 1900.[31] Early's attack—notable because it was the only battle that President Lincoln witnessed and came under enemy fire—reached the outskirts of Washington but failed to penetrate the city's defenses.

Early, aware of the claims that his troops were part of the plot, attempted to rebut them after the war, writing in the *Journal of the Southern Historical Society*: "I therefore deem it proper and necessary to ... disclaim all knowledge whatever of the alleged plot or conspiracy." The timing of his attack on Washington, he wrote, was totally dependent on his success in outmaneuvering Union forces in the Shenandoah Valley and Maryland. "I did not delay my attack on Washington, for I made none; but finding the defenses of that city occupied by a force much superior to my own.... I retired across the Potomac," Early wrote.[32]

According to the Sons of Liberty leaders with Vallandigham, at least two factors weighed in favor of starting the insurrection in Illinois. First, the Copperhead movement appeared to be stronger in Illinois than in any other northwestern state, with nearly five thousand members said to be in Chicago alone. Second, Camp Douglas itself held many prisoners who were former members of Morgan's raiders, hardened warriors who were almost always the ringleaders of escape plots at the prison.[33]

All those present at the meeting believed that the time was ripe to take action in the Northwest. Thompson summed up their rationale a few weeks later in a letter to

John Slidell, the Confederate minister to France, and James M. Mason, the Confederate minister to Great Britain:

> The severity of military orders, and a total disregard of private rights and personal liberty in the Western States of Kentucky, Missouri, Indiana, Illinois, and Ohio has aroused the people to madness, and prepared them in their desperation to seize upon the first glimmer of hope to dare all, and in doing so to regain what they have lost. In order to arouse the people, political meetings called "peace meetings" have been held and inflammatory addresses delivered, and whenever orators have expressed themselves for peace with the restoration of the Union, and if that can not be, then peace on any terms, the cheers and clamor of the masses have known no bounds.[34]

While Thompson, Hines and Vallandigham were beginning to formulate plans to coincide with the Democratic convention in July, leading Democrats were coming under pressure to postpone the political gathering. Many party members believed there was too much in flux—both on the battlefield and in the party—to come to agreement on a candidate or a platform.

The uncertain course of the war and unresolved issues between peace Democrats and war Democrats over the party platform gave rise to calls to delay the convention until September. By September, the thinking went, events on the battlefield might clarify the direction of the war in a way that would help unify the party's rank and file toward a war platform or a peace platform. Democrats could not defeat Lincoln if they remained divided over war and peace, party leaders agreed. By the end of June, a decision was made. The Democrats would put off the convention for eight weeks, until August 29.[35]

With the basic plans for the Chicago attack set in motion, Thompson turned to other matters, including purchasing arms to use in the Copperhead raids, attempting to buy influence with northern newspaper editors and meeting with anti-war politicians from the northern states.

When it came to purchasing arms and influencing Union newspapers and Democratic politicians, two brothers in New York provided a one-stop opportunity. Fernando and Benjamin Wood were influential Democratic politicians in New York City. Fernando had just stepped down as mayor and now served in Congress as a representative from New York. Benjamin also served in Congress from a neighboring district and ran the *New York Daily News*, an anti–Republican newspaper and also the city's largest.[36] Along with its news dispatches, the newspaper printed letters and classified ads with coded messages from Confederate spies in the North intended for Confederate leaders in the South.[37]

At some point during the summer of 1864, Hines and Thompson arranged for $25,000 to be transferred to the *Daily News*. Their intention was for the newspaper "to serve as the house organ for Confederate aims," a role that included trumpeting "peace, peace, peace" and continuing the newspaper's ongoing crusade against the war.[38]

The Confederate Commissioners' secretary, William Cleary, served as a go-between, meeting Fernando Wood at a violin shop near Washington Square in New York City. Cleary purchased a variety of arms and ammunition, including rifles, pistols, and components to make an incendiary weapon known as Greek Fire. It was a mixture of naptha and quicklime that would ignite on contact, developed by the Byzantine Greeks in the seventh century. The Confederates smuggled the armaments into Canada and then sent them back across the border into the Northern states packed in boxes labeled as "prayer books."[39]

At one meeting, Benjamin Wood apparently told Clay that, if an insurrection started in the northwestern states, he could virtually guarantee an uprising in New York City to add to the chaos.[40] The risks taken by the two Wood brothers in meeting with and assisting the rebel agents were incalculable. If their collusion were discovered, they could have been tried and executed for treason.[41]

* * * * *

One of the strangest episodes involving the Confederate Commissioners concerned a "Peace Conference" held on the Canadian side of Niagara Falls in July 1864. In early July, Horace Greeley, the editor of the staunchly Republican New York *Tribune* received a note from William Jewett, an American and ardent peace advocate in Canada, who knew Greeley and was in touch with George Sanders, the strong-willed "fourth commissioner." In the note, Jewett said the commissioners in Canada had "full and complete powers for peace" and asked Greeley to come to Canada for a meeting to discuss conditions for ending the war. Greeley, who also opposed the war, contacted Lincoln by letter, notifying him of Jewett's note and urging the president to make a peace offer, reminding him "that our bleeding, bankrupt, almost dying country also longs for peace."[42]

Greeley was an influential newspaper editor, not only in New York but throughout the Midwest. His *Weekly Tribune* had a circulation of two hundred thousand in the key states of Ohio and Illinois. Lincoln could hardly ignore Greeley's request. Lincoln needed to show the Democrats and the Confederates that he was willing to listen to reasonable peace proposals. If he rejected Greeley's request, the editor would likely portray Lincoln as determined to continue the bloodshed, potentially costing him the support of voters in the North who wanted an end to the war.[43]

Lincoln responded to Greeley but established firm guidelines for the negotiations. In a letter to Greeley, the president wrote that he would send his cabinet secretary, John Hay, to meet in Canada with "any person anywhere professing to have any proposition of Jefferson Davis in writing for peace." He attached two conditions to any agreement with Confederacy: "restoration of the union and abandonment of slavery."[44]

Greeley and Hay traveled to Niagara Falls where on July 20 they met with Holcombe and Sanders at the Clifton House on the Canadian side of the falls. The two other commissioners did not attend. Clay was out of town and Thompson wanted no part of the endeavor, believing it a waste of time since he knew neither he nor any of the other commissioners had authority from Richmond to negotiate with Lincoln.

Greeley also knew this and informed Lincoln but added that he believed the commissioners could quickly obtain negotiating authority if the discussions proved positive.[45]

Shortly after the meeting started, Hay handed Holcombe a note from Lincoln stating his conditions for any peace agreement, including the end of slavery and restoration of the union. Holcombe read the note and said he would confer with the other commissioners and respond the next day.[46]

In a letter to Greeley, the commissioners assailed Lincoln's conditions which they said "returns to the policy of no negotiations, no truce with the rebels until every man shall have laid down his arms … and sued for peace." They also denounced Greeley, saying he had misled them into believing the negotiations would have no conditions imposed in advance.[47] Although it embarrassed Lincoln and Greeley, the fiasco at Niagara Falls ended up as a minor footnote in the war.

On July 22, two days after the Niagara Falls conference, Thompson, Hines and Castleman traveled to St. Catherines where they met once more with several Sons of Liberty members. Many of these same Sons of Liberty members were also delegates to the Democratic convention, demonstrating the extent to which the Confederate clandestine efforts in Canada had succeeded in infiltrating the Democratic party itself.[48]

While many meetings between the commissioners and northern peace Democrats are reasonably well-documented, a less well-known series of meetings took place between the commissioners and disaffected Republicans, including persons representing members of Lincoln's own cabinet.

The meetings with Republicans were documented by Barry Sheehy, the Canadian-based writer and historian, who examined the archived guest register of St. Lawrence Hall, the hotel in Montreal that served as the key meeting spot in that city for Confederate agents during the Civil War years.

Sheehy's research shows that Thaddeus Stevens, the outspoken radical and anti-war Republican congressman from Pennsylvania, checked into Montreal's St. Lawrence Hall in August 1864 with several other Republicans.[49]

Their arrival coincided with what appeared to be the low-point of Lincoln's prospects for re-election. Grant's Union troops were stalled outside the city of Petersburg and the horrible losses already suffered by Union troops in Grant's spring offensive—more than 64,000 casualties—shocked Northerners.[50] Union General William Sherman had just suffered defeat at Kennesaw Mountain in Georgia. After more than three years of fighting, with seemingly no end in sight, the Union was war weary.[51]

On August 19, a group of radical Republicans met in New York to discuss calling for a new Republican convention and forcing Lincoln off the ticket.[52] Lincoln had been re-nominated in June at the Republican convention in Cincinnati.

New York *Tribune* editor Horace Greeley openly called for a replacement ticket. As substitute presidential candidates, he proposed Union Generals Ulysses Grant, Benjamin Butler or William Sherman and Navy Admiral David Farragut for vice president.[53]

Thurlow Weed, New York's Republican boss, was doubtful about Lincoln's chances, writing in August to Secretary of State Seward that Lincoln's re-election was an "impossibility…. The People are wild for Peace."[54]

Lincoln himself had doubts. On August 23, he wrote out a memorandum stating: "This morning, as for some days past, it seems exceedingly probable that this Administration will not be re-elected." In the document, Lincoln pledged that he would cooperate with the President-elect, assuming it was not going to be him. Lincoln asked the members of his cabinet to sign the back of the memorandum as witnesses without reading it.[55]

To make matters worse, in July Lincoln had ordered a call up of five hundred thousand additional volunteers and threatened to impose a new draft if the troop quotas were not met by early September. The move was wildly unpopular in the North where communities had already lost large numbers of men to the war.[56]

It was at this time that Montreal and Toronto were flooded with Democratic and Republican politicians, "all rubbing elbows with the Confederate Secret Service. Everyone was scrambling for safe ground," according to Sheehy.[57]

Also in August, Lincoln's Secretary of War Edwin Stanton went so far as to dispatch a friend, Jeremiah Black, to meet with Thompson in Toronto to discuss peace prospects before the election.[58] Black and Stanton had served together in the Buchanan administration—Black as Secretary of State and Stanton as Attorney General.

On August 20, the two men met at the Queen's Hotel. Stanton instructed Black to inquire about Southern morale, determination to fight and interest in peace.[59] Stanton also authorized Black to tell Thompson that restoration of the union would likely have to be part of any settlement. Thompson later wrote that, in addition to gauging "the state of feeling in the Confederate States," Black asked him "if negotiations for peace could be opened without the ultimatum of final separation."[60] Thompson added, "I am given to understand that a proposition will be considered which will secure us in all our rights, present and prospective," a somewhat vague reference that at least opens the possibility that Black went beyond his purview to suggest that ending slavery might not be required in a settlement.[61] The discussions between Black and Thompson ended after Thompson said he "was not authorized to make a direct and positive reply."[62]

It remains a mystery exactly why Stanton sent Black to Toronto. It is possible that he was unnerved by the possibility of having to leave office after Lincoln's expected defeat, fearing a backlash from a public angry about the administration's constraints on personal liberties, including the controversial imprisonment without trial of thousands of citizens and forced closure of several anti-war newspapers.[63] On August 22, *The New York Herald* reported Black's meeting with Thompson, suggesting that Stanton had authorized it. With Black's trip to Canada having been made public, Stanton denied he had approved it and rejected the idea of any armistice with the Confederacy.[64]

And Stanton was not the only Lincoln cabinet member who attempted to establish back-channel communications with the Confederate Commissioners during this time. Secretary of State William Seward, who was one of the Cabinet members closest to Lincoln, contacted the District Attorney in Detroit, Halmar H. Emmons, and asked him to act as an agent on his behalf to discuss peace prospects with Thompson and the other commissioners.[65] These discussions also failed to reap any significant results.

Thompson later alluded to the large number of Northerners making their way to Canada to confer with the Commissioners during this time. In a letter to the Confederate Secretary of State, Judah Benjamin, Thompson wrote: "I have so many papers in my possession, which in the hands of the enemy would utterly ruin and destroy very many of the prominent men in the North, that a due sense of my obligations to them will force on me the extremest caution in my movements."[66]

* * * * *

It was also in August 1864 when an event occurred—not reported at the time—that served as both an omen and a vivid example of the personal risks facing Lincoln. One warm evening, with his wife Mary out of town, Lincoln was riding alone on his way to the Soldiers' Home located on a hill outside Washington. Lincoln used the Soldiers' Home as an escape from the White House, which he called "the office." He particularly preferred the Soldiers' Home on hot summer nights where the air was cooler and the president found it easier to sleep.

As a guard at the Soldiers' Home, Private John W. Nichols, awaited the president's arrival, a gunshot rang out. Moments later, Lincoln and his horse came through the front gate. Nichols noticed that Lincoln was bareheaded and asked him what had happened. The president told him someone had fired a gun at the foot of the hill and caused his horse to bolt so suddenly that it "jerked his hat off."[67]

While Lincoln made his way to his quarters for the night, Nichols and another sentry went down the hill to look for the president's hat. They found the tall hat on the side of the road. It had holes on each side of the crown, showing that a bullet had pierced the hat inches above the president's skull. Lincoln told the guards he wanted the incident "kept quiet" and later said "No good can result at this time from giving it publicity."[68]

CHAPTER 14

A Gathering in Chicago

Toronto, Chicago, Sandusky—August 1864

They left Toronto in small groups—in pairs or parties of no more than five men—in order not to attract attention. Most of the men had served with Morgan's Confederate cavalry and would provide trained military leadership for the attack on Camp Douglas during the Democratic convention in Chicago. In all, seventy men would travel from Toronto as part of the squadron selected by Hines and his second-in-command, John Castleman.[1]

Each man was given a new pistol, ammunition, a train ticket to Chicago and a hundred dollars in cash for food and lodging. Some men departed Toronto as early as August 10 but most of them began their journey on August 24, five days before the Democratic convention was scheduled to begin.[2] Thompson had allocated $25,000 for the operation, which would pay for travel, living expenses, and firearms for the men involved in the Chicago attack and additional attacks and prison raids planned across the Northwestern states.[3]

Once in Chicago, Hines's men would join with members of the Sons of Liberty who were being recruited from downstate Illinois and Indiana. Charles Walsh, the Chicago-based brigadier general of the Sons of Liberty, told Hines and Thompson that he expected as many as two thousand members to be in Chicago to supply manpower to the core group that Hines and Castleman would bring from Canada.[4]

In order to maximize the element of surprise, the attack on Camp Douglas was to be made at night, most likely after the first day of the convention. To prevent or delay the dispatch of any Union troops sent as reinforcements for those already in Chicago, Hines assigned a team to cut the telegraph lines leading out of the city when the attack began.[5] Hines also made sure that word of the planned attack was communicated to prisoners in Camp Douglas so they would be ready to assist from inside the walls.

Once the prison was taken and secured, Castleman was to lead a column of liberated prisoners and attack a second Union prison at Rock Island, about 170 miles west of Chicago. They would release the prisoners held there and seize arms kept at the Union Army arsenal in the city.[6] At that point, the march would begin across the

Northwestern states with the aim of releasing more prisoners and triggering insurrection among the population.

In August 1864, Chicago was a hub of eleven railroad lines, every one of which was transporting hundreds of delegates, spectators, journalists and fast-buck merchants into the city for the convention. Hotels were filled with guests, boarding houses were booked to capacity and even private homes were opening their doors to accommodate the overflow.[7]

The Republican-leaning *Chicago Tribune* likened the convention delegates to a plague of locusts and called it the "National Copperhead Convention."[8] When Hines, Castleman and their men arrived in Chicago the city streets were filled with thousands of strangers, making it easy for the Confederates and Sons of Liberty members to blend easily among the crowds.[9]

The convention took place at the Wigwam, a huge two-story amphitheater on the shore of Lake Michigan near the center of the city. Constructed in 1860 for the Republican convention that year, it could hold up to fifteen thousand people.[10] On August 29, the first day of the convention, the doors to the Wigwam opened at 10 a.m. with a trumpet fanfare, allowing the delegates to enter and begin the day's proceedings. An hour later, spectators without tickets could enter and hundreds pushed their way in. They rushed to the main platform, causing its "fragile timbers" to "creak most ominously," according to the *Chicago Tribune*. Part of the platform collapsed under the weight of the crowd, burying about sixty people in the rubble. No one was reported to be seriously injured but the *Tribune* opined that the accident demonstrated "the instability of Democratic [party's] foundations generally."[11]

Clement Vallandigham, who was serving as a delegate from Ohio and led the Peace Democrats, took center stage on the convention's first day. On June 14, Vallandigham had re-entered the Union, unilaterally ending his exile in Canada. To aid his covert border crossing at Detroit, Vallandigham wore a disguise, stuffing a pillow under his coat to make him appear fat. The masquerade fooled no one, particularly the federal agents who were aware of his plans and followed his every step.[12]

He expected his arrival would provoke a violent response from Union authorities that could, in turn, trigger a retaliatory Copperhead rebellion. Nothing of the sort happened, however, because the Lincoln administration decided to simply ignore Vallandigham's return, much to his surprise and disappointment.[13] In fact, in a delicate political calculation, Lincoln told military authorities in Ohio and Illinois to watch Vallandigham closely but take no action unless they discovered "any palpable injury or imminent danger to the military proceeding from him."[14]

At the convention Vallandigham knew the odds were against him stopping the presidential nomination of former Union General George McClellan, who had wide support among the delegates. McClellan was considered the "war" candidate, in part because he could likely win the critical soldier vote against Lincoln. With even radical Republicans losing faith in the Lincoln administration, McClellan was favored to prevail in the fall election.

At the same time, the anti-war wing of the Democratic party, known as Peace Democrats or Copperheads, was at the height of its influence. With a prominent spot on the convention's resolution committee, Vallandigham pushed through what became known as the "war failure" plank of the party platform. It cited the "failure to restore the Union by the experiment of war" and called for "a cessation of hostilities, with a view to an ultimate convention of the States … to the end that at the earliest practicable moment peace may be restored on the basis of the Federal Union of the States."[15]

The resolution was read aloud to the assembled delegates. Halfway through the reading, cheers filled the Wigwam, rising to such a volume that the reading had to be suspended until order could be restored. It was but one example of the strength of the anti-war sentiment that pulsed through the Democratic party in 1864. The push for peace with the South was so strong during the convention that delegates cheered when the song "Dixie" was played but remained silent when the band struck up Union songs.[16] The War Democrats pushing McClellan's nomination did not seriously oppose the war failure plank, believing that securing McClellan's nomination was a higher priority.[17]

They achieved their objective, with McClellan winning the nomination with 174 votes, more than the 151 votes needed. In a gesture toward unity, Vallandigham stepped to the podium and urged the delegates to make the nomination unanimous, a move met with cheers throughout the Wigwam.[18]

Within days of McClellan's nomination, news arrived that Sherman had captured Atlanta and only a month earlier, Admiral David Farragut and his fleet had overtaken Confederate troops in Mobile, Alabama. The tide of the war had suddenly seemed to shift in favor of the North.[19] Democrats waited to hear from McClellan, who had not yet accepted the nomination. Would he stand behind the convention's peace platform?

On September 8, in a letter addressed to convention delegates, McClellan formally accepted the nomination and gave his answer. He would repudiate the party platform. "I could not look in the faces of my gallant comrades of the army and navy who have survived so many bloody battles and tell them that their labors and the sacrifices of so many of our slain and wounded brethren had been in vain; that we had abandoned that Union for which we have so often periled our lives," he wrote.[20]

* * * * *

Six weeks before the Chicago convention began, in his quarters at the Queen's Hotel in Toronto, Jacob Thompson issued an order that would eventually bring John Yates Beall into the Northwest Conspiracy and ultimately lead to Beall's planned attack on the Johnson's Island prison camp.

On July 14, as plans were being made for the attack on Camp Douglas and the follow-on raids across the Northwestern states, Thompson ordered an inspection of defenses of cities on the Great Lakes. Part of the inspection would also involve examining the feasibility of capturing the USS *Michigan*, the Union gunboat guarding Johnson's Island, and using it as part of the attack on Camp Douglas in Chicago.[21]

Thompson's interest in taking possession of the *Michigan* dated from his arrival in Canada in the spring of 1864. "It can be easily understood that the capture of the 'Michigan' by Confederates would have placed in large measure at our mercy all of the Lake towns," Castleman, the former Morgan raider now working with Thompson, wrote in his memoirs. He added, "The destructive agencies of an unopposed gunboat on the Lakes was inestimable."[22]

The man Thompson chose for the Great Lakes inspection tour was Charles H. Cole. After serving in the Confederate Army, Cole was either discharged or deserted and made his way to Canada. Cole was short and thin, about thirty-eight years old, with red hair and a long mustache.[23]

Earlier in July, Cole met with Holcombe at Niagara Falls. Knowing that Holcombe had originally been assigned to help former rebel soldiers return to the South, Cole asked Holcombe for assistance in arranging transportation to Virginia by way of Halifax and Wilmington. Based on what Cole told him about his background, however, Holcombe thought Cole might be of use to the commissioners. "Some Memphis people know him," Holcombe wrote to Clay on July 10. "He is not smart, but I suspect a bold and desperate fellow and I have detained him, thinking he might be useful."[24] Holcombe sent Cole to Toronto where he met with Thompson a few days later.[25]

Little is known for certain about Cole's background. The only fact people at the time and later historians seemed to agree on was that he was an inveterate liar about himself.[26] Some Confederate officers reported that Cole had fought in both the Union and Confederate armies and had deserted from both. Army records show that he served with Confederate General Nathan Bedford Forrest's cavalry in Tennessee, was captured by Union forces in April 1864 and then paroled on condition of not taking up arms again.[27]

In any event, after receiving Thompson's instructions, Cole booked passage on several excursion boats on Lake Erie and Lake Michigan, observing approaches to different harbors, and the location of bridges, sand bars and coal supplies.[28]

The report Cole sent to Thompson after his inspection tour included the following observations:

- "Lake Erie furnishes a splendid field for operation";
- "Buffalo is poorly protected: one regiment and a battalion of invalids";
- "Milwaukee is an easy place to take possession of. They have no fort"; and
- "There is little difficulty in bringing vessels to bear against Camp Douglas."[29]

Cole also reported that he had met John C. Carter, the captain of the USS *Michigan* in Sandusky—without explaining exactly how the meeting came about—and offered his personal assessment of the captain's character. "He is an unpolished man, whose pride seems to be touched for the reason that, having been an old United States naval officer, he is not allowed now a more extensive field of operation," Cole wrote, adding, "I do not think that he can be bought."[30]

In those two sentences, Cole accurately summarized Carter's career and current frustration. Carter, fifty-nine years old, was born in Fredericksburg, Virginia, in 1805. He began his career in the U.S. Navy in 1825 and over the next thirty-five years served on fourteen different war ships, using both sail and steam. His naval duties took him to the waters of the Atlantic, Pacific, Caribbean and Mediterranean. In 1855, he was promoted to the rank of commander.[31]

Carter took command of the USS *Michigan* in March 1861, one month before the Civil War began. It was not a prestigious assignment, but then such assignments were few and far between at that time in the U.S. Navy. In 1861, the Navy had only ninety vessels. Of that number, twenty-one were "little more than water-logged hulks," according to one account, and another twenty were not in service.[32] Many of the best warships were stationed in foreign ports far from the United States.[33]

Now Carter's sailing range extended barely beyond Lake Erie, the smallest of the Great Lakes. The USS *Michigan*, with its home port in Erie, Pennsylvania, was the only warship allowed to sail on the Great Lakes under the Rush-Bagot treaty signed by the U.S. and Great Britain after the War of 1812. During the first few years of the Civil War, the fourteen-gun warship had been used primarily for recruiting at various ports on the Great Lakes.

Carter dutifully navigated the *Michigan* through routine cruises on the lakes until October 1863 when Gideon Welles, Secretary of the Navy, ordered the gunboat to Sandusky where it would anchor off Johnson's Island, guarding against an attack across Lake Erie by Confederates from Canada. At the time, rumors were circulating that rebels in Canada were planning an attack to release prisoners on the island. The *Michigan* would remain there until the end of the war.

* * * * *

Beall arrived in Canada in mid–August 1864, following his release from incarceration at Fort McHenry. He had left Richmond in June and traveled north through Maryland and New York. Having learned about the Confederate commissioners during his stop in Richmond, Beall sought out Thompson in Toronto to volunteer his services.

Seeking to make use of his experience on Chesapeake Bay, Beall described his qualifications as an Acting Master in the Confederate Navy and offered to conduct a privateering operation on Lake Huron. Thompson rejected the offer, seeing no real value in such activity. Instead, Thompson informed Beall about Cole's recent surveillance of Lake Erie and the plan to capture the USS *Michigan* and release the Confederates confined at Johnson's Island. Hearing Thompson outline the very plan he had been trying to sell to Confederate officials in Richmond, Beall immediately accepted. He would set out for Ohio to meet with Cole in Sandusky.[34]

* * * * *

In Chicago, Hines and Castleman were adjusting to a stunning new development. They had settled into their quarters at the Richmond House, a grand hotel on the corner of Lake Street and Michigan Avenue, where they would stay for the duration of the Democratic convention. With many of their men from Canada, they had taken a block of rooms and—perhaps to disguise their frequent interactions—put up a sign in the hallway with the words "Missouri Delegation."[35] The hotel also served as the headquarters for Vallandigham and other Peace Democrat delegates.[36]

On the evening of August 28, with the convention set to begin the next morning, Hines and Castleman met with the Copperhead leaders at the Richmond House. They wanted to go over final plans for the attack on Camp Douglas which was to take place the next evening, following the first full day of the convention. The guns and other weapons needed for the attack had been secured; the prisoners at Camp Douglas had been alerted and were ready. Hines called the meeting so the leaders of the Copperheads and Sons of Liberty could inform him about exactly how many men they had in Chicago for the assault, allowing him to make final assignments.[37]

As soon as the leaders began to speak, Hines and Castleman realized their plans for an attack on Camp Douglas had just collapsed. Charles Walsh, the brigadier general of the Sons of Liberty in Illinois, admitted that he had failed to notify the thousands of down-state Copperheads when they should come to Chicago. The few dozen members who had arrived in Chicago on their own were ambling about aimlessly on the streets, waiting for instructions.[38]

Walsh had many excuses:

- his followers were not ready and needed more time for training;
- the Union Army's reinforcement of prison guards at Camp Douglas—with twelve hundred new troops—along with recent arrests of Copperhead leaders in Missouri and Kentucky caused a loss of confidence among many members; and
- the increasing likelihood of a Democratic victory in the election made an uprising unnecessary.

Walsh urged Hines and Castleman to postpone the attack until election day when his men would be better organized and trained. Hines nodded but made no firm commitment.[39]

In fact, Hines had come to the realization, perhaps belatedly, that his expectations about the fighting abilities of the Sons of Liberty were based more on hope than reality. While Vallandigham's estimate in June that there were as many as three hundred thousand Copperhead and Sons of Liberty members ready to be mobilized in the northwestern states may have seemed rational at the time, "they did not take into consideration the willingness of the individuals to be shot at," as one historian put it. Their idea of a well-drilled unit "was one that drilled once or twice a month. As a true military threat they were something of a joke."[40]

Hines gathered his men and told them the planned attack would not take place, explaining the lack of support from the Copperheads. The men were given the option of staying in the North, returning to Canada or going South. The majority chose Canada or the South.[41]

Had the attack gone forward, Hines and his compatriots would have encountered a fierce response from a beefed-up military force in Chicago. Days before the planned attack, a Confederate turncoat had informed the commander of Camp Douglas, Col. Benjamin Sweet, about the plot. Sweet, in turn, sent word to Union authorities in Washington and pleaded for reinforcements. On the eve of the convention, Major General Samuel P. Heintzelman, commander of the Department of the Ohio, responded to Sweet's request, sending 1,200 Union troops who arrived in Chicago on the eve of the convention. Sweet urged the troops to form patrols and make their presence known on the downtown streets, believing a show of force would discourage any uprising by Confederates and their Copperhead allies. The demonstration seemed to work, convincing Walsh in his meeting with Hines to emphasize the presence of troops as a reason to postpone the attack.[42]

In the end, the plot to launch an attack that would begin a new Confederacy in the Northwest states "never really advanced beyond the planning stages in a few hotel and barrooms in Canada," wrote historian Clint Johnson. "Middle-aged Midwestern farmers who read newspaper editorials raging at Lincoln's crackdown on dissent never knew that politicians they had never met counted them as would-be soldiers in a secret army ready to fight the Union."[43]

And what of the plans to capture the USS *Michigan* and bring it through the lakes to the shores of Chicago? It seems there was simply a lack of qualified personnel to execute Thompson's scheme in time for the Chicago convention. Although Thompson had sent Cole in July to examine the feasibility of capturing the *Michigan*, "A really competent and aggressive officer was, however, not found until Acting Master John Y. Beall was given authority," Castleman explained in his memoir.[44] Beall arrived in Canada and first met with Thompson only days before the convention began on August 29. In less than three weeks, Beall would have another chance.

CHAPTER 15

Hard Times on the Island

Johnson's Island—June–October 1864

By the early fall of 1864, daily life for the officers imprisoned on Johnson's Island had taken a turn for the worse. Among other hardships, food shortages were leading some prisoners to catch and eat rats. Prisoners in one blockhouse formed a group called the "Rat Club" and trained a terrier named "Nellie" to catch the rodents. They sold any excess rats they could not eat to other prisoners for ten cents apiece.[1]

"I can say with a clear conscience that I was as hungry when I left the table as I was when I went to my dinner," Major Edward Thomas Stakes of the 40th Virginia Infantry wrote in his diary September 12. After a fellow prisoner fried two rats, he wrote, "I ate the hind quarters of one which was as tender and good as a young squirrel. I have concluded in my mind not to suffer again while I am in this prison for the want of something as long as I [can] catch rats."[2]

And rats were not the only animals being caught and eaten on the island. One day, the prison commandant's large Newfoundland hound went missing. The commandant and guards searched the camp but the dog was never found. A while later, a note was found. It read: "Dear Col. For want of bread your dog is dead. For want of meat your dog is eat."[3]

In June 1864, daily food rations for Confederate prisoners in all Union prisons had been reduced by 20 percent. The cut in food rations was in retaliation for the poor treatment of Union prisoners held by the Confederacy. In May, Commissary-General William Hoffman had received a first-hand look at the condition of Union troops held in Confederate prisons when he visited a camp for returning Union Army prisoners of war near Annapolis, Maryland.

Hoffman was shocked by what he saw. "Some of these poor fellows were wasted to mere skeletons and had scarcely life enough remaining to appreciate that they were now in the hands of their friends…. Many faces showed that there was scarcely a ray of intelligence left," Hoffman wrote in a report to Secretary of War Edwin Stanton. "I would very respectfully urge that retaliatory measures be at once instituted by subjecting the officers we now hold as prisoners of war to a similar treatment."[4]

Hoffman, always the stickler for particulars, followed up by submitting a detailed proposal to Stanton, specifying the daily amounts of various foods

Confederate officers held as prisoners could receive. These included baked goods (flour or soft bread 16 ounces), meats (pork or bacon 10 ounces) and potatoes (15 ounces). Hoffman later expanded his initial recommendation to apply to all prisoners, not just officers.[5]

Stanton circulated Hoffman's recommendation to the military hierarchy, all of whom approved except for Major-General Henry Halleck, the Army Chief of Staff. Halleck suggested making the cutback on rations even more stringent by eliminating—not just reducing—all tea, coffee and sugar. On May 27, Stanton approved Hoffman's proposal along with Halleck's revision, making food cutbacks the official policy of the Union Army.[6]

* * * * *

Also, in May 1864, the military command in charge of the Johnson's Island prison camp changed leadership for the second time that year. The scare of a Confederate raid from Canada in November 1863 had touched off a series of leadership changes.

In January 1864, Hoffman ordered an increase in the troops guarding Sandusky and the prison. Replacing the original "Hoffman Battalion" was the 1st Brigade, 3rd Division of 6th Army Corps, five regiments in all, with about 1,500 men. The command was split between Brigadier General Henry D. Terry, who took charge of troops in Sandusky, and Colonel William Pierson, the prison's original commander, who remained in charge on Johnson's Island. Hoffman continued to be less than impressed with Pierson, writing to Ohio's Governor David Tod: "Col. Pierson is very attentive to his duties and very kind and courteous in his manners, but he has not sufficient force to meet the responsibilities of such a command."[7]

Terry remained until May when Colonel Charles W. Hill, commander of Ohio's 128th Volunteer Infantry, took charge of all troops, both in Sandusky and on Johnson's Island. Pierson resigned his commission in July. From the start, Hoffman had hoped for a prison commander who was both reliable and energetic. In Colonel Hill, Hoffman finally found a leader who, for the most part, met his expectations. Hill immediately issued a series of orders addressing issues ranging from the frequency of inspections at the prison to what items troops could take with them on furlough. Not even the ferry schedule between Sandusky and the island escaped the attention of the new commander. Hill modified the schedule to ensure more efficient loading and unloading of supplies for the prison.[8]

* * * * *

In June 1864, when the new policy limiting rations went into effect on Johnson's Island, prisoners saw a drastic shift in their daily food allotment. Prisoner Henry Shepherd described the meager rations that were handed out to prisoners every day at noon, the only time food would be provided for the day. "To each prisoner one-half loaf of hard bread, and a piece of salt pork, in size not sufficient for an ordinary meal. In taste the latter was almost nauseating, but it was devoured because there was no choice other than to eat it, or endure the tortures of prolonged starvation. Stimulants such as tea and coffee were rigidly interdicted."[9]

Shepherd continued, "Vegetable food was almost unknown, and as a natural result death from such diseases as scurvy carried more than one Confederate to a grave in the island cemetery.... The rations which were distributed at noon each day were expected to sustain life until the noon of the day following. During this interval, many of us became so crazed by hunger that the prescribed allowance of pork and bread was devoured ravenously as soon as received. Then followed an unbroken fast until noon of the day succeeding. For six or seven months I subsisted upon one meal in 24 hours, and that was composed of food so course and unpalatable as to appeal only to a stomach which was eating out its own life."[10]

A month later, to further implement the policy of retaliation, Hoffman took away two more privileges that had been allowed for Confederates held in Union prisons. On August 10, Hoffman issued an order prohibiting prisoners from purchasing food and clothing at prison sutler stands. The stands, operated by outside purveyors inside the prisons, had provided an outlet for prisoners with the financial means to supplement the food and clothing they received from prison authorities. In addition, Hoffman's order blocked all prisoners, except those who were sick, from receiving any packages of food or clothing from friends or relatives.[11]

The order contained an exception for clothing sent to prisoners who were "destitute," a condition that remained undefined. With the approval of the prison commandant, destitute prisoners would be allowed to receive packages of clothing, although Hoffman's order imposed strict limits on what type of clothing could escape confiscation by prison authorities. "Outer garments must be of gray or dark mixed color and of inferior quality," Hoffman's order stated with his characteristic specificity. "Only one suit of outer clothing and a change of underclothing will be allowed."[12]

Prisoner William Peel, who had at times been able to purchase items at the Johnson's Island sutler stand, noted how the new policy affected him. "I have been, for a week past, confined strictly to Govt rations, & my experience is that a man thus dependent, must be a very small eater not to suffer from hunger," he wrote in his diary in early August. The meat ration issued the previous Saturday—intended to last the prisoners three days—was gone after Sunday's breakfast, Peel noted.[13]

On August 22, the restrictions on packages sent to prisoners by friends and relatives took effect. Any packages arriving from that date forward were confiscated or returned to the senders. A relative of prisoner Henry Shepherd was a wealthy Southern planter. The relative, Shepherd's uncle, mailed his incarcerated nephew "a box of his finest hams renowned through all the land for their sweetness and excellence of flavor," Shepherd recounted. Upon arrival of the shipment, the Johnson's Island commandant promptly appropriated the hams for himself. Shepherd then received a delivery at his blockhouse of what remained: an empty box.[14]

Hygiene was also a problem on the island. In July, there was a sharp increase in prisoners stricken with dysentery. The chief causes of the outbreak were contaminated drinking water and widespread filth and inadequate housekeeping throughout the prison camp. Dysentery and chronic diarrhea were the leading causes of hospital admissions at the prison from November 1, 1863, to March 20, 1865. The cases comprised nearly a third of the 1,047 hospital admissions during that period and included forty-five deaths.[15]

Only one of the prison's two drinking water pumps was working, according to an inspection report from July 1864. The pumps were "of an inferior quality and frequently out of order," according to the report by Charles T. Alexander, acting medical inspector for the U.S. Army.[16] The island's pervasive limestone substrata prevented digging deep wells and caused poor drainage across the prison camp. In addition, efforts to pump water from the lake into the prison camp were hindered by water intakes positioned too close to shore.[17]

Alexander recommended adding an additional pump to the prison's water system, one that would send water 2,375 feet from the lake to the prison using a cast iron pipe, with an engine powered by oil or gasoline. In his report to Hoffman, Alexander anticipated the Commissary-General's tight-fisted response, writing, "As it involves a large expenditure, I doubt if you will approve so extensive a work, probably for only a temporary purpose. Such a structure would, without doubt, be very beneficial."[18] A proposal sent to Hoffman by the prison's commandant, Colonel Charles W. Hill, later in July estimated the new pump project would cost more than $7,000. Hoffman failed to respond to the proposal and it was never authorized.[19]

In his inspection report, Alexander also expressed disgust at the unsanitary conditions at the prison. "Seeing the camp, you would not know whether to be most astonished at the inefficiency of the officer in charge of the prisoners' camp or disgusted that men calling themselves gentlemen should be willing to live in such filth," he wrote.[20]

As an initial matter, officers in the Confederate military—in their positions of leadership—had little experience with or responsibility for performing clean up duties in their units. In addition, on Johnson's Island there was no main building where prisoners ate their meals, inspector Alexander noted. This resulted in the men using "small private cooking-stoves" in the same blockhouses where they slept. "I saw but few rooms which are not used as kitchen and mess-room, as well as sleeping apartment," Alexander reported, describing quarters littered with dirty dishes, food scraps and garbage. He recommended constructing two large mess-halls, each with a kitchen and storeroom, where the prisoners could eat. Such an arrangement would not only eliminate the haphazard dining practices but also free up space to house more prisoners in the blockhouses, he observed.[21]

While Hoffman had failed to respond to the recommendation for new water pumps, he quickly ordered construction of two new mess halls at the prison, just five days after receiving the inspection report. After first reprimanding Johnson's

Island commandant Hill for the "most censurable condition" at the prison, Hoffman instructed him to begin "immediately" the construction of two mess halls, each "210 feet long with four tables two and one-half feet broad" to accommodate two thousand men at two sittings. In a final admonition, he warned Hill to take care to prevent prisoners from appropriating tools or lumber that they "could make use of in effecting their escape."[22] By September 18, the mess halls and kitchens had been constructed and were operating, contributing to "a decided improvement" in the cleanliness at the prison, according to a follow up report sent to Hoffman.[23]

Despite the new mess halls, the retaliatory policy on food restrictions remained firmly in place. This, along with the continued halt in prisoner exchanges led an increasing number of Confederate prisoners to make a distasteful decision. The Union Army attempted to entice Confederate prisoners to take an oath of allegiance to the Union by allowing those who took the oath to receive extra rations and, in some cases, to be placed in better quarters. The hardships imposed across the Union Army prison system in the summer and fall of 1864 led to an increase in Confederates taking the oath of allegiance.[24]

The result, as might be expected, was enmity between prisoners who took the oath and those who did not. In early September 1864, officials at Johnson's Island reported a rise in incidents of abuse against oath takers. "There has been a persistent effort to intimidate men in the prison who show the least disposition to yield to the United States Government," Hill, the prison commandant, wrote to Hoffman. "Their roommates drive them out of quarters [during the] nights, and personal violence is not only threatened but often inflicted upon those who are suspected of wishing to take the oath of amnesty."[25]

At the time, it was not Union Army policy to release Confederates who took the oath of allegiance. As a result, one interim solution under discussion was to house such prisoners in separate quarters, away from other prisoners. Hill voiced support for separate barracks, suggesting such an option might create an incentive for more prisoners to take the oath. "Some better encouragement and more efficient protection for prisoners desirous to take the amnesty oath is undoubtedly required," he wrote Hoffman. "If they had one of the barracks by themselves, I presume it would be filled. At present but a very few dare let their sentiments be known."[26]

Hoffman agreed with the proposal for new quarters and suggested placing the quarters for oath takers near the blockhouses housing prison guards "where protection could more readily be extended to them."[27]

The effort to separate prisoners proceeded slowly, however with construction of the new quarters for oath-takers not completed until late January 1865. Prisoner Virgil Murphey described the scene when the oath-taking prisoners were transferred to their separate quarters:

"Crowds gathered upon the boulevard of the prison to scrutinize their faces, learn who they were and what states they presented," Murphey wrote. "They marched amid horrid groans and biting sarcasm with penitent heads abjectly bowed, eyes fastened intently upon the earth as if it would open its ponderous jaws and swallow them for apostasy, with pallid looks indicating their fear of vengeance."[28]

Yet another problem on Johnson's Island during the difficult summer of 1864 was overcrowding. The prison population grew from 2,251 in April to 2,444 by July and reached 3,231 by December.[29] Already in June, Hoffman had written to Hill, the commandant, telling him to expect the arrival of one thousand new prisoners. Aware that the existing living quarters were insufficient to house the additional Confederates, Hoffman advised Hill to "procure worn tents" that could be pitched in front of the blockhouses.[30]

With conditions on the island in steady decline, the interest among prisoners on the possibilities of escape was on the rise. Until July 1864, only three escapes had been reported from the prison in the twenty-seven months it had been in operation. Over the next six months, there would be nine prisoner escapes reported.[31]

Of particular value in escape attempts were parts of old Union Army uniforms often scavenged from dead Union troops on the battlefield. These fragments of clothing were pooled among the Johnson's Island prisoners to piece together almost complete federal uniforms that were then used to disguise potential escapees. The deception often worked. In early August, two prisoners, wearing Union uniforms, joined a work party hauling lumber in a wagon. They jumped aboard the wagon and rode it through the prison gates, past guards who barely gave them a second look.[32]

A more creative escape was accomplished by Lieutenant J.B. Murphy during construction of the new mess halls. Wearing a pair of Federal blue trousers with a blue shirt, Murphy followed an empty wagon as it left the prison to return to a nearby beach to load sand. Once outside the prison, he went to Colonel Hill's office and presented himself as a prison guard. Murphy then requested—and obtained—a pass to visit his "ailing mother" in Sandusky. The pass enabled him to board the ferry to Sandusky. Murphy was not heard from again until prison authorities received a letter from him, mailed from Toronto in late August, in which he apologized for not saying farewell and described himself as "the happiest man living."[33]

Captain Robert Cobb Kennedy, of the First Louisiana Infantry, had perhaps the most notorious escape during this period. On the night of October 4, 1864, Kennedy scaled the prison wall, using a ladder made of scrap lumber he had hidden under his bed in the blockhouse. He snuck past the guards' quarters and used a small skiff he found at the lakeshore to make his way off the island. Ten days later, Kennedy was in Canada.[34] Kennedy's escape was notorious not so much for the method he used but because of what he did after his escape.

The son of a doctor and wealthy landowner In Louisiana, the thirty-year old Kennedy had spent two years at West Point. He had been discharged just before the war began because of poor grades and what his superiors described as a tendency to be "inattentive to regulations."[35] Kennedy then joined the Confederate Army in Louisiana as a captain, serving in Florida and then in Georgia before he was captured by Union troops in November 1863.

After his escape from Johnson's Island, Kennedy went to Canada where he met up with Jacob Thompson and the other Commissioners in Toronto. He became embroiled in their plots and in November 1864 joined a group of Confederate agents in an attempt to burn New York City. The plot was part of the Confederacy's ongoing efforts to foment Northern opposition to the war. The plan was to set fire to New York City hotels, using a chemical concoction dating from ancient times known as Greek Fire, which contained a mixture of phosphorus and bisulfide of carbon. It was supposed to ignite spontaneously on contact with the air.[36]

The plot, which targeted thirteen major hotels, failed—but not before alarming hundreds of the city's hotel guests who ran from their rooms into the streets during the attacks. Unknown to the conspirators—who took pains to close windows and lock doors as they set fires in the hotels—Greek Fire required oxygen to burn. In the sealed rooms, the fires barely smoldered before being extinguished.[37] After the unsuccessful attack, Kennedy and the eight other men on the team returned to Toronto.

A month later, in December 1864, Kennedy would team up with another Confederate agent, John Yates Beall, and several other conspirators in yet another Confederate plot. This attack, set to take place near Buffalo, New York, would lead Kennedy and Beall—separately and at different times—to military court martial trials, followed by their imprisonment and death.

CHAPTER 16

"I Seize This Boat and Take You as Prisoner"

Detroit, Lake Erie Islands, Sandusky—September 1864

On Sunday, September 18, 1864, the *Philo Parsons* lay at anchor in the Detroit River at its berth on the Trowbridge & Wilcox dock, near the foot of Woodward Avenue in midtown Detroit.[1] The pleasure boat, a side-wheel steamer, ran daytrips regularly between Detroit and Sandusky, stopping at several of the Lake Erie islands popular with locals and visiting tourists.

The 136-foot-long vessel was well-appointed and designed for enjoyment, with a newly paneled passenger cabin equipped with a piano and bar. The main deck had a square-shaped wheelhouse sitting about twenty feet from the bow, followed by a large passenger cabin mid-deck. Then came a tall smokestack flanked by a large, enclosed paddlewheel on the boat's port side. There were chairs on deck along each side of the passenger cabin. About ten deck chairs sat on the ship's rear deck. Built in 1861, the *Philo Parsons* was named after a Detroit businessman who established and was president of the city's First National Bank.[2]

An advertisement that ran on the front page of the Sandusky *Daily Commercial Register* in September announced:

> The Philo Parsons has received a new engine the past winter, and undergone extensive repairs to her cabin, with new furniture, and she is now owned by parties who have it greatly to their interest to have a good steamer running between Sandusky and Detroit, she will positively remain on the route.[3]

The ad also described the boat's weekly schedule:

> Leave Sandusky for Detroit every Tuesday, Thursday, and Saturday at 8 o'clock am, connecting at Detroit with the Evening Trains over all the railroads for Chicago, Milwaukee, Saginaw, and all points west, north, and east. Leave Detroit for Sandusky every Monday, Wednesday and Friday at 8 o'clock am.[4]

The ad noted that the boat's excursions stopped "at all of the celebrated grape islands in Lake Erie, passing the famous Johnson's Island Depot for prisoners of war."[5]

At around 8 p.m. that Sunday evening, a young man in his mid-twenties boarded the *Philo Parsons* and called to Walter O. Ashley, a part-owner and clerk

Philo Parsons (Historical Collections of the Great Lakes, Bowling Green State University).

of the boat, who was in the cabin tending to some paperwork before the next day's departure to Sandusky.[6]

The young man was stout, "a little below" medium height, with a thin, light-colored beard. He had the air of a gentleman and spoke with an accent that Ashley later identified as English or Scottish. He asked Ashley if the *Philo Parsons* on the next day's trip could make an unscheduled stop at Sandwich, a town about three miles south of Detroit on the Canadian side of the river. He said he had three friends there who wanted to join him on the Monday excursion. One of the friends was lame, he said, and did not want to have to make the trip across the river by ferry to board the *Philo Parsons*. Ashley told him the boat could make the stop so long as he boarded at Detroit and confirmed the others would be at Sandwich.[7]

* * * * *

The visitor who came aboard the *Philo Parsons* that evening was Bennet Burley, Beall's right-hand-man during their privateering adventures on the Chesapeake Bay a year earlier. While Beall and most members of his team had been captured by Union forces in November 1863 and imprisoned at Fort McHenry in Baltimore, Burley had remained in Richmond, having come down with a bout of malaria. He recovered and by March 1864 Burley resumed privateering activities on the bay with a new band of marine raiders. Like Burley's days with Beall, Burley and his team had inflicted substantial damage to Union war efforts, cutting cables, destroying a lightship and capturing commercial vessels with cargoes of military supplies.[8]

In early May 1864, a Union infantry unit came upon Burley and several of the other privateers as they were laying mines in a Union-occupied area on the Virginia coast. The Union troops fired shots, killing several of Burley's men and wounding Burley. He and the other men were captured and taken to Fort Delaware, a Union Army prison about forty miles south of Philadelphia on the Delaware River.[9]

Fort Delaware did not hold Burley for long. The story of Burley's escape is recounted in a biography by a relative of Burley who was told stories of Burley's exploits by his grandmother, a great-granddaughter of Burley. According to the biographer, Graeden Greaves, in July 1864, Burley and several other prisoners pried off wooden planks from the floor of their cell and escaped into the fort's sewer system which ran beneath the floor. They crawled through muck and waste for 125 yards to where the sewer emptied into the Delaware river. Burley swam in the darkness for hours until he was rescued by boatmen who took him upriver to Philadelphia. From there, Burley headed north, making his way to Canada.[10]

At some point between August and September 1864, Beall and Burley were reunited after Beall "unexpectedly bumped into Burley whilst walking the streets of Toronto," according to Greaves.[11] By that time, Beall had already become involved in plans to capture the USS *Michigan* and free the prisoners on Johnson's Island.

Following the failure of the Chicago raid during the Democratic convention in August, Jacob Thompson, the lead Confederate commissioner, and Thomas Hines, his wily rebel agent, shifted their focus to Lake Erie. Capturing the *Michigan* and freeing the prisoners on Johnson's Island was a key piece of the larger attack on the North that was to begin in Chicago. Executing this part of the plan would now be their goal.

"After the fiasco at Chicago, it was determined to attempt, by means of the Lake, a descent upon Johnson's Island, capture the garrison, and carry off the prisoners," Hines wrote later.[12]

After their unexpected rendezvous in Toronto, Beall quickly enlisted Burley in the effort and began rounding up other members of a team to carry out the Sandusky raid. By mid–September, Beall, Burley and eighteen other Confederate veterans in Canada—including at least three who had traveled with Hines to Chicago in August—comprised the raiding force that would head for Sandusky.[13]

Another key member of the team was Charles Cole who had conducted the Great Lakes scouting mission for Thompson earlier in the summer of 1864. Following Cole's trip around the Great Lakes—in which he had noted the vulnerability of the *Michigan*—Thompson had sent him to live in Sandusky. From there, Cole would be able to assist in any Confederate effort targeting the *Michigan* and Johnson's Island.

By September, Cole had established himself as a figure in the community, posing as a wealthy oil baron. To aid in this masquerade, Cole had the help of several thousand dollars provided by Thompson who instructed him to spend it freely.[14] Cole impressed Sandusky residents with a cover story that he was the secretary of the nonexistent "Mount Hope Oil Company" headquartered in Titusville, Pennsylvania. He threw lavish parties, featuring the finest wines, whiskies and cigars. He made a particular effort to become familiar with crewmen and officers of the *Michigan* when they came ashore and even managed to accompany them on occasional sails, which had to be a violation of Navy rules.[15] Cole also linked up with Copperhead partisans in Sandusky.

As a site for his lodging and entertaining in Sandusky, Cole used the West House Hotel, located at the corner of Columbus Avenue and Water Street, directly across from the city docks. Opened in 1858, it was known as one of the premier hotels between New York and Chicago. It was owned, operated and had been constructed by W.T. and A.K. West, the same contractors who built the Johnson's Island prison.[16]

Staying with Cole in Sandusky was a woman variously known as "Annie Brown," "Annie Davis" or "Emma Bison," who Cole introduced as his wife. She was in fact his mistress. He had met her in Buffalo during his scouting tour of the Great Lakes. During their stay at the West House, Annie would serve as a messenger between Cole and Thompson in Toronto, making cross-border trips.[17]

Shortly after his arrival in Sandusky in August, Cole met with Beall at the West House. After Beall's initial meeting with Thompson in Toronto, Thompson had instructed Beall "to report" to Cole in Sandusky.[18] After they met up, however, it quickly became apparent that Beall had the focus and command authority to take charge of the entire operation, leaving Cole to play his part in Sandusky.

Cole's part was to befriend the crew and officers of the *Michigan* and establish contacts among the imprisoned Confederate officers on Johnson's Island. Most importantly, Cole needed to ensure that as many of the *Michigan*'s crew and officers as possible were incapacitated when the raid took place. He intended to accomplish this by luring officers and crewmen off the *Michigan* to attend an elaborate dinner and party onshore the day of the raid. The free-flowing wine and champagne to be served would be spiked with drugs.

Cole had contacted Copperheads in Sandusky who could provide additional manpower for the attack. Cole also claimed that he had enlisted the aid of Confederate prisoners inside the Johnson's Island prison camp.[19]

In fact, well before Cole arrived in Sandusky, the prisoners had plans in place for an insurrection and escape when and if they had the opportunity. Perhaps it was to be expected that, with more than two thousand Confederate military officers confined together for months, they would find themselves inclined to discuss and prepare strategies and tactics focused on escaping.

By early 1864, the prisoners had established a command structure led by General Isaac Trimble, the highest-ranking Confederate officer in the prison camp. The 61-year-old general had been one of three division commanders of the Confederacy's ill-fated Pickett's charge during the battle of Gettysburg in July 1863. Seriously wounded by a gunshot in his left leg, Trimble was taken prisoner and his leg was amputated. He was then taken to Johnson's Island. Four more generals among the prisoners were selected to command specific prison blocks housing prisoners.[20]

To help improve morale and unit cohesion, Trimble and the other commanders created a new organization among the prisoners known as the Order of the Brotherhood of the Southern Cross. Its symbol was a cross with the colors of the Confederate flag. Detailed contingency plans were drawn up with a variety of escape scenarios, including crossing over ice on a frozen Lake Erie to Canada, or reaching the shore near Sandusky and traveling through Toledo, Detroit and north to Canada, or marching east through Ohio to Cleveland, Pittsburgh and Wheeling to reach the Confederate states.[21]

The prisoners also made primitive weapons to aid in any escape attempt. "We were organized into companies and regiments and had armed ourselves with clubs, which were made of stove wood and other material at hand, with which to make the fight," prisoner Archibald S. McKennon, captain and assistant quarter master of the Sixteenth Arkansas Infantry, wrote in a letter.[22]

Meanwhile, in early September, Beall had returned to Canada and was meeting with Thompson in Windsor, directly across the river from Detroit. They sometimes were joined by a former Confederate Colonel, George Steele of Kentucky, who had relocated to Canada and helped organize meetings between Thompson and Copperhead dissidents. During these meetings, which sometimes took place at Steele's home near Windsor, they focused on the final plans for the attack.[23]

Beall and Thompson initially tried to find and purchase a suitable boat for their assault on the *Michigan* but were not successful. They ultimately concluded they would have to seize one, most likely one of the commercial vessels docked in Detroit, directly across the river from Windsor.[24]

The plan was for Beall and his team, with a cache of weapons, to sail from Detroit to Sandusky Bay and await a signal from Cole letting them know the *Michigan* crew had been immobilized. The *Philo Parsons* would cruise alongside the *Michigan*, allowing the men to capture the vessel. They would then fire a cannonball from the *Michigan* over the prison, letting the prisoners know it was time to launch an uprising and mass escape that would overwhelm the prison's guard force. Also responding to the *Michigan*'s cannon shot, the Copperhead partisans in Sandusky would cut telegraph wires, isolating the city.[25]

With the help of the freed prisoners and the band of Copperhead supporters from Sandusky, the escapees would loot the Sandusky arsenal for weapons. At the time of the attack in September, Beall and Cole considered the mostly likely route of escape would be for prisoners to head east on stolen horses toward Cleveland, then on to Pittsburgh, Wheeling and further South into Confederate territory.[26]

At the same time, the plan included using the captured gunboat *Michigan*, under Confederate command, to create havoc in cities along the Great Lakes, bombarding them with artillery or demanding tribute and contribution of money to avoid attack.[27]

At this stage of the war, with the Confederacy desperate to reverse its shrinking prospects for victory, even the originators of the plot knew the chances for success were slim. In an article published twelve years later, Hines called the plans for the

Lake Erie raid "audacious in the extreme," adding that it was "predicated upon the idea that courage and energy could in large measure, supply the lack of numbers."[28]

* * * * *

On Monday, September 19, promptly at 8 a.m., the *Philo Parsons'* captain, Sylvester Atwood, blew the boat's horn and crewmen cast off lines. With Bennet Burley and thirty-nine other passengers onboard, waters churned as the boat slowly steamed away from the dock and headed south on the Detroit River. At Sandwich, the unscheduled stop that Burley had requested, the boat took on four more passengers, one of whom was Beall, wearing a wide-brimmed cloth hat. Another of the boarding passengers was Burley's supposedly lame friend. Atwood noticed that, although the lame friend hobbled a bit as he got on board, after a short time he was moving quite spryly.[29]

At Malden (now Amherstburg), seventeen miles farther down the river, about twenty more passengers, mostly men, boarded the *Philo Parsons*. Malden, on the Canadian side of the river, was one of the *Philo Parsons'* regular stops. Two of the men who came aboard were carrying an old wooden trunk tied with ropes.

Ashley, the *Philo Parsons* clerk, noted differences between the group of men who boarded at Sandwich and those who boarded at Malden. Along with Burley, the four who boarded at Sandwich (including Beall) "appeared to be English gentlemen, all well-dressed in English clothes. Two were wearing kid gloves," Ashley recalled later. They inquired about the grapes and wines on the islands and were quite sociable with the other passengers. In fact, when a few women passengers entered the cabin to play the piano, Burley charmed them by offering to turn the pages of music.[30]

As Atwood conversed with the group of four, they told him that they were going to Kelleys Island to fish and "have a time." Atwood guessed that they were Southerners in disguise. It was not uncommon for draft-dodging troops from the North or South ("skedaddlers," Ashley called them) to board the *Philo Parsons* on its way either to or from Detroit.[31]

The men boarding at Malden had nothing to do with those who boarded at Sandwich and did not appear to recognize them, Ashley observed. "Their clothes were worn, ragged, men had seen hard service, the trunk was brought on by two of the hardest looking in the crowd," Ashley said later.[32]

From Malden, the *Philo Parsons* steamed across the lake to the islands, making its usual stops at North Bass and Middle Bass where Atwood disembarked. The captain was not feeling well and, because his home was on Middle Bass, he turned command of the boat over to the mate, DeWitt C. Nichols. It was not unusual for Atwood to disembark at Middle Bass and stay overnight at his residence, rejoining the *Philo Parsons* the next day on its return trip from Sandusky to Detroit.[33]

After a stop at Put-in-Bay, also known as South Bass—the southernmost of the islands—the *Philo Parsons* arrived at Kelleys Island around 4 p.m. Although it was supposedly the destination of Burley and the four men who had boarded at

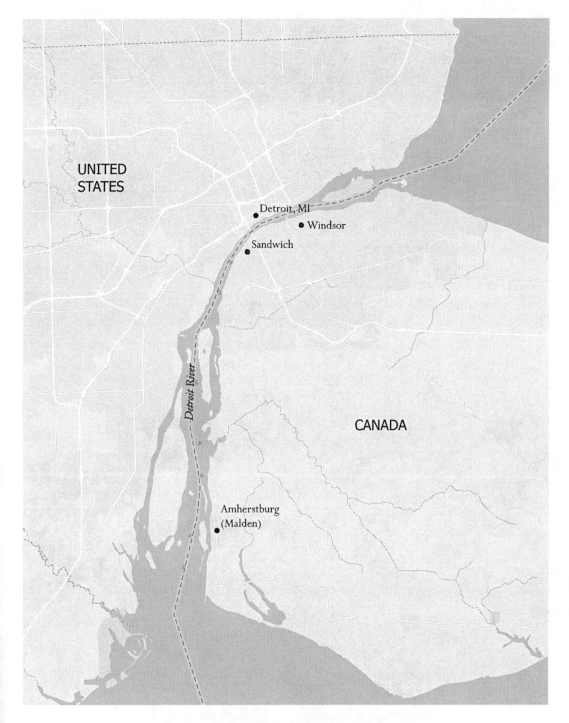

Detroit River Area.

Sandwich, the men remained on board, saying they had decided to go on to Sandusky without explaining why they had apparently given up their fishing plans.[34]

Several more passengers boarded the *Philo Parsons* at Kelleys Island. As part of the plot, Cole was supposed to have sent a messenger to meet Beall and the raiders on Kelleys Island, informing them about the status of Cole's planned dinner party with the *Michigan* crew. The messenger failed to appear during the brief stop, but Beall forged ahead with the attack plan, undaunted by the missing emissary.[35]

The *Philo Parsons* then headed for Sandusky, about eleven miles south. Twenty minutes later, Nichols was standing in the wheelhouse piloting the boat when a man stuck his head in the door and asked. "Are you captain of this boat?"[36]

"No, sir, I am mate," Nichols replied to the man, about thirty years of age, of medium height, with brown hair and wearing a wide-brimmed hat.[37]

"You have charge of her at present have you not?" said the man with an air of authority. Nichols later identified him as the leader of the group that boarded at Sandwich and Malden. Nichols said the men in the group called the man "Bell."[38]

"Yes, sir," Nichols said.

"Will you step back here a minute," Beall said to Nichols, gesturing toward the rear of the boat. "I want to talk to you."

Nichols walked with Beall toward the smokestack where they stopped. "I am a Confederate officer," Beall said. "There are thirty of us,[39] well-armed. I seize this boat and take you as a prisoner. You must pilot the boat as I direct—and here are the tools to make you," Beall said, as he slowly pulled out a revolver.[40]

CHAPTER 17

A Confederate Flag Flies
on Lake Erie

Onboard the Philo Parsons, *Lake Erie Near Sandusky—*
Monday, September 19, 1864

Around the same time that Beall confronted DeWitt C. Nichols, the pilot on the *Philo Parsons,* several men on Beall's team pulled out the battered trunk they had brought onboard at Malden. It sat with other passenger bags near the rear of the boat.

They slashed the ropes tied around the trunk, tore at buckles securing the lid and flipped it open, exposing the trunk's contents: dozens of long-barreled revolvers and steel-bladed hatchets. The raiders scrambled toward the trunk and quickly armed themselves, slipping the hatchet handles inside their belts and brandishing the revolvers.[1]

Passengers Frederick Hukill and Alfred Skinner, two Cincinnati businessmen, were returning to Ohio from a trip to Niagara Falls. They sat on the main deck, smoking cigars. "Something made me look up," Hukill said years later. "For an instant, I couldn't imagine what was happening. A man was holding a pistol to the pilot's (Nichols') head." Then another man yelled "Stand back. Stand back. In each hand he held one of the longest, prettiest revolvers it was my fortune to see," Hukill said. "And he had us covered to a nicety."[2]

Skinner, Hukill's colleague, called out, "What does this mean?"

"It means that we've captured this boat in the name of the Southern Confederacy," Beall responded. "You are our prisoners."[3]

The raiders were moving quickly to take control of the boat. Michael Campbell, the *Philo Parsons'* wheelman, was in the main cabin near the bar. He heard a shot, then a yell and another shot. He ran out on the main deck and saw a man with a cocked revolver in his hand chasing James Denison, the boat's fireman. The armed man shouted at Denison, ordering him to go down into the boat's hold and threatening to shoot him. As the fireman dodged out of the way, the same man turned his gun on Campbell and gave him the same order. Campbell told him to "go to hell" and the man fired at Campbell. The bullet missed, passing between Campbell's legs.[4]

At the rear of the boat, raiders hauled down the U.S. flag and hoisted up the

Confederate Stars and Bars, marking the only time a Confederate flag flew on any vessel in Lake Erie.[5]

Ashley, the clerk, was standing near his office next to the main cabin when Burley and three other men approached him and drew their revolvers. Burley told him if he offered any resistance, he "was a dead man." Two of the men kept their revolvers pointed at Ashley while the other two began rounding up the passengers. The passengers were herded into the main cabin and searched as women screamed and men backed against the wall.[6]

"Are you armed?" Beall asked Hukill.

"No sir, I'm not," Hukill replied in a sharp manner.

"I asked that in a gentlemanly way" Beall said to Hukill. "And it deserves a gentlemanly answer."[7]

Through the cabin window, Ashley could see Burley take an axe and smash open the luggage room door. Burley then moved forward on the deck and shattered the door to the saloon.[8]

Under gunpoint, the passengers and several crew members were directed out of the cabin and down a ladder into the boat's hold, which contained a storage area and engine room beneath the main deck. To ensure no one tried to escape, raiders hauled several heavy pieces of pig iron, part of the boat's cargo, across the deck and placed them on top of the hatch.[9]

With the passengers and most of the other crewmen confined in the boat's hold, Campbell, the wheelman, was steering the boat in an easterly direction as Beall stood nearby.[10] Burley ordered several of his men to throw overboard the rest of the pig iron cargo, some furniture and tobacco.[11] As they sailed past Sandusky Bay, the *Michigan* "was plainly visible" in the distance anchored off Johnson's Island.[12]

At around 5 p.m., Beall discovered he had a problem. Beall asked Nichols, the pilot of the *Philo Parsons*, how much fuel the boat carried. Nichols reminded him that the boat was a woodburner and it carried enough firewood to take them to Sandusky. Beall realized it was much too early in the day to attack the *Michigan*. Cole's dinner party for the ship's captain and crew—when they were to be drugged—was not scheduled to start until the evening. Beall knew they would need more wood to be able to sail the *Philo Parsons* for several more hours.[13]

After conferring with other raiders, Beall asked Campbell, at the wheel, where they could obtain more firewood. Campbell told him there was a wood stand at the dock on Middle Bass island. Beall ordered him to backtrack and return the *Philo Parsons* to Middle Bass.[14]

After passing Kelleys Island and Put-in-Bay, the *Philo Parsons* arrived at Middle Bass a little before 7 p.m. and tied up at Wehrle's dock on the south side of the island.[15] One of Beall's men fired shots in the direction of the owner of the wood stand and two other men standing on the dock. As the three men ran away, some of the *Philo Parsons* deckhands were released to carry firewood onboard.[16] After the crewmen had loaded about thirty cords of wood, passengers were ordered out of the hold and filed back into the cabin where they remained under guard.[17]

Around 7 p.m., the *Philo Parson's* captain, Sylvester Atwood, was at his home on Middle Bass, having left the boat at its earlier stop at Middle Bass that afternoon. A little boy ran up to the house and told Atwood that men were shooting at his father, who ran the wood stand, and were trying to kill him.[18]

Atwood immediately went to the Middle Bass dock where he saw the *Philo Parsons* and "men running about," as he described the scene later. The boat should be in Sandusky by now, he thought. "What in hell was up?" Atwood asked as he approached the men on the shore. The next thing he saw were three or four revolvers pointed in his direction. Two of the men shoved Atwood onto the gangplank leading to the *Philo Parsons* and he walked aboard. He was led to the cabin where he saw crew members and passengers under guard by men with pistols. Ashley, the boat's clerk, told Atwood Confederate pirates had captured the boat and there was no point in resisting.[19]

One of the raiders was sitting in the cabin and invited Atwood to sit beside him. The man, who was considerably older than the other raiders, introduced himself as a surgeon in the Confederate Army. He sympathized with Atwood, saying it was an unpleasant situation but that if Atwood and the other members of crew cooperated, they would not be hurt. The man told Atwood he thought he would regain possession of his boat when the raid was concluded.[20]

While not much is known about many on Beall's team, the man who spoke with Atwood was later identified as John Slick Riley, a fifty-year-old physician, born in Pennsylvania who attended the Medical College of Ohio in Cincinnati. He had served in the Mexican-American war and then headed west to participate in the California Gold Rush. It is unclear how or when he became associated with Beall.[21]

As Atwood sat down, he heard a boat's whistle. It was the *Island Queen*, another excursion boat, also making a stop at Middle Bass to take on more firewood.[22]

Like the *Philo Parsons*, the *Island Queen* was a sidewheel steamer. Slightly smaller in size, the *Island Queen* sailed from Sandusky each day at 3 p.m. and made stops at the various Lake Erie islands. More than two years earlier, the *Island Queen* had ferried the first Confederate prisoners to Johnson's Island from Sandusky. On this trip, the *Island Queen* was carrying about a hundred passengers.[23]

As the *Island Queen* pulled in beside the *Philo Parsons*, Beall and the other raiders saw an alarming sight: the deck of the *Island Queen* was swarming with Union soldiers, about thirty in all. Had they been sent to thwart the rebel raid? How had they found out? And why were so many soldiers on the relatively small boat?

In fact, the soldiers were unaware of the raid. They were not even armed. They were members of Ohio's 130th Infantry Regiment—"One Hundred Day Men," as they were called—from Toledo who were due to be mustered out of the military within days. As a celebration, the men had taken time off to spend a weekend on Kelleys Island, visiting friends and relatives.[24]

That Monday, the Union troops had expected to take the *Island Queen* back to Sandusky in the afternoon where they would board the train to Toledo. One of the soldiers was related to Alfred Kelley, the agent for the *Island Queen*.[25] As a favor, Kelley had told them that if they waited until the *Island Queen* returned to Middle Bass from Sandusky, he would send the *Island Queen* on to Toledo with the soldiers. The boat regularly came to Middle Bass to take on more firewood.[26]

As crewmen on the *Island Queen* began securing the lines, Beall observed the soldiers' carefree manner and quickly concluded they were not a threat. Seconds later, he and several other raiders jumped from the *Philo Parsons* and boarded the *Island Queen*. Some of the raiders continued swinging their hatchets, knocking down several *Island Queen* passengers. As the Sandusky *Daily Commercial Register* reported, "Some of the passengers, not obeying the orders of the raiders as quickly as they desired, were rather roughly used, the ruffians hitting them on the head with hatchets and revolvers."[27]

The raiders ordered the passengers off the *Island Queen*, and onto the *Philo Parsons*. Male passengers and crewmen were directed into the hold. Women and children were sent to the *Philo Parsons* cabin.[28]

The raiders called to the *Island Queen*'s engineer, Henry Haines, ordering him to come up from that boat's hold. He either failed to hear the command or ignored it. The next thing he heard was someone say, "Shoot the son-of-a-bitch." A gun fired and Haines was shot in the face. The ball passed through his nose and left cheek. Several other shots were fired indiscriminately into the group of passengers as they stepped off the *Island Queen*. A passenger from Put-in-Bay was wounded and many of the others were nearly in hysterics.[29]

Beall approached the captain of the *Island Queen*, George W. Orr, and demanded the boat's papers.

"What do you want with the papers?" Orr asked.[30]

"We want to send them as trophies to Jeff Davis," Beall replied.

"You can't run the boat without the papers," Orr told him.

"The boat isn't going to run much longer," Beall said.

Orr told Beall the papers were in the *Island Queen*'s office. When they reached the office, they found it had been broken open—most likely by other raiders—with the papers scattered on the floor. The money drawer had been rifled.[31]

Beall then ordered Orr, along with the *Island Queen*'s clerk, William Hamilton; and the engineer, Haines, who was bleeding profusely, back onto the *Philo Parsons* where they remained under guard.[32]

By now, it was becoming obvious that the *Philo Parsons* could not hold all the passengers, including the soldiers, from both boats. Beall and Burley gave the women and children permission to go ashore after they promised not to inform anyone about the raid for twenty-four hours. They then ordered the soldiers up on deck and told them they also could go ashore if they made the same promise as the passengers, along with a pledge not take up arms against Confederacy. Most of the passengers also left with their bags. There was no telegraph between the islands and the mainland.[33]

Beall asked Atwood, the *Philo Parson*'s captain, to go ashore and take charge of the passengers and crewmen who had been released. Beall promised that Atwood's quarters and possessions on the boat would not be disturbed.[34]

At this point, Ashley returned to his office onboard the *Philo Parsons* to retrieve some books and papers. Burley and Beall approached and told him not to remove anything from the boat. Ashley said he had some personal promissory notes in an envelope in his vest pocket and requested leave to take them. Beall then demanded that Ashley hand over the notes—totaling about $100—and ordered him to open the money drawer which contained about eight or ten dollars. Burley and Beall each took a portion of the money and told Ashley to join the rest of the passengers on shore.[35]

Shortly after 8 p.m., a bright moon appeared in the darkening sky. After clearing the vessels of passengers and most of the crewmen, the raiders lashed the two boats together, using the stern line, and got underway to Sandusky. Beall did not want to leave the *Island Queen* on Middle Bass where it could be used by the stranded passengers to escape. About four or five miles from Middle Bass, near Chickanolee Reef, a raider jumped from the *Philo Parsons* onto the *Island Queen*, went below and cut the steamer's water feed pipe, before returning to the *Philo Parsons*. The *Island Queen* was set adrift and slowly began to sink.[36]

The *Philo Parsons* continued on to Sandusky Bay with the boat's wheelman, Michael Campbell, guiding the boat. Shortly after leaving Middle Bass, it passed Ballast Island, a small uninhabited island about a mile east of Middle Bass, then Kelleys Island. A little before 10 p.m., the *Philo Parsons* was just off the Marblehead peninsula where the Marblehead lighthouse was clearly visible.

As the boat approached the entrance to Sandusky Bay, Campbell warned Beall that it was dangerous to enter the bay at night because the channel was narrow, and visibility was limited. Beall told Campbell to slow the boat. He expected to see a flare from Cole as soon as the *Philo Parsons* entered the bay, signaling that all was clear for the *Philo Parsons* to approach and capture the gunboat. There was no flare.[37]

Beall raised night glasses—a type of binoculars—and peered through the darkness, looking for the *Michigan* at anchor off Johnson's Island, about two miles away. Beall quickly located the gunboat, its hull gleaming in the moonlight. The *Michigan* had shifted its position from the afternoon and now was turned so its entire length was parallel to the island, "like a huge watch dog off the coast of Johnson's Island," as Daniel Lucas, Beall's lifelong friend and biographer wrote later.[38] The gunboat's decks were clear. Rather than being disabled, smoke from active steam engines was pouring from the *Michigan*'s stack, its guns ready to challenge any oncoming vessel.[39]

CHAPTER 18

A Telegram from Detroit

Detroit, Sandusky—September 17–19, 1864

On Saturday evening, September 17, 1864—two days before Beall and his team took over the *Philo Parsons*—Lieutenant Colonel Bennett J. Hill, the acting assistant provost marshal for the state of Michigan,* heard a knock on the door of his Detroit hotel room.

The man knocking on the door told Hill he was a former rebel soldier who knew about a plot to capture the USS *Michigan* by drugging the crew and officers. The plot would also involve releasing prisoners on Johnson's Island and attacking or demanding contribution from cities along the Great Lakes. The man said he had been asked to join the plot and would learn more details the next morning. He told Hill he would return to the hotel on Sunday night to brief him on additional details.[1]

After the man left, Hill immediately went to his office and sent a telegram to John C. Carter, captain of the *Michigan*: "It is reported to me that some of the officers and men of your steamer have been tampered with, and that a party of rebel refugees leave Windsor tomorrow with the expectation of getting possession of your steamer."[2]

Carter responded with a telegram of his own Sunday morning, writing to Hill: "Thanks for your dispatch. All ready. Cannot be true in relation to the officers or men."[3]

On Sunday evening September 18, the man returned and told Hill he had learned the plot now included seizure of the *Philo Parsons* after it left Detroit the next day and that certain officers and men on the *Michigan* had been co-opted by "a man named Cole."[4]

At 6 a.m. Monday September 19, Hill went to where the *Philo Parsons* was docked on the Detroit river. Seeing the boat for the first time, Hill decided it "was too small to be of any danger if taken by the persons, and after mature consideration, I came to the conclusion that it would be better to let the steamer go and place Captain Carter on his guard," he later wrote in a report. "These plots are being

---

*Provost marshals, stationed across the northern states during the war, were the military police of the Union Army. They were responsible for finding and arresting deserters, spies, and civilians suspected of disloyalty, in addition to handling the drafting of civilians into the military.

122

constantly made here," he added. "We had the information about this one, and the question was whether it would not be better to let it proceed, and make an example in this case, if the information really amounted to anything."[5]

That same morning, Hill sent Carter a second telegram, telling him that the plot to capture the *Michigan* would take place that day and that both he and his commander "look upon the matter as serious."[6]

Hill's second telegram prompted Carter to act. Leaving the *Michigan*, he took the Navy barge that tended the gunboat across the short distance to Johnson's Island, where he met with the prison's commandant, Charles W. Hill (no relation to Colonel Hill in Detroit), who had taken over command of the prison in May. After Carter told Hill about the telegram warnings he had received, they both agreed that Cole needed to be taken into custody and questioned.[7]

An ensign aboard the *Michigan,* James Hunter, knew Cole and was dispatched to apprehend him in Sandusky. On reaching the shore, Hunter had the barge's bow turned toward the lake—contrary to custom but useful for an expedited return trip—and told the crew to remain there.[8]

Arriving at the West House where Cole was staying, Hunter found Cole and his mistress, Annie Davis, with their bags packed and bills paid, prepared to make a quick departure later that day. Hunter decided to say nothing about it, at least for the time being. Hunter and Cole exchanged pleasantries and Cole offered Hunter a drink. Hunter, aware of the plot to drug *Michigan* officers and crew, declined, saying he preferred not to drink so shortly after chewing tobacco. But seeing Cole drink from the same bottle, after a while he followed his example.[9]

Cole invited Hunter to join the other *Michigan* officers at the party he had planned for later that day. It was to be held at the Seven Mile House, a suburban resort outside of Sandusky. Young, unattached women were also supposed to be in attendance. Hunter begged off, telling him he would be on duty. As the conversation continued, Hunter thought of a way he could lure Cole back to the *Michigan*. He suggested that Cole accompany him to the ship where he would seek leave from Captain Carter to attend the party.[10]

Hunter and Cole walked to the dock where the barge waited, with Hunter taking Cole by the arm in a friendly manner. When they reached the barge, Hunter gave Cole a vigorous push and he stumbled onto the boat. Hunter ordered the coxswain to push off immediately and they returned to the *Michigan*.[11]

Onboard the *Michigan,* Hunter took Cole to Carter's cabin. As Cole and Hunter entered, Carter barked out, "You are my prisoner, sir." They searched Cole and began interrogating him. Carter also sent the *Michigan's* executive officer, E.G. Martin, to return to Cole's room in the West House and seize his papers and baggage. Among the items found on Cole or in his hotel room were a pistol, a document identifying Cole as a major in a Confederate regiment in Tennessee, six hundred dollars in cash and several certified checks for five thousand dollars each, drawn on a Montreal bank. Also found was a paper showing that Cole had been captured in Memphis by

Union troops in April 1864, that he had been paroled and required to take an oath not to take up arms against the Union.[12]

Before a detailed interrogation of Cole began, Carter sent Ensign Hunter to Johnson's Island to notify Charles W. Hill, the prison commander, and bring him back to the *Michigan*. A short while later, the interrogation of Cole got underway, with Carter and Hill present. Cole denied knowing anything about a plot involving rebel conspirators to seize the *Michigan*. Carter then showed Cole a telegram found in Cole's coat pocket that read: "I send you today by messenger the thirty (30) shares of Mount Hope oil wells purchased as you previously advised." Cole said it was a private dispatch about his oil business.[13]

Under further questioning, Cole admitted that the "thirty shares" mentioned in the telegram referred to thirty men enlisted in the conspiracy who were supposed to arrive in Sandusky by train on Monday, September 19, the day of the raid.[14] The sender of the telegram is unidentified. In a later report, Hill, the prison commander, tied the telegram to a "W. Norris," again without further identification.[15] It is possible the telegram was sent to Cole by William Norris, the chief signal officer for the Confederacy which, if true, would implicate the highest levels of the Confederacy in planning for the Johnson's Island raid. "As head of the Signal Office, Norris oversaw a communications network that included the running of agents to and from Union territory."[16]

Cole also named seven Sandusky residents who were involved in the plot and had plans to seize the town's armory and cut telegraph wires.[17]

Hill told Carter he would organize his guard force at the prison to defend against any possible uprising among the prisoners. Hill also sent a detachment of soldiers from the island to the Sandusky train depot where they awaited the arrival of passenger trains with "suspicious characters" disembarking, as the Sandusky *Daily Commercial Register* reported.[18]

The effort to intercept conspirators arriving by train came to naught, principally because none seemed to have arrived. Hill's team rounded up about sixty male passengers whose "appearances gave the strongest indications that they were just the men that we were in quest of." Despite their "appearances," all the men were later found to be mechanics or laborers on their way to Nashville.[19]

Other soldiers began rounding up the seven Sandusky co-conspirators identified by Cole. They included two hardware merchants, a doctor, a clothing retailer and three other men. All were well-known Copperheads in Sandusky. They were arrested and placed under the custody of the Sandusky provost marshal. Cole was confined below deck aboard the *Michigan*.[20]

That same afternoon, Carter sent Lieutenant Colonel B.H. Hill, the assistant provost in Detroit, a telegram stating: "Your dispatch of 19th received. I have Cole and a fair prospect of bagging the party."[21]

* * * * *

The arrest of Cole in Sandusky on September 19 effectively made it impossible for Beall and the team of raiders to carry out the raid on Johnson's Island, although Cole's capture was unknown to them at the time. Who was responsible for informing Lieutenant Colonel Hill in Detroit about the plot two days before it began? There are several named, and unnamed, suspects. Conclusive proof identifying anyone, however, does not appear to exist and, as years turn to centuries after the event, the turncoat likely will never be known with any certainty.

One name that appears in many accounts is Godfrey J. Hyams, a trusted aide of Jacob Thompson, the lead Confederate commissioner in Toronto. Hyams, originally from Arkansas, was forced to leave the state after federal troops seized his property. Making his way to Toronto, he became involved with the Confederate commissioners and their plots. In various accounts, Hyams has been named as the informer not only for the Johnson's Island plot but also for the failed Chicago convention attack.[22]

Among other Confederate plots launched from Canada, Hyams was involved in a bizarre scheme during the summer of 1864 to attempt to spread yellow fever among the residents of Boston, Philadelphia and Washington, D.C. An early example of biological warfare, the plot involved trunks with clothing from Havana and Bermuda that was supposed to have been worn by people infected with yellow fever. One such trunk was to be delivered to President Lincoln as a "gift." The originator of the plot, Dr. Luke P. Blackburn, a Kentucky-born physician turned Confederate agent, was apparently unaware that the disease is spread through mosquito bites, not infected clothing.[23] There is some question whether Hyams was paid for his services in delivering the trunks to northern cities, possibly creating a motive for him to betray Thompson.

Maurice Langhorne is another Confederate conspirator mentioned as a possible betrayer of the plot. Langhorne, a Confederate artillery sergeant in John Hunt Morgan's cavalry command, arrived in Canada in 1863, most likely as a deserter. He became involved with Thomas Hines in planning the failed attack in Chicago during the 1864 Democratic convention. Langhorne testified as a government witness in the trial of several of the Confederates who were arrested for their involvement in the Chicago plot. Hines later called him a "traitor."[24]

Another name that appears as a suspected Confederate turncoat is a "Colonel Johnson" of Kentucky, without more description or background. The accounts say Johnson "dropped a paper" describing the plot on the wharf where the *Philo Parsons* was docked on the day of the raid, which contradicts the report of Lieutenant Colonel B.H. Hill, the assistant provost marshal in Detroit, who described his encounter with the informer in reports to the Union Army command. The same accounts go on to say Johnson felt remorse for his betrayal and committed suicide by cutting his throat while being held in prison.[25]

Another possible informer is an unnamed individual described as someone residing in a hotel where sixty Confederate refugees lived in Windsor, Canada across the river from Detroit. This person is said to have relayed every incriminating conversation he overheard to Lieutenant Colonel Hill, the assistant provost marshal of Detroit.[26]

Other accounts of the plot decline even to speculate on the identity of the informer. Jacob Thompson, writing to Confederate Secretary of State Judah P. Benjamin in December 1864 after the failure of the plot, assigns blame simply to "some treachery."[27] Similarly, Hines's comprehensive account of the Northwestern Conspiracy written in 1886, says only that plans for the *Michigan* attack "had been betrayed."[28]

Perhaps it was inevitable that plans for the *Michigan* and Johnson's Island attack would become known to Union authorities. The simple fact was that there were almost as many spies and detectives in Canada working for the Union as there were Confederate agents. They all frequented the same hotel lobbies and bars in Toronto and Montreal.

"It must have been comical with Federals and Confederates watching each other over their glasses of beer and whiskey," wrote one author. "Everyone in the bar either knew or suspected everyone else they did not know personally of being an enemy."[29]

Before the attempted raid in Chicago during the summer of 1864, Jacob Thompson cautioned Hines and his team to be careful about talking to strangers, warning they could be spies.[30] Ironically, Thompson himself was known to be dangerously loose-lipped, leading Hines to write years later that Thompson's subordinates "were kept in constant apprehension lest he compromise their efforts by indiscreet confidences."[31]

The combination of indiscreet remarks and deliberate treachery by those with knowledge of the planned attacks undermined more than a handful of plots hatched in Canada during these years. "Too many knew" of the projects, wrote one historian, "and most of those who did had nothing to do from one day to the next but sit in hotel lobbies, bars, and rooming houses, and talk. These tyros in the art of conspiracy were exiles and Southerners, and hence gregarious by definition and much too free with their confidences to fellow exiles, real or bogus."[32]

The proliferation of detectives and Union agents in Canada added another avenue for plans to become known. Federal detectives stood at bars in hotels learning secrets with dollars, liquor or simple sociability. Often, they knew as much about a conspiracy as the conspirators themselves.[33]

"The bane and curse of carrying out anything in this country is the surveillance under which we act," Thompson wrote, referring to Canada in his December 1864 letter to Benjamin, the Confederate Secretary of State. "Detectives, or those ready to give information, stand at every street corner. Two or three cannot interchange ideas without a reporter."[34]

Still another way for the Union to learn Confederate plans was by embedding agents inside Copperhead groups and anti–Union secret societies. I. Winslow Ayer, a medical quack and vendor of patent medicines, joined the Chicago branch of the Sons of Liberty for the specific purpose of monitoring their activities and reporting them to Union authorities. He provided early warning to the commander of Camp Douglas, Benjamin Sweet, about the planned attack on the fort during the Chicago convention.[35]

Similarly, Felix Stidger, a mild-mannered Kentuckian with Union sympathies, ingratiated himself into a leadership position with the Indiana Order of American Knights, the predecessor to the Sons of Liberty. From there, he gathered evidence about the growing Northwest Conspiracy targeting not only Chicago but other states in the northwest. He sent reports to the provost marshal in Indianapolis who, in turn, made sure the information made its way to Secretary of War Stanton in Washington. One of Stidger's most perilous moments as a double agent came when he was assigned to assassinate a fellow embedded agent, whose identity had become known to the Indiana Copperheads. Only a last minute change in assignments removed Stidger from the murder plot.[36]

* * * * *

Meanwhile, aboard the USS *Michigan*, in the late afternoon, Monday, September 19, Captain Carter, following his interrogation and the arrest of Cole, told the crew to prepare for action. He ordered up steam and had the crew take the exact elevation and range of the entrance to Sandusky Bay to accurately position the ship's guns. The *Philo Parsons'* usual arrival time in Sandusky was around 5 p.m. A dispatch received earlier in the day from Lieutenant Colonel Hill, the assistant provost marshal in Detroit, reported the boat had departed on time that morning. When it failed to arrive in Sandusky by evening, it became obvious to Carter and the *Michigan* crew something was amiss.[37]

About 7 p.m., the *Michigan's* crew spotted a small sloop sailing out of the bay. Because news of Cole's arrest was already circulating around Sandusky, Carter sent a barge to detain the sloop to prevent the news from traveling farther and possibly alerting the conspirators. After the barge made sure the sloop returned to the Sandusky docks, hours passed as the *Michigan* and its crew waited and watched to see if the rebel-controlled *Philo Parsons* would arrive in Sandusky Bay.[38]

CHAPTER 19

Chase and Escape

Sandusky Bay, Lake Erie, Detroit River—
September 19–September 21, 1864

Hours after Captain John Carter gave orders for the *Michigan* to prepare for action, Beall and his team were still aboard the *Philo Parsons* just outside the entrance to Sandusky Bay, rocking gently in the swells of Lake Erie. The night sky was clear, the moon shone brightly and a light wind came from the southwest.[1] Beall and his team had been surprised to see the *Michigan* with smoke coming out of its stack, no longer at rest.

Equally confounding was that no flare had come from Cole to signal that the gunboat's crew was disabled, leaving the vessel open to attack.[2] Beall wanted to wait, hoping the signal would appear. But the missing signal, together with the unexpected preparedness of the *Michigan*, unnerved Beall's team. It was now close to midnight. The men gathered with Beall in the main cabin and talked over their situation.

Beall tried in vain to convince the men to proceed with the plan. He emphasized their duty to the Confederacy, warning of their disgrace if it were later discovered the plan could have been executed. Several men voiced frustration that nothing had yet gone according to plan—noting the unexpected arrival of the *Island Queen* at Middle Bass with troops aboard, along with the missing messenger on Kelleys Island—arguing that it was simply too risky to proceed. At least one crew member used the term "slaughterhouse" in describing the dangers they faced, according to the recollections of a *Philo Parsons* crew member who was confined in the boat's hold.[3]

Finally, Beall relented. He would call off the raid. But, as a condition for the change in plans, he told the men they would have to sign "a memorial of their own insubordination."[4]

Written on the back of an old bill of lading, the memorial was one of the most extraordinary documents created during Beall's history as a Confederate raider. The paper Beall had his men sign not only declared the end to the attempted attack on Johnson's Island and the *Michigan*; it essentially amounted to an admission of mutiny by the men:

On Board the Philo Parsons
September 20, 1864.

    We, the undersigned, crew of the boat aforesaid, take pleasure in expressing our admiration of the gentlemanly bearing, skill, and courage of Capt. Beall as a commanding officer, and a gentleman; but believing, and being well convinced that the enemy is informed of our approach, and is so well prepared that we can not by possibility make it a success, and, having already captured two boats, we respectfully decline to prosecute it any further.[5]

Seventeen of the twenty men on Beall's team signed their names to the statement—all but Bennet Burley, Beall's second-in-command, and two other men.

    Beall then took the first steps to retreat from his planned attack. He directed DeWitt Nichols, the pilot of the *Philo Parsons*, to climb out of the hold and ordered him to chart a course back to Detroit. Nichols, George Orr, the *Island Queen's* captain, and Campbell, the *Philo Parsons'* wheelman, had been taken aboard the *Philo Parsons* before it left Middle Bass Island the previous afternoon. Despite having relinquished his plans to attack the *Michigan*, Beall's aggressive impulses had not entirely diminished. He told Campbell that every vessel they encountered on their way to Detroit "they were going to destroy."[6]

    The *Philo Parsons* cut through the waves at top speed, with the boiler "kept in a tremendous heat," Orr later recalled.[7] As the *Philo Parsons* passed Middle Bass, several of its former passengers were still on the shore. They saw the boat steam past in the darkness at about 1 a.m. Tuesday morning, with smoke pouring from its stack and Confederate flag flying.[8]

* * * * *

    As the *Philo Parsons* made its way to Detroit, passengers remaining on Middle Bass each had their own stories to tell about how they spent the night. Several of the women and children went with Sylvester Atwood, captain of the *Philo Parsons* who lived on Middle Bass, and spent the night at his house.[9] Most of the other women were able to find lodging with island residents.

    The men from the boats had to make do with less accommodating arrangements. Frederick Hukill, the Cincinnati businessman, and his colleague spent the night sleeping in a haystack at a local farm.[10]

    Beginning Tuesday morning around sunrise, several residents of Middle Bass who owned small boats began ferrying some of the passengers to Sandusky, about eighteen miles away. Hukill, along with several other passengers, crowded onto a small fishing sloop. "We were in need of elbow room and there was nothing to eat … except some herring and crackers," he recounted years later. "It wasn't exactly a pleasure trip." The wind died in the afternoon and they drifted for hours until a tugboat approached and towed them to Sandusky where they arrived at about 8 p.m.[11]

* * * * *

    Some passengers had escaped from Middle Bass just hours after they were released by Beall and the raiding team on Monday afternoon. Eight passengers, in two boats, rowed to South Bass Island, about a half mile directly south.[12]

When he arrived at the village of Put-in-Bay on South Bass, one of the passengers, George Magle, went door to door in the town to rouse the sleeping residents. "Get up!" he cried. "The steamers *Island Queen* and *Philo Parsons* are in the hands of the rebels! Secrete your money and valuables and if you have any firearms or ammunition in the house, get them together and hurry to the Bay."[13]

Residents quickly formed an ad hoc military company. The man chosen to lead the unit had already had his own brush with history. Captain John Brown, Jr., an island resident, was the eldest son of the notorious abolitionist who led the raid on the Harpers Ferry armory in 1859. Brown Jr., who was born in Hudson, Ohio, in 1841, had come to the island in 1862 with two wives in tow. Earlier in the war, Brown helped recruit abolitionists from Ohio and Michigan to move to Kansas. At the time, the Kansas-Nebraska Act of 1854 left the decision of whether Kansas would allow slavery to the state's citizens rather than Congress. In 1862, Brown Jr. left his recruiting position because of a severe case of arthritis and moved to South Bass. As an island resident, Brown Jr. operated a small museum and worked part-time as a surveyor.[14]

Brown possessed a significant arsenal of weapons, some of which had been used by his father during the Harpers Ferry raid, and they were distributed among men at Put-in-Bay. A cannon used during the War of 1812—known as the "Perry Victory" cannon after Commodore Oliver Hazard Perry's triumph over the British on Lake Erie—was wheeled into position in the harbor and filled with gunpowder, gravel and iron filings.[15]

After hearing Magle's cries of alarm, many of the island's residents did not know quite what to expect. Living on the peaceful island of South Bass, far from the scenes of battle to the south, they had little cause to imagine—let alone take steps to protect against—bands of Confederate raiders ransacking their homes.

In horse-drawn wagons, residents rumbled out of town in the darkness to wooded areas, carrying valuables they wanted to conceal from the rebel raiders. They hid their money, jewelry and other cherished personal items inside tree stumps and hollow logs. Several large caverns also perforated the island's limestone subsurface, providing refuge for those not wanting to remain in town.[16]

As word of the rebel raiders spread across the island, residents spent an uneasy night listening for the sound of explosions or gunfire, both near and far, but silence filled the hours.

After he was assured that adequate defenses were in place on the island, John Brown, Jr., decided it was imperative to alert the military authorities on Johnson's Island about the presence of rebel raiders on Lake Erie. With three other men, Brown took a small rowboat and set off for an area called Catawba Island, about two miles directly south of South Bass island. It barely qualified as an island, with only a narrow channel separating it from the rest of the Marblehead Peninsula. The wind had picked up, leaving Brown and his small crew struggling to make progress through the tossing waves. After several hours, they reached Catawba, wet and tired, and then began hiking south across the peninsula to a point opposite Johnson's Island. From there, they found a small boat and rowed the short distance to the prison camp where they arrived at about 7 a.m. Tuesday. Brown reported the seizures of the *Philo Parsons* and *Island Queen* to Colonel Hill, the prison camp's commander. It was the first such report to any Union authorities.[17]

* * * * *

About two hours earlier, at daybreak around 5 a.m. Tuesday, Captain Carter ordered the *Michigan* to leave its anchorage off Johnson's Island, sail out of Sandusky Bay into Lake Erie and begin searching for the *Philo Parsons*. The gunboat's first stop was Kelleys Island, the island closest to Sandusky. Several passengers from the excursion boats were on the shore. They had come from Middle Bass after being released the day before, trying to make their way back to Sandusky.[18]

As the *Michigan* approached, some of the passengers took cover, not knowing whether the Union Navy or the Confederacy had command of the vessel. But, as the ship glided closer to the dock, their fears eased when they recognized Captain Carter and the gunboat's pilot, William Hinton, standing on the deck. Hinton, in particular, was unmistakable because he weighed nearly three hundred pounds.[19]

Some of the passengers were taken aboard the *Michigan*. About halfway between Kelleys Island and Middle Bass, the *Michigan* approached a small boat sailing toward Sandusky with Thomas Ashley, the clerk of the *Philo Parsons*, a few other crew members and some passengers aboard. They were taken aboard the *Michigan*.[20]

* * * * *

With the *Michigan* having left its post guarding the Johnson's Island prison camp, Colonel Charles W. Hill, the prison camp's commandant, decided to take precautions in case the rebel raiders returned with reinforcements. Hill moved auxiliary cannons into position north of the prison—four Parrott cannons, capable of firing twenty-pound projectiles a distance of 2,000 yards—to defend the entrance to Sandusky Bay.[21]

Hill also ordered his quartermaster to take into service a small steamer, the *General Grant*, which cruised the waters of Sandusky Bay, and prepared to place on board one or two twenty-pound Parrot cannons, a twelve-pound howitzer and a small infantry force. At 115-feet in length, the *General Grant* was a much smaller vessel than the 165-foot-long *Michigan*, but Colonel Hill was hoping it could serve as a stand in, at least for few hours until the *Michigan* returned.[22]

* * * * *

After its stop at Kelleys Island, the *Michigan* steered toward the Detroit River, where it emptied into Lake Erie about thirty miles to the northwest. The journey across that expanse of Lake Erie turned up no signs of the *Philo Parsons*. As the *Michigan* approached the mouth of the river at about 10 a.m., it came near other tugs and vessels. Carter asked crew on each ship they encountered whether anyone aboard had seen the *Philo Parsons* within the last few hours. There were no sightings reported. In fact, Beall and his men aboard the *Philo Parsons* had arrived at the Detroit river in darkness several hours earlier.[23]

The *Michigan* turned about and headed back toward Sandusky, stopping at Middle Bass to pick up seven remaining passengers on that island. Soon after leaving Middle Bass, the *Michigan* crew spotted the *Island Queen* lying on Chickanolee Reef in about seven feet of water. With the shallow water making it unsafe to approach, the *Michigan* proceeded to Put-in-Bay on South Bass island where it picked up more passengers before arriving in Sandusky around 3 p.m. Tuesday.[24]

* * * * *

Earlier, after leaving Sandusky Bay on its way to Detroit Monday night, the *Philo Parsons* under the command of Beall, passed only one other ship. Beall told Campbell, the wheelman, to go alongside the other vessel to check on the possibility of an attack. As they approached, Beall asked Campbell what waters they were in. When Campbell told him they were in British waters in the northern part of Lake Erie, Beall backed off, saying the location was fortunate for the other ship, otherwise he would have boarded it.[25]

Between 4 a.m. and 5 a.m. Tuesday morning—several hours before the *Michigan* arrived—the *Philo Parsons* entered the Detroit River. As it passed the town of Malden south of Detroit—where Beall and three other men had boarded the *Philo Parsons* a day earlier—two of Beall's men filled a yawl, a small two-masted sailboat, with plunder. The plunder included a piano, trunks, chairs, mirrors and bedclothes. Beall's team had taken the yawl from the *Island Queen* the day before and had lashed it to the *Philo Parsons* as they headed toward the Detroit River.[26]

As the *Philo Parsons* approached Fighting Island, an uninhabited marshland in the middle of the river just south of Sandwich, Beall began preparing to scuttle the boat. He sent ashore Nichols, pilot on the *Philo Parsons* and the *Island Queen* crew members—Captain Orr, Haines, the engineer and Hamilton, the clerk. Orr told Beall's team, "We had rather be landed on the main shore." But Beall's team responded they "had rather we wouldn't."[27]

After their release, with help from the owners of a small boat, the *Island Queen*'s crew members quickly made their way to the mainland on the American side. Within hours, they had boarded a train, returning them to Sandusky.[28]

Around 8 a.m. on Tuesday, September 20, Beall and his team docked the *Philo Parsons* at Sandwich, near Windsor, across the river from Detroit. They unloaded their plunder, taking it ashore. Campbell, the *Philo Parsons* wheelman, and Denison, the boat's engineer, were still onboard. Beall ordered Denison to go below and cut the boat's injection pipes, allowing river water to rush in.[29]

The *Philo Parsons* slowly sank at the Sandwich dock. Its hull soon settled on the shallow river bottom, while its top deck and wheelhouse remained above water level. Nichols, the *Philo Parsons'* pilot, who had been released on Fighting Island, later spotted the boat and took possession of it. He arranged for a small steamer to tow the *Philo Parsons* back to the Trowbridge & Wilcox dock in Detroit where it had departed a little more than twenty-four hours earlier.[30]

Campbell, the *Philo Parsons'* wheelman, and Denison were among the last crew members released by Beall. As they stood on the dock at Sandwich, Beall approached Campbell and said he wanted to thank him for his help but regretted that he had no money. Instead, he handed Campbell a half dozen spoons and eight silver forks from the *Philo Parsons*.[31]

Then Campbell and Denison, along with Beall and members of his team started walking slowly north toward Windsor.[32]

Chapter 20

Aftermath

Sandusky, Canada, Vermont—September–October 1864

In the days following the raid, alarm spread across the Great Lakes states as officials in the Lincoln administration came to grips with the reality that an enemy force capable of launching attacks against key northern cities existed just across the U.S. border in Canada. Union Army leaders took steps to gauge the level of threat emanating from Confederates north of the border.

Secretary of War Edwin Stanton ordered Major-General Samuel P. Heintzelman, the commander of the military district encompassing Ohio, to go immediately to Sandusky and secure the Johnson's Island prison camp against any subsequent attacks. Heintzelman's office, in turn, sent telegrams to the mayors of Cleveland, Buffalo and Detroit, along with the commander of Camp Douglas in Chicago, warning them of the possibility of an attack by Confederates on the Great Lakes.[1]

Heintzelman commanded the Union Army's Northern Department, which included Ohio, Indiana, Illinois, and Michigan. He had taken the position—essentially a desk job in Columbus, Ohio—in October 1863 on orders of the War Department after his lackluster performance as a Union Army field commander in the Richmond peninsula campaign earlier in the war.[2]

Also ordered by Stanton to travel to Buffalo and Sandusky was Major General John Dix, commander of the Eastern Department, which included New York and New England. His jurisdiction included the border with Canada's eastern provinces. Dix, like Heintzelman, was in his sixties and past prime age for a field command. Earlier in the war he had negotiated the first prisoner exchange cartel, which was no longer in effect.

Before Dix arrived in Sandusky on September 26, he was preceded by Major General Ethan Allen Hitchcock, the Union Army's Commissioner in charge of prisoner exchanges. Both men spent several days interviewing Johnson's Island prison officials as well as crew on the *Michigan* and the two captured Lake Erie excursion boats, the *Philo Parson* and *Island Queen*.

Dix went first to Detroit and, ironically, traveled on to Sandusky aboard the *Philo Parsons*, which had been repaired and recommissioned within days of its seizure and abandonment by Beall and his team. The *Island Queen*, too, was refloated and sailing again a week after the attack.[3]

Dix's arrival in Sandusky was celebrated by the town's residents who gathered outside the West House hotel where he was staying. As Sandusky's Union Band played patriotic songs, the crowd began calling "Dix, Dix." The general stepped out onto the hotel balcony and addressed the citizens. Asserting "there could be no peace until the rebel armies were dispersed," Dix added, to great applause, that he could never agree to an armistice with the South, saying, "I have faith only in a steady, unceasing, unremitting prosecution of the war."[4]

Dix's visit to Sandusky was brief, lasting only a day and a night. Because of the investigative work already completed by Heintzelman and Hitchcock, Dix "deemed it unnecessary" to conduct his own review, as he wrote in a lengthy report to Stanton.[5]

Also contributing to the flurry of telegrams the day after the raid was the Commissary-General of Prisoners, William Hoffman. He wired Charles W. Hill, the Johnson's Island prison commander, complaining that Hill had delayed notifying him about the raid. "An event of this character should have been reported to this office by telegram immediately on its occurrence," Hoffman wrote. "Hereafter give me the earliest information of any such raid, or any rumor of preparations for such an undertaking that may reach you."[6]

In the next paragraph, Hoffman switched subjects entirely and, in characteristic fashion, focused on the minutiae of prison operations. He told Hill that he could authorize the prison sutler "to sell candles or oil to prisoners of war, but the use of them at night for lights must not be permitted beyond 9 o'clock, except in cases of sickness, when on the recommendation of the surgeons, you may extend the privilege at your discretion." He ended the three-paragraph telegram with an additional sentence: "Brooms may also be sold to prisoners."[7]

Inside the Johnson's Island prison, captured Confederate soldiers demonstrated varying degrees of awareness of what had transpired outside the gates on the night of the attempted raid. "Yankees terribly frightened at the discovery of a plot to capture the Michigan (Gun Boat) and release the prisoners confined here," Colonel Edmund DeWitt Patterson of the 9th Alabama Regiment wrote in his diary September 21. "The rebs and their sympathizers captured two steam boats up near the Canada shore but unfortunately for us the plot was exposed and the authorities put on their guard. It was a well laid plan and would have succeeded had they kept it secret; I hope they may try again."[8]

* * * * *

The attempted attack on Johnson's Island, originating on Canadian soil, roiled relations between the United States and Great Britain. Diplomacy between the two sovereigns had been unsettled since the *Trent* affair in 1861, when the U.S. Navy frigate *San Jacinto* seized two Confederate diplomats aboard a British vessel, the *Trent*.

The Lake Erie attack also exposed the irritation that had been building among U.S. officials over what they considered to be Great Britain's lax treatment of Confederate belligerents in Canada.

Dix, in his report to Stanton, referred to "a feeling of exasperation by the failure of Great Britain to prevent the arming in her ports of insurgent cruisers by which millions of our property have been destroyed on the ocean." He recommended organizing "a proper naval and military force" that could pursue any Confederate attackers "into the Canadian territory."[9]

Major General Hitchcock joined Dix in urging a buildup of military capabilities on the Great Lakes. Writing to Stanton on September 23, Hitchcock called for the placement of "several armed vessels" on the lakes to protect commerce and cities on the shore. He pointed to the actions of Commissioner Jacob Thompson in Canada "in setting on foot expeditions of the most dangerous character."[10]

Stanton replied the same day, telling Hitchcock to make a thorough inspection of the defenses on the lakes, including the "force, the vigilance and qualifications of commanders." Stanton's reply resulted in Hitchcock's trip to Johnson's Island where he was joined by Heintzelman and then followed by Dix.[11]

In Canada, Charles Monck, the governor-general of the British territory, was aware of the growing concern among U.S. officials. To discourage any effort by the United States to retaliate militarily in the days following the raid, he ordered Canadian troops to Windsor, across the border from Detroit. "In the present excitable condition of the public mind in the States, it is wise to take every precaution against anything that may give them a handle against us," Monck wrote to his military commander, Sir Fenwick Williams.[12]

Born in Ireland, Monck, the forty-five-year-old leader, had taken office in 1861. At the time, the provinces in Canada were just beginning their drive to become a confederation, a drive inspired, in part, by the civil war south of the Canadian border. Establishing a confederation was seen as a way to discourage any plans by the North or the South to extend the war into Canada. Monck would later serve as the first governor of Canada after it formally established the confederation in 1867.

The Lincoln administration also took concrete steps to bolster defenses along the Great Lakes. Days after the attack, Secretary of State William Seward informed the British Charge' d' Affaires in Washington that, in view of the hostilities on Lake Erie, the United States would have to breach the Rush-Bagot treaty, which limited naval operations on the Great Lakes to one armed vessel each for the U.S. and Britain.[13]

Major General Dix, following his survey and investigation of defenses on the lakes, recommended that five tugboats be armed and positioned at harbor entrances of major cities on the U.S. side of the Great Lakes. In addition, construction of a revenue cutter to patrol the lakes was hastily completed. Normally unarmed, the cutter would now carry six guns. Union Army troop regiments were also sent to Detroit and Buffalo. "By early autumn the Canadian-American border was an armed frontier in nearly every sense of the word," according to Canadian historian Robin W. Winks.[14]

While repercussions from the attack played out in the U.S. and Canada, Beall, the leader of the attack, returned to Canada. After leaving the *Philo Parsons* partially submerged in the Detroit River, Beall met with Commissioner Jacob Thompson in Toronto. Thompson advised Beall to distance himself as much as possible from the prying eyes and sensitive ears of Union detectives and agents on duty in Canada's cities along the American border. Beall went to Balsam Lake in the Kawartha Lakes region about eighty miles north of Toronto where he spent two weeks at a hunting and fishing camp.[15]

Shortly after his arrival in Canada following the raid, Beall became incensed after he saw an editorial in one of the Toronto newspapers accusing him of stealing $80,000 during the seizures of the *Philo Parsons* and *Island Queen*. He wrote a letter to the editor denying the accusation and defending his actions in connection with the raid.

"The United States is carrying on war on Lake Erie against the Confederates … by transportation of men and supplies on its waters; by confining Confederate prisoners on its islands, and lastly, by the presence of a 14-gun steamer patrolling its waters," Beall wrote. He denied violating any laws of Canada, emphasizing that the seizures of the *Philo Parsons* and *Island Queen* took place entirely within waters of the United States. Moreover, no one was killed, and no one was robbed, Beall asserted.[16]

Addressing the plan to take over the *Michigan*, Beall pointed out that its guns exceeded the limit on arms allowed for lake vessels under the Rush-Bagot treaty between the U.S. and Great Britain. "England allows this boat to remain guarding Confederate prisoners, though she carries an armament in violation of the treaty," he wrote.

Defending his men, Beall concluded, "These men were not 'burglars,' or 'pirates,' enemies of mankind, unless hatred and hostility to the Yankees be taken as a sin against humanity, or a crime against civilization."[17]

Little more is known about Beall's activities in the period immediately following the raid other than the fact that he was not considering abandoning his efforts on behalf of the Confederacy. In early October, Beall wrote to a friend: "You know that I am not one of the giving-up kind. We are going to try again on my plan."[18]

After his return to Canada, Bennet Burley, Beall's co-leader during the raid, headed to Guelph, a town about sixty miles west of Toronto, where he stayed with a cousin, Adam Robertson. Like Burley, Robertson was an emigrant from Scotland. He ran the town's foundry. Soon after Burley's arrival, Robertson expanded production at the foundry which until that time had turned out mostly farm implements. Under Burley's influence, Robertson started to make munitions for the Confederacy, including cannons, cannonballs, grenades and torpedoes, similar to the torpedo that Burley unsuccessfully attempted to explode in New York harbor in 1863. They planned to smuggle the weaponry into the South, using either a sea route or by land, with the munitions packaged in falsely labeled crates.[19]

Charles Cole, the only member of the raiding team who had been apprehended, remained under guard at Johnson's Island prison camp. The day after the raid, Cole's mistress, Annie Davis, traveled to Toronto where she met with Jacob Thompson and informed him about the events on Lake Erie in the preceding days. She returned to Sandusky on September 25, carrying a letter from Thompson addressed to Colonel Hill, commandant of the Johnson's Island prison.[20]

In the letter, signed by both Thompson and Clement Clay, the two commissioners challenged the Union Army's contention that Cole was a spy and should be tried as one. "If you can justly condemn Captain Cole as a spy, every soldier and officer of the United States caught within the lines of the armies coming within the lines of the armies and limits of the Confederate States would be tried and condemned as spies," they wrote. Cole also was not guilty of violating any laws of the United States, they argued, adding that—even if he had planned to—he failed to carry out any such offense.[21] The letter was not persuasive to Union authorities and Cole would remain in Union Army custody for another sixteen months.

* * * * *

In early October, a little more than two weeks after Beall's raid, two young men entered a hotel in the small town of St. Albans, Vermont, located on Lake Champlain, a few miles south of the Canadian border. They asked for a room, saying they were members of a hunting and fishing club in Montreal. They had come to St. Albans, they said, for an outing to the large lake in Vermont. In the days that followed, additional members of the sporting club arrived in town, with several more showing up every few days.[22]

By October 19, twenty-one members of the club had gathered in St. Albans. The leader of the group was a twenty-one-year-old Kentuckian named Bennett H. Young. In addition to fishing and hunting experience, Young had a military background. He had been a lieutenant with Confederate General John Hunt Morgan and had participated in Morgan's cavalry raid across Ohio in July 1863. Young was captured—along with Morgan, Thomas Hines and John Castleman—and imprisoned at Camp Douglas, the Union Army prison in Chicago. He escaped a few months later, fled from Illinois and ultimately arrived in Canada.[23]

Before Young relocated to Canada, he met with Confederate War Secretary James Seddon in Richmond. There, Seddon and Young agreed on a plan in which Young would inspect areas along the U.S.-Canadian border, looking for towns that could be sacked and burned in an attempt to replicate the campaign of destruction then being waged in Georgia by Union General William Sherman. "It is but right that the people of New England and Vermont especially, some of whose officers and troops have been foremost in these excesses, should have brought home to them some of the horrors of such warfare," Seddon wrote in a letter to Young.[24]

On October 19 at around 3 p.m., Young stepped onto the porch of the St. Albans hotel, displayed a Navy Colt revolver and declared: "In the name of the Confederate states, I take possession of St. Albans."[25] As Young made his announcement, thirteen other members of the group busted through the doors of the three banks in town and, at gunpoint, took a total of approximately $208,000 (worth nearly $4 million today).[26] As the robberies proceeded, the remaining men, including Young, herded any passersby onto the town green where they were kept under guard.[27] Other villagers saw what was happening and fired on the raiders. The Confederates returned fire, wounding two men and killing one.[28]

As the Confederates retreated with their stolen cash, Young and his men hurled bottles of Greek Fire—the naptha and quicklime incendiary weapon—onto the roofs and through windows of nearby buildings, attempting to set them ablaze. The men then regrouped, jumped on horses and fled across the border into Canada. By the next morning, thirteen of the raiders, including Young, had been captured by a pursuing posse from St. Albans. Because they were still in Canadian territory, the posse turned the raiders over to Canadian authorities. About $90,000, or a little less than half of the money, was eventually recovered.[29]

The Greek Fire used by Young and his men largely failed to ignite. Although fires did burn in a couple of St. Albans buildings, prompt action by townsfolk and sufficient amounts of water kept damage to a minimum. The failure to wreak destruction in the town made the episode appear more like "a large-scale bank robbery" than an act of war, in the words of one author.[30] Nonetheless, the St. Albans attack is considered by historians to be the most northerly engagement of the Civil War.

What became known as the St. Alban's raid had been commissioned by Confederate Secretary of War James Seddon and at least one of the Confederate Commissioners, Clement Clay. It followed an earlier, planned raid on a bank in Calais, Maine, that never was carried out because Union authorities learned of the plans and alerted bank officials.[31]

Like the Lake Erie raid a month earlier, the attack on St. Albans had international ramifications. Major General John Dix, commander of the Union Army's Department of the East, ordered troops into Canada to find the raiders still at large. He justified the order under the doctrine of "hot pursuit," which ostensibly allowed raids by U.S. authorities into Canada that were close-in-time to the actual offense.[32]

Dix's order, which had not been approved by higher levels of the Union military command, risked open conflict with Canadian troops and, therefore, Great Britain. Such a development would be welcome news in Richmond. A war between the United States and England "would be our peace," wrote a clerk in the Confederate War Department, referring to how a U.S.-England conflict would relieve military pressure on the Confederacy.[33]

Secretary of State Seward recognized the dangers posed by Dix's order but, at that point in the war, he did not object to placing Great Britain under increasing pressure to control Confederate belligerents in Canada. Moreover, the Lake Erie raid one month earlier, together with the raid on St. Albans, provided Seward and the Lincoln administration justification for abrogating the Rush-Bagot treaty and placing more arms on the Great Lakes. Seward took no immediate action to rescind Dix's order, reminding Canadian officials that they had yet to respond to his request for extradition of the captured St. Albans raiders to the U.S.[34]

The St. Albans raid also contributed to a rift among the Confederate Commissioners in Canada. Thompson, the senior commissioner, had been scrupulous in following the instructions he had received from Jefferson Davis not to violate British neutrality in the war. He had rejected proposals to rob banks in Buffalo and other border towns. "I knew nothing whatever of the raid on Saint Albans until after it transpired," he wrote in a December letter to Judah P. Benjamin, the Confederate Secretary of State.[35]

The raid had been planned by Seddon, Jefferson's Secretary of War (raising questions about policy coherence within the Confederate cabinet at that stage of the war), and had been approved in Canada by Commissioner Clement Clay. As a subordinate of Thompson, Clay lacked authority to approve the raid but nonetheless allowed Young to proceed without Thompson's knowledge.[36]

Thompson, for his part, was working on plans of his own during this time. The plans included another mission involving ships on the Great Lakes. And this mission would, for a second time, involve John Yates Beall.

CHAPTER 21

A Visitor to Montreal

Montreal—October 1864

St. Lawrence Hall was the favored hotel and gathering spot for Confederates in Montreal. Located on St. James Street in a fashionable section of town, it catered to its southern clientele by being the only hotel in Canada to serve mint juleps, which were available at Dooley's Bar in the hotel basement.[1]

The drawing room at "The Hall," as it was known, was wide and spacious. A grand piano sat near the center of the room, surrounded by plush chairs and upholstered benches where men sat, some smoking cigars, some reading newspapers, some doing both. Where the walls met the ceiling, scalloped-shaped plaster moldings made the high ceiling seem even higher. Double doors made of dark mahogany opened to the hotel lobby.[2]

Through those doors, entering the drawing room after checking in on October 18, 1864, was a twenty-six-year-old man, about five-foot-eight in height, of compact build, with curled, jet-black hair of medium length, a mustache and dark eyes. His name was John Wilkes Booth.[3]

The young actor had arrived in Montreal that evening, after traveling by train from Newburgh, New York, on the Hudson River. Before traveling to Montreal, Booth had been in Pennsylvania and New York City to close out an unsuccessful venture into the oil business. Several months earlier, Booth, with two partners, had formed the Dramatic Oil Company and purchased drilling rights on land in western Pennsylvania. At the time, the area was booming with the recent discovery of oil. Booth was quickly discouraged, however, after his holdings failed to produce any oil. In late September, Booth disposed of his interest in the venture, with his investment of about $6,000 (about $100,000 in today's dollars) a total loss.[4]

Exactly what drew Booth to Canada in October 1864 has never been adequately explained. But by the time he had arrived in Montreal he had decided to devote the next few months arranging for the kidnapping of Lincoln, according to an entry in his diary.[5]

Booth told friends that his visit to Montreal, his first trip outside the United States, was to arrange for the transport of his theatrical wardrobe to the South, bypassing or evading the Union navy's blockade.[6] It is possible this was just a cover story, however, as ships sailed daily from New York City to ports in Nassau, Bermuda and Havana where cargo could be transferred onto smaller, faster blockade-running vessels and into the Confederacy.[7]

Like many Canadians, residents of Montreal were generally sympathetic to the Confederacy, not because they favored slavery but rather as a shrewd assessment that a divided United States was less a threat than a united neighbor with a powerful military.[8] The fact that some American newspapers advocated and politicians—including members of Lincoln's cabinet—had talked openly about annexing Canada's maritime provinces did little to assuage Canadian anxieties.[9]

By October 1864, Montreal had become a hub of Confederate activity in Canada, attracting so-called "skedaddlers" evading the military draft, escaped prisoners of war, soldiers-of-fortune, blockade runners, arms-sellers and spies.

So pervasive was the influx of Southerners into "Canada West" (which later became the province of Ontario) that *The New York Herald* described it as a "rebel colony" where it was difficult for outsiders—particularly detectives or other agents representing interests of the Northern states—to penetrate.

"All over Canada—since it has become a rebel colony—where these desperadoes made their headquarters, the rebels have instituted a police system of their own, and no stranger is permitted to inhabit the place an hour before he is, to use police parlance, 'stood up,' and rebel detectives are at once put upon his trail, and until the object of his visit is satisfactorily ascertained, a constant surveillance is kept over him," wrote the *Herald Tribune*.[10]

The dates of Booth's visit to Montreal happened to coincide with what was a burgeoning—and rapidly coalescing—plot by Confederates to kidnap President Lincoln. Exactly when the plotting began and who was involved in pushing it forward is still open to historical examination and speculation. But the weight of the evidence appears to show that much of the planning took place in Canada—and specifically in Montreal—in late 1864.

Over the course of his ten-day stay in Montreal, Booth frequented the public rooms at St. Lawrence Hall, where he was seen engaging with other guests and visitors, many of whom were involved with Confederate plots against the North.

Booth was seen playing cards with Dr. Luke Blackburn, the Kentucky-born physician who had plotted to send clothing supposedly infected with yellow fever to Lincoln and other Washington officials.[11]

Booth also met with George Sanders, the unofficial "fourth commissioner" for the Confederacy in Canada, who associated closely with commissioners Jacob Thompson, Clement Clay and James Holcombe. Sanders, one of the most radical of the Confederates in Canada at that time, was a proponent of political assassination and an admirer of the 1848 revolutions that toppled monarchies across Europe. Sanders had arrived in Montreal a few days after Booth to begin arranging legal representation for Bennett Young and other raiders of St. Albans, Vermont, who had just been captured. The raid occurred the day after Booth arrived in Montreal.[12]

Booth and Sanders were observed in confidential conversation on the portico of St. Lawrence Hall. Shortly thereafter, Sanders told a correspondent for the London *Daily Telegraph* that the Confederate Secret Service was going to execute a plan that "would make the world shudder."[13]

Booth also played billiards at St. Lawrence Hall, enjoying games in the hotel's billiards room with the manager and other hotel guests. One guest was struck by what he called Booth's "derangement or excitement" after remarks Booth made during their game. The subject of the approaching U.S. presidential election came up. Booth told the guest that the outcome of the election "made damned little difference [because] head or tail, Abe's contract was near up and whether elected or not, he would get his goose cooked." After the guest noted Booth's skill at knocking balls into the table's corner pockets, Booth raised his cue and exclaimed, "Do you know I have got the sharpest play laid out ever done in America? I can bag the biggest game this side of ----- You'll hear of a double carom one of these days."[14]

Booth also visited Patrick C. Martin, a senior Confederate agent in Montreal and blockade runner who had left Baltimore early in the war. Martin, who also operated a liquor importing business, had his hand in a variety of Confederate operations originating in Canada, including the first aborted raid on Johnson's Island in late 1863, nearly a year before Beall's raid in 1864.[15]

Booth sought out Martin in hopes of finding their mutual friend George Kane, another former Baltimore resident, who had fled to Canada early in the war. Kane had been living with Martin in Montreal but had returned to the Confederacy by the time Booth arrived. Kane was a former Marshal of Police in Baltimore with Southern sympathies. In 1861, Kane was believed to have been part of an attempted plot to assassinate Lincoln when the newly elected president stopped in Baltimore on his way to Washington for his inauguration. The plot was never carried out because Alan Pinkerton, then the head of the National Detective Agency, arranged for Lincoln's train to pass through Baltimore in the middle of the night, earlier than expected.[16]

During Booth's stay in Montreal, Booth and Martin were seen entering the Ontario Bank at least once a day, and sometimes more often. It is unclear exactly why Booth and Martin made so many trips to the Ontario Bank during this time but, among other things, the bank was known to launder money for Confederates in Canada.[17]

Booth went to the Ontario Bank with Martin again on October 27, near the time he departed Montreal for the U.S. During that final visit, Booth opened an account in his own name and deposited $455 (about $8,000 today). He also purchased a bill of exchange, similar to a cashier's check and cashable anywhere, with a value of about sixty-one British pounds (about $7,000 today). These bank transactions show that Booth was thinking ahead, establishing a comfortable "nest egg … if he needed to make a hasty retreat across the border to Canada," according to a Booth biographer, Terry Alford.[18]

Martin also assisted Booth in transporting his theater wardrobe—which was considerable—back to the South. Packed into two trunks and one large box, it consisted of velvet suits, crowns, caps, plumes, doublets, shoes, stage swords and pistols. There were also fifty-six volumes of plays, correspondence, photographs, and clippings of old reviews.[19]

Originally from Baltimore, Martin had acquaintances throughout Maryland. He gave Booth letters of introduction to rebel agents and Confederate couriers in southern Maryland. Included among the contacts were two doctors, William Queen and Samuel Mudd, who used the cover of their profession to transport people and correspondence through southern Maryland to Virginia and into the Confederacy. The rebel contacts Martin provided to Booth happened to be located along the escape route in Maryland that Booth would take the night he assassinated Lincoln.[20]

Martin also owned a seventy-three-foot schooner, the *Marie Victoria*, which he used to sail through the Union blockade to southern ports. With Booth's wardrobe on board and a crew of six, including Martin, the *Marie Victoria* set sail from Montreal on October 24. Two weeks later, on November 7, the vessel foundered in a storm near Pointe au Pere on the St. Lawrence River and ran aground. When rescuers arrived, they found the bow smashed and no one on board, with the crew and Martin presumed dead.[21]

One other name that comes up in connection with Booth's visit to Montreal in October 1864 is John Yates Beall. It is unclear whether Booth and Beall actually met during this period but there is evidence that Beall was in the vicinity. Booth checked in to room No. 150 at St. Lawrence Hall on October 18 and checked out on October 28. Beall checked in to room No. 149 on November 2, according to the hotel's guest register. Also checking in with Beall on November 2 was Thomas Hines, the rebel agent who conspired in many plots against the North, including the failed raid on Chicago in August 1864.[22] Booth's alleged connection to Beall would stir controversy following Lincoln's assassination and remains a topic of controversy among some historians of the period.

The parade of Confederate agents and southern sympathizers who associated with Booth during his visit show that he was surrounded by rebel conspirators, many of whom were or had recently been engaged in plots against the North and Lincoln specifically. It does not require a great leap to conclude that Booth himself knew about or was personally involved in some of these same endeavors.

If nothing else, the mix of high-level Confederate agents traveling through Montreal in the fall of 1864 suggests that plans were afoot for a major undertaking, even if its ultimate manifestation had not yet taken shape. Montreal historian and writer Barry Sheehy states:

It is likely Booth was in Montreal to meet with members of the Confederate Secret Service and senior Confederate Commissioners to discuss a plan for kidnapping President Lincoln. The genesis of the Lincoln assassination can be traced directly to these meetings.[23]

The initial inspiration for a Confederate plot against Lincoln, which originally contemplated a kidnapping, is often traced to a Union cavalry raid near Richmond in early 1864. On March 3, 1864, Union Colonel Ulric Dahlgren led an advance column, with five hundred supporting troops, behind Confederate lines on the outskirts of Richmond. Dahlgren's advance was part of a larger Union attack on Richmond aimed at freeing Union soldiers held in the city's prisons. It was an attack that ultimately failed.[24] Dahlgren was killed in a crossfire with Confederate troops. Papers found on Dahlgren's body by the rebel forces included the draft of an address Dahlgren had apparently planned to deliver to the troops under his command:

> We hope to release the prisoners from Belle Island first, and having seen them fairly started, we will cross the James River into Richmond, destroying the bridges after us and, exhorting the released prisoners to destroy and burn the hateful city, and do not allow rebel leader Davis and his traitorous crew to escape.[25]

A second document found on Dahlgren was even more specific about the attack's objectives: "The men must keep together and well in hand, and, once in the city, it must be destroyed and Jeff Davis and Cabinet killed."[26]

What made public disclosure of the orders especially damaging were further revelations that the plans had been approved by Secretary of War Edwin Stanton, one of Lincoln's senior cabinet officials. This led to speculation that the plans against Davis must have been known by President Lincoln. Southern sentiments were inflamed after news came out about the Union Army plans, with Richmond newspapers holding Lincoln and his administration fully responsible for the raid. The Richmond *Sentinel* wrote:

> Dahlgren's infamy did not begin or die with him ... he was but the willing instrument for executing an atrocity which his superiors had carefully approved and sanctioned. Truly there is no depth of dishonor and villainy to which Lincoln and his agents are not capable of descending.[27]

The Lincoln administration denied any involvement in a plot to decapitate the Confederate leadership and claims of forgery about Dahlgren's papers spread through the Northern press. But the damage had been done and there was now open discussion in the South about striking back at Lincoln.[28]

Following the Dahlgren raid—in an odd historical footnote—three of Beall's close associates were selected by Confederate leaders to interview prisoners at Richmond's notorious Libby prison. On March 30, Bennet Burley, John Maxwell and Daniel Lucas were provided with passes to enter the prison and interrogate Union prisoners about their knowledge of the raid and its scope. Burley was Beall's right-hand man during their time as raiders on Chesapeake Bay and Johnson's Island. Maxwell also served with Beall on the Chesapeake. And Lucas was Beall's boyhood friend and a well-connected Richmond lawyer who would later write Beall's "memoir."[29]

As the months of 1864 wore on and the South's prospects in the war looked increasingly dire, Jefferson Davis no longer dismissed out of hand schemes proposed to retaliate against Lincoln, as he had done earlier in the war.[30] The idea of an abduction of the President became a subject of discussion in high Confederate circles. If Lincoln were a captive of the South, he would be a highly valuable hostage, one that could possibly be used by Confederate negotiators as leverage to force an exchange of prisoners that would replenish Southern ranks. Such negotiations might also lead to relief from the Union Army's tightening grip around Richmond and Sherman's destructive march through Georgia.[31]

One focus of Confederate plotters was Lincoln's practice of traveling alone by horse cart, or with only a single military escort, through the streets of Washington to a cottage near the Soldiers' Home on the outskirts of the city. During Washington's hot summer months, Lincoln would make the four-mile trip to spend the night on the Soldiers' Home grounds, high on a hill where the air was cooler. It was unremarkable for Lincoln to travel this way, at a time before the Secret Service was established and assigned responsibility for protecting the president's personal safety.[32]

It was not far-fetched for Confederates to contemplate the possibility of several armed men overpowering Lincoln's military escort—if there was one—snatching the president and spiriting him away to Confederate-friendly Maryland or across the Potomac into Virginia.

As a professional actor with little or no military background or training, Booth seemed an unlikely candidate to participate in a plot against Lincoln. At the same time, he was an avowed advocate of the Confederate cause and spoke openly about his distress when news broke about the Dahlgren raid and the captured orders describing plans to kill Jefferson Davis and his cabinet. There is no question that Booth had opportunities not available to the average citizen at the time. His life as a well-known actor allowed him to travel between the North and South, even to Canada, with few questions asked. "I have a free pass everywhere, my profession, my name is my passport," Booth told his sister, as she recounted in a memoir.[33]

It appears that, even before there were plans under discussion to take action against Lincoln, Booth was involved in clandestine activity on behalf of the Confederacy. He smuggled drugs, principally quinine used as medicine, into the South. Booth's sister, Asia Booth Clarke, wrote of her brother's activities as a drug smuggler in her memoir, *The Unlocked Book*. Booth confided to her that his knowledge of drugs was "invaluable," saying it was "one of the means by which I serve the South."[34]

Malaria was prevalent throughout the South during the Civil War. Quinine, the only effective treatment, was scarce and found only in the bark of cinchona trees in Central and South America. Although troops on both sides suffered from the disease, particularly during the 1863 Vicksburg campaign in Mississippi, Union troops had easier access to quinine and, as a result, had fewer cases and resulting casualties from the disease.[35]

Booth was able to obtain high-grade quinine from a Washington druggist and transported it into the South, initially concealed in horse collars.[36] The smuggling route was roundabout, across Chesapeake Bay on brigs and schooners and into hidden coves. From there, it went to Nassau and through the Union blockade to southern states on blockade-running vessels.[37] This clandestine activity was lucrative for both Booth and the druggist, who shared the profits after receiving payment from the Confederacy. After a single trip, Booth could collect as much as one thousand dollars (approximately $19,000 in today's dollars).[38]

Exactly when Booth became involved in the planning for kidnapping Lincoln is unclear, but it appears likely that he could have been actively engaged in the plot as early as July 1864. By that time, Booth had effectively abandoned his career as a traveling actor. After an appearance on the stage in Boston in May 1864, he would perform publicly only three more times, in benefits.[39]

On July 26, 1864, Booth was in Boston, staying at the stylish Parker House hotel. During his visit, he met with four men, three claiming to be from Canada and one from Baltimore, according to the Parker House guest register. One of the men signed in as H.V. Clinton, apparently an alias that would also show up several times in the register of St. Lawrence Hall in Montreal between May and August 1864. At least one of Clinton's arrivals at St. Lawrence Hall coincided with the arrival of Confederate Commissioner Jacob Thompson. H.V. Clinton was almost certainly a member of the Confederate Secret Service operating out of Montreal, based on examinations of his travels and hotel registrations by Montreal historian Barry Sheehy and William A. Tidwell, a Lincoln assassination authority.[40]

* * * * *

Perhaps it was due to the speed with which Confederate war objectives unraveled in late 1864 and early 1865, but at some point Booth's plans shifted from an abduction to an assassination of the President. Indeed, Booth wrote in his diary, "[F]or six months we had worked to capture. But our cause being almost lost, something decisive and great must be done."[41]

Following the fatal gunshots at Ford's Theater on April 14, 1865, the federal government attempted to prove that Lincoln's assassination had been planned and carried out by the Confederate government and its agents in Canada. During the trial of Booth's conspirators in May 1865, Union prosecutors spent several days putting on testimony from witnesses who said they observed Booth in Canada in October 1864 associating with known Confederate agents.

The prosecutors were unable to prove their allegations that Confederate officials in Canada and Richmond were involved in the assassination, however, in part because of the chaotic state of Confederate records after the war. In addition, some government witnesses were found to have made false statements, which served to taint even some of the government's factually-supported evidence. As a result, many details about the involvement of Confederates in Canada and their links to Booth's activities during this time have faded into the mists of history.[42]

After the collapse of the government's attempt to tie Lincoln's assassination to Confederates in Canada, the public came to accept the conclusion that Lincoln's death was the result of a rash act by a single man—John Wilkes Booth, ignoring much of the activity in Canada that had preceded the assassination. By not focusing on Confederate activity in Canada relating to the assassination, such a view managed to avoid creating discord between the U.S. and Great Britain, serving interests on both sides of the U.S.-Canadian border after the war had concluded.

* * * * *

The visit of John Wilkes Booth was not the only notable event that took place at St. Lawrence Hall in the month of October 1864. The hotel was also the venue for a clandestine meeting between representatives of the Lincoln administration and the Confederate government in Richmond. This was not another attempt at a "peace conference" such as the one that occurred in Niagara Falls in July 1864. The focus of this gathering was on money and trade, both of which were in short supply in the North and South. The purpose of the meeting in Montreal was to work out the details of what would be the largest exchange of Southern cotton for northern goods and dollars ever carried out—worth as much as one billion dollars in 1864 currency.[43]

The discussions at St. Lawrence Hall were an attempt to rectify some of the economic damage the war had inflicted on both sides of the Mason-Dixon line by disrupting the trade in cotton, one of the country's largest exports before the war began. The trade in cotton—principally with textile manufacturers in New England and Britain—provided profits for northern shipping and banking interests. Profits also went to planters in the South, which had no industrial base of its own, thereby helping southerners to purchase food and other supplies. Moreover, the cotton commerce funded much of the federal budget through taxes and helped to maintain the U.S. balance of trade between imports and exports.

The war had ruptured this mutually beneficial economic relationship. The war prevented the South from shipping cotton to foreign manufacturers through northern ports such as New York and Boston and from southern ports closed by the Union Navy's blockade. The halt in trade had the effect of cutting the South off from profits in the textile trade; it also sharply reduced payments to northern manufacturers, shippers and bankers. The scarcity of cotton on the market resulted in skyrocketing cotton prices, which rose by more than 1000 percent by 1864—from ten cents a pound to nearly $1.90 a pound.[44]

The loss of cotton sale payments had different—but equally adverse—consequences in the North and South. In the North, the Lincoln administration needed to buy arms and other supplies to conduct the war. The loss of funds from the cotton trade meant payments would have to be made with gold. By 1864, the U.S. had significantly depleted its gold supply. This had the effect of reducing federal reserves and weakening the value of U.S. currency.

In the South, the loss of trade had a more physical impact: the Confederacy was critically short of food, especially meat. The discussions in Montreal, if they went well, would provide the South with a massive supply of meat and other foodstuffs in return for cotton.

Earlier in the war, Lincoln had gone along with sales of cotton between the North and South, rationalizing that they would help the balance of trade, shore up the federal gold supply and minimize devaluation of the U.S. currency. Expecting these sales to be minimal, he put the Treasury Department in charge of issuing licenses for selling cotton to any citizen claiming loyalty to the Union. In regions of the South occupied by the Union Army, cotton sales often became the chief means by which poor whites and former slaves were able to support their families.[45]

With the huge increases in cotton's sale price, the licenses to sell cotton quickly led to speculation and corruption. Lincoln administration officials made scores of patronage appointments, selecting friends and relatives to be Treasury agents authorized to issue licenses. Many of these agents would go on to engage in illicit profit-making, taking bribes for the sale of licenses.[46]

One of the lead negotiators at the cotton sale conclave in Montreal was Beverley Tucker, a former newspaper editor who supported the Southern cause. Before the war, Tucker had founded and edited *The Washington Sentinel*, a Democratic-leaning newspaper that supported states' rights. When the war started, Tucker left Washington for Richmond where he fought with a local militia to defend the Confederate capital.

Another key negotiator was James Virgul Barnes, a thirty-year-old agent for international merchant banks, including the Brown Brothers New York financial house which had long been involved in the cotton trade. Barnes, born in Canada but raised in the United States, had been on his way to seek a fortune in the California gold fields when political tensions in the 1850s created opportunities for money-making in merchant banking which he decided to pursue.[47]

Also present and representing U.S. interests were three key Treasury agents, Hanson Risley, G.H. Ellery and G.M. Lane. Risley, later revealed to be corrupt, singlehandedly issued special Treasury permits for nearly a million bales of Southern cotton.[48]

In addition to the lead negotiators, the talks in Montreal attracted an assembly of bankers, cotton speculators, shipping magnates, politicians and lobbyists. These included stockbroker and Erie Railroad baron James "Diamond Jim" Fisk, Jay Cooke of Cooke Brothers Bank, William Fargo, founder of Wells Fargo, and financier Jay Gould, according to St. Lawrence Hall's registration records for the later months of 1864. Of this period, one Montreal historian wrote:

> The hard truth is that fabulous fortunes were made during the war. Some of this wealth represented profits from war-time commerce but some of it came from cotton trading and inter-belligerent commerce. The war launched a great many fortunes. It is no accident that many great commercial dynasties of the late nineteenth and early twentieth centuries date back to this period.[49]

In sanctioning the cotton deal, Lincoln took a major political risk. While sales of cotton between the North and South were not a secret, a transaction of this magnitude—in effect "trading with the enemy" for almost a billion dollars—could have crushed Lincoln's re-election chances in November 1864 had it become widely-known among voters in the northern states. There was a reason the negotiations over the sale were held in Montreal.[50]

Along with promoting the economic interests of the northern states and the federal treasury, Lincoln had practical political reasons for allowing the sale to go forward. Massachusetts and New York were critical states for Lincoln and the Republican party in the 1864 election. Owners of New England textile manufacturing plants required cotton to continue their operations and Lincoln could not ignore their interests. New York's thirty-five electoral votes had ensured Lincoln's election in 1860. He could not afford to alienate such powerful New York Republicans as Thurlow Weed, editor of the *Albany Evening Journal*, who effectively controlled the Republican party in New York, or Edwin Morgan, a New York senator and former Governor. Both were involved in trading cotton. Morgan made numerous trips to Montreal during the summer and fall of 1864, registering at St. Lawrence Hall at least a dozen times during this period, according to hotel records.[51]

While there is no question that the trade in cotton benefited certain interests of the North, it also likely had the perverse effect of prolonging the war. The military strategy being pursued by Union military commander Ulysses S. Grant involved smashing Lee's army and cutting supply lines to the Confederacy. Cotton sales between the North and South undermined this effort by providing the South with both money and supplies.[52]

Little information is available to reveal exactly how much of the cotton sale arranged in Montreal was completed. In the later months of 1864, Generals Grant and Sherman made steady gains against Confederate troops near Richmond and in Georgia, putting an end to the war within sight. The price of cotton was dropping, and many parts of the South were enveloped in chaos. Even if the sale were fully executed, it would be too late to save the Confederacy. By the time news of the Montreal negotiations became public in 1865, the war was over, Lincoln was dead and trading with the enemy did not carry the same weight of scandal that it might have in the months leading up to the 1864 election.[53]

CHAPTER 22

The Ill-Fated Voyage
of the CSS *Georgian*

Toronto, Lake Erie, Lake Huron, Washington, D.C.—
November–December 1864

After the failure of the Lake Erie raid on Johnson's Island in September 1864, Jacob Thompson, the lead Confederate commissioner in Canada, decided to try a different approach. He would purchase his own vessel and outfit it with weaponry. According to Thompson's plan, once he had one warship he could use it to capture additional ships, thus acquiring a fleet that could be used to overpower the USS *Michigan* and attack shipping on the Great Lakes and cities along the shore.

Thompson already had in mind the man who would serve as commander of the operation. It would be John Yates Beall, leader of the Johnson's Island raid, who had experience attacking Union commercial vessels on the Chesapeake Bay and could put his experience to use once again on the Great Lakes. Joining Beall would be two former Morgan's raiders sent by Confederate officials in Richmond to assist Thompson: John W. Headley and Robert M. Martin. Although both were still in their twenties, the two had served as officers under Morgan's command and were experienced in conducting raids behind enemy lines. In addition, a young courier who had served with Headley and Martin in Morgan's cavalry, George S. Anderson, signed on to the venture.[1]

Thompson's plan would be for the "Confederate fleet" to conduct raids on Buffalo and other U.S. cities along the Lake Erie shore. These attacks would likely trigger a response from the USS *Michigan*, drawing it away from its position at Johnson's Island. This would create an opening for one or more of the Confederate ships to attack the Union guard force on the island and release the prisoners. The vessels would then turn their firepower on the *Michigan*. Headley, writing in his memoirs, described the plan:

> It was intended that Beall should shell and capture Buffalo, if possible, or make the authorities ransom the city. He would at all events capture several other good steamers at Buffalo and destroy all the others at the wharf. Then our navy would take the towns along the shore to Cleveland, where a few additional Confederates would come aboard at each place to help man the vessels. At the earliest moment, after two or more vessels could be equipped, the fleet

151

would be divided and the one under Beall would make straight along the Canadian shore for the west, destroying every vessel he met. He would reach Toledo as soon as possible unless, by a scouting vessel, which he would send to Sandusky, he found the gunboat *Michigan* had gone east to capture us about Buffalo. In such event he could go direct to Johnson's Island before the garrison could be reinforced and release the Confederate prisoners by attacking with the guns of two vessels. It was understood that every available Confederate soldier in Canada or Kentucky would come to join the crews.[2]

In an example of the inflated Confederate expectations for the success of the operation, Headley estimated that within a week after attacking Buffalo, their Confederate naval force would include at least four warships and number between three to four hundred men.[3]

In late October, Dr. James Bates, acting as a proxy for Thompson, purchased a 130-foot lake steamer named the *Georgian*, paying $16,500 for the vessel with money provided by Thompson. Bates, a former Mississippi riverboat captain who had joined other Confederate expatriates in Toronto, took delivery of the ship on November 1 at Port Colborne, a city on the Canadian side of Lake Erie, about fifteen miles west of Buffalo. It was located at the southern end of the Welland Canal, the shipping passage near Niagara Falls linking Lake Erie with Lake Ontario.[4]

The *Georgian*, constructed in 1864, was propeller-driven and had a shallow draft to carry heavy loads for the lumber trade, which meant it only needed a few feet of water to remain afloat. This feature also meant the *Georgian* could attack other vessels, then run for cover in shallower waters where many similar-sized ships could not follow.[5]

Bates quickly got to work converting the *Georgian* into a ship ready for battle. He arranged to have the hull reinforced and planned to have a ram attached to the bow for use in attacking vessels, including the *Michigan*, on the Great Lakes.

Assisting in the effort to prepare the *Georgian* for battle was Bennet Burley who by this time was working at his cousin's foundry in Guelph, a town in Canada about sixty miles west of Toronto. Burley had already convinced his cousin to shift production at the foundry from farm implements to armaments, including cannon and torpedoes. As the ordnance was produced, it was shipped to various ports on the lakes. The plan was to have the *Georgian* pick up armaments in stages at different ports so as not to arouse suspicion.[6]

Soon after taking possession of the *Georgian*, Bates discovered the propeller was loose and the ship had to make an unscheduled trip to Buffalo for repairs. On November 3, the *Georgian* returned to Port Colborne where it was met by Headley and Martin who expected to rendezvous with Beall and begin the vessel's inaugural voyage as a Confederate warship. Beall, however, was nowhere to be seen. After waiting two days with no sign of Beall, Headley, Martin and Anderson returned to Toronto.[7]

The record is murky regarding exactly where Beall was and what he was doing at this time. It is possible he engaged in scouting missions, checking vulnerabilities of towns along Lake Erie on the American side. A young Confederate named Charles C. Hemming, who had escaped in September from the federal prison at

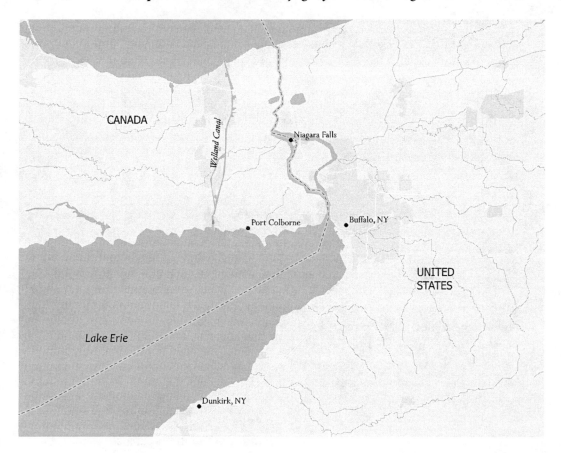

Niagara Falls–Buffalo Area.

Rock Island, Illinois, wrote an unpublished memoir in which he recounted travels with Beall around this time.

After Hemming arrived in Toronto, Jacob Thompson recruited him to conduct reconnaissance regarding federal troop levels in Buffalo, Toledo and Cleveland. Hemming writes of meeting Beall "who was preparing an expedition to raid the lakes by armed steamers…. Beall from the first seemed to take a strong liking to me, and we soon became intimate, and every time he crossed the line, I was with him, and the same blanket covered us both."[8]

Another reason for Beall's absence could have been that he was aware of the extraordinary level of surveillance that Union and Canadian authorities focused on the *Georgian,* almost from the day it passed into Confederate hands.

On November 3, the same day the *Georgian* returned to Port Colborne after its propeller repair, a U.S. consular agent in Toronto sent word to the federal Provost Marshal in Buffalo that he had received information—from four separate sources—that Confederate agents had purchased the *Georgian* for "a cruise of destruction" on the Great Lakes. This information was passed on to the U.S. Vice-Consul General in Montreal who, in turn, notified Secretary of State Seward in Washington.[9]

On Saturday, November 5, the *Georgian* left Port Colborne and headed west across Lake Erie. Its destination was Sarnia, a town in Canada on the St. Clair River where it connects with Lake Huron north of Detroit. At the helm of the ship was its original captain, a man named Milne, who was a known Confederate sympathizer.[10] Bates apparently remained aboard, retaining overall command of the ship. The record is unclear with respect to the makeup of the crew at this point—with neither Beall, Headley, Martin nor Anderson aboard. Bates's decision to retain the *Georgian's* previous captain, however, suggests it is likely he kept the original crew as well, at least to sail to other ports on the lakes where Confederate crew and weapons could be gathered.

Also on November 5, the mayor of Buffalo, William Fargo, telegraphed John C. Carter, Commander of the *Michigan* at Johnson's Island, informing him of the *Georgian's* purchase and departure from Buffalo for what he called "piratical and predatory purposes."[11] Fargo also sent warnings to city officials in other towns along the lake shore, including Erie, Cleveland, Sandusky and Detroit.[12] Fargo received information about the *Georgian* from one of his own spies who worked under the code-name "Fides." Carter, aboard the *Michigan*, forwarded the information to Navy Secretary Gideon Welles who responded, ordering Carter to capture the *Georgian* if he found it "in American waters or on the open lake."[13]

In a curious coincidence, that same month, Fargo was in Montreal and registered as a guest at St. Lawrence Hall while the negotiations over a cotton deal between the North and South were taking place. The reason for Fargo's visit is unclear. The Buffalo mayor could have been in Montreal in his capacity as mayor or, in his role as the head of Wells Fargo bank, Fargo could have somehow been involved in the cotton sale. In any event, during his time in Montreal there is no question that Fargo was rubbing shoulders with Confederate agents and operatives, the very people he took pains to warn against while he was in Buffalo.

If Confederate agents in Canada had any hope of concealing their purchase and outfitting of the *Georgian* with weapons, it was quickly dashed. News of the vessel's transfer into Confederate hands not only reached Union military and cabinet officials but quickly spread among the general public. "A good deal of excitement prevails in Buffalo with reference to the supposed mission of the propeller [boat] *Georgian*," wrote the *Buffalo Commercial Advertiser*. On November 7, the newspaper ran a front-page, thirteen-paragraph story outlining details of the ship's sale, describing the ship's size, tonnage and sailing capabilities, and expressing uncertainty about the ship's true purpose:

> Whether Mr. Bates bought the *Georgian* for the purpose, as is supposed in Buffalo, of converting her into a privateer, to encounter and destroy the *Michigan*, and liberate the rebel prisoners on Johnson's Island—or whether, as he asserted here, he made the purchase for the purpose of using the vessel in the lumber trade—we shall not pretend to decide. A day or two more will no doubt clear up the whole mystery.[14]

Soon after the *Georgian* set sail, communities along the lake quickly took steps to defend against any attack by the Confederate warship. In Buffalo, two tugs armed with cannon began patrolling the harbor and were prepared to fire rockets as a warning to residents if any "suspicious craft" were observed. In Detroit, church bells rang, warning of a potential attack.[15]

Public concern about the *Georgian* was so intense that, after the ship had sailed less than twenty miles from Buffalo on Lake Erie, it was stopped and boarded by the captain and crew of the *Pacific*, a lake steamer. While the legal authority is questionable for one commercial vessel to stop, board and search another, the *Georgian* apparently did not resist. The *Pacific* crew promptly reported their contact with the *Georgian* to Union Army authorities in Cleveland, noting the vessel had "a crew of eight men, six of them drunk." The men aboard the *Georgian* told the *Pacific's* crew that they were going to Sarnia to pick up lumber and deliver it to Chicago where they would load grain for their return trip. "[We] saw nothing to excite suspicion, and let her go," the *Pacific* reported.[16]

After encountering propeller problems for a second time near Port Stanley on the northern shore of Lake Erie, about 130 miles west of Buffalo, the *Georgian* continued slowly cruising west, until it reached Malden (now Amherstburg) on the Detroit River. There, Lieutenant Colonel Bennet H. Hill, the acting assistant provost marshal for the state of Michigan, ordered two tugboats from Detroit to stop and search the *Georgian*. Just two months earlier, after a mysterious visit from an informer, Hill had been instrumental in alerting the Johnson's Island commandant about Beall's planned raid. The search of the *Georgian* again failed to reveal any suspicious cargo and the ship was allowed to proceed to Sarnia, about seventy miles north.[17]

On November 11, the *Georgian* arrived at Sarnia near the southern shore of Lake Huron. It was searched again, this time by Canadian authorities.[18] Canada's leader, Governor General Charles Monck, knew that American officials were beginning to question Canada's neutrality in the wake of Beall's attempted raid on Johnson's Island and the Confederate raid on St. Albans, Vermont. Monck was determined to demonstrate his vigilance against Confederate operations originating in Canada and used the arrival of the *Georgian* in Canadian waters to continue the intense surveillance of the vessel that began in Buffalo.[19]

With the *Georgian* docked at Sarnia, Bates left the ship to travel to Toronto and order a new propeller. It was to be delivered to the *Georgian's* next port of call at Collingwood, a town on Georgian Bay in the eastern part of Lake Huron. Collingwood had a shipyard where repairs could be done.[20]

While the *Georgian* was waiting for repairs, Canadian authorities—with the help of the American consul in Toronto—had tracked down Bennet Burley at the foundry in Guelph. He had been wanted by Union authorities since his capture on the Chesapeake Bay in May 1864 and subsequent escape from Fort Delaware. On November 19, they placed Burley under arrest. He was taken to

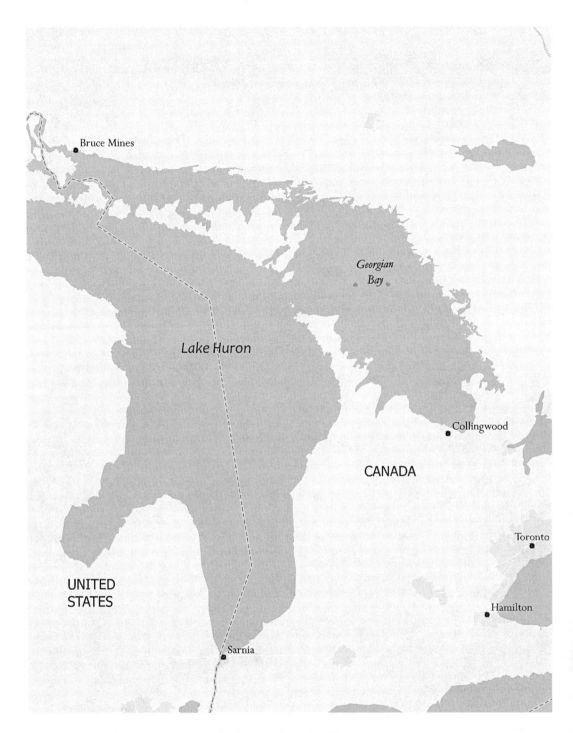

Lake Huron–Georgian Bay Area.

Toronto where proceedings for his extradition to the United States were initiated.[21]

Along with arresting Burley, the Canadian authorities were also able to intercept several shipments from the Guelph foundry intended to be loaded onto the *Georgian*.[22] One shipment, consisting of two barrels and a large box labeled "POTATOES," was found at Lexington, a town in Michigan on the western shore of Lake Huron. Packed inside the barrels and boxes officials found munitions.[23]

A few days after the *Georgian* arrived at Collingwood, Bates took the ship north in Georgian Bay to an area known as Bruce Mines, about 175 miles north of Collingwood. Bates told Canadian customs officials the *Georgian* was involved in the lumber trade and he intended to load timber at ports in Georgian Bay. It was unclear whether the new propeller was ever delivered or installed on the ship.[24]

The *Georgian's* trip north was likely a feint to mislead Canadian officials. Apparently unknown to Bates and the rest of the crew aboard the *Georgian*, the USS *Michigan* had left its position at Johnson's Island and had been shadowing the *Georgian* the entire time it had sailed across the lakes.[25]

On December 6, the new commander of the *Michigan*, Francis Asbury Roe, wrote to Navy Secretary Welles, stating the *Georgian* "has not carried a pound of freight or earned a dollar in legitimate trade since she fell into her present owner's hands."[26] Roe had replaced John Carter as the *Michigan's* commander in mid-November. Carter had been forced into retirement, in part, because of certain actions he took during the attempted raid on Johnson's Island. The day following the raid, Carter had taken the *Michigan* from its anchorage at Johnson's Island to search for the *Philo Parsons* on Lake Erie, sailing as far north as Detroit. Navy Secretary Welles considered Carter's actions to have violated his instruction to Carter to remain with the *Michigan* at Johnson's Island until reinforcements arrived.[27]

In his report to Welles, Roe summarized his view that the *Georgian* was unlikely to pose a threat to other vessels or cities on the lakes, writing, "The derangement of her propeller, the watch kept over her, and the notoriety she has along the Canada and American shores have frustrated all her intentions."[28]

As winter arrived in the upper Great Lakes, ice was forming, and navigation was becoming increasingly difficult. The *Georgian* would likely be forced to remain at Collingwood until the spring. "The advanced state of the season renders it almost certain that no attempt will be made by her this winter," Roe noted.[29]

By the time Roe sent his report to Welles, Jacob Thompson had already concluded that his planned mission for the *Georgian* had failed. In a December 3 message to Judah Benjamin, the Confederacy's Secretary of State, Thompson complained about the pervasive spying conducted on Confederate operations in Canada. "The bane and curse of carrying out anything in this country is the surveillance under which we act. Detectives, or those ready to give information, stand at every street corner. Two or three cannot interchange ideas without a reporter," Thompson wrote.[30]

The following spring, on April 7, 1865, Canadian customs officials seized the *Georgian*. The ship was eventually turned over to the U.S. government. It was later sold and would continue to sail on the Great Lakes as a private vessel for more than twenty years.[31]

* * * * *

In Washington, on Tuesday, November 8, it was raining. As darkness fell, Lincoln walked from the White House to the telegraph office in the War Department building next door where he would monitor election returns with his aide John Hay and others. Despite threats and rumors of disruption and violence, the election of 1864 had gone smoothly in a nation at war and cleaved between states in the north and west and the eleven states in the Confederacy, which did not participate.

By midnight, it appeared as if Lincoln had won all of New England, Wisconsin, and Maryland. Strong Republican majorities were also being counted in Ohio, Indiana, Michigan—states where Copperhead and anti-war sentiment had been particularly strong. A little while later, news came from Chicago that Lincoln held a 20,000-vote margin statewide, meaning he would likely carry Illinois, another state with significant Copperhead support. New York was still a question mark, with George McClellan, the Democratic presidential nominee, winning every city but Rochester. An aide entered, carrying a tray of fried oysters and Lincoln began serving out the late-night meal.[32]

A little after 2 a.m., a messenger told Lincoln and the others gathered around him that a crowd had formed in front of the White House to congratulate him. Lincoln returned to the Executive Mansion and, standing on the front steps still wet with rain, told those assembled:

> I am thankful to God for this approval of the people…. But while deeply grateful for this mark of their confidence in me, if I know my heart, my gratitude is free from any taint of personal triumph. I do not impugn the motives of any one opposed to me. It is no pleasure to me to triumph over any one; but I give thanks to the Almighty for this evidence of the people's resolution to stand by free government and the rights of humanity.[33]

When all the votes were counted, Lincoln won 55 percent of the popular vote. In the electoral college, Lincoln prevailed over McClellan by an overwhelming majority, 212 to 21. McClellan won just three states: Kentucky, Delaware, and his home state of New Jersey. In a surprise for the former Union Army General, McClellan lost the support of Union solders by a substantial margin, winning only 30 percent of their votes.[34]

The South's hopes for victory had been diminishing for months. By late summer, Union Army victories under General Sherman in Georgia and General Sheridan in the Shenandoah Valley caused anti-war and pro–Copperhead sentiment in the Northwestern states to plummet. Lincoln's victory at the ballot box now showed unmistakably that the long-held plans of Confederate leaders in Richmond and Montreal—to inflame Copperhead anti-war sentiment and defeat Lincoln—had failed. Yet, despite the almost impossible odds they now faced, Confederate Commissioner Jacob Thompson and John Yates Beall were preparing to launch one more raid in the North. This time it would be on land.

CHAPTER 23

A Train from Sandusky

Toronto, Buffalo, Niagara Falls—December 13–16, 1864

In the 1860s, what became known as the Lake Shore Railway was one of the most profitable rail lines in the United States. Stretching 536 miles from Chicago to Buffalo, its route ran along the Michigan-Indiana border into Ohio where it traced the Lake Erie shoreline. Trains made stops at South Bend, Toledo, Sandusky, Cleveland, and Erie before reaching Buffalo. The railway began in the 1830s with shorter rail segments in Illinois, Indiana, Ohio, Michigan, and Pennsylvania. The lines were eventually merged and connected with rail lines in New York. The railway's construction and consolidation had been heavily promoted by business and civic leaders in Chicago and Cleveland because, among other things, the railway gave factories and farmers in the Midwest quick and easy access to east coast cities and ports.[1]

The railroad also served as a passenger line. In early December 1864, Confederate Commissioner Jacob Thompson received news about a group of passengers scheduled to travel on the Lake Shore Railway, departing Sandusky around December 15, headed for Buffalo and, from there, on to New York City and Boston. The passengers were seven Confederate generals imprisoned at Johnson's Island who were to be transferred east to Fort Lafayette, a prison for Confederates in New York City, and Fort Warren, a military prison in Boston.[2] Rebel prisoners were often shuttled between locations depending on space and overcrowding considerations. The train carrying the generals might be vulnerable to attack and Thompson knew that if an attack on the train was successful in freeing the generals, they could rejoin the Confederate army in the South and fortify a rapidly deteriorating fighting force.

Among the generals to be transferred was Major General Isaac Trimble, one of the highest-ranking Confederate officers at Johnson's Island. He had been captured at the battle of Gettysburg in July 1863 and lost a leg during Pickett's charge, the unsuccessful rebel attack on the last day of the battle.

Within a short time of his arrival at Johnson's Island, Trimble—an imposing West Point graduate who now used a crutch—became the leader of the secret group of prisoner-conspirators at Johnson's Island known as the Order of the Brotherhood of the Southern Cross. Trimble and other members of the group had been instrumental in planning the aborted escape attempt from the island prison in the fall of 1863. They had also worked with Charles Cole, the Sandusky-based conspirator, as he helped plan the Lake Erie attack launched by John Yates Beall in September 1864.[3]

In Toronto, Thompson began assembling a team to conduct the raid on the Lake Shore Railway. To lead the group, Thompson chose John Yates Beall, Robert Martin and John W. Headley. Martin and Headley, former Confederate officers in their early twenties, had served as scouts with the notorious rebel cavalry officer John Hunt Morgan. Known as Morgan's raiders, the cavalry had conducted daring raids into Indiana and Ohio during the summer of 1863. Both Martin and Headley seemed to thrive on risky, high-adrenaline adventures and were attracted to the bold plots planned by Thompson. Earlier in 1864, both men had left Morgan's command and joined the Confederate Secret Service in Canada. Beall apparently was not in Toronto at the time but would meet up with the group enroute to the attack site, which would be in New York.[4]

In just the past few weeks, Martin and Headley had participated in two of Thompson's more audacious schemes. In early November, the two had traveled to Port Colborne on the Canadian side of Lake Erie. They had expected to join John Yates Beall on the Confederate warship, the *Georgian,* and conduct raids on shipping and ports on the Great Lakes. Beall's failure to make the rendezvous, combined with the unrelenting surveillance of the *Georgian*'s cruise by Union and Canadian authorities, had caused the plot to founder before it ever really began.

And only three weeks earlier, on the evening of November 25, Martin and Headley had led another group of Confederate raiders in New York City where they attempted to set fire to several of the city's major hotels. The attack, conducted in retaliation for the devastation in the South wreaked by Union Generals William T. Sherman in Georgia and Phillip Sheridan in the Shenandoah Valley, also failed. Greek Fire, a bottled incendiary concoction the rebels tossed into hotel rooms, failed to ignite or cause any significant damage.

The group that would launch the attack on the Lake Shore Railway included seven other men, three of whom had also taken part in the New York firebombing plot. One was Robert Cobb Kennedy, a thirty-year-old West Point dropout who had fought with the Confederate Army in Tennessee. After being captured in October 1863, Kennedy was sent to Johnson's Island. A year later, he escaped from the prison, one of only twelve prisoners to do so during the entire war. He traveled to Toronto where he joined Thompson's group of Confederate raiders and became involved in the New York City attack. It was the first operation that Kennedy took part in following his escape. Several months later, he would be the only person captured, tried and executed for the attack.[5]

Two other rebel agents, James T. Harrington and John T. Ashbrook, had also participated in the New York City attack before they joined the train plot. Also in the group of ten were Charles C. Hemming, who had written of scouting trips with Beall along the Great Lakes before the *Georgian* episode; George S. Anderson, who had been involved with the *Georgian* the previous month; and two others, W.P. Rutland and Forney Holt.[6]

The men left Toronto in pairs, traveling by train to Buffalo on the night of December 13 and the following day, December 14. Martin and Headley were among the first to depart on December 13 and left the train late in the evening at Hamilton, a small town on the western edge of Lake Ontario about halfway between Toronto and Buffalo. When they arrived at their hotel, they were told Beall was staying there but had already retired for the night.[7]

The next morning, Headley and Martin greeted Beall, whom they had heard much about but had never met. Headley, in a memoir, recollected his first impression of Beall:

> We had never met Beall before, but fell in love with him at once. He was a modest, unassuming gentleman. I soon observed that he did not talk to entertain but was a thinking man and was resourceful and self-possessed. He did not get excited in relating an exciting episode and only smiled at amusing stories when others laughed aloud. And yet he was an interesting companion.[8]

The three men spent the morning in Beall's room going over their final plans. They would capture the train outside Buffalo, disarm the guards and detach all but one of the passenger cars from rest of the train, leaving the engine and a passenger car for the raiding party and the generals. Because there was also a chance that the train would be transporting a safe for the American Express Company, founded in Buffalo, they would bring tools to crack open the safe.[9] After taking civilian clothing from some of the passengers for use by the generals (and reimbursing the passengers), they would cut the telegraph wires that ran parallel to the tracks and force the train crew to take the engine and express car closer to Buffalo. From there, the ten raiders and seven generals would leave the train and walk to the Buffalo train depot where—posing as regular passengers—they would board trains to Canada, arriving eventually in Toronto.[10]

Passengers on the train were not to be robbed or otherwise molested unless they resisted or interfered, according to the plan. In that case, "We would shoot them the same as we would shoot the federal guards of the prisoners," Headley wrote in his memoir.[11]

On the afternoon of December 14, Martin, Headley and Beall traveled from Hamilton to Buffalo where they checked into the Genesee House for the night. The hotel, built in 1842 and located on Genesee Square in the center of town, was one of the premier hotels in Buffalo, with five stories and shops on the street level. At the hotel, Martin, Headley and Beall met up with the seven other members of the raiding party. Headley noted that he and the other men took care not to speak with each other in public or otherwise indicate that they knew each other. "I saw George Anderson in the office and gave him a sign to follow me outside, which he did, and then upstairs to our room where Colonel Martin posted him on plans for capturing the train," Headley wrote.[12]

The next morning, December 15, as the members of the raiding party left their rooms and came down to the hotel lobby, they were greeted by ominous news in the Buffalo newspaper. The day before, Major General John Dix, commander of the Union Army's Department of the East, had issued an order in response to the October raid in St. Albans, Vermont, and other cross-border "acts of depredation," as the order put it, instigated by Jacob Thompson and members of the Confederate Secret Service in Canada.[13]

Dix's General Order No. 97 stated that Union military commanders on the northern frontier would shoot on sight any "perpetrators" from Canada conducting attacks across the border. Moreover, the commanders were authorized to cross into Canada in pursuit of attackers and, if the attackers were apprehended, under no circumstances were they to be released.[14]

The raiding party quickly realized the new order put them in greater peril. Nonetheless, Martin, Beall and Headley decided to go ahead with their plan. From the Buffalo depot, the ten men boarded a westbound train—again in pairs—and all but Martin disembarked at Dunkirk, New York, a small town on the Lake Shore line about forty miles southwest of Buffalo.

Martin remained on the train because a glaring hole had emerged in the plan for the train attack—one that revealed either the inadequacies in communications of the day or negligence by those planning the raid. Perhaps both. With more than one eastbound train traveling on the Lakeshore line each day, the raiding team did not know which eastbound train from Sandusky the generals would be traveling on. As a result, Martin decided to remain aboard the westbound train from Buffalo and disembark at Erie. There he would attempt to find out more about the generals' scheduled arrival from Sandusky the next day. Beall and Headley would make similar inquiries at Dunkirk.[15]

Later in the day, Martin returned to Dunkirk from Erie and, after exiting the train, reported he had learned the generals had not yet departed from Sandusky. Snow blanketed the ground and the raiding party had been out in the cold for hours. At that point, Martin, Beall and Headley decided that the members of raiding party would return to the Buffalo depot where they would await the arrival of the trains from points west, including Sandusky. When a train did arrive with the generals on board, the rebel raiders would board it and execute their plan.[16]

The generals were not aboard the first eastbound Lake Shore train that arrived in Buffalo the next morning, December 16. The raiding team knew that, with the Dix order in effect, they were at risk if they remained too long in any one place. They decided that when darkness fell at around 5 p.m., the group would leave town again and travel, in horse-drawn sleighs, to an uninhabited area in a forest a few miles west of Buffalo where a country road crossed the Lake Shore tracks. There they would attempt to derail the last train heading for Buffalo that day from the west, betting that the generals would be onboard.[17]

They arrived at the spot in darkness and hid the sleighs and horses in the nearby

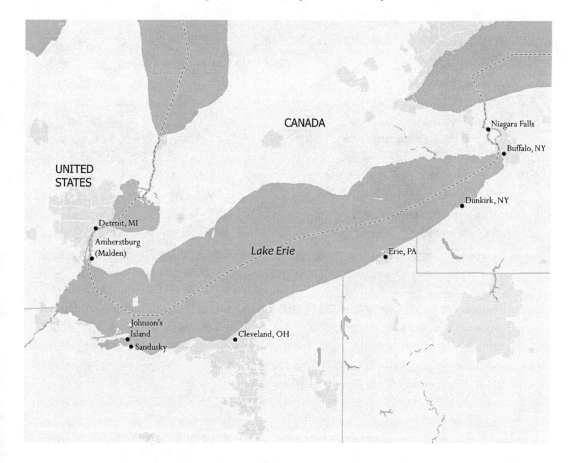

Towns Along Lake Erie Shoreline.

woods. Martin and other members of the team walked to the tracks, used a sledge-hammer and chisel to dislodge an iron rail, and placed it across the tracks. Martin planned to use a lantern to signal the train to stop before it reached the rail. If that failed, the rail would either derail the train or otherwise force it to stop. At least that was the plan.[18]

However, before they had positioned the rail in the exact spot where they wanted it, a fast-moving eastbound train came upon them, apparently ahead of schedule. The train hit the rail hard, knocking it into the air. The train remained on the tracks but stopped about fifty yards from the point of impact. The raiding team could see men with lanterns jump down from the train and start to walk toward them. Although it was dark, the men from the train appeared to be soldiers, surprising the rebel raiders. Fearing that the train might hold a significant Union military force, the rebels abandoned their plan. They scattered into the woods, retrieved the horses and sleighs and returned to the Buffalo depot as quickly as they could. The members of the raiding party apparently were never able to determine whether the generals were passengers on any of the eastbound trains that passed by them.[19]

Realizing their action in stopping the train would likely trigger a major law enforcement response throughout the area, the group decided to flee to Canada in separate groups. After arriving at the Buffalo depot, Martin and Headley waited an hour for a Central Railroad train from New York City that would take them about twenty-three miles north to the Niagara depot where they could leave the train and walk across the Suspension Bridge over the Niagara River into Canada. The elevated bridge—828 feet long—had been designed and constructed in 1855 by John Roebling, who would later gain fame for building the Brooklyn Bridge in New York City.[20]

In all, six members of the raiding team would manage to reach Canada the night of December 16. Headley and Martin, who walked across the Suspension Bridge, were followed by Ashbrook, Kennedy, Holt and Rutland. The six arrived in Toronto the following day, December 17, and were joined a while later by Hemming and Harrington. Reunited, the team then discovered that two of their members were missing—Anderson and Beall.[21]

* * * * *

On the night of December 16, Beall and Anderson had arrived at the Niagara depot on the same Central Railroad train from Buffalo with Martin and Headley. Martin and Headley decided to go on foot across the Suspension Bridge. Once in Canada, they could walk the two miles to Clifton, the first station stop for the Great Western train leaving from Niagara Falls and heading west.[22]

Beall had been assigned to accompany Anderson, the young courier, who was exhausted after the events of the day and apparently was unwilling to walk with the others across the Suspension Bridge. As a result, Beall and Anderson remained in the station to wait for the train into Canada expected later that evening.[23]

Sometime between 9 p.m. and 10 p.m., when the train into Canada arrived, Beall quickly exited the station and took a seat in one of the train cars. He looked around and discovered that Anderson was nowhere to be seen. Beall left the train and re-entered the station where he saw Anderson asleep on a bench in the eating area where they had been sitting.[24]

At that moment, two Niagara city policemen entered the room, spotted Beall and Anderson, and approached the bench where Anderson lay. The officers asked Beall and Anderson for their names. Beall first murmured "Beall" but when one of the policemen, David H. Thomas, asked for his full name, Beall said "W.W. Baker," giving the name of one of his compatriots on the Chesapeake Bay during the summer of 1863.[25]

Thomas told Beall he was under arrest. When Beall asked what he was being arrested for, the officer said he was "an escaped rebel prisoner." Beall asked where he had escaped from. Thomas said it did not matter so long as Beall was an escaped rebel prisoner. Since Beall's raid on Lake Erie in September, law enforcement authorities in cities along the Great Lakes had been on the lookout for members of the raiding party.[26]

In fact, following the firebombing of New York City hotels on November 25, efforts to apprehend renegade Confederates had intensified. John A. Dix, the Union

Commander of the Department of the East, enlisted the aid of local police departments to monitor several key border crossings, including the Niagara Falls Suspension Bridge, with the aim of arresting Confederate raiders attempting to escape into Canada. While the identities of the rebels responsible for the New York firebombing were still being sought, local police had been given descriptions of other rebel raiders already known to U.S. authorities, including Beall.[27]

The police officers took Beall and Anderson into the depot's telegraph room and searched them and a carpet bag they had with them. In the bag they found a dirty shirt and pair of socks, five or six tallow-candles, some matches and a box of paper collars—a cheap, disposable alternative to freshly-laundered shirts commonly used during the nineteenth century.[28]

On Beall, they found a fully-loaded Colt pistol in a sheath attached to his belt, a two-ounce vial of the pain-killer laudanum—which Beall said he used for a toothache—two ten-dollar American gold pieces, a Canadian two-dollar note and six dollars in American bills. Beall told Thomas that had he not acted so quickly in making the arrests, Beall would have shot him, adding, he "had fully resolved never to be taken alive."[29]

Under guard, Beall and Anderson were put on a train heading south. They soon arrived at police headquarters on Mulberry Street in New York City and were placed in separate jail cells. It was Beall's second arrest in a little over a year. It would also be his last.

CHAPTER 24

Behind Bars on Mulberry Street

New York City—December 18, 1864–January 5, 1865

John Yates Beall's jail cell at the central police station in New York City measured about eight-feet by five-feet. Located on the ground floor of the station at 300 Mulberry Street, the cell had a mattress and blanket, along with water and a sink. Through an open grate on the upper half of his cell door, made of solid iron, Beall could see three other cells and a passageway illuminated by two large windows and a gas lantern at night. Meals came three times a day, at 9 a.m., 3 p.m. and 9 p.m. He had a copy of the New Testament and was making attempts to obtain a Book of Common Prayer.[1]

New York City's police headquarters had moved to its Mulberry Street location just two years earlier, in 1862. The four-story building, which occupied most of the block, was later called simply "The Block" and would become notorious as the place of incarceration for many of the city's most hardened criminals. In late 1864, as Beall remained incarcerated, a twenty-two-year-old police officer named Thomas F. Byrnes was just starting his law enforcement career at the station on Mulberry Street. Byrnes would remain with the force and rise steadily in its ranks until, in 1880, he would be appointed Chief of the Detective Bureau. In the years that followed, Byrnes would put in place crime-fighting measures that acquired their own notoriety, giving rise to slang terms that are commonly used to this day. Byrnes established an extensive photographic file of criminal suspects that became known as the "rogues gallery" and used intensive interrogation techniques—which critics said bordered on torture—that came to be called the "third degree."[2]

In his cell, Beall began writing in a small diary, about the size of a modern-day passport, with lined pages and a hard-paper cover. In neat handwriting, using a pencil, Beall wrote descriptions of his surroundings, and professed his loyalty to Virginia and the Confederacy. He also expressed his views about other prisoners and their lack of remorse for their crimes: "At first, I took an interest in their cases, but now I do not; they all have been guilty, I believe.... Nearly every one I have met with seems to regard society as his enemy and a just prey. They look on an offence [as] simply a skirmish. Profane, lying and thieving, what a people!"[3]

Beall wrote about how he had been taken by the police "some half dozen times" to appear in lineups where victims would attempt to identify their offenders. "The modus operandi is this: The prisoner, unkempt, roughly clad, dirty, and bearing marks of confinement, is placed among well-dressed detectives, and the recognizer is shown in. As a matter of course he can tell who is the stranger."[4]

On New Year's Eve, as a cold rain fell, the words Beall wrote in his diary revealed a growing awareness of the life and death stakes that faced him as he remained behind bars.

"Today I complete my twenty-ninth year. What have I done to make this world any wiser or better? May God bless me in the future; be it in time or eternity…. Will I see the year 1865 go out? Or will I pass away from this world of sin, shame, and suffering?"[5]

On January 1, his thirtieth birthday, Beall was even more contemplative:

Today I enter my thirtieth year of pilgrimage…. Has my life been so crowded with pleasure or good deeds that I need desire to prolong it? Alas no! Though well reared, and surrounded with very many advantages, I have not done anything to give me particular pleasure; nor, on the other hand, have I been remarkable for the opposite…. This far on life's way I have lived an honest life, defrauding no man. Those blows that I have struck have been against the society of a hostile nation; not against the society of which I am a member by right or vs. mankind generally.[6]

On January 2, prison authorities conducted a thorough search of Beall's cell as well as the clothing he wore. It appears that either at the time of the search or shortly thereafter, the authorities confiscated Beall's diary.[7]

Around this time, Beall had an encounter with one of the prison guards, Edward Hays. When Hays came to his cell, Beall asked for some paper so he could write a letter to Confederate officials in Canada who "might do some good for him to get him out." Hays told Beall that there were too many detectives in the office at the time and suggested waiting until the office cleared. At that point in the conversation, Beall made a more direct appeal: "Hays, I tell you what you can do for me," he said. "You can let me go."[8]

When Hays declined the offer, Beall went a step further, saying, "If you do, I will give you $1,000 in gold" (about $19,00 in present day value). Hays asked Beall if he had that amount of money. Beall said he did not while in jail but that he could get it in Canada. Beall told Hays about the letter he had written to Confederate officials while he was imprisoned at Fort McHenry a year earlier. In that letter, Beall described his imprisonment and told about being chained. The letter had resulted in quick retaliation by the Confederates, who promptly placed several Union Army prisoners of war in chains. News of the retaliatory action resulted in federal troops quickly removing the chains on Beall and his team at Fort McHenry.[9]

With Beall seemingly at ease conversing with Hays, the prison guard decided to ask Beall whether he had been involved in the firebombing of New York City hotels a few weeks earlier. Beall denied having any involvement but acknowledged that he knew the men responsible, adding that they had escaped into Canada.[10]

Hays said, "I suppose if your government found out that you were in prison here now that they would try to get you out in some way."[11]

Beall said he doubted that would happen because he was now charged with different crimes than when he was held at Fort McHenry. He also noted the Confederacy was not as strong as it had been a year earlier.[12]

Later in the conversation, Hays brought up Beall's idea of writing a letter but Beall apparently had lost interest in the possibility at that point, saying it would take too long to result in any action.[13]

Beall again encouraged Hays to release him. "You know you can," Beall said. Hays asked him what time in the night he would like to be released. Beall said he would prefer the early hours of the night. He had friends living on Thirtieth Street in the city who could supply him with weapons and funds to pay Hays, "probably half of it in greenbacks, if not in gold," Beall said.[14]

Hays asked Beall how he would plan to flee from New York if he was released. Beall replied that he would start by going to his friends' house on Thirtieth Street and, from there, go to New Jersey where another friend lived. Hays asked Beall for the names of his friends and their addresses. "I think you are a very smart man, and you must have done a good deal of harm to our Government since this commenced," Hays told Beall, seeming to try to play to his ego.[15]

"Yes, I have taken hundreds and hundreds of prisoners," Beall responded falsely. "I have done Lincoln's Government a good deal of harm and they know it."[16]

Beall rebuffed Hays' request for information about his friends but told him he knew something "that would be worth $30,000 to any one in the detective's office" and "things that would be worth millions of dollars to the Government." But he said he "would die first," before providing such information.[17]

Returning once again to Hays helping him escape, Beall told the prison guard, "You can rest assured that you can get the $1,000 and get it in gold, as I own more than that myself."[18]

Hays told him he "would see what he could do" but made no commitment.[19]

The next time Hays went to Beall's jail cell, Beall was gone. He had not escaped. Instead, at the request of Union Army officials, on January 5, 1865, city police authorities had transferred Beall to Fort Lafayette, a Union Army fort in New York harbor which now housed military prisoners, where he would stand for trial.

CHAPTER 25

The Trial

Fort Lafayette, New York Harbor—
January 5–February 8, 1865

Fort Lafayette, known at the time as the "American Bastille," would serve as the location for Beall's trial by a military commission which would deliberate the charges brought against him by the Union Army.[1] During the Civil War, the fort held both Confederate prisoners and civilians considered disloyal to the Union. Completed in 1822, the fort was named in honor of the Marquis de Lafayette, a Frenchman who aided the American revolution and was touring the country that year. The fort was built on Hendrick's Reef, a two-acre site in the narrows of New York Harbor where the modern-day Verrazano Narrows Bridge now stands. At the time of Beall's arrival, the fort held about sixty prisoners.[2]

On January 17, 1865, Major General John A. Dix, commander of the Union Army's Department of the East, issued an order listing the charges against Beall. There were two charges: violation of the laws of war and acting as a spy and guerrilla. Each of the charges included specific factual allegations against Beall stemming from his actions in Ohio and New York. These included the seizure of the *Philo Parsons* and the seizure and sinking of the *Island Queen* during his September 1864 raid on Lake Erie, as well as his attempt to derail the train near Buffalo in December 1864.[3]

Dix's order also set Beall's trial date as January 20 and named the members of the military tribunal that would hear the charges. The six-man commission was to be headed by Brigadier General Fitz-Henry Warren. A former journalist and politician originally from Massachusetts, Warren had run unsuccessfully for governor of Iowa in 1863.[4] The other members of the commission were Brigadier General William Hopkins Morris, a West Point graduate and former editor at the New York *Home Journal*; Colonel M.S. Howe, of the 3rd U.S. Cavalry; Colonel H. Day, U.S. Army; Brevet Lieutenant R.F. O'Bierne of the 14th U.S. Infantry; and Major George W. Wallace, of the 6th U.S. Infantry.[5]

Two months later, in March, this same commission would also hear the case of Confederate prisoner Robert Cobb Kennedy, who had escaped from Johnson's Island, linked up with other Confederates in Canada and was to be the only rebel conspirator arrested, tried and convicted for the fire bombings of hotels in New York City in November 1864.[6]

* * * * *

Until the Civil War, military commissions—also known as war courts, or military courts—had been used only sporadically by the American military to prosecute crimes committed during war by enemy combatants—either uniformed or non-uniformed. This changed during the Civil War when more than 2,000 trials by military commissions took place, including the trial of the conspirators charged in the assassination of Lincoln.[7]

The use of military commission trials expanded during the Civil War, in part, because of the unique conditions existing in the country during the conflict. Union troops occupied vast areas of territory in the South and West where the local population was unfriendly, if not rebellious. Actions against Union troops and property also took place even in northern states such as Illinois, Iowa, Ohio, and Indiana which were populated by large numbers of war opponents and anti–Union citizens, or Copperheads. The laws of war were simply inadequate to address transgressions and crimes directed at Union troops and property.[8]

The focus of the military commission trials were actions considered to be outside the scope of normal war conduct, actions which would later come to be known as "war crimes." While difficult to define, actions constituting war crimes included such conduct as rape, pillaging, intentionally killing civilians, torture, hostage-taking, theft and the destruction of civilian property.

Prosecutions of individuals, including Beall, during the Civil War helped develop and define the concept of war crimes that would later be embodied in such international protocols as the Geneva Conventions. One legal commentary called the criminal liability standards established in Beall's trial "one of the American Civil War's most significant contributions to the history of international law."[9]

During the Civil War, the laws of war in the U.S. were governed by what was known as the "Lieber Code," a set of legal principles written by Francis Lieber, a German émigré who arrived in the United States in the 1820s after fighting as a recruit in the Prussian Army during the Napoleonic wars. Lieber taught history and political science in South Carolina and, later, at Columbia University for more than twenty years. During this time, he gained recognition as a leading thinker about issues such as the rights of soldiers taken as prisoners of war and what acts by soldiers were punishable as war crimes. In December 1862, War Secretary Stanton summoned Lieber to Washington and requested that he draft a code of regulations for the Army, in effect a "plain English" document that could guide the actions of military officers engaged in active operations.[10]

Lieber submitted his draft code in February 1863 and Lincoln adopted the regulations, formally issuing them in April in the form of General Orders No. 100, Instructions for the Government of Armies of the United States in the Field. The

War Department printed copies in small pamphlets and distributed them to officers in the field.[11]

Lieber's concepts would be used and further developed in later prosecutions that took place at such tribunals as the Nuremberg trials after World War II, the International Criminal Court at The Hague after the Yugoslavia breakup in the 1990s and, in the present day, in prosecutions of Al Quaeda enemy combatants at the U.S. Guantanamo Naval Base in Cuba.

* * * * *

At 11 a.m. on January 20, 1865, the military commission hearing Beall's case officially convened. Major John Bolles, with the title of Judge Advocate, would manage the prosecution of Beall on behalf of the military. An accomplished legal scholar, Bolles was in his mid-fifties, with a thatch of straight brown hair and a neatly-trimmed mustache. He was the son of an abolitionist preacher and had served a term as Secretary of State for Massachusetts in the 1840s. Bolles had offered his services to the Union Army when the war began and was commissioned as a Major, Judge Advocate and Aide-de-Camp of Volunteers. He served on the staff of Major General John A. Dix, commander of the Union Army's Department of the East, who also happened to be his brother-in-law.

As the hearing got underway, Bolles stood between the six commission members and Beall, who sat alone before the panel. Bolles began by asking Beall two questions: whether he objected to any members on the commission and whether he was ready to proceed. In responding, Beall rose to his feet and told Bolles and the commission he had no objection to any specific member of the commission but objected to being tried by a military commission generally. As to whether he was ready for trial, Beall said:

> I am a stranger in a strange land; alone and among my enemies; no counsel has been assigned me, nor has any opportunity been allowed me either to obtain counsel or procure evidence necessary for my defence. I would request that such counsel as I may select in the South be assigned me, and that permission be granted him to appear, and bring forward the documentary evidence necessary for my defence. If this can not be granted, I ask further time for preparation.[12]

The commission agreed to postpone the trial, giving Beall four days, until January 25, to obtain counsel and prepare his defense. As it happened, Beall had already made known his desire to be represented by Roger A. Pryor, one of his cellmates at Fort Lafayette. A lawyer and former newspaper editor who had also served as a member of Congress from Virginia, Pryor was a rabid secessionist and had joined the Confederate military when the war began. He was captured in November 1864 and taken to Fort Lafayette where he was confined as a suspected spy.[13]

After learning of Beall's interest in retaining Pryor as his lawyer, on January 17 Dix sent Beall's request on to Secretary of War Stanton and recommended that it be granted.[14] Two days later, the assistant secretary of war, Charles A. Dana, responded on behalf of Stanton, writing "Under no circumstances" could prisoners of war be allowed to act as counsel.[15]

With his request to be represented by a lawyer from "the South" having been denied, Beall next wrote to an eminent lawyer from the North, James T. Brady, asking that he agree to defend him in the trial.

Brady, a well-known criminal defense lawyer in New York City, had been practicing law for nearly thirty years. "Hardly a criminal case of any note has been tried in the city during the past quarter of a century in which he did not figure either as the leading or the associate counsel for the defense," *The New York Times* would write in Brady's obituary in 1869.[16]

Brady, fifty years old, had a piercing gaze and booming voice that filled the courtroom. He was a former Democrat who had switched parties when the war began and became a firm supporter of Lincoln and the Republicans. Even so, Brady agreed to represent Beall without compensation, believing every defendant deserved the best legal representation available. He would do the same for Jefferson Davis after the war.

While he waited to hear from Brady, Beall took steps to gather evidence for his defense. To refute the charges of being a spy guilty of war crimes, Beall sought to obtain proof that he carried out his actions in Ohio and New York as an officer of the Confederate Navy, pursuant to official orders from Richmond.

On January 22, Beall sent letters to Daniel B. Lucas, his boyhood friend who practiced law in Richmond; Alexander R. Boteler, also a friend and a congressman from Virginia serving in the Confederate legislature; and Jacob Thompson, the Confederate commissioner in Toronto. Beall requested that they send "certificates or other evidence" showing that he was acting under authority of the Confederate government. In his letter to Thompson, Beall conveyed unusual optimism, writing: "The commission so far have [sic] evidenced a disposition to treat me fairly and equitably. With the evidence you can send, together with that I have a right to expect from Richd [sic] and elsewhere, I am confident of an acquittal."[17]

When the military commission reconvened on January 25, Judge Advocate Bolles again asked Beall whether he was ready to proceed to trial. Beall responded that he had sent a letter to Brady requesting that he represent him but had not received a reply.

At this point, Bolles announced that a letter from Brady had arrived at Fort Lafayette that morning. In his written reply, Brady noted that he was currently involved in another trial, that he had attempted unsuccessfully to obtain other representation for Beall and asked the commission whether Beall's trial could be postponed for a week at which time he would be available to assist Beall with his defense. The commission agreed to postpone the trial for a week, until February 1.[18]

Bolles brought out the three letters Beall had written to Lucas, Boteler and Thompson. The letters were never mailed, Bolles revealed. Instead, Bolles offered Beall what amounted to an evidentiary short-cut: the prosecution would not object if

Beall simply wrote out an affidavit stating the facts he wanted to prove with the "certificates or other evidence" he had requested in the letters. Because it was likely the witnesses and documents Beall sought in the letters would support Beall's defense, Bolles said, an affidavit from Beall would suffice. Beall agreed to Bolles' proposal. What Beall did not appreciate at the time was that Bolles' offer contained a chilling implication: Whatever factual evidence Beall might be able to produce in his defense would be of little concern to the prosecution or the commission.[19]

One week later, on February 1, 1865, the trial began. In the courtroom were the six commission members, Bolles, and Beall, accompanied by his recently-retained lawyer, Brady. The hearing was closed to the public. Warren, the commission president, read the formal charges. Beall pleaded not guilty. Warren then turned the proceedings over to Bolles for the prosecution.

The prosecution's case would be based on the testimony of five witnesses who would appear at the trial: Walter Ashley, the *Philo Parsons* clerk and part-owner; William Weston, a fireman on the *Philo Parsons*; David H. Thomas, the Niagara Falls detective who arrested Beall; Edward Hays, the guard at the Mulberry Street police station in New York; and George S. Anderson, the young Confederate courier arrested with Beall at the Niagara Falls train station. Anderson had arranged a plea deal with the prosecution to testify in exchange for having the charges against him dropped.

While no mention of it was made during the trial, the entire proceeding was being conducted under what was essentially a news "black-out," with no press in attendance or, apparently, even aware that the trial was taking place. By keeping the public and Confederate authorities in Richmond in ignorance of the trial, Union officials were able to prevent any attempts by the Confederacy to retaliate or take other action, at least while the trial was being conducted. As it turned out, the first newspaper account about the trial would not appear until February 15, a week after it ended.[20]

Under questioning by Bolles, Ashley, the first witness to testify, recounted the events leading up to and including the capture of the *Philo Parsons* and the scuttling of the *Island Queen* by Beall and the other raiders.

Brady then conducted a brief cross-examination. It was not clear whether Brady had been given access to the sworn affidavit Ashley had prepared shortly after the Lake Erie raid in September 1864 in which he described Beall's actions. Brady did not attempt to impeach the testimony Ashley gave in his direct examination by Bolles. Instead, and somewhat surprisingly, Brady elicited testimony from Ashley that identified Beall as the man who led the Lake Erie raid. In Brady's cross-examination, Ashley acknowledged that he had been brought to New York several weeks earlier to identify Beall in a lineup at the Mulberry Street police station. The only difference in Beall's appearance since the September raid, Ashley said in response to Bolles' questions, was that Beall now had a full beard instead of a mustache.[21]

The next witness was William Weston, a fireman aboard the *Philo Parsons* during the raid. Oddly, Weston's name does not appear in any of the affidavits or news accounts written close in time to the Lake Erie raid. It was unclear how or why he was selected as a witness for the prosecution. Bolles' direct examination of Weston was brief, consisting of just twelve questions. Critical facts brought out in Weston's direct testimony were that Beall participated in the capture of the *Philo Parsons* and that he was dressed in civilian clothing at the time, a fact the prosecution apparently wanted in evidence to support the charge that Beall was acting as a spy.[22]

In his brief cross examination of Weston, Brady again did not attempt to refute or discount much of the witness's testimony. In one question, he asked Weston whether he had identified another man as Beall by mistake in a lineup at Fort Lafayette, a contention Weston denied.[23]

The third witness, David H. Thomas, the Niagara Falls detective, described the actions and statements of Beall and Anderson when Thomas and his partner, a Mr. Saule, apprehended them at the Niagara train station. Thomas testified that Beall was dressed in civilian clothing, carried a loaded revolver, and gave a false name when Thomas asked his identity.[24]

In a perfunctory cross-examination, Brady asked Thomas what time of night the arrest occurred, whether Beall had said anything about being a Confederate officer and what kind of cap Beall wore. Thomas responded that the arrest occurred around 10 p.m., that Beall claimed (falsely) to be a sergeant in the Second Virginia Infantry and wore a cloth "citizen's cap." At that point, the commission adjourned for the day.[25]

On February 2, the second day of Beall's trial, two more witnesses testified: Edward Hays, the guard at the Mulberry Street police station, and George S. Anderson, the young courier who was captured with Beall at Niagara Falls. Hays told of Beall's attempt to bribe him to gain release from custody in New York. Hays also testified about Beall's denial of any role in the New York City fire bombings but mentioned that Beall admitted knowing the parties responsible.[26]

Brady's cross-examination of Hays lasted slightly longer than that of the other witnesses. It focused on the circumstances that led to Beall's attempt to bribe Hays, whether Hays had said or done anything to try to win Beall's confidence beforehand, and whether he knew Beall had no money to pay a bribe. Hays described Beall as the initiator of the bribe attempt, saying he had no prior dealings with Beall, nor had his police supervisor given him any suggestions on how to extract information from Beall about his background.[27]

George Anderson's testimony on direct examination by Bolles covered how and when he became acquainted with Beall, the circumstances that led to the attempt to derail the train at Dunkirk, New York, the details of the train attack and what he remembered about his arrest at the Niagara Falls train station.

Although he was not asked directly, Anderson's testimony made it clear there was no mistake about Beall's identity and his participation in the raids referenced in the charges against him. Anderson apparently had reached an agreement with Union authorities that, in return for his testimony, he would be released from federal custody.[28]

Brady's cross-examination brought out only one point moderately helpful to Beall's defense. Anderson testified that, although Beall participated, it was Robert Martin, the former Morgan's raider, not Beall, who was the leader of the group that attacked the train. Brady tried to get Anderson to say that Beall or others in the group had indicated that Beall was a Confederate officer and that they addressed him as "captain." Anderson denied hearing anything related to Beall's role in the Confederate military and said he never heard Beall addressed as captain.[29]

With Anderson's testimony completed, Bolles next introduced into evidence the three letters Beall had written requesting exculpatory evidence. Bolles also read into evidence the small pocket diary Beall had started keeping at the Mulberry Street police station. The diary had apparently been taken from Beall when he was searched before arriving at Fort Lafayette. With the submission of these exhibits, the prosecution rested its case. When Beall was asked if he was ready to proceed with his defense, Brady said Beall was not ready and asked for a postponement until the following week. The commission agreed and set the February 7 as the date the trial would resume.[30]

* * * * *

Five days later, when the trial reconvened, Brady began Beall's defense by introducing two exhibits. The first was a certified copy of a warrant dated March 5, 1863, signed by Confederate Navy Secretary Stephen R. Mallory, appointing Beall as an Acting Master of the Confederate Navy. The second was a copy of a document signed by Jefferson Davis confirming that Beall's raid on Lake Erie was ordered by and undertaken under the authority of the Confederate States of America.[31]

Brady said the defense would not call any witnesses. This decision, together with Brady's somewhat lackluster questioning of the prosecution's witnesses, was perhaps a sign that Brady recognized the evidence in Beall's case was not really in dispute. The real question was what the military commission would make of it in deciding whether Beall was guilty of the charges against him.

On that score, Brady knew he faced an uphill battle. The raids coming from Canada over the past year—on Lake Erie, in St. Albans, Vermont; the *Georgian* on the Great Lakes and at Dunkirk, New York—had enraged, if not embarrassed, Major General Dix. All the attacks had occurred within the region Dix commanded, the Army's Department of the East. Brady knew it was likely that Dix expected the military commission he had appointed to send a clear warning to other potential raiders, a warning in the form of a guilty verdict.

In presenting Beall's defense, Brady decided to rely on his skills in oral argument. For the next hour and a half, Brady would deliver an address of over 10,000 impassioned words to the commission, speaking in carefully-crafted sentences that touched on all the charges against his client and attempted to refute each one of them.

Brady began by assuring the commission that Beall had not been involved in the New York City hotel fire bombings, saying such rumors were "without foundation."[32]

Brady next focused on the military commission's jurisdiction, arguing that Beall was being improperly prosecuted under two contradictory legal regimes. On the one hand, he was charged as an individual having committed offenses against the public at large and, on the other, he was charged in his military capacity as having violated the laws of war. Brady argued:

> If what is here presented against him in the proof shows that he has only committed some offence against general society cognizable in the ordinary courts of judicature, then he would be entitled under the Constitution of the United States to a trial by jury. That right accompanies him as a citizen of the United States, without any reference to what any revolting States may declare.[33]

As for the charge of violating the laws of war, Brady argued that it was simply too broad, vague and did not "conform to the requirements of the law applicable to cases of this character."[34]

Brady then proceeded to address the most serious charges against Beall—that he was a spy and a guerrilla. Beginning with spy, Brady read the definition of "spy" contained in legislation passed by Congress in 1863 which said:

> All persons who in time of war or rebellion against the Supreme authority of the United States, shall be found lurking or acting as spies in or about any of the fortifications, posts, quarters or encampments of any of the armies of the United States, or elsewhere, shall be triable by general court martial or military commission, and shall, upon conviction, suffer death.[35]

Brady questioned whether the types of locations for spying described in the legislation applied in Beall's case. By definition, he said, there had to be limits. "What are, in a military sense, the lines of the United States Army for the purpose of determining the question of one's being a spy?" Brady asked. "You may make a city a camp or an entire district, but I don't know that you can make a whole country a camp."[36]

As for the matter of disguise in the context of spying, Brady asserted that the mere fact that Beall was in civilian clothing was not evidence he was a spy:

Brady continued: "I think, therefore, that I am warranted in saying, that the charge of being a spy is not only not sustained, but entirely disproved. He did not come as a spy; he did not lurk as a spy; he sought no information; he obtained none; he communicated none."[37]

On the charge of Beall being a guerrilla, Brady argued the line was blurred between what was considered legal and illegal warfare:

> It is death, desolation, mutilation, and massacre that you are permitted to accomplish in war. And you look at it not through the medium of philanthropy, not through the Divine precept that tells you to love your neighbors as yourself, but through the melancholy necessity that characterizes the awful nature of war.... Where do you draw the line of distinction between the act of one you call a guerrilla and the act of one you call a raider.... Where do you make

the distinction between the march of Major-General Sherman through the enemy's country, carrying ravage and desolation everywhere, destroying the most peaceable and lawful industry, mills and machinery, and everything of that nature—where do you draw the line between his march through Georgia and an expedition of twenty men acting under commission who get into any of the States we claim to be in the Union, and commit depredations there?[38]

Beall was not a guerrilla, Brady maintained, "because he was a commissioned officer in the Confederate service, acting under authority of that government during war, in connection with other military men, for an act of war."[39] As a result, he was not properly before the military commission and should be treated as any other soldier captured in battle. With that, Brady concluded the defense's case and told the commission, "I leave his fate in your hands."[40]

General Warren, president of the commission, turned his attention to Bolles, the Judge Advocate, who rose to his feet and began his closing argument to the military panel. His address on behalf of the prosecution would rival Brady's in length, lasting more than an hour.

On jurisdiction, Bolles said that although certain actions taken during a time of peace would be triable by a jury in a civil court of law, those same actions performed during wartime become acts of war:

> Murder, which is a civil offence under ordinary circumstances, may and does, in time of war, when committed for disloyal and treasonable purposes, become a military offence and may then be tried by a military court.... In this case it is very clear that personal advantage was not the motive that led to the seizure of the steamboats, or the attempt on the railroad.[41]

Bolles also sought to refute Beall's defense that his actions were legally authorized. He discounted the documents Beall introduced that showed he had been appointed as a Confederate Naval officer and that his actions were performed pursuant to orders from the Confederate president, Jefferson Davis. Bolles argued that not only were Beall's actions illegal but that the orders underlying them were unlawful as well:

> I was willing to admit that Beall was a rebel officer, and that all he did was authorized by Mr. Davis; because, in my view of the case, all that was done by the accused, being in violation of the law of war, no commission, command, or manifesto could justify his acts.... A solider is bound to obey the lawful commands of his superior officer.... His superior officer cannot require or compel any soldier to act as a spy or as an assassin. If then such unlawful command be given and obeyed, its only effect is to prove that both he who gave and he who obeyed the command are criminals.[42]

Bolles next took up the issue of spying, asserting that spying "within our lines" was an expansive concept:

> Every man is within our lines who enters a loyal State by sea or land with hostile purposes. Any rebel emissary who has first violated the rights of Canadian neutrality, and then in the guise of a peaceful citizen crossed into our territory along the whole northern frontier of which are military posts and garrisons, is within our lines.[43]

Bolles quoted from several legal dictionaries to show that Beall's actions, including his wearing of civilian clothing, constituted the acts of a spy:

The accused came aboard the *Philo Parsons* clandestinely, with the heart and hate of an enemy, but in the dress and with the profession of a friend; so did he clandestinely enter the *Island Queen*; so did he clandestinely visit Buffalo. Deception, disguise, concealment, falsehood, stamp their guilty image and superscription on all his acts, and on all his declarations. "His dress belies and disguises his real character," Bolles asserted.[44]

Bolles contended that it was not necessary for the prosecution to prove, with separate evidence, that Beall was also a guerrilla, saying the word was "mere surplusage" in the charges. "If the evidence in this case shows that the accused engaged in hostile acts which are forbidden by the law of war, you may call him brigand or raider, guerrilla or guerrillero, prowler or robber, he is still amendable to this Court," Bolles said.[45]

Finally, Bolles forcefully argued that Beall was being properly tried in a military court and was guilty as charged. In his summation, he wrapped all of Beall's actions into a comprehensive description of what, in the military context, had yet to be formally recognized as "war crimes":

"The piracy on the lake and the outrage on the railroad were parts of that system of irregular warfare, under the fear of which no man, woman, or child can sleep with any feeling of security in our midst. Such atrocities are attempts, on the part of the rebel officers and soldiers who engage in and countenance them, to bring back war to its old condition of barbarism— to imitate the stealthy cruelty of the North American savage, who creeps under the cover of midnight upon his unsuspecting victim, and smites him to death…. With the accused, this savage purpose takes form in the robbery of steamboats and the destruction of railroad trains and travellers," Bolles contended.[46]

The prosecution rested and the case was submitted to the military commission for decision.

* * * * *

On February 8, the military commission met to consider the evidence and render its verdict. The deliberations did not take long. The commission found Beall guilty and sentenced him to death by hanging. The execution was to take place February 18 at Fort Columbus on Governor's Island, another military prison in New York harbor.[47]

CHAPTER 26

Cries for Mercy

Fort Lafayette, New York Harbor; Washington, D.C.—
February 1865

On February 13, 1865, five days after the military commission reached its verdict, John Yates Beall was summoned to the commandant's office at Fort Lafayette. Beall had not yet been told of his conviction.[1] Beall entered the commandant's office and stood before Colonel Martin Burke, a tall, white-haired, career military officer in his mid-sixties. Burke, a veteran of the Mexican-American war, had been appointed commandant at Fort Lafayette in 1861, shortly after the war began. A stickler for following orders and keeping the fort spotless and freshly-painted, Burke was famous for never leaving his post. Over the previous four years, Burke had ventured off the island only twice. It was rumored that his reluctance to leave the fort was to avoid being served with a summons to one of the courtrooms in New York City. Burke routinely ignored writs of habeas corpus issued by the city's judges in cases filed by prisoners challenging their incarceration. Process servers were not allowed onto fort property.[2]

"I have bad news for you, Captain," Burke told Beall. "But I know you are a brave man and can stand it." Although quite frail from his weeks behind bars, Beall stood straight and asked the colonel to continue. Burke then read Major General Dix's order adopting the commission's guilty verdict and sentencing Beall to death by hanging. The order set Beall's execution to take place on Saturday, February 18 "between the hours of 12 and 2 in the afternoon." Beall, expressionless, was taken back to his cell.[3]

Shortly after meeting with Burke, Beall sent a letter to a close friend, James McClure, a classmate at the University of Virginia who practiced law in Baltimore. Beall asked McClure to find out what expenses James Brady had incurred in representing him at trial so he could reimburse him—apparently unaware or having forgotten that Brady had represented him without charge. Beall also gave instructions for his burial, requesting that his body be buried in New York rather than in Virginia, at least until the war was over.[4]

Word of Beall's conviction quickly spread among his friends and associates. They organized a wide-ranging campaign—which spread from Washington to New

York—to save Beall from death. On February 15, the day after Dix issued his order scheduling Beall's execution, McClure and Albert Ritchie, another lawyer and University of Virginia classmate, contacted Andrew Sterrett Ridgely, also a University of Virginia graduate and Baltimore lawyer, who knew Lincoln. Ridgeley's assignment would be to meet personally with the president, urging him to postpone and ultimately commute Beall's sentence.[5]

Attempting to involve the nation's highest elected official in overturning Beall's death sentence was a bold, but not unprecedented, move. Two years earlier, Lincoln had intervened on behalf of a respected Virginia physician who had shot and killed a Union officer in cold blood as he led a column of Black troops from the U.S. Colored Infantry Regiment in Norfolk, Virginia. After the physician, David M. Wright, was convicted and sentenced to death by hanging, Lincoln requested a copy of the trial transcript. "Do not let the execution be done upon him, until my further order," Lincoln directed. Ultimately, Lincoln allowed the execution to proceed but his involvement had been noted in the North and South.[6]

On February 16, Ridgeley traveled to Washington. Lincoln offered Ridgeley no encouragement, telling him he had already rebuffed appeals by others on Beall's behalf, adding that he had no reason to reject the judgment and order of Dix.[7]

Also on February 16, a tug arrived at Fort Lafayette to take Beall to Fort Columbus, the largest Union fort in New York harbor, about seven miles north of Fort Lafayette, located on Governors Island just off Battery Park. It was where Beall was to be executed. A Confederate prisoner recalled Beall's departure: "When he walked from his cell into the yard he saluted me and several others. He spoke pleasantly to me and walked with a steady step to the tug that was to bear him to his place of execution"[8]

The next day, February 17, Ritchie and another prominent Baltimore resident, Francis L. Wheatly, decided to seek the assistance of another close Lincoln acquaintance. They contacted Orville H. Browning, one of Washington's preeminent lawyer-lobbyists.[9] Browning, a former Whig-turned Republican, had served as a U.S. senator from Illinois. He had a career that roughly paralleled Lincoln's. Born in Kentucky, Browning moved to Illinois as a young man where he fought in the Black Hawk War and then became a successful attorney. He served in the Illinois state legislature and, in 1861, was appointed to fill the U.S. Senate seat left vacant after the death of Stephen A. Douglas. After leaving the Senate in 1863, Browning established a successful law and lobbying practice, in part because of his close personal relationship with Lincoln. Among other interactions with the president, Browning and his wife had stayed in the White House to console Lincoln and his wife while their son, Willie, lay dying.[10]

Browning prepared a letter to Lincoln, noting that Dix's order had set the date for Beall's execution as the next day, February 18. To buy time and mount a more substantial appeal, Browning's letter sought only what he called a "respite" from carrying out Beall's death sentence rather than an outright commutation. At the same time, the letter noted:

The friends of Capt. Beall desire to appeal to your clemency for a commutation of the sentence from death to imprisonment and that they may have the opportunity to prepare and present to your consideration the reason which they hope may induce to a commutation.[11]

That same day, February 17, Browning carried his letter to the White House and met with Lincoln for more than an hour. Along with the letter, Browning presented the president with a petition signed by ninety-one members of Congress—eighty-five members of the House of Representatives and six senators—asking Lincoln to commute Beall's death sentence. Among those signing was a future president, Ohio Congressman John A. Garfield.[12] A local Presbyterian minister, Dr. John J. Bullock, had been instrumental in circulating the petition among the lawmakers at the U.S. Capitol.[13]

Shortly after Browning met with Lincoln, he reported his impressions to Ritchie and Wheatly, telling them he thought it was unlikely that Beall would be executed the next day.[14] As it turned out, Browning's prediction was accurate—but the reason for the delay in Beall's execution was because of a technical error in the charges against him. The specification charging Beall with spying in New York stated incorrectly that the spying took place in September, instead of December 1864. As a result, the commission had found Beall "not guilty" of that particular charge.

Also on February 17, in light of the charging error, Major General Dix issued an order staying Beall's execution, which was to be the next day. He also directed the commission to reconvene and reconsider a revised charge, which had been changed to reflect the correct date.[15]

Ritchie and Wheatly, buoyed by the delay in Beall's execution, met with Browning again the next day, February 18. He told them if they could obtain the approval of Major General Dix, he felt confident that Lincoln would commute the sentence. Hearing that assessment from Browning, Ritchie and Wheatly returned to Baltimore to prepare a direct appeal to Dix.[16]

On Monday, February 20, the Commission reconvened and, with the date corrected for the spying charge, found Beall guilty a second time. Major General Dix approved the conviction the next day and rescheduled Beall's execution for Friday, February 24.[17]

Over the next four days, a parade of high-level lobbyists, politicians, editors and one former cabinet member besieged the White House, all asking to meet with the president to plead for the commutation of Beall's death sentence. Among those making attempts to see Lincoln on Beall's behalf were Francis P. Blair, the former postmaster-general; Thaddeus Stevens, a staunch abolitionist and a Republican Congressman from Pennsylvania; Richard S. Spofford, the Librarian of Congress; Governor John Andrews of Massachusetts; John W. Forney, Secretary of the U.S. Senate; and Washington McLean, editor of the Democratic-leaning *Cincinnati Enquirer*.[18]

It is unclear how many of the people wishing to make appeals to the president were able to meet with him. One who did was Roger A. Pryor, the former Confederate general and congressman who was imprisoned with Beall at Fort Lafayette.

Pryor, who had been Beall's first choice as lawyer to represent him at the military commission trial, had been released in a recent prisoner exchange. A memoir later recounted Lincoln's reaction to Pryor's appeal:

> Although Mr. Lincoln evinced the sincerest compassion for the young man, and an extreme aversion to his death, he felt constrained to yield to the assurance of Gen. Dix, in a telegram just received, that the execution was indispensable to the security of the Northern cities—it being believed though erroneously, that Capt. Beall was implicated in the burning of the New York hotels.[19]

Why did so many high-ranking national figures with no direct connection to Beall come to his aid? The historical record provides no clear answer. While it appears that none of those advocating on behalf of Beall sought his outright release, they did ask Lincoln to commute Beall's death sentence, urging Beall's imprisonment instead. Their motivations were likely varied, with some advocates thinking Beall's trial and conviction were conducted in haste, and others perhaps wishing to allow Beall more time to mount an appeal or at least prepare for the end of his life. Another motivation could have been fear that Confederates would retaliate against Lincoln, who had already received threatening letters saying he would pay with his life if Beall were executed.[20]

For others, it could have been nothing more than a desire on the part of members of a certain class of society to save one of their own, putting aside whatever acts of "mischief" against the North he may have engaged in along the way. Such a rationale is at least hinted at by Daniel Lucas, Beall's life-long friend, in his book, *The Memoir of John Yates Beall*:

> We heard through every hour of the day, also, of the interest manifested, and exertions made by others—strangers to us, and strangers to John, except so far as he was known to them by the appreciation they had formed of his character, and by those sympathetic ties which unite the generous and high-toned, no matter what may be the differences of political or religious creed.[21]

Indeed, Isaac Markens, who as a young reporter covered the efforts to save Beall, attributed Lincoln's interest in the case to Beall's "social standing and high reputation."[22]

The six-day reprieve of Beall's execution also provided an opportunity for his mother—having received word of his death sentence—to travel from Charles Town, West Virginia, to New York to meet with her son in his cell at Fort Columbus. Beall and his mother had no privacy, with several Army officers standing watch over their brief time together. According to one account, Beall and his mother revealed little outward emotion during their reunion, with both exhibiting "that degree of composed fortitude which might have been expected by those acquainted with their characters."[23]

Beall was comforted by his mother's stoic demeanor because it demonstrated to him that she had the inner strength to carry on after his death. His father had died years earlier and Beall was the oldest son. "I saw the moment she entered the cell that she could bear it, and that it made no difference to her whether I died upon the scaffold, or fell upon the field," Beall said after her visit.[24]

The evening of Wednesday, February 22, Ritchie left for New York to meet with Dix. When he arrived early the next day, he was startled to discover that Dix had ordered Beall's execution to take place on February 24. With only one day to spare, Ritchie rushed to Dix's office at Army headquarters in New York City. Dix saw Ritchie immediately upon his arrival, but Dix had no words of encouragement, telling him "there was not ... a gleam of hope" to save Beall from execution.[25]

At the same time, Dix handed Ritchie a pass to witness the hanging, saying "any one whom Capt. Beall wished to see, would be permitted to go to the Island."[26] Markens, in his account of Ritchie's meeting with Dix, noted, "In striking contrast with Dix's firm stand against Beall was his complaisance in the distribution of passes to witness the execution. These were given out without question, promiscuously and for the mere asking."[27] In fact, Dix had an interest in publicizing Beall's execution, anticipating that word of the hanging would travel to Confederates in Canada and serve as a warning against further attacks.

Following his discouraging meeting with Dix, Ritchie telegraphed McClure, advising him to come to join him New York immediately, so that "should it be impossible to arrest the coming of that hour [for Beall's execution], to at least share it with him if permitted."[28]

In Washington, on the evening of February 23—now only hours before Beall's scheduled execution—a few more petitioners appeared outside the White House to deliver appeals on Beall's behalf. By this time, however, Lincoln had effectively stepped away from the controversy, directing his private secretary to tell any visitors that Beall's case "was closed."[29]

CHAPTER 27

The Execution

Fort Columbus, Governors Island, N.Y.—
February 24, 1865

On Friday, February 24, at 1 p.m., three men entered Beall's cell at Fort Columbus where he sat quietly. They were the Provost Marshal of Governors Island, Lieutenant A.L. Tallman; the U.S. Marshal, Robert Murray; and the executioner, a Union army deserter working off his crime. Beall looked toward the executioner and said, "Let this thing be as brief as possible," referring to his hanging, which was about to occur within the next hour. "It is to me a mere muscular effort. Make it as short as you can when you get there."[1]

As Beall rose to his feet, the executioner placed a loose-fitting, black drape-cap on his head. It was elongated and would be pulled over his eyes when he stood on the gallows. Beall's hands were tied behind his back and a section of rope with a noose on the end was placed around his neck. As Beall stepped out of his cell into the hallway, Tallman, who had acquired a certain respect for Beall in their encounters, took off his military cloak and threw it onto Beall's shoulders. Beall was accompanied by the Rev. S.H. Weston, an Episcopal minister assigned to the Seventh New York Infantry who had been with Beall in his cell and administered last rights in the previous hours.[2]

Standing outside Beall's cell were his two friends, James McClure and Albert Ritchie, who had come to Governors Island to be with Beall during his final hours. McClure, not noticing that Beall's hands were tied, offered his hand. "I cannot shake hands," Beall said, smiling. "I am pinioned!"[3]

Ritchie had spent the night in the fort and had been with Beall until midnight. He recalled that Beall had complained of a bad toothache and was tempted to use some of the laudanum pain killer he had used earlier during his prison stay. On this night, however, Beall had refrained from requesting the pain drug for fear his use of it—on the night before his death—would be misunderstood.[4]

Ritchie also recalled another disclosure Beall had made the previous night. Just before the jailer took Ritchie to Beall's cell, he had requested that Ritchie not furnish the prisoner with any instrument he could use to take his own life. When Ritchie informed Beall of the request, Beall had bent over, lifted his left shoe and plucked out from the upper layer of leather a small metal saw blade made from a steel watch spring. "I could have opened a vein at any moment had I wished to do so," Beall said.[5]

Now led by the three men who had come to his cell, Beall walked through the fort's east gate into the frigid air and bright sunshine. Several soldiers drew up on each side of him as a drum rolled out the death march. Beall walked in step with his military escort and approached the fort's parade ground. A scaffolding with the gallows was visible on the southerly slope of the island. Surrounding the gallows structure was a crowd of about five hundred people who had arrived on the island in tugs and ferries earlier in the day. Beall could also see people in boats on the water, bobbing near the shore, hoping to get a view of the hanging. Dix had succeeded in his efforts to publicize the execution.[6]

A reporter with the New York *World* described the scene near the gallows: "The most variegated and characteristic crowd ever seen out of Dante was assembled around the machine of death—officers of staff and of the regular and volunteer services, sick soldiers in pale blue breeches and miserable civilian laborers in gray and mud, reporters in straggling beards."[7]

About three hundred yards from the scaffolding, Beall and the military procession came to a halt as soldiers at the gallows made last-minute preparations. Gazing upward, Beall said to the Reverend Weston, still at his side, "This is the last time I shall see the sun." Looking into the distance across the harbor, Beall asked about the location of Fort Lafayette, his previous quarters, saying he had "many kind friends there." After about five minutes, the march continued and Beall arrived at the gallows scaffolding. He stepped forward onto the wooden platform and saw a plain, pine box at the foot of it which would be his coffin.[8]

The structure erected for Beall's hanging was not the traditional "drop" type gallows. Rather, it used a taut rope wound through weights and pulleys to jerk the condemned victim off the ground, with a motion so violent that it would dislocate vertebrae in the neck and cause instant death. The name given to the contraption described its function: "upright jerker." Beall sat down in a chair that had been placed directly under the rope hanging from the gallows. After sitting a moment, he rose and pushed the chair aside with his foot.[9]

Provost Marshall Tallman stepped forward and began reading the order of Major General Dix, setting forth the charges against Beall and the findings of the military commission. As the reading of the lengthy document continued for almost nine minutes, Beall took his seat again, turning his chair so his back was to the Provost Marshall and his face was turned to the South. Beall smiled "derisively" once or twice when particular parts of Dix's order were read, according to a newspaper account. For the most part, however, his countenance remained unemotional.[10]

When the provost marshal finished reading, the Reverend Weston took a step toward Beall and spoke briefly, offering a prayer for the dead as Beall closed his eyes. When Weston finished, Beall uttered, "Amen."[11]

The provost marshal then asked Beall whether he had anything to say. Beall, in a calm, firm voice, responded, "All I have to say is that the execution of this sentence is murder, absolute murder. I die in the service and defense of my country. I have nothing more to say."[12]

At 1:13 p.m., the provost marshal and Weston stepped back, and the executioner came forward. He removed the cape from Beall's shoulders and attached the noose that hung around his neck to the longer rope hanging from the scaffolding. He pulled down the black drape-cap over Beall's head, covering his face. The executioner then moved out of public view into a small wooden hut-like structure next to the scaffolding. The hut had a small peephole, allowing the executioner to see the gallows. Seconds later, Provost Marshall Tallman signaled to the executioner by raising his sword, its steel blade flashing in the sunlight. A loud thump came from inside the hut as the executioner's axe sliced through rope, dropping a weight to the ground. Beall's body heaved upward toward the sky.[13]

Epilogue

Beall and Booth—A Connection?

The assassination of Abraham Lincoln—coming less than two months after John Yates Beall's execution—gave rise to what one author called a "weird and lurid story"[1] that captivated conspiracy theorists for decades following the war. In brief, the story held that John Wilkes Booth and Beall were longtime friends, even "comrades in arms," having been at the University of Virginia at the same time and sharing a strong belief in the Confederate cause. When Booth learned that Beall had been captured and was about to be hanged as a Confederate spy, he appealed directly to Lincoln, with some accounts describing Booth as pleading on bended knee before the president.

The story continues, saying that Lincoln promised Booth he would intervene to save Beall from death. Some accounts also involved Secretary of War Edwin Stanton who, after learning of Lincoln's pledge to Booth, purportedly stormed into Lincoln's office and threatened to resign if Lincoln commuted Beall's death sentence. Beall must hang, Stanton insisted, adding that public sentiment in the North demanded that the Confederate raider should face the maximum punishment for his commando attacks. Some accounts have Secretary of State William Seward joining Stanton in the revolt against Lincoln's potential pardon of Beall. In response to Stanton and Seward's demands, Lincoln failed to follow through on his earlier pledge and the assassination followed, as an act of vengeance by Booth for Beall's execution, according to the story. A few accounts also tell of Beall and Booth being cousins, while other versions say Booth was engaged to Beall's sister, Elizabeth.

Immediately following Lincoln's assassination on April 14, 1865, suspicions in the U.S. were pervasive about the involvement of Confederates in Canada in the plot. On May 2, 1865, President Andrew Johnson issued a proclamation offering a reward of $25,000 for the capture and arrest of Confederate Commissioners Jacob Thompson, Clement Clay and two of their close associates, George N. Sanders and Beverley Tucker, identifying each of them as having "incited, concerted, and procured … the atrocious murder of the late President Abraham Lincoln, and the attempted assassination of the Hon. William H. Seward, Secretary of State."[2]

A flood of letters also poured into the office of Secretary of War Stanton from citizens claiming to have overheard discussions among conspirators describing plans to take some action against Lincoln. Lafayette Baker, who headed the Lincoln administration's spying efforts against the Confederacy at the National Detective Bureau, quoted from several of the letters in his memoir, *History of the United States Secret Service*, published in 1867.

Among the letters cited in the book was one written by "G.S.C.," identified only as "a respected lawyer" in Buffalo, New York, dated April 18, 1865, four days after the assassination. In the letter, G.S.C. reported that, in recent weeks, he was at the Queen's Hotel in Toronto, another favorite Confederate gathering spot. "I was informed at that time that the friends of Beale [sic] were banded together for the double purpose of avenging his death and aiding the Rebel Government." In addition, G.S.C. said he overheard conversations in which rebel sympathizers were "mourning over the late rebel reverses," including "the execution of Beale." The comments went further, G.S.C. wrote, and included vague references to a planned operation expected to take place in Washington. These statements were along the lines of: "We'll make the damned Yankees howl yet," "We'll get better news in forty-eight hours," and "We'll have something from Washington that will make people stare," according to G.S.C.[3]

The letter continued: "Their words at the time appeared to me to be simply profane and vulgar, implying idle threats which could never have been executed…. The next morning (Saturday, April 15), when I received the news of the assassination, I could not help feeling that the party [sic] I had heard the night before were implicated in the act."[4]

Allegations of a connection between Beall's execution and Booth's assassination of Lincoln also emerged early in the trial of the Lincoln conspirators which took place in May 1865, as Government prosecutors attempted to prove that the assassination plot began in Canada.

On May 13, Judge Advocate Joseph Holt, the government's lead prosecutor, called as a witness James B. Merritt, who said he met Booth in Montreal and associated with other rebel agents in Canada. Referring to George N. Sanders, the unofficial fourth Confederate commissioner who favored political assassinations, Holt asked Merritt if he remembered Sanders saying that one of Booth's motivations for assassinating Lincoln was that he was related to Beall who was hung in New York?[5]

Merritt replied: "Sanders said that Booth was heart and soul in this project of assassination, and felt as much as any person could feel, for the reason that he was a cousin to Beall that was hung in New York."[6] Part of Merritt's testimony regarding his time in Canada was later revealed to be false and, as a result, his entire testimony, including his statements regarding Beall and Booth, has been heavily discounted by historians.[7]

Various versions of the story linking Beall and Booth continued to appear in the decades after the war, particularly in journals popular among former members of the Confederate military. In the January 1901 edition of the *Confederate Veteran*, a journal featuring personal reminiscences of rebel soldiers, Dr. John Slick Riley, one of the raiders who accompanied Beall on the Johnson's Island raid, presented his account of Beall and Booth.

Riley, the oldest member of the raiding team and a surgeon, wrote that he became acquainted with Beall in Canada and learned that Beall and Booth were "sworn friends." Booth was "overwhelmed with grief" after learning of Beall's execution, Riley wrote, and "swore in his wrath that he would take the life of Lincoln if it cost him his own." Booth enlisted others in the plot to take the lives of Seward and Stanton as well, Riley recounted.[8]

In the same edition of *Confederate Veteran*, an unnamed writer, claiming to be "intimately acquainted" with Beall in Canada, wrote that Beall told him of his close friendship with Booth. "I have no doubt in my mind ... that Booth really killed President Lincoln on account of Capt. Beall's execution and the President's failure to commute his punishment or pardon him," the unnamed writer asserted.[9]

A third account was contributed by the son of another physician who claimed to have been in an adjoining cell with Beall at Fort Columbus on Governor's Island. It appeared in the July 1911 edition of *Confederate Veteran*. The son said he found the account in papers left by his father, Dr. George Foote, a surgeon in the Confederate Army. "The war had nothing to do with the assassination of the President," wrote the son, who did not provide or quote from the papers themselves. "It was due solely to revenge, which enmity was intensified by Booth's love and admiration for his friend."[10]

Beall's execution did, in fact, receive widespread publicity in the South and generated calls for retaliation. On March 3, 1865, just a week after Beall's hanging, the Virginia House of Delegates unanimously adopted a resolution condemning Beall's execution and recommended that steps be taken to retaliate. "No purer, no more patriotic and honorable man ever existed than John Yates Beall," the resolution stated. It recommended "the adoption of such steps as may be necessary in retaliation for the offence."[11]

A headline in *The New York Herald* for March 7, 1865, declared: "Excitement Over the Execution of Beall—Threats of Retaliation by His Friends."[12] With a Richmond, Virginia, dateline, the newspaper reported:

> The murder by hanging of Captain John Y. Beall ... is exciting deep indignation in this community where deceased had many friends.... Threats were made yesterday looking to the hanging, summarily upon the first lamp post, of any of the Yankee officers now on their parole and who might be found at large.[13]

As an initial matter, there is little question that Booth likely knew about Beall's execution, if not before, then shortly after it occurred. Indeed, historian Terry Alford, in his biography of Booth, *Fortune's Fool*, wrote that news of Beall's death "hit him hard," noting that Beall's fiancée, Martha O'Bryan, later said that Booth fainted and had an attack of "brain fever" when he learned of Beall's execution.[14]

Alford quotes an actor friend of Booth, John McCullough, as saying Booth received news of Beall's hanging on the day it occurred. "Booth damned Old Lincoln for a murderer," McCullough reportedly said, adding Booth warned, "Somebody would one day give it to him."[15]

Many efforts made by historians over the years to examine the accuracy of the claims connecting Booth and Beall have concluded that, while intriguing, they are essentially baseless. One of the first to address the controversy was Frederick J. Shepard, who wrote about Beall's raid on Lake Erie and its aftermath in the 1906 house organ of the Buffalo Historical Society. "Once in a while a story goes the rounds of the newspapers connecting the assassination of Lincoln with Beall's execution," Shepard wrote. "And a Philadelphia auctioneer is quoted as professing to own documents which prove that Booth was impelled to his act by his friendship for Beall and a desire to avenge him."[16]

Shepard apparently did not do extensive research into the topic, however, noting only that he had corresponded with Daniel Lucas, the Richmond lawyer who wrote Beall's "memoir" and was his lifelong friend. "Judge Lucas does not believe that Beall ever saw Booth and remarks that there was no similarity of conduct between the two, Beall having no fancy for the sports that attracted Booth," Shepard wrote, adding, "while there is not the slightest evidence that they were in Canada at the same time."[17]

In fact, there is evidence that Booth and Beall not only were in Montreal around the same time in the fall of 1864 but that they both stayed in the same hotel, St. Lawrence Hall, which was the gathering place for Confederates in that city. According to the hotel's guest register, Booth checked in to room No. 150 on October 18 and checked out on October 27. Beall checked in to room No. 149 on November 2.[18]

While the dates of Booth's visit to Montreal in October 1864 are well-documented, the exact dates of Beall's time in the city are murky. With other hotels and accommodations available in town at the time, which could provide alternate lodgings for Beall, it is at least possible that the visits of Beall and Booth could have overlapped, allowing them to have met or attended the same gatherings with other conspirators.

The New York journalist Isaac Markens also examined the Beall-Booth controversy in his short book, *President Lincoln and the Case of John Y. Beall,* published in 1911. In his book, which largely covers the extensive appeals to Lincoln following Beall's conviction, Markens traced the origin of the story connecting Beall and Booth. He attributes it to Marcus M. Pomeroy who, during the war years, was editor of the notoriously anti–Lincoln newspaper, the *La Crosse Democrat* in Wisconsin. Without providing a specific date, Markens states that Pomeroy published the first public account making the claim that Booth sought to avenge Beall's execution by killing Lincoln. The account appeared in *Pomeroy's Democrat,* a weekly publication that Pomeroy started shortly after the war.[19] The historian Terry Alford agreed with the finding that Pomeroy was one of the first to write about the Beall-Booth story, writing, "If the editor Mark Pomeroy, a veteran Lincoln hater, was not the father of this story, he was its favorite uncle."[20]

In the face of the many accounts linking Beall and Booth, family and friends of Beall took steps to disprove the story. In 1927, Virginia Lucas, the daughter of Beall's friend Daniel Lucas, attempted to refute the allegations in an article she wrote for the *Confederate Veteran* titled, "John Yates Beall: An Appreciation." Lucas explained that one reason she wrote her essay was to show "how unlikely it would be that a serious, orderly, and high-principled young man, such as all accounts show Beall to have been, that such an [sic] one would have been the intimate and boon companion of that dissipated, handsome, and, perhaps to some extent, charming young Marylander, John Wilkes Booth. And the evidence is all the other way."[21]

Among the evidence that Lucas offered in support of her argument were statements by her father, Daniel, a life-long friend of Beall. She quoted from a letter her father sent in response to a query asking about Beall and Booth. "The whole story about John Wilkes Booth and his connection with Beall is a fabrication without a particle of truth," Daniel Lucas wrote.[22]

In the article, Virginia Lucas also quoted from a letter written by another close Beall friend, Albert Ritchie, who was with Beall at Fort Columbus just before his execution. Ritchie was responding to a letter from Daniel Lucas asking whether Ritchie had any knowledge of Dr. Foote, who claimed to have been in an adjoining cell with Beall at the prison and said he had heard Beall talk about his relationship with Booth. As for Dr. Foote, Ritchie wrote, "Who is Dr. Foote? If he had an adjoining cell, I knew nothing of it, nor did John speak of it." And with respect to Booth, Ritchie wrote: "I have seen this Booth business referred to two or three times before. Is there anything in it? … I never heard of Booth's intimacy with John, nor do I remember John's speaking of him."[23]

Others who have examined the controversy note that Booth never attended the University of Virginia, or any college for that matter, let alone shared time on the campus with Beall.[24]

Cameron Moseley, Beall's first cousin twice removed, wrote of the controversy in his self-published biography of Beall, *John Yates Beall—Confederate Commando*. In the book, he quotes Alford, the Civil War historian and Booth biographer, as providing an "admirable summary of the probabilities" of the Booth-Beall connection. In a letter to Moseley, Alford wrote, "The Beall-Booth matter apparently has a grain of truth but has been much embellished." Booth and Beall likely met when they both served with Virginia militia units present at the hanging of John Brown in Charles Town, Virginia, in late 1859, Alford noted, a conclusion consistent with other historical accounts.[25]

Alford added:

Their relationship could not have been close. The execution of Beall did anger Booth. Two of Booth's closest friends, actor John McCullough and business partner Joe Simonds, both said so. It is doubtful if Booth appealed directly to Lincoln for clemency, but there can be no doubt the hanging formed an element in Booth's volatility which led to the president's murder.[26]

In sum, the weight of the available evidence seems to point to the absence of any strong Beall-Booth bond.

At the same time, there are suggestions in the words and writings of some Beall family members—and those who have known them—that much of the existing evidence of a relationship between the two men was intentionally destroyed. It is possible the nation's first presidential assassination sent such a shockwave through the American public that exhaustive efforts were made by Beall's family and friends to erase any proof that the name John Yates Beall had connection with the death of a president.

"There are many who believe that Booth, who had toyed with the idea of assassinating Lincoln for months, was spurred to action by the death of Beall," noted Louise Littleton Davis, a Nashville journalist-historian who wrote about Beall's fiancée and Nashville native, Martha O'Bryan, and interviewed her family members. "From that moment, it became doubly dangerous to have known Beall. Family and friends, for their own safety, had to 'clam up,' as one of them said. Letters vanished," Littleton wrote. "Possible proof of the courtship between Beall's sister and Booth vanished. And that girl, Elizabeth Beall, became a recluse, seeing few people and saying little, even to her relatives, throughout her long life."[27]

Littleton continued:

> The savagery of the trials of Booth's accomplices … is one of the disgraceful pages in American history. It was too dangerous for anyone who had known Booth or his friends to speak up or to keep any correspondence. But relatives of Beall in Virginia and West Virginia are convinced that the assassination of Lincoln grew out of the indignation of Beall's friends over his unjust trial and death. Cheap exploitation of the story by writers for sensational newspapers over the years have discredited the theory for many. Beall's family … are convinced that there is only one weakness in the story: the written, tangible evidence vanished because it was too dangerous to possess.[28]

Moseley, Beall's distant cousin and biographer, supported Littleton's view, writing in his Beall biography, "The brutality and seeming unfairness of Beall's execution and the possibility that it was linked directly to Booth's assassination of Lincoln were strong reasons for family, friends, pundits, and officials both North and South to lock the Booth/Beall skeleton in a closet."[29]

In the end, with respect to any purported Beall-Booth connection, perhaps it is enough to say that historical conclusions—after more than 150 years—are difficult to reach even when substantial evidence is available. With the possibility that evidence was purposely expunged in the case of Beall and Booth, the safest conclusion may be the axiom that "absence of evidence is not necessarily evidence of absence."

Their Later Lives

John Yates Beall

On Saturday, February 25, 1865, the day following the execution of John Yates Beall, his friends James McClure and Albert Ritchie buried his body in a small plot at Greenwood Cemetery in Brooklyn, overlooking New York Harbor. A front-page account of Beall's execution appearing that day in the New York *World* ended, saying, "Let those of us who must die for the right side do so as well as he who died for the wrong side."[30]

In 1870, five years after the war ended, Beall's relatives removed his body from the Greenwood Cemetery and reinterred it in the cemetery of Zion Episcopal Church in Charles Town, West Virginia. It remains there in a line of burial plots with other deceased members of the Beall family. A raised placard near the cemetery entrance describes notable figures buried in the cemetery, including Beall as well as several relatives of George Washington. Inscribed on Beall's tombstone are the words he requested just before his death: "He died in the service and defense of his country."

Bennet Burley

After the raid on Lake Erie in September 1864, Bennet Burley returned to Canada and began working at a foundry owned by his cousin in the town of Guelph, north of Toronto. When Burley arrived, the foundry expanded its production to include munitions for the Confederacy.[31]

On November 19, 1864, Canadian authorities discovered Burley's location and placed him under arrest. Burley, who was not interested in helping the authorities, allowed them to believe—at least for a time—that they had captured John Yates Beall. After he was correctly identified, Burley was transferred to Toronto for a hearing on his extradition to the United States.[32]

Burley's arrest and hearing, conducted by a special panel of judges from the Queen's Bench and Court of Common Pleas, generated widespread publicity and strong passions among Canadian citizens. The issues were complex, in part because Burley was a British citizen.[33]

U.S. authorities faced the challenge of deciding exactly what charges to bring against Burley. Piracy was considered but rejected to avoid offending the British and Canadian governments, which did not recognize the crime of piracy on the Great Lakes. Their rationale was that piracy could only occur on the "high seas." The charges ultimately brought were limited to robbery at gunpoint, based on Burley's participation with Beall in taking money and notes from Walter Ashley, the clerk of the *Philo Parsons*, during the boat's seizure.[34]

After several delays, in late January 1865 the panel ordered Burley's extradition to the United States and he was taken to Detroit and placed in the city's house of correction.[35] During his nearly six months of incarceration in Detroit, Burley spent time learning French and German from books he had ordered. In June, he was indicted by a grand jury in Port Clinton, Ohio—the county seat of Ottawa County where the seizures of the *Philo Parsons* and *Island Queen* took place. Burley was then taken from Detroit to Port Clinton, sailing across Lake Erie aboard the *Philo Parsons*, the same tourist boat he had captured with Beall nearly a year earlier.[36]

In July, Burley's first trial ended in a hung jury. Lacking bail money, Burley was returned to the county jail. The jail in Port Clinton lacked security and Burley's cell on the ground floor had a window through which he could converse with passersby. Soon, Burley's gregarious personality won him a group of friends including, as it turned out, the county sheriff, James Lattimore. Lattimore and his wife lived in private quarters adjacent to the jail. Burley and Lattimore became so friendly that the sheriff would sometimes take Burley with him on errands outside the jail.[37]

On September 17, 1865, almost exactly one year after the raid on Lake Erie, Lattimore and his wife left town, leaving Burley—the only prisoner in the jail—with access to a hallway near Lattimore's private quarters. Burley managed to obtain a key to Lattimore's quarters and escaped through a window.[38]

Before he left the jail, Burley wrote a note to Lattimore: "I have gone out for a walk, perhaps (?) I will return shortly. B.G. Burley."[39]

Burley headed back to Canada and, from Windsor, sent a letter to Lattimore, asking him to return the books Burley had collected during his time in jail. After Burley sent Lattimore money to cover the shipping charges, Burley's prison library was sent to him in Canada.[40]

Burley then returned to Scotland, where he changed the spelling of his name to "Burleigh," which he considered to be the correct spelling, according to a biographer.[41] Another, unspoken, motivation could have been Burley's desire to disassociate himself from his previous career as a Confederate pirate and raider.

By the early 1870s, he was back in the U.S., working in Texas as a journalist for the Houston *Telegraph.* Burley also spent several years as a reporter for the New York *Sun* before continuing his journalism career on the other side of the Atlantic. Around 1882, he joined the staff of the London *Daily Telegraph* as a foreign correspondent.[42]

Covering the British invasion of Egypt in 1882, Burley quickly gained fame as a fearless and competitive war correspondent. Journalists in the Victorian era depended on telegraph wires to send their dispatches back to the home office. As a result, there was competition among correspondents to be the first to reach the nearest telegraph office. After observing a battle fought near the Suez Canal, Burley beat other correspondents to the local wire office, but had not yet finished his report. Calling on his competitive instincts, Burley persuaded the telegraph operator to copy and send the first chapter of the Book of Genesis over the wire while Burley wrote his dispatch, thereby blocking the telegraph from use by other correspondents. On another occasion, to prevent a competitor from joining in an interview with a dignitary traveling by train, Burley threw the correspondent's luggage off the train, forcing the other correspondent to disembark.[43]

As a correspondent with the British press corps, Burley also covered the Boer War in South Africa, the Russo-Japanese War and the Greco-Turkish War, among others. He became friends with Winston Churchill and Rudyard Kipling, who were also working as correspondents at the time.

Despite having little time for family life, Burley married three times and had ten children over forty years. Living into his late seventies, Burley died in London on June 17, 1914, just before the start of World War I. In an obituary, the London *Daily Telegraph* wrote that Burley "had probably seen more warfare than any other living man over the last fifty years."[44]

Capt. John Carter

Captain John Carter was forced to retire from the U.S. Navy in October 1864, the month after the Johnson's Island raid. When Carter sailed the USS *Michigan* as far as Detroit to search for the *Philo Parsons* the day after the raid, Navy Secretary Gideon Welles considered Carter to have violated his instructions to remain at Johnson's Island to guard against any follow-on attack.[45]

Although he was never court-martialed or otherwise disciplined, Carter was relieved of command, ending his career with the U.S. Navy. Carter's wife made efforts to have him restored to active duty, going so far as to hire an attorney. In June 1866, President Andrew Johnson agreed to meet personally with the former captain to hear his grievances. Following the meeting, Carter was restored to active duty and received an appointment as Light House Inspector for the 12th Naval District in northern California. Four years later, he was detached from the California inspector post and ordered to New York where he died on November 24, 1870, at age 66, while awaiting orders.[46]

Clement Clay

In early 1865, Clement Clay, one of the three Confederate Commissioners, left Toronto and went to Halifax, Nova Scotia, with plans to return to the South. He boarded a mail boat headed for Nassau and, from there, attempted to sail aboard a blockade runner to Wilmington, North Carolina. By that late stage of the war, however, the Union Naval blockade of the South made it almost impossible to reach Wilmington where Clay's original voyage to Canada had started nine months earlier. Aboard the blockade-runner *Rattlesnake,* Clay was forced to switch his destination to Charleston, South Carolina. The *Rattlesnake* encountered a violent storm and ran aground, leaving Clay to make his way to shore in a lifeboat. Clay eventually arrived in Macon, Georgia, where he was reunited with his wife.[47]

After learning that President Andrew Johnson had issued a proclamation in May 1865, offering a reward for the arrest and capture of the Confederate Commissioners, Clay turned himself in to Union Army officials in Georgia. He was arrested and imprisoned in Fort Monroe in Hampton, Virginia, until April 1866 when he was released. Clay returned to Alabama and attempted to resume his law practice but ill health interfered with his efforts to return to his former profession. He died in 1882 at age 65.[48]

Charles Cole

Following his arrest in Sandusky, Ohio, on September 19, 1864, the day of the planned raid on Johnson's Island, Cole was imprisoned at the Johnson's Island prison camp. At the time of his arrest, Cole named several Sandusky residents, mostly Copperheads, as co-conspirators in the raid plot. Cole's reputation for truth-telling was already tainted after his time spent in Sandusky before the raid posing as a wealthy oil baron.

After Union Army officials interrogated the suspects named by Cole, four were released, leaving only three remaining Sandusky residents and Cole under arrest. In June 1865, Cole appeared as a witness at the trial of two of the Sandusky residents. Cole's testimony was exposed by the defense attorneys as false and the jury returned a not guilty verdict for both men. In July, the Judge Advocate General of the Union Army determined that Cole should be tried as a spy by a military commission and he was transferred to Fort Lafayette, the same military prison in New York harbor where John Yates Beall had been held. No trial was ever conducted but Cole remained at Fort Lafayette until he was released in February 1866.[49]

After he was freed from Fort Lafayette, Cole drifted to Mexico and then went to Texas, where he reportedly went into the railroad business.[50]

Major General John A. Dix

In 1863, Major General John A. Dix was named president of the Union Pacific Railroad, a position he held even as he was also serving as commander of the Union Army's Department of the East, the administrative district covering New York, New Jersey, and New England. During his time at Union Pacific, Dix oversaw construction of the nation's first transcontinental railroad. After the war, Dix remained with Union Pacific until 1868. From 1866 to 1869, Dix served as the United States Minister to France in the administration of Andrew Johnson.

In 1872, Dix entered New York state politics when he was nominated to run for governor on the Republican ticket. He won the election, serving one term before he was defeated in his bid for reelection in 1874 by Democrat Samuel Tilden. In 1876, Dix ran unsuccessfully for the mayor of New York City. He died in 1879 at the age of eighty.[51]

Thomas Hines

When the Civil War ended in April 1865, Thomas Hines was in Canada, splitting his time between Toronto and Windsor just across the Detroit River from the city of Detroit. Two days after Lincoln was shot, Hines was spotted in Detroit and—because of his resemblance to John Wilkes Booth—was mistaken for the assassin who was the focus of a nationwide manhunt. With a crowd gathering to apprehend him, Hines escaped to the city's wharf area and forced a ferry captain at gunpoint to transport him across the river to Canada. Hines's adventure resulted in an erroneous report that Booth had escaped to Canada. Hines returned to Toronto and wrote to his wife in Kentucky, asking her to join him.[52]

On July 20, 1865, Hines returned to Detroit to take an oath of allegiance to the United States as part of an amnesty program for former Confederate soldiers and agents initiated by President Andrew Johnson. After being warned that U.S. officials still planned to arrest him despite his taking the oath, Hines remained in Toronto until May 1866. During his time in Canada, Hines enrolled at the University of Toronto to study French and literature.[53] He also began to study law under the guidance of Joshua Bullitt, the former Chief Justice of the Kentucky Court of Appeals (the state's highest court). Bullitt, a Confederate sympathizer, had fled to Canada in June 1865 after U.S. officials sought his capture and arrest. In March 1866, Hines and his wife returned to Kentucky where he passed the bar that June.[54]

Hines set up his law practice in Bowling Green, Kentucky. As he settled into the community, Hines remained aloof from other Confederate veterans and rarely spoke about his days with Morgan's cavalry and as a Confederate agent. He spent quiet evenings at home with his wife and children, often reading classics in French when he could obtain them.[55]

After years as a well-respected attorney, in 1878 Hines was elected to the Kentucky Court of Appeals and, in 1884 was elevated to serve as Chief Justice. He left the court in 1886 and returned to the practice of law in Frankfort, Kentucky. He died in 1898 at the age of fifty-nine.[56]

Commissary-General William Hoffman

In February 1865, near the end of the Civil War, Clara Barton, already famous for her nursing activities during the war, approached William Hoffman, the Union Army's Commissary General in charge of prisoners of war. Barton expressed concern about the number of soldiers who were unaccounted for. Many soldiers had been buried in unmarked graves on the battlefield or captured without any information provided to their families. Barton asked Hoffman for permission to go to Camp Parole in Annapolis, Maryland, where many former Union Army soldiers were being brought for care after their release from Confederate prisons. She proposed to conduct inquiries among the returning prisoners, asking them about missing soldiers and to deliver any news of the missing men to their families. Hoffman offered support for Barton's proposal and, as a result, helped establish what became the Missing Soldiers Office which Barton operated for the next four years. The office ultimately helped locate more than 20,000 missing Union Army soldiers.[57]

Hoffman, who by 1865 had been promoted to the rank of Brevet Brigadier General, then went west to serve as the commander of Fort Leavenworth in Kansas. In that position, Hoffman stirred controversy when he objected to efforts by some officers to organize one of the new regiments of Black soldiers serving during peacetime (regiments which later became known as the "Buffalo Soldiers"). Hoffman harassed the officers attempting to establish the new regiment with complaints and criticism, which ended in a public confrontation between Hoffman and the organizing officers on the parade fields of the fort. The new unit of Black soldiers was ultimately created and Hoffman retired from the military in 1870. He resettled in Rock Island, Illinois, and died there in 1884 at age seventy-six.[58]

James Holcombe

After the war, James Holcombe, one of the three Confederate Commissioners, started a school for boys on a six-hundred-acre farm he had purchased near Bellevue in Bedford County, Virginia. The school attracted students from prominent Southern families. The school's motto, authored by Holcombe, was "learn or leave." After a few years, however, enrollment decreased because of Holcombe's failing health and lack of business acumen. The school continued to operate until 1910. Holcombe died in 1873 at the age of fifty-three.[59]

Edwin Gray Lee

After leaving John Yates Beall and his team on the Chesapeake Bay in the summer of 1863, Edwin Gray Lee—a longtime friend of Beall and a relative of Robert E. Lee—took on a series of military assignments in Richmond and the Shenandoah Valley. He continued to be plagued by health problems, however, and in November 1864 requested leave from the Confederate military.[60] He planned to relocate in Canada where he hoped the dryer weather in the North would relieve some of his lung ailments, which were made worse by the hot, humid weather in the South.

In December 1864, Lee was assigned by Confederate Secretary of State Judah P. Benjamin to replace Jacob Thompson as the lead Confederate Commissioner, directing actions of the Confederate Secret Service originating in Canada. That same month, Lee and his wife boarded a blockade runner in Wilmington, North Carolina, and sailed for Canada.[61]

Lee was soon joined in Canada by his cousin Daniel Lucas, Beall's longtime friend who also wrote Beall's "memoir." As of late 1864, Lucas had also become part of the Confederate Secret Service. In February 1865, Lee and Lucas learned of Beall's death sentence. They took steps to achieve Beall's release, steps that included attempting to bribe guards at Fort Lafayette, Beall's place of incarceration, with Confederate gold. Ultimately, their efforts were unsuccessful. In 1890, Lee died of lung disease at the age of 34.

Martha O'Bryan

Following the death of John Yates Beall, his fiancée Martha O'Bryan dressed herself in mourning until the end of her life forty-five years later. In a pendant around her neck, she also kept a lock of Beall's hair taken from him the night before his hanging. At the end of the war, she returned to Nashville, Tennessee, and resumed her teaching career.[62]

She later retired from teaching and devoted her time to church and charity work in Nashville, focusing on the plight of the city's poor. In a one-horse surrey, she traveled Nashville's streets, collecting old clothes and food from fellow church members to distribute to the poor.[63]

After she died in 1910, her fellow church members founded a settlement house in her memory. It became a center for home-making instruction, childcare and Bible study.[64] Today, the Martha O'Bryan Center in Nashville continues to operate and serves over 15,000 children, youth and adults with food banks, community meals, and educational programs.[65]

George Sanders

In November 1865, after President Andrew Johnson issued a reward for his arrest, George Sanders, the Confederacy's unofficial "fourth commissioner" in Canada, fled to Europe. Rather than go into hiding, however, he became involved in schemes and plots by revolutionaries in Italy and France. In 1870, during the Prussian Army's siege of Paris, Sanders took an active role in aiding the city's defenders, designing a system of rifle pits and trenches.[66]

Sanders returned to the United States in 1872, reuniting with his family for the first time since he left for Canada in 1864.

At least one scholar credits Sanders with helping to discredit part of the legal case prosecuted by U.S. authorities against the Lincoln assassination conspirators—specifically, the claims that the assassination plot was initiated by Confederates in Canada with the knowledge of Confederate officials in Richmond. "As a result of Sanders' machinations, a series of the prosecution's witnesses were discredited, and then Sanders' rebel associates dispersed Confederate propaganda that further disproved any involvement," wrote Melinda Squires at Western Kentucky University. "Consequently, Sanders influenced a tragic event in American history by perpetuating the belief that the Confederacy had nothing to do with Lincoln's death."[67]

Sanders died of heart disease in New York City in August 1873 at the age of sixty-one.[68]

Jacob Thompson

In January 1865, Jacob Thompson, the lead Confederate Commissioner, received word from the Confederate leadership in Richmond that his services in Toronto were no longer needed, in part because, by then, his role and activities in Canada were under close watch by Union agents. A letter from Confederate Secretary of State Judah Benjamin informed Thompson, "We are satisfied that so close an espionage is kept upon you that your services have been deprived of the value which we attached to your further residence in Canada."[69]

In April 1865, Thompson and his wife sailed to Europe where they spent the next several years living in London and Paris. In late 1869 or 1870, Thompson returned to his home in Oxford, Mississippi, and discovered that it had been destroyed by the Union Army in 1864, after having been used for a time as a military hospital. He and his wife then moved to Memphis, Tennessee, where he became a wealthy businessman. He served as a trustee of the University of the South in Sewanee, Tennessee. He died in March 1885 at the age of seventy-four.[70]

Clement Vallandigham

After the Civil War, Clement Vallandigham became active as a leader of the Democratic Party in Ohio, serving as chairman of the state Democratic Party's convention in 1865. While opposing most Reconstruction policies of the Republicans, Vallandigham promoted the so-called "New Departure" efforts of the Democratic Party in the northern states, which called for the end of slavery and equal rights for Blacks. In 1868, he ran an unsuccessful race in Ohio for a U.S. Senate seat and in 1870 he ran unsuccessfully for the U.S. House of Representatives.[71]

Vallandigham returned to the practice of law but his life was cut short in a bizarre accident. In 1871, while serving as a defense counsel for a murder suspect, the fifty-year-old Vallandigham attempted to enact for his defense team what he planned to demonstrate to the jury the following day. He would argue that the murder victim, in fact, accidentally shot himself when he drew a pistol from his pocket while rising from a kneeling position. Vallandigham picked up a pistol he believed to be unloaded and proceeded to act out the events as he thought they had transpired. As he drew the gun from his pocket, it snagged on his coat and discharged a bullet into his stomach. He was fatally wounded and died the next day. With Vallandigham's unfortunate accident proving his theory of the case, his client, the murder suspect, was acquitted by the jury and released.[72]

Johnson's Island

News of the surrender of Confederate General Robert E. Lee at Appomattox Court House in Virginia on April 9, 1865, reached Sandusky, Ohio, later that day. Rebels on Johnson's Island could hear the city's church bells ringing and bands playing in celebration of the surrender. The next day, two hundred guns were fired across the prison yard to commemorate the Union Army's victory. A U.S. flag was raised and cheered by the prisoners in Blockhouse No. 1 which housed those who had taken the oath of allegiance to support the Union. Other prisoners hissed.[73] When the war ended in April 1865, there were 2,806 prisoners held on Johnson's Island.[74] Within a month, all but thirty-five of the rebels at the prison had taken the oath.[75]

Over the next several months, the prison population steadily declined as prisoners were released. Beginning in late 1864, as both sides understood the end of the war was approaching, Union and Confederate officials agreed to start releasing prisoners who were injured, ill or otherwise unlikely to return to active duty within a six-month period.[76] On July 20, 1865, President Andrew Johnson called for the immediate release of all Confederate prisoners remaining in Union Army prisons.[77] In July 1865, the Johnson's Island prison population stood at 119. By August, just seven prisoners remained on the island.[78]

On September 1, 1865, Commissary General William Hoffman ordered the few remaining prisoners on Johnson's Island to be transferred to Fort Lafayette in New York Harbor. Among them was Charles H. Cole, who had been arrested for his involvement in the September 1864 raid. Over the next several months, advertisements in the Sandusky *Register* announced auctions of government property at the prison, with tools, kitchen equipment, furniture, and building materials offered for sale. The owner of the island, Leonard B. Johnson, purchased most of the prison buildings. By June 1866, the prison was abandoned. The remaining guards and Union troops on duty were transferred to Columbus, Ohio.[79]

Today, Johnson's Island is considered a prime vacation spot on Lake Erie. A two-lane bridge now links the island to the mainland. Summer homes owned by residents of cities in the area—Detroit, Toledo and Cleveland—ring the island's shoreline. Commercial establishments are few. A small marina with dockage for pleasure boats occupies a spot near the center of the island, once the location of a limestone quarry that began after the Civil War.

All that remains of the former prison site is a tree-shrouded cemetery with a grassy lawn surrounded by a tall wrought-iron fence, painted black. Administered by the Department of Veterans Affairs and the Ohio Western Reserve National Cemetery, the cemetery contains 206 graves of Confederate soldiers who died during their imprisonment. Marble head stones, spaced in neat rows, mark each grave. A nineteen-foot statue of a Confederate soldier, named "The Lookout," stands at the cemetery's entrance gate. Placed there in 1910 by the United Daughters of the Confederacy, the stone soldier grips a bayonetted rifle in his right hand. His left hand is raised to his forehead, shielding his eyes from the sun, as he looks toward the South.[80]

Chapter Notes

ABBREVIATIONS

OR   U.S. War Department. *The War of the Rebellion: A Compilation of the Official Records of the Union and Confederate Armies*. Washington, D.C.: Government Printing Office, 1880–1901.

ORN   United States Department of the Navy. *Official Records of the Union and Confederate Navies in the War of the Rebellion*. Washington, D.C.: Government Printing Office, 1894–1927.

Chapter 1

1. Barbara Yocum, "Fort Jay: Historic Structure Report," Governors Island National Monument, National Parks of New York Harbor (National Park Service, 2005), p. xix.
2. *The New York Times*, February 25, 1865.
3. *The War of the Rebellion: A Compilation of the Official Records of the Union and Confederate Armies* (Washington, D.C.: Government Printing Office, 1880–1901), Ser. 2, Vol. 8, pp. 998, 1000. Hereinafter cited as OR, followed by the series number, volume number, and page number.
4. *Trial of John Y. Beall as a Spy and Guerrillero by Military Commission* (New York: D. Appleton, 1865), p. 94.
5. Upon the death of Beall's father, George Brook Beall, in 1855, ownership of the family's slaves was divided among the surviving family members, according to George Beall's will, although it appears the slaves remained at the family plantation. https://www.ancestry.com/-discoveryui-content/view/532474:9087?tid; accessed July 25, 2022; Slave Schedule, 1850 U.S. Federal Census, George B. Beall; https://search.ancestry.com/cgi-bin/sse.dll?_phsrc=nHH28&_phstart=successSource&usePUBJs=true&indiv=1&dbid=8055&gsfn=George&gsln=Beall&_83004003-n_xcl=f&msrpn__ftp=charles%20town,%20jefferson,%20west%20virginia,%20usa&msrpn=24681&_80100003=Beall&new=1&rank=1&uidh=6g2&redir=false&msT=1&gss=angs-d&pcat=35&fh=0&h=92811127&recoff=&ml_rpos=1&queryId=2ce962a6a1178b17ee00912efcafff3b; accessed July 24, 2022; Slave Schedule, 1860 U.S. Federal Census, John Yates Beall, https://www.ancestry.com/imageviewer/collections/7668/images/vam653_1392-0323?treeid=&personid=&hintid=&queryId=341945742bdbfe1af2e31a51f439329c&usePUB=t rue&_phsrc=nHH36&_phstart=successSource&usePUBJs=true&pId=91145079; accessed July 25, 2022; Cameron S. Moseley, *John Yates Beall: Confederate Commando* (Great Falls, VA: Clan Bell International, 2011), pp. 2–5.
6. Daniel Lucas, *Memoir of John Yates Beall: His Life; Trial; Correspondence; Diary and Private Manuscript Found Among His Papers, Including His Own Account of the Raid on Lake Erie* (Montreal: John Lovell, 1865), p. 2.
7. Moseley, *John Yates Beall: Confederate Commando*, p. 2; Cassandra Luca, "A History of the Land, Labor, and People of the Dumbarton Oaks Estate Until 1920" (June–August 2019); chrome-extension://efaidnbmnnnibpcajpcglclefindmkaj/https://www.doaks.org/research/garden-landscape/summer-internship-program/luca-2019-gls-intern-report.pdf; accessed July 24, 2022.
8. Moseley, *John Yates Beall: Confederate Commando*, p. 3; Lucas, *Memoir of John Yates Beall*, pp. 3, 5–6.
9. Lucas, *Memoir of John Yates Beall*, pp. 4–5.
10. *Ibid.*, p. 7.
11. Thomas Hines, "The Northwestern Conspiracy," *Southern Bivouac* 2 (1886), p. 702.
12. Lucas, *Memoir of John Yates Beall*, p. 76.
13. *Ibid.*
14. *Ibid.*, p. 67.
15. *Ibid.*, p. 78.
16. *Ibid.*
17. *The Tennessean*, February 5, 1950.
18. *The New York Times*, February 25, 1865.

Chapter 2

1. Chad Fraser, *Lake Erie Stories: Struggle and Survival on a Freshwater Ocean* (Toronto: Dundurn, 2008), p. 98.

2. Thomas Watson Jernigan, "Death at Elmira, William Hoffman and the Union Prison System" (M.A. thesis, East Tennessee State University, 2005), p. 33.

3. OR, Ser. 2, Vol. 3, p. 8; Guy Gugliotta, *Freedom's Cap* (New York: Hill and Wang, 2012), pp. 145–146.

4. Jernigan, *Death at Elmira*, p. 31.

5. *Ibid.*, p. 32.

6. OR, Ser. 2, Vol. 3, p. 8.

7. W.W. Williams, *History of the Firelands, Comprising Huron and Erie Counties, Ohio* (Cleveland: Press Leader Printing Co., 1879), pp. 436–437.

8. Sandusky *Daily Commercial Register*, October 1, 1861.

9. *Ibid.*

10. "Lost to the Lake: Story of the Island Queen," accessed June 14, 2014, http://www.lakeeffectliving.com/Jun14/Shipwrecks-Island_Queen.html.

11. OR, Ser. 2, Vol. 3, p. 54.

12. *Ibid.*

13. *Ibid.*

14. *Ibid.*, p. 55.

15. Phillip B. Shriver and Donald J. Breen, *Ohio's Military Prisons in the Civil War* (Columbus: Ohio State University Press 1964), p. 29.

16. OR, Ser. 2, Vol. 3, p. 56.

17. *Ibid.*

18. *Ibid.*, p. 55.

19. *Ibid.*, pp. 122–123.

20. Terry Alford, *Fortunes Fool: The Life of John Wilkes Booth* (Oxford: Oxford University Press, 2015), p. 70.

21. Moseley, *John Yates Beall: Confederate Commando*, p. 7; Alford, *Fortune's Fool*, p. 75.

22. Moseley, *John Yates Beall: Confederate Commando*, p. 8.

23. Lucas, *Memoir of John Yates Beall*, p. 13.

24. *Ibid.*, p. 14.

25. *Ibid.*

Chapter 3

1. Harold Mytum and Gilly Carr, eds., *Prisoners of War: Archeology, Memory, and Heritage of 19th and 20th Century Mass Internment* (New York: Springer Science and Business Media, 2013), p. 62.

2. Leslie Gene Hunter, "Warden for the Union: General William Hoffman" (PhD diss., University of Arizona, 1971), pp. 25–26.

3. Mytum and Carr, eds., *Prisoners of War*, p. 63.

4. OR, Ser. 2, Vol. 3, p. 58.

5. Charles E. Frohman, *Rebels on Lake Erie* (Columbus: Ohio Historical Society, 1965), p. 2.

6. Mytum and Carr, eds., *Prisoners of War*, p. 64.

7. *Ibid.*; Hunter, "Warden for the Union," p. 38.

8. Mytum and Carr, eds., *Prisoners of War*, p. 64.

9. *Ibid.*

10. *Ibid.*

11. David R. Bush, Alan C. Tonetti, and Ed Bearss, National Historic Landmark Nomination Submitted to U.S. Department of the Interior, National Park Service, National Register of Historic Places Registration Form, "Johnson's Island Civil War Prison," January 1990; OR, Ser. 2, Vol. 3, pp. 57–58; Frohman, *Rebels on Lake Erie*, pp. 3–5; Shriver and Breen, *Ohio's Military Prisons*, p. 30.

12. Mytum and Carr, eds., *Prisoners of War*, p. 62.

13. Roger Long, "Johnson's Island Prison," *Blue and Gray* 4, no. 4 (February–March 1987), p. 11.

14. Ron Davidson, *Images of America, Sandusky Ohio* (Mount Pleasant, SC: Arcadia, 2002), p. 17.

15. Frohman, *Rebels on Lake Erie*, p. 4; Roger Pickenpaugh, *Captives in Gray* (Tuscaloosa: University of Alabama Press, 2009), p. 5.

16. Hunter, "Warden for the Union," p. 3.

17. *Ibid.*, p. 13.

18. OR, Ser. 2, Vol. 3, p. 129.

19. *Ibid.*, p. 123.

20. *Ibid.*, p. 124; Fraser, *Lake Erie Stories*, p. 100.

21. OR, Ser. 2, Vol. 3, p. 171.

22. Long, "Johnson's Island Prison," p. 13.

23. Pickenpaugh, *Captives in Gray*, p. 5.

24. OR, Ser. 2, Vol. 3, p. 163.

25. Pickenpaugh, *Captives in Gray*, p. 5; Frohman, *Rebels on Lake Erie*, p. 6.

26. Frohman, *Rebels on Lake Erie*, p. 4.

27. OR, Ser. 2, Vol. 3, p. 317.

28. *Ibid.*

29. Hunter, "Warden for the Union," p. 42.

30. Bruce Catton, *Grant Moves South* (Boston: Little, Brown, 1960), p. 175.

31. *Ibid.*, p. 176.

32. Hunter, "Warden for the Union," p. 40.

33. "Harpers Ferry During the Civil War," Encyclopedia Virginia, https://encyclopediavirginia.org/entries/harpers-ferry-during-the-civil-war/; accessed July 14, 2015.

34. Moseley, *Confederate Commando*, p. 8.

35. *Ibid.*; *Biographical Souvenir of the States of Georgia and Florida* (Chicago: F.A. Battey & Co., 1889), p. 851, https://babel.hathitrust.org/cgi/pt?id=wu.89072984412&view=1up&seq=13.

36. Moseley, *Confederate Commando*, p. 8; Lucas, *Memoir of John Yates Beall*, p. 14.

37. *The Tennessean*, February 5, 1950; *National Register of Historic Places Registration Form, George O'Bryan House, Nashville, Tenn.* (U.S. Department of the Interior, January 24, 1989).

38. Moseley, *Confederate Commando*, p. 8; Lucas, *Memoir of John Yates Beall*, p. 15.

39. Moseley, *Confederate Commando*, p. 8; *The Tennessean*, February 5, 1950.

40. Lucas, *Memoir of John Yates Beall*, pp. 16–17.

41. *Ibid.*, p. 6.

42. *Ibid.*, pp. 6–7.

Chapter 4

1. Frohman, *Rebels on Lake Erie*, p. 7.

2. Sandusky *Daily Commercial Register*, April 11, 1862.

3. *Ibid.*

4. *Ibid.*

5. OR, Ser. 2, Vol. 3, p. 384.

6. Frohman, *Rebels on Lake Erie*, p. 7.

7. OR, Ser. 2, Vol. 3, p. 448.

8. Mytum and Carr, eds., *Prisoners of War*, p. 66.

9. Roger Pickenpaugh, *Johnson's Island* (Kent: Kent State University Press, 2016), p. 11.

10. *Ibid.*, p. 12.

11. Mytum and Carr, eds., *Prisoners of War*, p. 65.

12. Frohman, *Rebels on Lake Erie*, p. 11.

13. OR, Ser. 2, Vol. 3, pp. 479–480.

14. OR, Ser. 2, Vol. 4, p. 42.

15. *Ibid.*

16. Moseley, *Confederate Commando*, pp. 8–9.

17. Dubuque County Genealogy, "Cascade Shelters a Confederate Spy, Extracted from 1834–1984: Cascade Iowa, First 150 Years," http://sites.rootsweb.com/~iadubuqu/civilwar/cwspy.html, accessed December 13, 2015.

18. Interview with S. Keyron McDermott, August 30, 2017 (McDermott is a Cascade resident who has researched Beall's time in Cascade and written a theatrical play about it, *The True Story of John Yates Beall*).

19. Jennifer L. Weber, *Copperheads: The Rise and Fall of Lincoln's Opponents in the North* (New York: Oxford University Press, 2006), p. 48.

20. *Ibid.*, p. 22.

21. Lucas, *Memoir of John Yates Beall*, p. 254.

Chapter 5

1. OR, Ser. 2, Vol. 8, p. 986.

2. Sandusky *Daily Commercial Register*, June 26, 1862.

3. Pickenpaugh, *Captives in Gray*, p. 100.

4. *Ibid.*

5. Frohman, *Rebels on Lake Erie*, p. 15.

6. *Ibid.*

7. Pickenpaugh, *Johnson's Island*, p. 46.

8. Long, "Johnson's Island Prison," p. 16.

9. Pickenpaugh, *Johnson's Island*, p. 15.

10. Long, "Johnson's Island Prison," p. 16.

11. Shriver and Breen, *Ohio's Military Prisons*, p. 34

12. Frohman, *Rebels on Lake Erie*, p. 15.

13. Professor David Bush, Heidelberg University, Johnson's Island Dig, Field Report 4, July 1, 2006.

14. Frohman, *Rebels on Lake Erie*, p. 15.

15. Shriver and Breen, *Ohio's Military Prisons*, p. 33.

16. Pickenpaugh, *Captives in Gray*, p. 109.

17. Pickenpaugh, *Johnson's Island*, p. 49.

18. Long, "Johnson's Island Prison," p. 20

19. Shriver and Breen, *Ohio's Military Prisons*, p. 37.

20. Pickenpaugh, *Johnson's Island*, p. 56; Robert C. Crouch, "Picture Made on Johnson's Island," *Confederate Veteran* XVII (1909), pp. 28–29.

21. Jernigan, *Death at Elmira*, p. 27.

22. William Best Hesseltine, *Civil War Prisons* (New York: Ungar, 1930) pp. 14–17; Jernigan, *Death at Elmira*, p. 37.

23. Pickenpaugh, *Captives in Gray*, p. 46.

24. OR, Ser. 2, Vol. 3, p. 157.

25. Jernigan, *Death at Elmira*, p. 27.

26. Hesseltine, *Civil War Prisons*, p. 25.

27. *The New York Times*, July 9, 1862.

28. OR, Ser. 2, Vol. 4, p. 174.

29. John A. Dix, *Memoirs of John Adams Dix* (New York: Harper & Brothers, 1883), Vol. I, p. 371.

30. Hal Bridges, "D.H. Hill's Anti-Yankee Algebra," *The Journal of Southern History* 22 (May 1956), pp. 220–222.

31. OR, Ser. 2, Vol. 4, pp. 265–268.

32. *Ibid.*

33. Pickenpaugh, *Captives in Gray*, p. 49.

34. Pickenpaugh, *Johnson's Island*, pp. 24, 27; OR, Ser. 2, Vol. 8, p. 987.

Chapter 6

1. Moseley, *Confederate Commando*, p. 9; Lucas, *Memoir of John Yates Beall*, pp. 18, 264.

2. Robin Winks, *The Civil War Years: Canada and the United States* (Montreal: McGill-Queen's University Press, 1998), p. 141.

3. *Ibid.*, p. 2.

4. *Ibid.*, p. 133.

5. *Ibid.*, pp. 135–136.

6. Lucas, *Memoir of John Yates Beall*, pp. 17–18.

7. Barry Sheehy, *Montreal, City of Secrets* (Montreal: Baraka Books, 2017), p. 45.

8. *Ibid.*, p. 25.

9. Alford, *Fortune's Fool*, pp. 185–186.

10. "St. Lawrence Hall: Higgins & Cooper Proprietors, Montreal, 1898," Advertisement, https://archive.org/details/cihm_44387/page/n3/mode/2up; accessed September 9, 2017.

11. Adam Mayers, *Dixie & the Dominion: Canada, the Confederacy and the War for the Union* (Toronto: Dundurn, 2003), p. 39.

12. Winks, *The Civil War Years*, p. 1.

13. Sheehy, *Montreal, City of Secrets*, p. 37.

14. Winks, *The Civil War Years*, p. 7.

15. Sheehy, *Montreal, City of Secrets*, p. 32.

16. Mayers, *Dixie & The Dominion*, p. 53.

17. Winks, *The Civil War Years*, pp. 23–24.

18. *Ibid.*, p. 28.

19. *Ibid.*, p. 70.

20. Nathaniel Philbrick, *Sea of Glory: America's Voyage of Discovery, the U.S. Exploring Expedition* (London: Penguin Random House, 2003), pp. xvi, xxiii, 281–282.

21. Sheehy, *Montreal, City of Secrets*, p. 41; Winks, *The Civil War Years*, p. 98.

John Bell, *Rebels on the Great Lakes* (Toronto: Dundurn, 2011), p. 12.

22. *Ibid.*

Chapter 7

1. Encyclopedia Virginia, "Richmond During the Civil War," https://www.encyclopediavirginia.org/Richmond_During_the_Civil_War; accessed February 13, 2017.

2. Lucas, *Memoir of John Yates Beall*, pp. 19–20, 288.

3. Alexandra Lee Levin, *This Awful Drama: General Edwin Gray Lee, C.S. A. and His Family* (New York: Vantage Press, 1987), p. 60.

4. *Ibid.*

5. Moseley, *Confederate Commando*, p. 11.

6. Ernest B. Furgurson, *Ashes of Glory: Richmond at War* (New York: Vintage, 1997), p. 90.

7. Lucas, *Memoir of John Yates Beall*, pp. 19–20.

8. Thomas R. Campbell, *Fire and Thunder: Exploits of the Confederate States Navy* (Shippensburg, PA: Burd Street Press, 1997), p. 1; William Morrison Robinson, Jr., *The Confederate Privateers* (New Haven: Yale University Press, 1928), p. 13.

9. David J. Murphy, "Naval Strategy During the American Civil War," Air War College, Air University, Research Report (Maxwell Air Force Base, Alabama, 1999), pp. 23–26; accessed March 6, 2017, chrome-extension://efaidnbmnnnibpcajpcglclefindmkaj/https://apps.dtic.mil/sti/pdfs/ADA395177.pdf.

10. Beall's plan was similar to a proposal made to Davis just a few weeks earlier by William H. Murdaugh, an ambitious young officer in the Confederate Navy. Murdaugh was a member of the James River Squadron, a motley collection of converted tugboats and other watercraft charged with protecting Richmond from attack by Union ships. Murdaugh's plan did not include a release of prisoners on Johnson's Island but it did contemplate a raid from Canada and capturing the USS *Michigan*, then docked at Erie, Pennsylvania. The Confederate-controlled *Michigan* would then embark on a voyage of destruction up and down the Great Lakes, bombarding cities and destroying locks and canals to impose maximum damage on Great Lakes commerce. ORN, Ser. 1, Vol. 2, pp. 828–830.

11. Lucas, *Memoir of John Yates Beall*, pp. 19–20.

12. *Ibid.*; ORN, Ser. 1, Vol. 2, pp. 828–830.

13. ORN, Ser. 1, Vol. 2, pp. 828–830.

14. Moseley, *Confederate Commando*, p. 11.

Chapter 8

1. Clement Laird Vallandigham, "The Constitution—Peace—Reunion," Appendix, *Congressional Globe: Containing the Speeches, Important State Papers and the Laws of the Third Session Thirty-seventh Congress*, edited by John C. Rives (Washington, D.C.: Globe Office, 1863), pp. 52–60.

2. James D. Horan, *Confederate Agent* (Allentown, PA: The Fairfax Press, 1954), p. 18.

3. Frank Abail Flowers, *Edwin McMasters Stanton, the Autocrat of Rebellion, Emancipation and Reconstruction* (Boston: George M. Smith & Co., 1905), p. 252.

4. Spencer C. Tucker, ed., *American Civil War: The Definitive Encyclopedia and Document Collection* (Santa Barbara: ABC-CLIO, 2013), p. 2465.

5. Weber, *Copperheads*, p. 3.

6. Wood Gray, *The Hidden Civil War: The Story of the Copperheads* (New York: Viking Press, 1942), pp. 140–141.

7. Weber, *Copperheads*, pp. 17–18, 27–28.

8. *Ibid.*

9. *Ibid.*

10. *Ibid.*, pp. 81–82.

11. *Ibid.*, p. 63.

12. *Ibid.*

13. Stephen W. Sears, *Landscape Turned Red: The Battle of Antietam* (Boston: Ticknor & Fields, 1983), pp. 294–296.

14. Weber, *Copperheads*, p.63.

15. *Ibid.*

16. *Ibid.*, p. 80.

17. Gray, *The Hidden Civil War*, p. 90.

18. *Ibid.*

19. *Ibid.* p. 99.

20. *Ibid.*, p. 100.

21. Weber, *Copperheads*, p. 51.

22. *Ibid.*, p. 53.

23. OR, Ser. 3, Vol. 2, pp. 321–322.

24. Weber, *Copperheads*, p. 53.

25. *Ibid.*; Gray, *Hidden Civil War*, p. 88.

26. James Patrick Morgans, *John Todd and the Underground Railroad: Biography of an Iowa Abolitionist* (Jefferson, NC: McFarland, 2006), p. 180.

27. Gray, *Hidden Civil War*, p. 132.

28. Weber, *Copperheads*, p. 103.

29. *The New York Times*, May 13, 2013.

30. Geoffrey R. Stone, *Perilous Times: Free Speech in Wartime* (New York: W.W. Norton, 2004), p. 101.

31. *Ibid.*; *The Fremont Journal* (Ohio), May 8, 1863; *The Daily Ohio Statesman* (Columbus), May 7, 1863.

32. *The Daily Ohio Statesman* (Columbus), May 7, 1863; Stone, *Perilous Times*, p. 106.

33. Stone, *Perilous Times*, p. 101; *The New York Times*, May 13, 2013.

34. Stone, *Perilous Times*, pp. 108–109.

35. Weber, *Copperheads*, p. 104.

36. Stone, *Perilous Times*, p. 109; *The New York Times*, May 13, 2013.

37. Dickenson College Civil War Research Engine, "In Tennessee, exiled U.S. Congressman Clement Vallandigham is delivered to the Confederate lines," https://hd.housedivided.dickinson.edu/node/39579.

38. Stone, *Perilous Times*, p. 118.

39. Mayers, *Dixie & the Dominion*, p. 42.

40. Weber, *Copperheads*, p. 118.

41. Gray, *Hidden Civil War*, pp. 151–153.

Chapter 9

1. ORN, Ser. 1, Vol. 4, pp. 420, 430.
2. Lucas, *Memoir of John Yates Beall,* p. 23.
3. David A. Sutherland, "Wood, John Taylor," in *Dictionary of Canadian Biography,* Vol. 13 (University of Toronto/Université Laval, 2003), http://www.biographi.ca/en/bio/wood_john_taylor_13E.html; accessed August 5, 2019.
4. Levin, *This Awful Drama,* p. 61.
5. *Ibid.*
6. Moseley, *Confederate Commando,* p. 12.
7. W.W. Baker, *Memoirs of Service with John Yates Beall* (Richmond: The Richmond Press, 1910), p. 16.
8. *Ibid.*
9. *Ibid.*, pp. 15–16.
10. *Ibid.*, p. 16.
11. Lucas, *Memoir of John Yates Beall,* p. 21.
12. *Ibid.*
13. *Ibid.*
14. *Ibid.*, pp. 21–22.
15. Levin, *This Awful Drama,* p. 62.
16. Eric Mills, *Chesapeake Bay in the Civil War* (Centreville, MD: Tidewater, 1996), p. 215; Levin, *This Awful Drama,* p. 62.
17. Eric Foner, *Reconstruction: America's Unfinished Revolution* (New York: Harper Perennial Modern Classics, 1988), pp. 7–8.
18. Levin, *This Awful Drama,* p. 63; Moseley, *Confederate Commando,* p. 14.
19. Matthew Ostergaard Krogh, "The Eastern Shore of Virginia in the Civil War" (Master of Arts thesis, Virginia Polytechnic Institute and State University, 2006), p. 66.
20. Lucas, *Memoir of John Yates Beall,* p. 24.
21. *Ibid.*, pp. 24–25; Moseley, *Confederate Commando,* p. 15.
22. Lucas, *Memoir of John Yates Beall,* p. 25; Mills, *Chesapeake Bay in the Civil War,* p. 215; The names are perhaps a reference to the Aesop's fable about the black raven who saw a white swan in a pond and, hoping to change his black feathers to white like the swan's, jumped into the pond but soon died because he did not know how to feed himself by catching fish.
23. Baker, *Memoirs of Service,* p. 18.
24. *Ibid.*, pp. 19–20; Lucas, *Memoir of John Yates Beall,* pp. 25–26.
25. Mills, *Chesapeake Bay in the Civil War,* p. 218.
26. John Pelzer and Linda Pelzer, "The Ghost of the Chesapeake," *Civil War Times Illustrated* 26 (1987), pp. 38–43.
27. Mills, *Chesapeake Bay in the Civil War,* p. 219; Baker, *Memoirs of Service,* p. 18.
28. Mills, *Chesapeake Bay in the Civil War,* p. 219; Lucas, *Memoir of John Yates Beall,* p. 27; "Bay Attacks Spark Wistar's Raid," Hampton Roads *Daily Press,* October 5, 2013.
29. "An Extensive Raid in Matthews County—Another Instance of Yankee Atrocity," *Richmond Enquirer,* October 16, 1863; Pelzer and Pelzer, "The Ghost of the Chesapeake," p. 41.

30. Mills, *Chesapeake Bay,* p. 218.
31. Baker, *Memoir of John Yates Beall,* p. 26.
32. *Ibid.*
33. Mills, *Chesapeake Bay in the Civil War,* p. 220.
34. *Baltimore Sun,* February 28, 1885, p. 5.
35. F. Lauriston Bullard, *Famous War Correspondents* (Boston: Little, Brown, 1914), p. 193; https://archive.org/details/famouswarcorresp00bulluoft/mode/1up?ref=ol&view=theater.
36. Baker, *Memoirs of Service,* pp. 27–28; Mills, *Chesapeake Bay,* p. 219.
37. Richmond *Daily Dispatch,* October 16, 1863.
38. *Ibid.*
39. Baker, *Memoirs of Service,* p. 29.
40. *Ibid.*
41. *Ibid.*, p. 31; Mills, *Chesapeake Bay in the Civil War,* p. 221.
42. Lucas, *Memoir of John Yates Beall,* p. 28, Baker, *Memoirs of Service,* p. 31.
43. *Richmond Enquirer,* February 26, 1864.
44. *Ibid.*
45. *Ibid.*
46. *Ibid.*
47. *Ibid.*
48. OR Ser. 1, Vol. 29, Part 1, pp. 639–640.

Chapter 10

1. Pickenpaugh, *Johnson's Island,* p. 39; OR, Ser. 2, Vol. 8, p. 991.
2. Frohman, *Rebels on Lake Erie,* p. 15.
3. Pickenpaugh, *Johnson's Island,* p. 39.
4. OR, Ser. 2, Vol. 8, pp. 987–91.
5. *Ibid.*
6. Pickenpaugh, *Johnson's Island,* pp. 28, 31.
7. OR, Ser. 2, Vol. 5, pp. 940–41.
8. *The New York Herald,* August 2, 1863.
9. Hesseltine, *Civil War Prisons,* pp. 114–125; Lonnie R. Speer, *Portals to Hell: Military Prisons of the Civil War* (Mechanicsburg, PA: Stackpole Books, 1997), pp. 119–126.
10. OR, Ser. 2, Vol. 5, p. 487.
11. Pickenpaugh, *Johnson Island,* p. 29.
12. Frohman, *Rebels on Lake Erie,* p. 15.
13. Pickenpaugh, *Johnson's Island,* p. 52.
14. Although this anecdote is reported in several prisoner diaries, the three dollar amount charged seems excessive. Adjusted for inflation, the value of three dollars in 1864 is equal to approximately ninety dollars today.
15. Pickenpaugh, *Johnson's Island,* p. 53.
16. OR, Ser. 2, Vol. 6, p. 161.
17. *Ibid.*, pp 192–193.
18. *Ibid.*, p. 330.
19. Pickenpaugh, *Johnson's Island,* p. 91; Shriver and Breen, *Ohio's Military Prisons,* p. 37.
20. ORN, Ser. 1, Vol. 2, pp. 478–479.
21. Herbert Reynolds Spencer, USS *Michigan* (The Erie Book Store, 1966), p. 23; Steven Selenfriend and Ted Myers, "The Iron Lady of Erie," American Society of Arms Collectors, Saratoga Springs, N.Y., *Bulletin* No. 79 (Fall 1998),p. 41, chrome-exten

sion://efaidnbmnnnibpcajpcglclefindmkaj/https://
americansocietyofarmscollectors.org/wp-content/
uploads/2019/06/1998-B79-The-Iron-Lady-of-Erie.
pdf.

22. ORN, Ser. 1, Vol. 2, pp. 474, 478–479; OR,
Ser. 2, Vol. 6, p. 435.

23. ORN, Ser. 1, Vol. 2, pp. 822–827.

24. *Ibid.*

25. J. Wilkinson, *The Narrative of a Blockade-
Runner* (New York: Sheldon & Company, 1877), p.
184, https://archive.org/details/narrativeofblock
0000wilk.

26. ORN, Ser. 1, Vol. 2, p. 474.

27. ORN, Ser. 1, Vol. 2, p. 825.

28. Winks, *The Civil War Years*, pp. 146–147.

29. OR, Ser. 3, Vol. 3, pp. 1013–1015. Bell, *Rebels
on the Great Lakes*, p. 36.

30. ORN, Ser. 1, Vol. 2, p. 496.

31. OR, Ser. 2, Vol. 6, p. 500.

32. Letter from William F. Hoffman to Edwin
Stanton, December 3, 1863, NARA, Record Group
249.

33. ORN, Ser. 1, Vol. 2, p. 508.

34. Horace Carpenter, "Plain Living at Johnson's Island," *The Century Illustrated Monthly
Magazine* XLI (November 1890–April 1891), p. 711.

35. *Ibid.*

36. Long, "Johnson's Island Prison," p. 15.

37. Pickenpaugh, *Johnson's Island*, p. 65.

38. OR, Ser. 2, Vol. 8, pp. 986–1003.

39. Pickenpaugh, *Johnson's Island*, p. 68.

40. *Ibid.*, pp. 69–70.

41. Henry E. Shepherd, *Narrative of Prison Life
at Baltimore and Johnson's Island Ohio*, 1917, University of North Carolina, electronic edition, 1998,
p. 10; https://docsouth.unc.edu/fpn/shepherd/
shepherd.html.

42. *Ibid.*, p. 16.

43. Carpenter, "Plain Living," p. 710.

44. Pickenpaugh, *Johnson's Island*, p. 90.

45. *Ibid.*

46. OR, Ser. 2, Vol. 8, p. 994.

Chapter 11

1. The Richmond *Daily Dispatch*, January 6,
1864.

2. Thomas Hines, "The Northwestern Conspiracy," p. 438. This multi-part article appeared under
the byline of Thomas Hines but it was apparently
written by John B. Castleman, a member of Morgan's raiders who went to Canada and worked
with Thompson and Hines. In his own account
of his exploits during and after the war, Castleman explains that Hines asked him to write the
Southern Bivouac article for him. John Breckinridge Castleman, *Active Service in the Confederacy
and Spanish War* (Louisville: Courier Journal Job
Printing Co., 1917), p. 137.

3. *Ibid.*

4. John C. Waugh, *Re-Electing Lincoln* (Boston:
Da Capo Press, 1997), p. 149.

5. Winks, *The Civil War Years*, p. 265.

6. *Ibid.*

7. John G. Nicolay and John Hay, eds., *Abraham
Lincoln: Complete Works, Comprising His Speeches,
Letter, State Papers, and Miscellaneous Writings*, Vol.
II (New York: The Century Company, 1894), p. 39.

8. Clint Johnson, *A Vast and Fiendish Plot* (New
York: Citadel Press, 2010), p. 115.

9. Weber, *Copperheads*, pp. 79–80.

10. Stephen Z. Starr, *Colonel Grenfell's Wars*
(Baton Rouge: Louisiana State University Press,
1971), p. 146.

11. Weber, *Copperheads*, p. 124.

12. *Ibid.*

13. *Ibid.*, p. 118.

14. Hines, "The Northwestern Conspiracy," p. 440

15. Castleman, *Active Service in the Confederacy and Spanish War*, p. 143.

16. Weber, *Copperheads*, p. 124.

17. "The Baltimore Bastille," National Park Service online pamphlet, https://www.nps.gov/fomc/
learn/historyculture/the-baltimore-bastille.htm.

18. Lucas, *Memoir of John Yates Beall*, p. 29.

19. Daniel Carrol Toomey, "Where the Civil
War Began," *Baltimore Magazine*, April 2011,
https://www.baltimoremagazine.com/section/
historypolitics/where-the-civil-war-began-2/.

20. Moseley, *Confederate Commando*, p. 17;
Baker, *Memoir of Service*, p. 40.

21. Gray, *Hidden Civil War*, p. 167.

22. *Ibid.*

23. Horan, *Confederate Agent*, p. 33; Hines,
"The Northwestern Conspiracy," p. 442.

24. Weber, *Copperheads*, p. 113; "Morgan's Raid,"
Ohio History Central, www.ohiohistorycentral.
org/w/Morgan%27s_Raid.

25. David Meyers, Elise Meyers and James Dailey II, *Inside the Ohio Penitentiary* (Mount Pleasant, SC: History Press, 2013), p. 21.

26. Horan, *Confederate Agent*, p. 36.

27. *Ibid.*

28. *Ibid.*

29. *Ibid.*, p. 43.

30. *Ibid.*, p. 45.

31. *Ibid.*, pp. 52–55.

32. *Ibid.*, pp. 55–57.

33. *Ibid.*, pp. 57–58, 68.

34. Starr, *Colonel Grenfell's Wars*, p. 147.

35. *Ibid.*

36. *Ibid.*, p. 144.

37. Hines, "The Northwestern Conspiracy," p. 443.

Chapter 12

1. Robert K. Krick, *Civil War Weather in Virginia* (Tuscaloosa: University of Alabama Press,
2007), p. 121.

2. Waugh, *Re-Electing Lincoln*, p. 150.

3. Hines, "The Northwestern Conspiracy," p. 441.

4. Sheehy, *Montreal, City of Secrets*, p. 49.

5. Oscar Kinchen, *Confederate Operations in
Canada and the North* (North Quincy, MA: Christopher Publishing House, 1970), p. 36.

6. Mayers, *Dixie & the Dominion*, p. 26.

7. *Ibid.*

8. *Ibid.*

9. *Ibid.*, p. 27.

10. Johnson, *A Vast and Fiendish Plot*, p. 113.

11. Waugh, *Re-Electing Lincoln*, p. 154.

12. Mayers, *Dixie & the Dominion*, p. 28.

13. Castleman, *Active Service in the Confederacy and Spanish War*, p. 133.

14. Mayers, *Dixie & the Dominion*, p. 29.

15. Hines, "The Northwestern Conspiracy," p. 444.

16. *Ibid.*

17. *Ibid.*

18. Mayers, *Dixie & the Dominion*, pp. 21–22.

19. Hines, "The Northwestern Conspiracy," p. 445.

20. *Ibid.*

21. Kinchen, *Confederate Operations*, p. 36.

22. Mayers, *Dixie & the Dominion*, p. 36.

23. *Ibid.*, p. 37.

24. Kinchen, *Confederate Operations*, p. 48; Ruth Ketrig Nuermberger, *The Clays of Alabama—A Planter, Lawyer, Politician Family* (Lexington: University of Kentucky Press, 1958), p. 235.

25. "Our History: Former Faculty, Holcombe, James P. (1851–1861)," University of Virginia School of Law, https://libguides.law.virginia.edu/faculty/holcombe; accessed January 30, 2022.

26. Nuermberger, *The Clays of Alabama*, p. 236.

27. Lucas, *Memoir of John Yates Beall*, p. 29; Baker, *Memoirs of Service*, p. 44; Moseley, *Confederate Commando*, p. 17.

28. OR, Ser. 2, Vol. 6, pp. 711–712.

29. Hesseltine, *Civil War Prisons*, p. 210.

30. OR, Ser. 2, Vol. 6, pp. 711–712.

31. Hesseltine, *Civil War Prisons*, pp. 210–211.

32. Lucas, *Memoir of John Yates Beall*, p. 30.

33. Waugh, *Re-Electing Lincoln*, pp 166–167.

34. David J. Eicher, *The Longest Night: A Military History of the Civil War* (New York: Simon & Schuster, 2001), p. 673.

35. *Ibid.*

36. Shelby Foote, *The Civil War, a Narrative, Red River to Appomattox* (New York: Random House, 1974), p. 232.

37. Lucas, *Memoir of John Yates Beall*, p. 31.

38. The information is conflicting on the sequence of Beall's activities following his release. Lucas, Beall's biographer and boyhood friend, writes in Beall's "memoir" that he spent the two weeks in Georgia immediately following his release but then has him participating in the Yellow Tavern battle, which occurred only a few days following his release on May 5.

39. Lucas, *Memoir of John Yates Beall*, p. 30.

40. Moseley, *Confederate Commando*, p. 18.

41. Lucas, *Memoir of John Yates Beall*, p. 31.

Chapter 13

1. "The Queen's Hotel Then and Now," http://torontothenandnow.blogspot.com/2011/08/26-queens-hotel-then-and-now.html; accessed June 13, 2018.

2. Horan, *Confederate Agent*, p. 80.

3. Kinchen, *Confederate Operations*, p. 40; Hines, "The Northwestern Conspiracy," p. 445.

4. Mayers, *Dixie & the Dominion*, p. 39.

5. Horan, *Confederate Agent*, pp. 78–79.

6. Johnson, *A Vast and Fiendish Plot*, p. 114.

7. Starr, *Colonel Grenfell's Wars*, p. 149.

8. Hines, "The Northwestern Conspiracy," p. 500.

9. Kinchen, *Confederate Operations*, p. 47.

10. Sheehy, *Montreal, City of Secrets*, p. 66.

11. Winks, *The Civil War Years*, p. 275.

12. John Boyko, *Blood and Daring: How Canada Fought the American Civil War and Forged a Nation* (Toronto: Vintage Canada, 2014), p. 165.

13. Sheehy, *Montreal, City of Secrets*, p. 58.

14. Winks, *The Civil War Years*, pp. 275–276.

15. Sheehy, *Montreal, City of Secrets*, p. 58.

16. Castleman, *Active Service in the Confederacy and Spanish War*, p. 166.

17. *Ibid.*, pp. 166–167.

18. *Ibid.*, p. 167.

19. *Ibid.*, pp. 168–169.

20. Sheehy, *Montreal, City of Secrets*, p. 54.

21. Starr, *Colonel Grenfell's Wars*, p. 155; Hines, "The Northwestern Conspiracy," p. 500.

22. Starr, *Colonel Grenfell's Wars*, p. 155.

23. Horan, *Confederate Agent*, p. 90.

24. Weber, *Copperheads*, p. 150; Boyko, *Blood and Daring*, p. 176.

25. Charles Bracelen Flood, *1864: Lincoln at the Gates of History* (New York: Simon & Schuster, 2009), p. 129.

26. Johnson, *A Vast and Fiendish Plot*, p. 141; OR, Ser. 2, Vol. 8, p. 997.

27. Waugh, *Re-Electing Lincoln*, p. 209.

28. *Ibid.*

29. Johnson, *A Vast and Fiendish Plot*, p. 117.

30. Weber, *Copperheads*, p. 150.

31. William H. Knauss, *The Story of Camp Chase* (Publishing House of the Methodist Episcopal Church, 1906), p. 215.

32. Jubal Early, "The Story of the Attempted Formation of a Northwest Conspiracy," *Southern Historical Society Papers* X, no. 4 (April 1882), p. 155.

33. Starr, *Colonel Grenfell's Wars*, p. 154.

34. Hines, "The Northwestern Conspiracy," p. 509.

35. Waugh, *Reelecting Lincoln*, pp. 207–208.

36. Johnson, *A Vast and Fiendish Plot*, pp. 107–108.

37. Mayers, *Dixie & the Dominion*, p. 39.

38. Horan, *Confederate Agent*, p. 94.

39. Mayers, *Dixie & the Dominion*, p. 56.

40. Johnson, *A Vast and Fiendish Plot*, p. 119.

41. *Ibid.*

42. Flood, *1864: Lincoln at the Gates of History*, p. 186.

43. *Ibid.*

44. Waugh, *Re-Electing Lincoln*, p. 249.

45. Waugh, *Reelecting Lincoln,* pp. 246–254; Weber, *Copperheads,* pp. 154–155; Hines, "The Northwestern Conspiracy," p. 501.

46. Waugh, *Re-Electing Lincoln,* p. 253.

47. *Ibid.*

48. Hines, "The Northwestern Conspiracy," p. 507; Boyko, *Blood and Daring,* p. 177.

49. Sheehy, *Montreal, City of Secrets,* p. 62.

50. Weber, *Copperheads,* p. 139.

51. *Ibid.*

52. Waugh, *Re-Electing Lincoln,* p. 270.

53. *Ibid.*

54. Weber, *Copperheads,* p. 158.

55. Flood, *1864: Lincoln at the Gates of History,* pp. 272–273.

56. Gray, *The Hidden Civil War,* p. 176; Weber, *Copperheads,* p. 151.

57. Sheehy, *Montreal, City of Secrets,* p. 62.

58. Larry E. Nelson, *Bullets, Ballots and Rhetoric: Confederate Policy for the United States Presidential Contest of 1864* (Tuscaloosa: University of Alabama Press, 1980), pp. 107–108; Hines, "The Northwestern Conspiracy," p. 509.

59. Mayers, *Dixie & the Dominion,* pp. 69–70.

60. Hines, "The Northwestern Conspiracy," p. 509.

61. *Ibid.*

62. *Ibid.*

63. Sheehy, *Montreal, City of Secrets,* p. 62.

64. Walter Stahr, *Stanton: Lincoln's War Secretary* (New York: Simon & Schuster, 2017), p. 364.

65. Sheehy, *Montreal, City of Secrets,* p. 63.

66. OR, Ser. 1, Vol. 43, Part II, p. 935.

67. Flood, *1864: Lincoln at the Gates of History,* pp. 266–267.

68. *Ibid.*

Chapter 14

1. Horan, *Confederate Agent,* p. 123; Gray, *The Hidden Civil War,* p. 181.

2. Horan, *Confederate Agent,* pp. 123–124.

3. Kinchen, *Confederate Operations,* pp. 66–68.

4. Starr, *Colonel Grenfell's Wars,* p. 173.

5. *Ibid.,* p. 166.

6. *Ibid.*

7. Waugh, *Reelecting Lincoln,* p. 278.

8. *Chicago Tribune,* August 27, 1864.

9. Starr, *Colonel Grenfell's Wars,* p. 173.

10. Waugh, *Re-Electing Lincoln,* p. 282; Flood, *1864: Lincoln at the Gates of History,* p. 274.

11. *Chicago Tribune,* August 30, 1864.

12. Robert S. Harper, *Ohio Handbook of the Civil War* (Columbus: Ohio Historical Society, 1961), pp. 3–4.

13. Starr, *Colonel Grenfell's Wars,* p. 159.

14. Flood, *1864: Lincoln at the Gates of History,* p. 128.

15. *Official Proceedings of the Democratic National Convention* (The Times Steam Book and Job Printing House, 1864), pp. 27–28, https://quod.lib.umich.edu/m/moa/AEW7007.0001.001/1?rgn=full+text;view=image; John Nicolay and John G.

Hay, "Abraham Lincoln: A History. The Chicago Surrender," *The Century* 38, Issue 4 (August 1889), p. 550.

16. Johnson, *A Vast and Fiendish Plot,* p. 132.

17. Waugh, *Re-Electing Lincoln,* p. 286.

18. *Ibid.,* p. 291.

19. Johnson, *A Vast and Fiendish Plot,* p. 133.

20. *Official Proceedings of the Democratic National Convention* (1864), pp. 60–61.

21. Hines," The Northwestern Conspiracy," p. 567.

22. Castleman, *Active Service in the Confederacy and Spanish War,* p. 161.

23. Victor Speer, ed., *Memoirs of a Great Detective: Incidents in the Life of John Wilson Murray* (New York: The Baker & Taylor Co., 1904), p. 20.

24. Mayers, *Dixie & the Dominion,* p. 79.

25. *Ibid.;* Kinchen, *Confederate Operations,* pp. 104–105.

26. Frederick J. Shepard, "The Johnson's Island Plot," *Publications of the Buffalo Historical Society* IX (1906), p. 21, fn. 19.

27. Bell, *Rebels on the Great Lakes,* pp. 69–70.

28. Hines, "The Northwestern Conspiracy," pp. 567–568.

29. *Ibid.*

30. *Ibid.*

31. David W. Francis and Virginia E. McCormick, "The United States Navy and the Johnson's Island Conspiracy: The Case of John C. Carter," *Northwest Ohio Quarterly,* Summer 1980, p. 230.

32. *Ibid.*

33. *Ibid.*

34. Lucas, *Memoir of John Yates Beall,* p. 296.

35. Starr, *Colonel Grenfell's Wars,* p. 173.

36. *Ibid.,* p. 171.

37. *Ibid.,* p. 173.

38. *Ibid.*

39. Hines, "The Northwestern Conspiracy," pp. 573–574; Starr, *Colonel Grenfell's Wars,* p. 177; Gray, *The Hidden Civil War,* p. 185.

40. William A. Tidwell, James O. Hall and David Winfred Gaddy, *Come Retribution: The Confederate Secret Service and the Assassination of Abraham Lincoln* (Jackson: University Press of Mississippi, 1988), p. 195.

41. Starr, *Colonel Grenfell's Wars,* p. 177.

42. *Ibid.,* p. 176.

43. Johnson, *A Vast and Fiendish Plot,* p. 121.

44. Castleman, *Active Service in the Confederacy and Spanish War,* p. 161.

Chapter 15

1. Shriver, Breen, "Ohio's Military Prisons," p. 39.

2. Edward T. Stakes, *A True Account of His Suffering While a Prisoner of War—Fortieth Virginia Infantry,* edited by Martin Stakes Lane (n.p.: Martin Stakes Lane, 2000), p. 27.

3. Horan, *Confederate Agent,* p. 36.

4. OR, Ser. 2, Vol. 7, pp. 110–111.

5. *Ibid.,* pp. 183–184.

6. *Ibid.*, pp. 150–151.

7. Pickenpaugh, *Johnson's Island*, pp. 58–59.

8. *Ibid.*, pp. 58–60.

9. Shepherd, *Narrative of Prison Life*, p. 14.

10. *Ibid.*, p. 15.

11. OR, Ser. 2, Vol. 7, pp. 573–574.

12. *Ibid.*

13. Pickenpaugh, *Captives in Gray*, p. 191.

14. Shepherd, *Narrative of Prison Life*, p. 14.

15. Frohman, *Rebels on Lake Erie*, p. 37.

16. OR, Ser. 2, Vol. 7, p. 484–485.

17. Shriver and Breen, *Ohio's Military Prisons*, p. 37.

18. OR, Ser. 2, Vol. 7, p. 485.

19. Pickenpaugh, *Johnson's Island*, pp. 91–92.

20. OR, Ser. 2, Vol. 7, p. 484.

21. *Ibid.*

22. *Ibid.*, pp. 504–505.

23. *Ibid.*, p. 840.

24. Pickenpaugh, *Johnson's Island*, p. 84.

25. OR, Ser. 2, Vol. 7, p. 766.

26. *Ibid.*, pp. 803–804.

27. *Ibid.*, p. 811.

28. Pickenpaugh, *Johnson's Island*, p. 85.

29. OR, Ser. 2, Vol. 8, pp. 995–999.

30. OR, Ser. 2, Vol. 7, p. 184.

31. Shriver and Breen, *Ohio's Military Prisons*, p. 39.

32. Pickenpaugh, *Johnson's Island*, p. 71.

33. Shriver and Breen, *Ohio's Military Prisons*, p. 40.

34. Nat Brandt, *The Man Who Tried to Burn New York* (Lincoln: toExcel, 1986), p. 61.

35. *Ibid.*, p. 32.

36. *Ibid.*, p. 77.

37. *Ibid.*, p. 129.

Chapter 16

1. Frank B. Woodford, *Father Abraham's Children: Michigan Episodes in the Civil War* (Detroit: Wayne State University Press, 1961, 1999), pp. 141–142.

2. Digital Traveler, https://lemacks.com/2019/07/18/who-was-philo-parsons-of-brush-park-detroit-a-steamship-bearing-his-name-was-featured-in-the-civil-war/; July 18, 2019.

3. Sandusky *Daily Commercial Register*, September 1, 1864.

4. *Ibid.*

5. *Ibid.*

6. OR, Ser. I, Vol. 43, Part II, p. 242.

7. *Ibid.*

8. Graeden Greaves, *Wild Bennet Burleigh* (CreateSpace, 2012) p. 12; Shepard, "The Johnson's Island Plot," p. 28.

9. Shepard, "The Johnson's Island Plot," p. 28.

10. Greaves, *Wild Bennet Burleigh*, pp. 13–14.

11. *Ibid.*, p. 15.

12. Hines, "The Northwestern Conspiracy," p. 699.

13. Lucas, *Memoir of John Yates Beall*, p. 296; Bell, *Rebels on the Great Lakes*, p. 88; John W. Headley, *Confederate Operations in Canada and New York* (New York: The Neale Publishing Company, 1906), p. 228; I. Winslow Ayer, *The Great Northwestern Conspiracy* (Chicago: John R. Walsh, Baldwin & Bamford, 1865), p. 66; also available at https://www.gutenberg.org/ebooks/8543.

14. Kinchen, *Confederate Operations*, p. 105.

15. R.A. Brock, "Johnson's Island," *Southern Historical Society Papers* 30 (1902), p. 259.

16. "The West House Hotel," last modified November 14, 2009, Sanduskyhistory.blogspot.com/2009/11/west-house-hotel.htm.

17. Kinchen, *Confederate Operations*, p. 105; Brock, "Johnson's Island," p. 259; Fraser, *Lake Erie Stories*, p. 108.

18. Hines, "The Northwestern Conspiracy," p. 568.

19. Headley, *Confederate Operations in Canada and New York*, p. 234.

20. Bell, *Rebels on the Great Lakes*, pp. 49–51.

21. *Ibid.*, pp. 54–56.

22. Shepard, "The Johnson's Island Plot," p. 10.

23. Ayer, *The Great Northwestern Conspiracy*, p. 66; Sheehy, *Montreal, City of Secrets*, p. 63.

24. Greaves, *Wild Bennet Burleigh*, p. 17.

25. Woodford, *Father Abraham's Children*, pp. 138–139; Headley, *Confederate Operations in Canada and New York*, pp. 234–236; "The Copperheads—Lake Erie Conspiracy," Ohio Historical Society (1961), p. 5.

26. Headley, *Confederate Operations in Canada and New York*, p. 235; Kinchen, *Confederate Operations*, p. 108.

27. William H. Knauss, *The Story of Camp Chase* (Publishing House of the Methodist Episcopal Church, 1906), p. 221.

28. Hines, "The Northwestern Conspiracy," p. 700.

29. OR, Ser. 1, Vol. 43, Part II, p. 238.

30. *Ibid.*, pp. 243–244; Frohman, *Rebels on Lake Erie*, p. 76.

31. OR, Ser. 1, Vol. 43, Part II, pp. 238, 243.

32. *Ibid.*, pp. 243–244.

33. *Ibid.*, p. 243; Woodford, *Father Abraham's Children*, p. 143; Long, "Johnson's Island Prison," p. 50.

34. Kinchen, *Confederate Operations*, p. 109.

35. OR, Ser. 1, Vol. 43, Part II, pp. 226–227; Headley, *Confederate Operations in Canada and New York*, p. 250; Bell, *Rebels on the Great Lakes*, p. 77.

36. OR, Ser. 1, Vol. 43, Part II, p. 240.

37. *Ibid.*

38. *Ibid.*

39. Beall's claim that he had thirty men on board appears to have been an exaggeration in light of other evidence about the raid revealed later.

40. OR, Ser. 1, Vol. 43, Part II, p. 240.

Chapter 17

1. OR, Ser. 1, Vol. 43, Part II, p. 243; Kinchen, *Confederate Operations*, p. 110.

2. *The New York Times*, August 11, 1895.

3. *Ibid.*

4. OR, Ser. 1, Vol. 43, Part II, p. 237.

5. Lucas, *Memoir of John Yates Beall*, p. 35; Shepard, "The Johnson's Island Plot," pp. 32–33; Brock, "Johnson's Island," p. 260.

6. OR, Ser. 1, Vol. 43, Part II, p. 243; Fraser, *Lake Erie Stories*, p. 110.

7. *The New York Times*, August 11, 1895.

8. Fraser, *Lake Erie Stories*, p. 111.

9. OR, Ser. 1, Vol. 43, Part II, pp. 235–236.

10. *Ibid.*, p. 237.

11. Fraser, *Lake Erie Stories*, p. 111; OR, Ser. 1, Vol. 43, Part II, p. 244.

12. OR, Ser. 1, Vol. 43, Part II, p. 240.

13. *Ibid.*, pp. 240–241; Woodford, *Father Abraham's Children*, p. 144.

14. OR, Ser. 1, Vol. 43, Part II, p. 237.

15. *Ibid.*, p. 241; Michael Gora, *Lake Erie Islands, Sketches and Stories* (Put-in-Bay, OH: Lake Erie Islands Historical Society, 2004), pp. 207–208; Frohman, *Rebels on Lake Erie*, p. 78.

16. OR, Ser. 1, Vol. 43, Part II, p. 237.

17. *Ibid.*; Knauss, *The Story of Camp Chase*, p. 209.

18. OR, Ser. 1, Vol. 43, Part II, p. 238.

19. *Ibid.*, p. 239.

20. *Ibid.*; Frohman, *Rebels on Lake Erie*, p. 78.

21. Kathleen Endres, "A Pirate, A Prison, A Plot," Rebels on Lake Erie Blog, http://rebelsonlakeerie.com/blog/, University of Akron, June 10, 2012.

22. OR, Ser. 1, Vol. 43, Part II, p. 239.

23. Gora, *Lake Erie Islands, Sketches and Stories*, p. 211.

24. William Frank Zornow, "Confederate Raiders on Lake Erie," *Inland Seas* 5, no. 1 (Spring 1949), pp. 46–47; Frohman, *Rebels on Lake Erie*, p. 78.

25. Frohman, *Rebels on Lake Erie*, p. 79.

26. *Ibid.*

27. Sandusky *Daily Commercial Register*, September 21, 1864; Shepard, "The Johnson's Island Plot," p. 30.

28. OR, Ser. 1, Vol. 43, Part II, p. 239.

29. Gora, *Lake Erie Islands, Sketches and Stories*, p. 211; OR, Ser. 1, Vol. 43, Part II, pp. 244–245.

30. Gora, *Lake Erie Islands, Sketches and Stories*, p. 211.

31. *Ibid.*

32. *Ibid.*

33. Sandusky *Daily Commercial Register*, September 21, 1864.

34. Frohman, *Rebels on Lake Erie*, p. 79; OR, Ser. I, Vol. 43, Part II, p. 239.

35. *Trial of John Y. Beall as a Spy and Guerrillero*, p. 12.

36. Sandusky *Daily Commercial Register*, September 21, 1864; OR, Ser. 1, Vol. 43, Part II, pp. 227, 239; Fraser, *Lake Erie Stories*, p. 113; Long, "Johnson's Island Prison," p. 55; Headley, *Confederate Operations in Canada and New York*, p. 250.

37. Frohman, *Rebels on Lake Erie*, pp. 79–80; OR, Ser. 1, Vol. 43, Part II, p. 237.

38. Lucas, *Memoir of John Yates Beall*, p. 37.

39. Kinchen, *Confederate Operations*, p. 112.

Chapter 18

1. OR, Ser. 1, Vol. 43, Part II, p. 233.

2. *Ibid.*, p. 234.

3. *Ibid.*, p. 235.

4. *Ibid.*, p. 233.

5. *Ibid.*

6. *Ibid.*, p. 235.

7. OR, Ser. II, Vol. 7, p. 901; Speer, *Portals to Hell, Military Prisons of the Civil War*, p. 237.

8. Shepard, "The Johnson's Island Plot," p. 36.

9. *Ibid.*, pp. 36–37.

10. Lucas, *Memoir of John Yates Beall*, p. 39; Shepard, "The Johnson's Island Plot," pp. 36–37; Mayers, *Dixie & the Dominion*, pp. 87–88. There are conflicting accounts about where Cole's party was to take place, with some sources saying the party was to be onboard the *Michigan* and others saying the party was to be at a location onshore. I chose to rely on the accounts written by Daniel Lucas in his *Memoir* of Beall as well as Frederick Shepard's "The Johnson's Island Plot," and Adam Mayers *Dixie & the Dominion*, because I found their accounts on other related events to be the most reliable among the sources I examined.

11. Shepard, "The Johnson's Island Plot," p. 37; Mayers, *Dixie & the Dominion*, p. 88.

12. Shepard, "The Johnson's Island Plot," pp. 37–38; Sandusky *Daily Commercial Register*, September 22, 1864; Speer, *Memoirs of a Great Detective*, p. 25; Adam Mayers, "Confederacy's Canadian Mission: Spies Across the Border," *Civil War Times*, June 2001; accessed online, https://www.historynet.com/confederacys-canadian-mission-spies-across-the-border.

13. Sandusky *Daily Commercial Register*, September 22, 1864.

14. OR, Ser. 2, Vol. 7, p. 901.

15. *Ibid.*, p. 904.

16. Tidwell, *Come Retribution*, p. 49; Mark C. Hageman, "Espionage in the Civil War," Signal Corps Association, http://www.civilwarsignals.org/pages/spy/spy.html; accessed January 6, 2022.

17. OR, Ser. 2, Vol. 7, p. 900, 905; Sandusky *Daily Commercial Register*, September 22, 1864.

18. Sandusky *Daily Commercial Register*, September 22, 1864.

19. OR, Ser. 2, Vol. 7, pp. 901–902.

20. *Ibid.*, p. 902; *Cleveland Plain Dealer*, September 20, 1864; Long, "Johnson's Island Prison," pp. 52–53; Kinchen, *Confederate Operations*, p. 114; Knauss, *The Story of Camp Chase*, p. 208.

21. OR, Ser. 1, Vol. 43, Part II, p. 235.

22. Pickenpaugh, *Johnson's Island*, pp. 75–76; Woodford, *Father Abraham's Children*, p. 139; Mayers, "Confederacy's Canadian Mission."

23. Tidwell, *Come Retribution*, p. 186; *The New York Times*, May 26, 1865.

24. Starr, *Colonel Grenfell's Wars*, p. 185; Nuernberger, *The Clay's of Alabama*, p. 253.

25. Brock, "Johnson's Island, p. 261; Knauss, *The Story of Camp Chase*, p. 216; T.A. Burr, "A Romance of the Great Rebellion," *Firelands Pioneer* 1 (June 1882), p. 87.

26. Kinchen, *Confederate Operations*, pp. 112–113.

27. OR, Ser. 1, Vol. 43, Part II, p. 932.

28. Hines, "The Northwestern Conspiracy," p. 700.

29. Johnson, "A Vast and Fiendish Plot," p. 118.

30. Headley, *Confederate Operations in Canada and New York*, p. 215.

31. Hines, "The Northwestern Conspiracy," p. 502.

32. Starr, *Colonel Grenfell's Wars*, p. 168.

33. *Ibid.*, p. 169.

34. OR, Ser. 1, Vol. 43, Part II, p. 934.

35. Starr, *Colonel Grenfell's Wars*, p. 161.

36. Horan, *Confederate Agent*, pp. 97–100.

37. Shepard, "The Johnson's Island Plot," p. 34; Sandusky *Daily Commercial Register*, September 22, 1865.

38. Sandusky *Daily Commercial Register*, September 22, 1865.

Chapter 19

1. Logbook Entry, September 19, 1864, 8 p.m.–12 a.m., USS *Michigan*, Logbooks of U.S. Navy Ships 1801–1940, National Archives and Records Administration, Record Group 24.

2. Lucas, *The Memoir of John Yates Beall*, p. 39. Accounts differ on whether the signal flare was to come from the *Michigan* or from the Johnson's Island prison camp. I chose to rely on the account written by Daniel Lucas, Beall's longtime friend and author of Beall's "memoir."

3. *Ibid.*, p. 42; Kinchen, *Confederate Operations*, p. 112; Headley, *Confederate Operations in Canada and New York*, p. 251; Shepard, "The Johnson's Island Plot," p. 31; Bell, *Rebels on the Great Lakes*, p. 88; Fraser, *Lake Erie Stories*, p. 113; Woodford, *Father Abraham's Children*, p. 145; Sandusky *Daily Commercial Register*, September 21, 1864.

4. Lucas, *The Memoir of John Yates Beall*, p. 40.

5. *Ibid.*

6. OR, Ser. 1, Vol. 43, Part II, p. 237.

7. Lydia J. Ryall (as Theresa Thorndale), *Sketches and Stories of the Lake Erie Islands* (Sandusky, OH: I.F. Mack & Brother, 1898), p. 79.

8. Constance Woolson, "The Wine Islands of Lake Erie," *Harper's Magazine* 47 (June 1873), p. 33; Frohman, *Rebels on Lake Erie*, p. 80.

9. OR, Ser. 1, Vol. 43, Part II, p. 239.

10. *The New York Times*, August 11, 1895.

11. *Ibid.*

12. Sandusky *Daily Commercial Register*, September 21, 1864.

13. Thorndale, *Sketches and Stories of the Lake Erie Islands*, pp. 70–71.

14. *Ibid.*, pp. 71–72; Ruth Dickerman Moizuk, *The Put in Bay Story*, self-published, publication date unknown, https://archive.org/details/putinbaystory00moiz, p. 21.

15. Thorndale, *Sketches and Stories of the Lake Erie Islands*, p. 72.

16. *Ibid.*, p. 73.

17. Bell, *Rebels on the Great Lakes*, p. 84; OR, Ser. 2, Vol. 7, p. 903.

18. Shepard, "The Johnson's Island Plot," p. 38; Knauss, *The Story of Camp Chase*, p. 209.

19. Shepard, "The Johnson's Island Plot," p. 38.

20. Knauss, *The Story of Camp Chase*, p. 209; Sandusky *Daily Commercial Register*, September 21, 1864; Long, "Johnson's Island Prison," p. 59.

21. OR, Ser. 2, Vol. 7, p. 903.

22. *Ibid.*; Frohman, *Rebels on Lake Erie*, p. 85.

23. Sandusky *Daily Commercial Register*, September 22, 1864.

24. *Ibid.*, September 21, 1864; Knauss, *The Story of Camp Chase*, p. 210; Frohman, *Rebels on Lake Erie*, pp. 85–86.

25. OR, Series 1, Vol. 43, Part II, pp. 237, 241; Frohman, *Rebels on Lake Erie*, p. 80.

26. Kinchen, *Confederate Operations*, p. 114; OR, Ser. 1, Vol. 43, Part II, p. 238.

27. OR, Ser. 1, Vol. 43, Part II, p. 241; Thorndale, *Sketches and Stories of the Lake Erie Islands*, p. 79.

28. OR, Ser. 1, Vol. 43, Part II, p. 236; Thorndale, *Sketches and Stories of the Lake Erie Islands*, pp. 79–80; Woodford, *Father Abraham's Children*, p. 145.

29. OR, Ser. I, Vol. 43, Part II, p. 238; Frohman, *Rebels on Lake Erie*, p. 81.

30. OR, Ser. 1, Vol. 43, Part II, p 227. Within a few days, the *Philo Parsons* had been pumped out, repaired and, by September 24, was back in operation.

31. OR, Series 1, Vol. 43, Part II, pp. 237–238; Frohman, *Rebels on Lake Erie*, p. 81.

32. OR, Series 1, Vol. 43, Part II, p. 238; Fraser, *Lake Erie Stories*, p. 114; Kinchen, *Confederate Operations*, p. 114.

Chapter 20

1. OR, Series 1, Vol. 39, pp. 426–428.

2. "Samuel Peter Heintzelman (September 30, 1805–May 1, 1880)," *Ohio Civil War Central*, https://www.ohiocivilwarcentral.com/samuel-peter-heintzelman/.

3. OR, Ser. 2, Vol. 43, p. 228.

4. Sandusky *Daily Commercial Register*, September 27, 1864.

5. *Ibid.*, OR, Ser. 2, Vol. 43, p. 229.

6. OR, Ser. 2, Vol. 7, p. 853. The telegram traffic shows that Hill notified the War Department by contacting Heintzelman's office in Columbus on September 20, 1864, the day following the raid. Hill's report made its way to Stanton and Hoffman later that day. OR, Ser. 2, Vol. 7, p. 850.

7. *Ibid.*, p. 853.

8. John G. Barrett, ed., *Yankee Rebel: The Civil War Journal of Edmund DeWitt Patterson* (Chapel Hill: University of North Carolina Press, 1966), p. 195.

9. OR, Ser. 1, Vol. 43, Part II, p. 232.

10. OR, Ser. 1, Vol. 39, Part II, p. 448.
11. *Ibid.*
12. Mayers, *Dixie & The Dominion*, p. 89.
13. *Ibid.*, p. 90; Winks, *The Civil War Years*, p. 293.
14. Winks, *The Civil War Years*, p. 293.
15. Bell, *Rebels on the Great Lakes*, p. 92; Lucas, *The Memoir of John Yates Beall*, p. 45.
16. Lucas, *The Memoir of John Yates Beall*, pp. 296–297.
17. *Ibid.*, p. 297.
18. *Ibid.*, p. 45.
19. Greaves, *Wild Bennet Burley*, p. 25; "The Robertson Foundry and Ferndell," https://cms.driftscape.com/feature/5394e6de-f4df-11ea-8000-bc1c5a8f0f67
20. Kinchen, *Confederate Operations*, pp. 114–115.
21. OR, Series 2, Vol. 7, p. 864.
22. Winks, *The Civil War Years*, p. 299; Mayers, *Dixie & the Dominion*, p. 107.
23. Headley, *Confederate Operations in Canada and New York*, p. 257.
24. Mayers, *Dixie & the Dominion*, pp. 101–102.
25. Winks, *The Civil War Years*, p. 299.
26. *Ibid.* Calculating the total amount taken from the St. Albans banks involves "guess work," as Winks points out, noting estimates range from $186,133 to the $208,000 claimed by Bennett Young.
27. Mayers, *Dixie & the Dominion*, pp. 108–109.
28. Winks, *The Civil War Years*, p. 300.
29. Mayers, *Dixie & the Dominion*, pp. 109–110.
30. Tidwell, *Come Retribution*, p. 201.
31. Tidwell, *Come Retribution*, p. 190.
32. Winks, *The Civil War Years*, p 302.
33. *Ibid.*, p. 303.
34. *Ibid.*, pp. 304–305.
35. OR, Ser. 1, Vol. 43, p. 934.
36. Winks, *The Civil War Years*, p. 306

Chapter 21

1. Sheehy, *Montreal, City of Secrets*, p. 113.
2. *Ibid.*, p. 117.
3. Wanted Poster for John Wilkes Booth, 1865, Library of Congress; Alford, *Fortune's Fool*, p. 185.
4. Alford, *Fortune's Fool*, pp. 171, 183–184.
5. Bell, *Rebels on the Great Lakes*, p. 163.
6. *Ibid.*, p. 161; Alford, *Fortune's Fool*, p. 185.
7. Barry Sheehy, "Conspiracy in Montreal 1864–1865: The Confederate Secret Service in Canada and the Lincoln Assassination," *North & South*, May-June 2019, p. 49.
8. Alford, *Fortune's Fool*, p. 186.
9. Sheehy, *Montreal, City of Secrets*, pp. 21, 137.
10. *The New York Herald Tribune*, February 5, 1865.
11. Alford, *Fortune's Fool*, p. 186.
12. *Ibid.*, p. 187.
13. *Ibid.*; Sheehy, *Montreal, City of Secrets*, p. 140.
14. Alford, *Fortune's Fool*, p. 188.

15. *Ibid.*, p. 185; Sheehy, *Montreal, City of Secrets*, p. 76.
16. Alford, *Fortune's Fool*, p. 185; Sheehy, *Montreal, City of Secrets*, p. 138.
17. Sheehy, *Montreal, City of Secrets*, p. 139.
18. Alford, *Fortune's Fool*, p. 188.
19. *Ibid.*, p. 185.
20. *Ibid.*, pp. 188–189; Bell, *Rebels on the Great Lakes*, p. 166; Tidwell, *Come Retribution*, pp. 330–332.
21. Tidwell, *Come Retribution*, p. 331; Bell, *Rebels on the Great Lakes*, pp. 166–167.
22. Guest Register, St. Lawrence Hall, November 2, 1864. As was typical at the time, both Beall and Hines used aliases, with Beall signing as "J. Yates" and Hines signing as "Thomas Haines."
23. Sheehy, *Montreal, City of Secrets*, p. 132.
24. Lonnie Speer, *Portals to Hell*, p. 238.
25. "The Dahlgren Papers Revisited," History-Net, June 12, 2016, https://www.historynet.com/-the-dahlgren-papers-revisited/; James O. Hall, "The Dahlgren Papers," *Civil War Times Illustrated*, November 1983, pp. 30–39.
26. Edward Steers, Jr., *Blood on the Moon* (The University Press of Kentucky, 2001), p. 45.
27. Richmond *Sentinel*, March 7, 1864; Joseph George, Jr., "Black Flag Warfare: Lincoln and the Raids Against Richmond and Jefferson Davis," *The Pennsylvania Magazine of History and Biography*, Vol. 115, No. 3 (July 1991), p. 313.
28. Tidwell, *Come Retribution*, p. 246; Sheehy, *Montreal, City of Secrets*, p. 134.
29. Sheehy, *Montreal, City of Secrets*, p. 59.
30. Tidwell, *Come Retribution*, p. 251.
31. *Ibid.*, p. 18.
32. Ironically, Lincoln signed legislation creating the Secret Service on the day he was assassinated. After it began operation, the agency's primary duty was to combat counterfeit currency which, in the year's following the Civil War, was proliferating across the country. The agency was not assigned responsibility for protecting the president until after the assassination of President William McKinley in 1901.
33. Asia Booth Clarke, *The Unlocked Book, A Memoir of John Wilkes Booth* (New York: G.P. Putnam's Sons, 1938), pp. 113–114.
34. *Ibid.*, p. 114.
35. Anuraag Bukkuri, "The History of Malaria in the United States: How It Spread, How It Was Treated, and Public Responses," *MOJ Anat Physiol.* University of Minnesota (April 28, 2016), https://medcraveonline.com/MOJAP/the-history-of-malaria-in-the-united-states-how-it-spread-how-it-was-treated-and-public-responses.html.
36. Alford, *Fortune's Fool*, p. 235.
37. *Ibid.*
38. *Ibid.*
39. Tidwell, *Come Retribution*, p. 261.
40. Sheehy, *Montreal, City of Secrets*, p. 133; Tidwell, *Come Retribution*, pp. 262–263.
41. *The New York Times*, May 22, 1867.
42. Tidwell, *Come Retribution*, p. 3.

43. Sheehy, *Montreal, City of Secrets,* p. 107.
44. *Ibid.*
45. *Ibid.*, p. 108; "Trading with the Enemy," *The New York Times,* October 28, 2012.
46. Sheehy, *Montreal, City of Secrets,* p. 107.
47. *Ibid,* p. 112.
48. *Ibid.*, p. 116.
49. *Ibid.*, p. 111.
50. *Ibid.*, p. 110.
51. Milledge L. Bonham Jr., "New York and the Election of 1860," *New York History,* Vol. 15, No. 2 (April 1934), p. 142; accessed June 20, 2021 at https://www.jstor.org/stable/23134496?read-now=1&refreqid=excelsior%3A893d65af1a9a28d352ea f9625a047850&seq=21#page_scan_tab_contents; Sheehy, *Montreal, City of Secrets,* pp. 99, 203.
52. David G. Surdam, "Traders or Traitors: Northern Cotton Trading During the Civil War," *Business and Economic History,* Vol. 28, No. 2 (Winter 1999), p. 310; Sheehy, *Montreal, City of Secrets,* pp. 117–118.
53. Sheehy, *Montreal, City of Secrets,* pp. 117–118.

Chapter 22

1. Bell, *Rebels on the Great Lakes,* p. 97.
2. Headley, *Confederate Operations in Canada and New York,* p. 254.
3. *Ibid.*
4. Kinchen, *Confederate Operations,* pp. 116–117; Bell, *Rebels on the Great Lakes,* p. 96; Winks, *The Civil War Years,* p. 308.
5. "Georgian (1864, Propeller)," Alpena County George N. Fletcher Public Library, Great Lakes Maritime Collection, https://greatlakeships.org/2904656/data?n=4.
6. Kinchen, *Confederate Operations,* p. 117.
7. Headley, *Confederate Operations in Canada and New York,* p. 255; Bell, *Rebels on the Great Lakes,* p. 97.
8. "Charles C. Hemming, A Confederate Odyssey," *American Heritage Magazine,* Vol. 36, Issue 1 (1984), https://www.americanheritage.com/-confederate-odyssey, accessed July 12, 2021.
9. ORN, Ser. 1, Vol. 3, pp. 371–372; U.S. Department of State, Office of the Historian, "Papers Relating to Foreign Affairs, Accompanying the Annual Message of the President to the Second Session, Thirty-eighth Congress, Part II, Document 561"; accessed July 13, 2021, https://history.state.gov/historicaldocuments/frus1864p2/d561.
10. Bell, *Rebels on the Great Lakes,* p. 96; ORN, Ser. 1, Vol. 3, p. 349.
11. ORN, Ser. 1, Vol. 3, p. 349.
12. *Ibid.*, p. 375.
13. Kinchen, *Confederate Operations,* p. 119; OR Ser. 1, Vol. 3, p. 374.
14. *Buffalo Commercial Advertiser,* November 7, 1864.
15. "Georgian (Propeller) 1864," *Maritime History of the Great Lakes,* https://images.maritimehistoryofthegreatlakes.ca/26776/data?n=3; *The*

New York Herald, November 9, 1864; OR, Ser. 1, Vol. 43, Part II, p. 934.
16. OR, Ser. 1, Vol. 39, Part III, p. 694.
17. Kinchen, *Confederate Operations,* p. 120.
18. *Ibid.*
19. Winks, *The Civil War Years,* p. 308.
20. Kinchen, *Confederate Operations,* p. 120.
21. Mayers, *Dixie & the Dominion,* p.135; Bell, *Rebels on the Great Lakes,* p. 98.
22. Bell, *Rebels on the Great Lakes,* p. 98; Mayers, *Dixie & the Dominion,* p. 133.
23. Bell, *Rebels on the Great Lakes,* p. 98, Kinchen, *Confederate Operations,* p. 121.
24. Kinchen, *Confederate Operations,* p. 121.
25. *Ibid.*
26. ORN, Ser. 1, Vol. 3, p. 388.
27. David Francis and Virginia McCormick, "The United States Navy and the Johnson's Island Conspiracy: The Case of John C. Carter," *Northwest Ohio Quarterly* 52, no. 3 (Summer 1980); ORN, Ser. 1, Vol. 3, pp. 218–219.
28. ORN, Ser. 1, Vol. 3, p. 389.
29. *Ibid.*
30. OR, Ser. 1, Vol. 43, p. 934.
31. Kinchen, *Confederate Operations,* pp. 122–123; "Georgian (1864, Propeller)," Alpena County George N. Fletcher Public Library, Great Lakes Maritime Collection, https://greatlakeships.org/2904656/data?n=4.
32. Waugh, *Re-Electing Lincoln,* pp. 351–355.
33. *Ibid.*, p. 355.
34. *Ibid.*, p. 354.

Chapter 23

1. "History of the Lake Shore and Michigan Southern Railway Company," excerpt from the 1913 Annual Report of the New York Central Railroad System, https://web.archive.org/web/20131215142554/http://www.s363.com/dkny/lsms.html.
2. Bell, *Rebels on the Great Lakes,* p. 101.
3. Apart from Trimble, there is some question as to the identities of the other generals who were to be transferred from Johnson's Island at this time. The leading, and most often cited, authority is John W. Headley's account in his memoir, *Confederate Operations in Canada and New York.* In addition to Trimble, Headley lists Major General Edward Johnson and Brigadier General J.J. Archer. However, Johnson was not captured until December 16 at the Battle of Nashville, which came after the planned attack on the train. Archer was part of a prisoner exchange in October 1864, returned to the Confederate Army and died in October 1864, two months before the planned train attack. The other generals listed by Headley as transferees were M. Jeff Thompson, J.R. Jones, W.N.R. Beall and I.W. Frazier. Headley, *Confederate Operations in Canada and New York,* p. 301.
In addition, Frederick Shepard, another authority on Johnson's Island, wrote in his account for the Buffalo Historical Society, "The Johnson's Island Plot,"

that Confederate generals John Marmaduke and William Cabell were also included among the generals to be transferred. This is also inaccurate. Marmaduke and Cabell had been captured and were in Union hands in December 1864. However, they were in Missouri on December 16, 1864, and had not yet arrived as prisoners on Johnson's Island. *Daily Alta California* 16, no. 5400 (December 16 1864), https://cdnc.ucr.edu/?a=d&d=DAC18641216.2.14&e=en--20--1--txt-txIN--------1.

4. Bell, *Rebels on the Great Lakes*, p. 102.

5. Edward O. Cunningham, "In Violation of the Laws of War: The Execution of Robert Cobb Kennedy," *Louisiana History, the Journal of the Louisiana Historical Association* 18, no. 2 (Spring 1977), pp. 189–201.

6. Headley, *Confederate Operations in Canada and New York*, p. 301.

7. *Ibid.*, p. 302.

8. *Ibid.*

9. *The New York Herald*, February 5, 1865.

10. Bell, *Rebels on the Great Lakes,* p. 103, Headley, *Confederate Operations in Canada and New York*, p. 302.

11. Headley, *Confederate Operations in Canada and New York*, p. 302.

12. *Ibid.*, pp. 302–303.

13. OR, Ser. 1, Vol. 43, Part II, p. 789.

14. *Ibid.*

15. Kinchen, *Confederate Operations*, p. 188; Headley, *Confederate Operations in Canada and New York*, p. 304.

16. Headley, *Confederate Operations in Canada and New York*, p. 304; Kinchen, *Confederate Operations*, pp. 188–189.

17. Headley, *Confederate Operations in Canada and New York*, pp. 305–306.

18. Bell, *Rebels on the Great Lakes,* p. 106.

19. *Ibid.*; Headley, *Confederate Operation in Canada and New York*, p. 306; *The New York Herald*, February 5, 1865.

20. Headley, *Confederate Operation in Canada and New York*, p. 306; Bell, *Rebels on the Great Lakes*, p. 106.

21. Headley, *Confederate Operations in Canada and New York*, p. 307.

22. *Ibid.*; Lucas, *Memoir of John Yates Beall*, pp. 47–48.

23. Lucas, *Memoir of John Yates Beall*, p. 47.

24. *Ibid.*

25. *Trial of John Y. Beall as a Spy and Guerrillero*, p. 23.

26. *Ibid.*

27. *The New York Herald*, February 5, 1865; *The New York Times*, February 6, 1865.

28. *Trial of John Y. Beall as a Spy and Guerrillero*, pp. 23–25.

29. *Ibid.*, p. 24.

Chapter 24

1. Lucas, *Memoir of John Yates Beall*, p. 51.

2. *The New York Times*, November 28, 1909; *San Francisco Call* 106, no. 104 (September 12, 1909), p. 6.

3. Lucas, *Memoir of John Yates Beall*, p. 52.

4. *Ibid.*, pp. 51–52.

5. *Ibid.*, p. 54.

6. *Ibid.*, pp. 54–55.

7. *Trial of John Y. Beall as a Spy and Guerrillero*, p. 47; Lucas, *Memoir of John Yates Beall*, p. 51.

8. *Trial of John Y. Beall as a Spy and Guerrillero*, p. 26.

9. *Ibid.*

10. *Ibid.*

11. *Ibid.*

12. *Ibid.*

13. *Ibid.*

14. *Ibid.*, p. 27.

15. *Ibid.*

16. *Ibid.*

17. *Ibid.*

18. *Ibid.*, p. 28.

19. *Ibid.*

Chapter 25

1. Lucas, *Memoir of John Yates Beall*, p. 56.

2. Bell, *Rebels on the Great Lakes,* p. 129.

3. *Trial of John Y. Beall as a Spy and Guerrillero*, pp. 6–7.

4. Edward H. Stiles, "General Fitz Henry Warren" *The Annals of Iowa* 6, no. 7, 3rd Series (October 1904), pp. 493–494.

5. *Trial of John Y. Beall as a Spy and Guerrillero*, pp. 3–4.

6. Brandt, *The Man Who Tried to Burn New York*, p. 169.

7. Michael O. Lacy, "Military Commissions: A Historical Survey," *The Army Lawyer*, March 2002, p. 43.

8. *Ibid.*

9. Jessica Laird and John Fabian Witt, "Inventing the War Crime: An Internal Theory," *Virginia Journal of International Law* 60 (2019–2020), p. 53.

10. Stahr, *Stanton: Lincoln's War Secretary*, pp. 274–275.

11. *Ibid.*

12. *Trial of John Y. Beall as a Spy and Guerrillero*, p. 4; Lucas, *Memoir of John Yates Beall*, p. 57.

13. Lucas, *Memoir of John Yates Beall*, pp. 56–57.

14. OR, Ser. 2, Vol. 8, pp. 83–84.

15. *Ibid.*, p. 91.

16. *The New York Times*, February 10, 1869.

17. Lucas, *Memoir of John Yates Beall*, pp. 60–62.

18. *Trial of John Y. Beall as a Spy and Guerrillero*, pp. 5–6.

19. *Ibid.*

20. Headley, *Confederate Operations in Canada and New York,* pp. 342, 368.

21. *Trial of John Y. Beall as a Spy and Guerrillero*, p. 18.

22. *Ibid.*, pp. 20–21.

23. *Ibid.*, p. 21.

24. *Ibid.* pp. 22–24.

25. *Ibid.*, pp. 24–25.
26. *Ibid.*, p. 26.
27. *Ibid.*, pp. 28–33.
28. Lucas, *Memoir of John Yates Beall*, pp. 50–51; Headley, *Confederate Operations in Canada and New York,* p. 340.
29. *Trial of John Y. Beall as a Spy and Guerrillero*, pp. 39–40.
30. *Ibid.*, p. 41.
31. *Ibid.*, pp. 42, 48–50.
32. *Ibid.*, p. 50.
33. *Ibid.*, p. 53.
34. *Ibid.*, p. 55.
35. *Ibid.*, p. 58.
36. *Ibid.*, pp. 59–60.
37. *Ibid.*, p. 62.
38. *Ibid.*, pp. 64–65.
39. *Ibid.*, p. 69.
40. *Ibid.*, p. 70.
41. *Ibid.*, pp. 77–78.
42. *Ibid.*, p. 72.
43. *Ibid.*, p. 76.
44. *Ibid.*, p. 79.
45. *Ibid.*, pp. 82–83.
46. *Ibid.*, p. 88.
47. *Ibid.*, p. 91; Bell, *Rebels on the Great Lakes,* p. 141.

Chapter 26

1. Lucas, *Memoir of John Yates Beall*, p. 66; *Trial of John Y. Beall*, p. 89; Horan, *Confederate Agent*, p. 257.
2. *The New York Times,* March 17, 1865; Brandt, *The Man Who Tried to Burn New York,* p. 209; John Strasbaugh, *City of Sedition: The History of New York City During the Civil War* (New York: Hachette, 2016), p. 199.
3. Horan, *Confederate Agent*, p. 257; *Trial of John Y. Beall*, p. 91.
4. Lucas, *Memoir of John Yates Beall*, pp. 66–67.
5. *Ibid.,* p. 68.
6. *Virginian-Pilot*, March 18, 2021.
7. Lucas, *Memoir of John Yates Beall*, p. 69.
8. Horan, *Confederate Agent,* pp. 257–258.
9. Lucas, *Memoir of John Yates Beall*, p. 70.
10. Flood, *1864: Lincoln at the Gates of History,* p. 270.
11. Isaac Markens, "President Lincoln and the Case of John Y. Beall," *Americana Illustrated, National Americana Society* 6 (January–December 1911), pp. 4–5.
12. *Ibid.*, p. 6; Alford, *Fortune's Fool*, p. 219.
13. Lucas, *Memoir of John Yates Beall*, p. 70.
14. *Ibid.*
15. *Trial of John Y. Beall as a Spy and Guerrillero*, pp. 91–94.
16. Lucas, *Memoir of John Yates Beall*, p. 71.
17. *Trial of John Y. Beall as a Spy and Guerrillero*, pp. 93–94.
18. Lucas, *Memoir of John Yates Beall,* pp. 72–73; John Grady, "Trial of a Confederate Terrorist," *Civil War Monitor,* June 1, 2015, https://www.civilwarmonitor.com/blogs/trial-of-a-confederate-terrorist.
19. Sara A. Pryor, *Reminiscences in Peace and War* (New York: Macmillan, 1905), pp. 340–342.
20. Alford, *Fortune's Fool*, pp. 219–220.
21. Lucas, *Memoir of John Yates Beall,* p. 70.
22. Markens, "President Lincoln and the Case of John Y. Beall," p. 8.
23. Lucas, *Memoir of John Yates Beall*, p. 75.
24. *Ibid.*
25. *Ibid.*, p. 72.
26. *Ibid.*
27. Markens, "President Lincoln and the Case of John Y. Beall," p. 9.
28. Lucas, *Memoir of John Yates Beall*, p. 72.
29. *Ibid.*, p. 73.

Chapter 27

1. *The New York Times,* February 25, 1865; *The New York Herald,* February 25, 1865; New York *World,* February 25, 1865.
2. *The New York Times,* February 25, 1865; *The New York Herald,* February 25, 1865; New York *World,* February 25, 1865.
3. Lucas, *Memoir of John Yates Beall*, p. 79.
4. *Ibid.*, p. 78.
5. *Ibid.*, p. 77.
6. Horan, *Confederate Agent,* pp. 258–259; New York *World,* February 25, 1865; *The New York Times,* February 25, 1865; *The New York Herald,* February 25, 1865.
7. New York *World,* February 25, 1865.
8. New York *World,* February 25, 1865; *The New York Times,* February 25, 1865; *The New York Herald,* February 25, 1865; Lucas, *Memoir of John Yates Beall,* p. 83.
9. *The New York Herald,* February 25, 1865; New York *World,* February 25, 1865.
10. Horan, *Confederate Agent,* pp. 258–259; New York *World,* February 25, 1865; *The New York Times,* February 25, 1865; *The New York Herald,* February 25, 1865; Lucas, *Memoir of John Yates Beall,* p. 84.
11. New York *World,* February 25, 1865.
12. New York *World,* February 25, 1865; *The New York Times,* February 25, 1865; *The New York Herald,* February 25, 1865; Lucas, *Memoir of John Yates Beall,* p. 87.
13. *The New York Herald,* February 25, 1865; New York *World,* February 25, 1865; Lucas, *Memoir of John Yates Beall,* p. 88.

Epilogue

1. Markens, "President Lincoln and the Case of John Y. Beall," p. 10.
2. OR, Ser. 1, Vol. 49, Part II, pp. 566–67.
3. L.C. Baker, *History of the United States Secret Service* (L.C. Baker, Publisher, 1867), pp. 544–545.
4. *Ibid.*
5. *The Assassination of President Lincoln and the Trial of the Conspirators* (New York: Moore,

Wilstach & Baldwin, 1865), p. 35, https://hdl.loc.gov/loc.law/llds.00120275616.2; accessed June 14, 2021.

6. *Ibid.*

7. Steers, *Blood on the Moon*, pp. 224–225.

8. "Why Booth Killed President Lincoln," *Confederate Veteran* 9, no. 1 (January 1901), pp. 3–4.

9. *Ibid.*, p. 4.

10. "Testimony as to Cause of Lincoln's Murder," *Confederate Veteran* 19 (July 1911), p. 343.

11. *The New York Herald*, March 7, 1865.

12. *Ibid.*

13. *Ibid.*

14. Alford, *Fortune's Fool*, p. 221.

15. *Ibid.*

16. Shepard, "The Johnson's Island Plot," pp. 43–44.

17. *Ibid.*, p. 44.

18. Alford, *Fortune's Fool*, pp. 185, 188; St. Lawrence Hall Guest Register, November 2, 1864, accessed by Barry Sheehy, author of *Montreal, City of Secrets.*

19. Markens, "President Lincoln and the Case of John Y. Beall," p. 11.

20. Alford, *Fortune's Fool*, p. 399, note 3.

21. Virginia Lucas, "John Yates Beall: An Appreciation," *Confederate Veteran* 35, no. 8 (August 1927), p. 301.

22. *Ibid.*, p. 338.

23. *Ibid.*, p. 337.

24. Ron Soodalter, "Murder with a Vengeance: John Yates Beall, John Wilkes Booth and the Killing of a President," https://www.historynet.com/-murder-with-w-vengeance.htm; accessed October 21, 2021.

25. Moseley, *Confederate Commando*, p. 39.

26. *Ibid.*

27. Louise Littleton Davis, *More Tales of Tennessee* (New Orleans: Pelican, 1978), p. 173.

28. *Ibid.*, pp. 176–176.

29. Moseley, *Confederate Commando*, p. 40.

30. New York *World*, February 25, 1865.

31. Greaves, *Wild Bennet Burleigh*, p. 23.

32. Bell, *Rebels on the Great Lakes*, p. 98.

33. *Ibid.*, pp. 115–116.

34. *Ibid.*; Bullard, *Famous War Correspondents*, p. 195.

35. Bell, *Rebels on the Great Lakes*, pp. 118–121.

36. *Ibid.*, pp. 121–122.

37. *Ibid.*, p. 123; Shepard, "The Johnson's Island Plot," p. 50.

38. Bell, *Rebels on the Great Lakes*, p. 123.

39. Frohman, *Rebels on Lake Erie*, p. 120; Bell, *Rebels on the Great Lakes*, p. 123.

40. Shepard, "The Johnson's Island Plot," pp. 149–151.

41. Greaves, *Wild Bennet Burleigh*, p. 49.

42. *Ibid.*, p. 53; Bullard, *Famous War Correspondents*, p. 197.

43. Tom Rowley, "Bennet Burleigh: The Wild Man of the Victorian Press," June 13, 2013, https://www.telegraph.co.uk/history/10132546/-

Bennet-Burleigh-the-wild-man-of-theVictorian-press.html; accessed December 29, 2021.

44. Greaves, *Wild Bennet Burleigh*, pp. 177–179.

45. Francis and McCormick, "The United States Navy and the Johnson's Island Conspiracy," pp. 231–232.

46. *Ibid.*, pp. 232–233.

47. Mayers, *Dixie & the Dominion*, pp. 201–202.

48. Brandt, *The Man Who Tried to Burn New York*, p. 237.

49. Bell, *Rebels on the Great Lakes*, pp. 109–114; Headley, *Confederate Operations*, pp. 236–240.

50. Adam Mayers, "Confederacy's Canadian Mission."

51. Brandt, *The Man Who Tried to Burn New York*, p. 237.

52. Horan, *Confederate Agent,* pp. 261–262.

53. Martha Luan Carter Brunson, "Confederate Activities from Canada: A Study in Canadian-American Relations" (M.A. thesis, Texas Technological College, 1958), p. 112.

54. Horan, *Confederate Agent*, pp. 272, 285.

55. *Ibid.*, p. 286.

56. *Ibid.*, pp. 288, 292.

57. Ida Husted Harper, "The Life and Work of Clara Barton," *The North American Review* 195, no. 678 (May 1912), pp. 703–704; Michael Hoffman, "William Hoffman's Encounters with History," National Museum of Civil War Medicine, https://www.civilwarmed.org/surgeons-call/hoffman/; accessed January 29, 2022.

58. Hoffman, "William Hoffman's Encounters with History."

59. John Salmon, National Register of Historic Places Registration Form, "Bellvue," September 29, 1989, accessed December 13, 2022, https://web.archive.org/web/20120926203837/http://www.dhr.virginia.gov/registers/Counties/Bedford/009-0003_Bellevue_1990_Final_Nomination.pdf; University of Virginia School of Law, "Our History: Former Faculty, Holcombe, James P." (1852–1861), https://libguides.law.virginia.edu/faculty/holcombe; accessed January 30, 2020.

60. Levin, *This Awful Drama*, pp. 120–121.

61. *Ibid.*, pp. 122, 132–134.

62. *The Tennessean*, February 5, 1950.

63. *Ibid.*

64. *Ibid.*

65. https://marthaobryan.org/; accessed October 31, 2022.

66. Melinda Squires, "The Controversial Career of George Nicholas Sanders" (M.A. thesis, Western Kentucky University, 2000), pp. 143–144. https://digitalcommons.wku.edu/theses/704/.

67. *Ibid.*, pp. 147–148.

68. *Ibid.* pp. 144–145.

69. Levin, *This Awful Drama*, pp. 134–135.

70. Richard G. Stone, Jr., "Jacob Thompson," (ncpedia 1996), accessed February 1, 2022, https://www.ncpedia.org/biography/thompson-jacob; "Jacob Thompson (1810–1885) Lawyer and Political Leader," accessed February

1, 2022, https://mississippiencyclopedia.org/entries/jacob-thompson/.

71. "Clement Vallandigham," Ohio History Central, accessed February 2, 2020, https://ohiohistorycentral.org/w/Clement_Vallandigham.

72. Roger Long, "Copperhead Clement Vallandigham," *Civil War Times Illustrated* XX, no. 8 (December 1981), p. 29.

73. Frohman, *Rebels on Lake Erie*, p. 67.

74. OR, Ser. 2, Vol. 8, p. 1001.

75. Frohman, *Rebels on Lake Erie*, p. 68.

76. Pickenpaugh, *Johnson's Island*, p. 97.

77. *Ibid.*, p. 103.

78. OR, Ser. 2, Vol. 8, pp. 1001, 1003.

79. Frohman, *Rebels on Lake Erie*, pp. 69–70.

80. "Confederate Stockade Cemetery," U.S. Department of Veterans Affairs, National Cemetery Administration, https://www.cem.va.gov/cems/lots/Confederate_Stockade.asp; accessed February 9, 2022.

Bibliography

Alford, Terry. *Fortunes Fool: The Life of John Wilkes Booth*. Oxford: Oxford University Press, 2015.

The Assassination of President Lincoln and the Trial of the Conspirators. New York: Moore, Wilstach & Baldwin, 1865. https://hdl.loc.gov/loc.law/llds.00120275616.2.

Ayer, I. Winslow. *The Great Northwestern Conspiracy*. Chicago: John R. Walsh, Baldwin & Bamford, 1865. https://www.gutenberg.org/ebooks/8543.

Baker, L.C. *History of the United States Secret Service*. L.C. Baker, Publisher, 1867.

Baker, W.W. *Memoirs of Service With John Yates Beall*. Richmond: The Richmond Press, 1910.

"The Baltimore Bastille." National Park Service online pamphlet. https://www.nps.gov/fomc/learn/historyculture/the-baltimore-bastille.htm.

Barret, John G., ed. *Yankee Rebel: The Civil War Journal of Edmund DeWitt Patterson*. Chapel Hill: University of North Carolina Press, 1966.

Bell, John. *Confederate Seadog: John Taylor Wood in War and Exile*. Jefferson, NC: McFarland, 2002.

Bell, John. *Rebels on the Great Lakes*. Toronto : Dundurn, 2011.

Biographical Souvenir of the States of Georgia and Florida. Chicago: F.A. Battey & Co., 1889. https://babel.hathitrust.org/cgi/pt?id=wu.89072984412&view=1up&seq=13.

Blue, Charles S. "Famous Canadian Trials." *Canadian Magazine* XLV (July 1915).

Boaz, Thomas. *Guns for Cotton: England Arms the Confederacy*. Shippensburg, PA: Burd Street Press, 1990.

Bonham, Milledge L., Jr. "New York and the Election of 1860." *New York History* 15, no. 2 (April 1934).

Botsford, David P. "The Port of Amherstburg, A Century Ago and Now." *Inland Seas* 5, no. 2 (Summer 1949).

Boyko, John. *Blood and Daring: How Canada Fought the American Civil War and Forged a Nation*. Toronto: Vintage Canada, 2014.

Brandt, Nat. *The Man Who Tried to Burn New York*. Lincoln: toExcel, 1986.

Bridges, Hal. "D.H. Hill's Anti-Yankee Algebra." *The Journal of Southern History* 22 (May 1956).

Brock, R.A. "Johnson's Island." *Southern Historical Society Papers* 30 (1902).

Brunson, Martha Luan Carter. "Confederate Activities From Canada: A Study in Canadian-American Relations." M.A. thesis, Texas Technological College, 1958.

Bukkuir, Anuraag. "The History of Malaria in the United States: How it Spread, How it Was Treated, and Public Responses." *MOJ Anatomy and Physiology*, April 28, 2016. https://medcraveonline.com/MOJAP/the-history-of-malaria-in-the-united-states-how-it-spread-how-it-was-treated-and-public-responses.html.

Bullard, F. Lauriston. *Famous War Correspondents*. Boston: Little, Brown, 1914. https://archive.org/details/famouswarcorresp00bulluoft/mode/1up?ref=ol&view=theater.

Burr, T.A. "A Romance of the Great Rebellion." *Firelands Pioneer* 1 (June 1882).

Bush, David R. Heidelberg University, Johnson's Island Dig, Field Report 4, July 1, 2006.

Bush, David R., Alan C. Tonetti, and Ed Bearss. National Historic Landmark Nomination Submitted to U.S. Department of the Interior, National Park Service, National Register of Historic Places Registration Form, "Johnson's Island Civil War Prison," January 1990.

Campbell, Thomas R. *Fire and Thunder: Exploits of the Confederate States Navy*. Shippensburg, PA: Burd Street Press, 1997.

Carpenter, Horace. "Plain Living at Johnson's Island." *The Century Illustrated Monthly Magazine* XLI (November 1890–April 1891).

"Cascade Shelters a Confederate Spy." 1834–1984: Cascade, Iowa—First 150 Years. Accessed December 13, 2015. http://sites.rootsweb.com/~iadubuqu/civilwar/cwspy.html.

Castleman, John Breckinridge. *Active Service in the Confederacy and Spanish War*. Louisville: Courier Journal Job Printing Co., 1917.

Catton, Bruce. *Grant Moves South*. Boston: Little, Brown, 1960.

"Charles C. Hemming, A Confederate Odyssey." *American Heritage Magazine* 36, no. 1 (1984). https://www.americanheritage.com/confederate-odyssey.

Clarke, Asia Booth. *The Unlocked Book: A Memoir of John Wilkes Booth*. New York: G.P. Putnam's Sons, 1938.

"Clement Vallandigham." Ohio History Central. Accessed February 2, 2020. https://ohiohistorycentral.org/w/Clement_Vallandigham.

"Confederate Stockade Cemetery." U.S. Department of Veterans Affairs. https://www.cem.va.gov/cems/lots/Confederate_Stockade.asp.

Court Martial of John Yates Beall. National Archives and Records Administration. Records of the Judge Advocate General (Army), File No. NN-3513.

Crouch, Robert C. "Picture Made on Johnson's Island." *Confederate Veteran* XVII (1909).

Cunningham, Edward O. "In Violation of the Laws of War: The Execution of Robert Cobb Kennedy." *Louisiana History, the Journal of the Louisiana Historical Association* 18, no. 2 (Spring 1977).

"The Dahlgren Papers Revisited." HistoryNet. https://www.historynet.com/the-dahlgren-papers-revisited/.

Daily Alta California 16, no. 5400, December 16 1864. https://cdnc.ucr.edu/?a=d&d=DAC18641216.2.14&e=en--20--1--txt-txIN--------1.

Davidson, Ron. *Images of America, Sandusky Ohio.* Mount Pleasant, SC: Arcadia, 2002.

Davis, Louise Littleton. *More Tales of Tennessee.* New Orleans: Pelican, 1978.

Davis, William C. *An Honorable Defeat: The Last Days of the Confederate Government.* New York: Harcourt, 2001.

"Depot of Prisoners of War on Johnson's Island, Ohio." ww.johnsonsisland.org/history/war.htm.

Dix, John A. *Memoirs of John Adams Dix.* New York: Harper & Brothers, 1883.

Durham, Roger S. *High Seas and Yankee Gunboats.* Columbia: University of South Carolina Press, 2005.

Early, Jubal. "The Story of the Attempted Formation of a Northwest Conspiracy." *Southern Historical Society Papers* X, no. 4 (April 1882).

Eicher, David J. *The Longest Night: A Military History of the Civil War.* New York: Simon & Schuster, 2001.

Eicher, John H., and David J. Eicher. *Civil War High Commands.* Stanford: Stanford University Press, 2001.

Endres, Kathleen. "A Pirate, A Prison, A Plot." University of Akron. Accessed June 17, 2018. http://rebelsonlakeerie.com/blog/.

Flood, Charles Bracelen. *1864: Lincoln at the Gates of History.* New York: Simon & Schuster, 2009.

Flowers, Frank Abial. *Edwin McMasters Stanton, the Autocrat of Rebellion, Emancipation and Reconstruction.* Boston : George M. Smith & Co., 1905.

Foner, Eric. *Reconstruction: America's Unfinished Revolution.* New York: Harper Perennial Modern Classics, 1988.

Foote, Shelby. *The Civil War, a Narrative, Red River to Appomattox.* New York : Random House, 1974.

Foreman, Amanda. *A World on Fire: Britain's Crucial Role in the American Civil War.* New York: Random House, 2010.

Francis, David W., and Virginia E. McCormick. "The United States Navy and the Johnson's Island Conspiracy: The Case of John C. Carter." *Northwest Ohio Quarterly,* Summer 1980.

Fraser, Chad. *Lake Erie Stories: Struggle and Survival on a Freshwater Ocean.* Toronto: Dundurn, 2008.

Frohman, Charles E. *Rebels on Lake Erie.* Columbus: Ohio Historical Society, 1965.

Furgurson, Ernest B. *Ashes of Glory: Richmond at War.* New York: Vintage, 1997.

George, Joseph, Jr. "Black Flag Warfare: Lincoln and the Raids Against Richmond and Jefferson Davis." *The Pennsylvania Magazine of History and Biography* 115, no. 3 (July 1991).

"Georgian (1864, Propeller)." Great Lakes Maritime Collection. https://greatlakeships.org/2904656/data?n=4.

"Georgian (Propeller) 1864." Maritime History of the Great Lakes. https://images.maritimehistoryofthegreatlakes.ca/26776/data?n=3.

Goodwin, Doris Kearns. *Team of Rivals: The Political Genius of Abraham Lincoln.* New York: Simon & Schuster, 2005.

Gora, Michael. *Lake Erie Islands, Sketches and Stories.* Put-in-Bay, OH: Lake Erie Islands Historical Society, 2004.

Gott, Kendall D. *Where the South Lost the War: An Analysis of the Fort Henry—Fort Donelson Campaign.* Mechanicsburg, PA: Stackpole Books, 2003.

Grady, John. "Trial of a Confederate Terrorist." *Civil War Monitor.* https://www.civilwarmonitor.com/blogs/trial-of-a-confederate-terrorist.

Gray, Wood. *The Hidden Civil War: The Story of the Copperheads.* New York: Viking Press, 1942.

Greaves, Graeden. *Wild Bennet Burleigh.* CreateSpace, 2012.

Gugliotta, Guy. *Freedom's Cap.* New York: Hill and Wang, 2012.

Hageman, Mark C. "Espionage in the Civil War." Signal Corps Association. Accessed January 6, 2022. http://www.civilwarsignals.org/pages/spy/spy.html.

Hall, James O. "The Dahlgren Papers." *Civil War Times Illustrated,* November 1983.

Harper, Ida Husted. "The Life and Work of Clara Barton." *The North American Review* 195, no. 678 (May 1912).

Harper, Robert S. *Ohio Handbook of the Civil War.* Columbus: Ohio Historical Society, 1961.

"Harpers Ferry During the Civil War." Encyclopedia Virginia. Accessed July 14, 2015. https://encyclopediavirginia.org/entries/harpers-ferry-during-the-civil-war/.

Hatch, Frederick. *Protecting President Lincoln.* Jefferson, NC: McFarland, 2016.

Headley, John W. *Confederate Operations in Canada and New York.* New York: The Neale Publishing Company, 1906.

Hesseltine, William Best. *Civil War Prisons.* New York: Ungar, 1930.

Hines, Thomas [and John B. Castleman]. "The Northwestern Conspiracy." *Southern Bivouac* 2 (1886).

"History of the Lake Shore and Michigan Southern Railway Company." New York Central Railroad System. 1913 Annual Report. https://web.archive.org/web/20131215142554/http://www.s363.com/dkny/lsms.html.

Hoffman, Michael. "William Hoffman's Encounters With History." National Museum of Civil War Medicine. Accessed January 29, 2022. https://www.civilwarmed.org/surgeons-call/hoffman/.

Horan, James D. Horan. *Confederate Agent*. Allentown, PA: The Fairfax Press, 1954.

Hundley, D.R. *Prison Echoes of the Great Rebellion*. New York: S.W. Green, 1874.

Hunter, Leslie Gene. "Warden for the Union: General William Hoffman." PhD diss., University of Arizona, 1971.

"In Tennessee, Exiled U.S. Congressman Clement Vallandigham is Delivered to the Confederate Lines." Dickenson College Civil War Research Engine. https://hd.housedivided.dickinson.edu/node/39579.

Jernigan, Thomas Watson. "Death at Elmira, William Hoffman and the Union Prison System." M.A. thesis, East Tennessee State University, 2005.

Johnson, Johnson. *A Vast and Fiendish Plot*. New York: Citadel Press, 2010.

Kinchen, Oscar. *Confederate Operations in Canada and the North*. North Quincy, MA: Christopher Publishing House, 1970.

Klement, Frank L. *Dark Lanterns: Secret Political Societies, Conspiracies, and Treason Trials in the Civil War*. Baton Rouge: Louisiana State University Press, 1984.

Kline, Michael J. *The Baltimore Plot: The First Conspiracy to Assassinate Abraham Lincoln*. Yardley, PA: Westholme, 2008.

Krick, Robert K. *Civil War Weather in Virginia*. Tuscaloosa: University of Alabama Press, 2007.

Krogh, Matthew Ostergaard. "The Eastern Shore of Virginia in the Civil War." Master of Arts thesis, Virginia Polytechnic Institute and State University, 2006.

Lacy, Michael O. "Military Commissions: A Historical Survey." *The Army Lawyer*, March 2002.

Laird, Jessica, and John Fabian Witt. "Inventing the War Crime: An Internal Theory." *Virginia Journal of International Law* 60 (2019–2020).

Langlois, Thomas Huxley, and Marina Holmes Langlois. *South Bass Island and Islanders*. Columbus: Ohio State University Press,1948.

Letter from William F. Hoffman to Edwin Stanton. December 3, 1863, NARA, Record Group 249.

Levin, Alexandra Lee. *This Awful Drama: General Edwin Gray Lee, C.S.A. and His Family*. New York: Vantage Press, 1987.

Logbook Entry, September 19, 1864, 8 p.m.–12 a.m., USS *Michigan*, Logbooks of U.S. Navy Ships 1801–1940. National Archives and Records Administration. Record Group 24.

Long, Roger. "Copperhead Clement Vallandigham." *Civil War Times Illustrated* XX, no. 8 (December 1981).

Long, Roger. "Johnson's Island Prison." *Blue and Gray* 4, no. 4 (February–March 1987).

"Lost to the Lake: Story of the Island Queen." Accessed June 14, 2014. http://www.lakeeffectliving.com/Jun14/Shipwrecks-Island_Queen.html.

Luca, Cassandra. "A History of the Land, Labor, and People of the Dumbarton Oaks Estate Until 1920." June–August 2019. Accessed July 24, 2022. chrome-extension://efaidnbmnnnibpcajpcglclefindmkaj/https://www.doaks.org/research/garden-landscape/summer-internship-program/luca-2019-gls-intern-report.pdf.

Lucas, Daniel. *Memoir of John Yates Beall: His Life; Trial; Correspondence; Diary and Private Manuscript Found Among His Papers, Including His Own Account of the Raid on Lake Erie*. Montreal: John Lovell, 1865.

Lucas, Virginia. "John Yates Beall: An Appreciation." *Confederate Veteran* 35 (August 1927).

Lucas, Virginia. "John Yates Beall: An Appreciation" *Confederate Veteran* 35 (September 1927).

Lupold, Harry F., and Gladys Haddad, eds. *Ohio's Western Reserve: A Regional Reader*. Kent, OH: Kent State University Press, 1988.

Mahan, Bruce. "A Confederate Spy." Ed. John Ely Briggs. *The Palimpsest* IV (February 1923).

Markens, Isaac. "President Lincoln and the Case of John Y. Beall." *Americana Illustrated, National Americana Society* 6 (January–December 1911).

Markle, Donald E. *Spies and Spymasters of the Civil War*. New York: Barnes and Noble, 1994.

Marvel, William. *Lincoln's Autocrat: The Life of Ewin Stanton*. Chapel Hill: University of North Carolina Press, 2015.

Mayers, Adam. "Confederacy's Canadian Mission: Spies Across the Border." *Civil War Times*, June 2001. https://www.historynet.com/-confederacys-canadian-mission-spies-across-the-border/.

Mayers, Adam. *Dixie & the Dominion: Canada, the Confederacy and the War for the Union*. Toronto: Dundurn, 2003.

McDermott, S. Keyron. Interview by Ralph Lindeman, August 30, 2017 (McDermott is a Cascade, Iowa, resident who has researched Beall's time in Cascade and written a theatrical play about it, *The True Story of John Yates Beall*.)

Meyers, David, Elise Meyers, and James Dailey II. *Inside the Ohio Penitentiary*. Mount Pleasant, SC: History Press 2013.

Mills, Eric. *Chesapeake Bay in the Civil War*. Centreville, MD: Tidewater, 1996.

Moizuk, Ruth Dickerman. *The Put in Bay Story*. Self-published, publication date unknown, https://archive.org/details/putinbaystory00moiz.

Morgans, James Patrick. *John Todd and the Underground Railroad; Biography of an Iowa Abolitionist*. Jefferson, NC: McFarland, 2006.

"Morgan's Raid." Ohio History Central. www.ohiohistorycentral.org/w/Morgan%27s_Raid.

Moseley, Cameron S. *John Yates Beall: Confederate Commando*. Great Falls, VA: Clan Bell International, 2011.

Murphy, David J. "Naval Strategy During the American Civil War." Air War College, Air University, Research Report (Maxwell Air Force Base, Alabama, 1999), chrome-extension://efaidnbmnnnibpcajpcglclefindmkaj/https://apps.dtic.mil/sti/pdfs/ADA395177.pdf.

Mytum, Harold, and Gilly Carr, eds. *Prisoners of War: Archeology, Memory, and Heritage of 19th and 20th Century Mass Internment*. New York: Springer Science and Business Media, 2013.

Nelson, Larry E. *Bullets, Ballots and Rhetoric: Confederate Policy for the United States Presidential Contest of 1864*. Tuscaloosa: University of Alabama Press, 1980.

Nicolay, John, and John G. Hay. "Abraham Lincoln: A History. The Chicago Surrender." *The Century* 38, Issue 4 (August 1889).

Nicolay, John G., and John G. Hay, eds. *Abraham Lincoln: Complete Works, Comprising His Speeches, Letter, State Papers, and Miscellaneous Writings*. New York: The Century Company, 1894.

Nuermberger, Ruth Ketrig. *The Clays of Alabama—A Planter, Lawyer, Politician Family*. Lexington: University of Kentucky Press, 1958.

Official Proceedings of the Democratic National Convention. The Times Steam Book and Job Printing House, 1864. https://quod.lib.umich.edu/m/moa/AEW7007.0001.001/1?rgn=full+text;view=image.

"Our History: Former Faculty, Holcombe, James P. (1851–1861)." University of Virginia School of Law. Accessed January 30, 2022. https://libguides.law.virginia.edu/faculty/holcombe.

Papers of Gen. William F. Hoffman. National Archives and Records Administration, Records of the Office of Commissary General. Record Group 249. File 16.

"Papers Relating to Foreign Affairs, Accompanying the Annual Message of the President to the Second Session, Thirty-eighth Congress, Part II, Document 561." U.S. Department of State, Office of the Historian. Accessed July 13, 2021. https://history.state.gov/historicaldocuments/frus1864p2/d561.

Pelzer, John, and Linda Pelzer. "The Ghost of the Chesapeake." *Civil War Times Illustrated* 26 (1987).

Philbrick, Nathaniel. *Sea of Glory: America's Voyage of Discovery, the U.S. Exploring Expedition*. London: Penguin Random House, 2003.

Pickenpaugh, Roger. *Captives in Gray*. Tuscaloosa: University of Alabama Press, 2009.

Pickenpaugh, Roger. *Johnson's Island*. Kent, OH: Kent State University Press, 2016.

Pryor, Sara A. *Reminiscences in Peace and War*. New York: Macmillan, 1905.

"The Queen's Hotel Then and Now." Toronto Then and Now. Accessed June 13, 2018. http://torontothenandnow.blogspot.com/2011/08/26-queens-hotel-then-and-now.html.

"Richmond During the Civil War." Encyclopedia Virginia. Accessed February 13, 2017. https://www.encyclopediavirginia.org/Richmond_During_the_Civil_War.

Rives, John C., ed. Clement Laird Vallandigham, "The Constitution—Peace—Reunion," Appendix. *Congressional Globe: Containing the Speeches, Important State Papers and the Laws of the Third Session Thirty-seventh Congress*. Washington, D.C.: Globe Office, 1863.

"The Robertson Foundry and Ferndell." Guelph Downtown. https://cms.driftscape.com/feature/5394e6de-f4df-11ea-8000-bc1c5a8f0f67.

Robinson, William Morrison, Jr. *The Confederate Privateers*. New Haven: Yale University Press, 1928.

Rodgers, Bradley A. *Guardian of the Great Lakes: The U.S. Paddle Frigate*. Ann Arbor: University of Michigan Press, 1996.

Ross, Carolyn J. "Jacob Thompson (1810–1885) Lawyer and Political Leader." Accessed February 1, 2022. https://mississippiencyclopedia.org/entries/jacob-thompson/.

Rowley, Tom. "Bennet Burleigh: The Wild Man of the Victorian Press." June 13, 2013. Accessed Dec. 29, 2021. https://www.telegraph.co.uk/history/10132546/Bennet-Burleigh-the-wild-man-of-theVictorian-press.html

Ryall, Lydia J. (as Theresa Thorndale). *Sketches and Stories of the Lake Erie Islands*. Sandusky, OH: I.F. Mack & Brother, 1898.

"St. Lawrence Hall: Higgins & Cooper Proprietors, Montreal, 1898." Advertisement. Accessed September 9, 2017. https://archive.org/details/cihm_44387/page/n3/mode/2up.

The St. Lawrence Hall Montreal City Guide: 1885. Montreal: Canada Bank Note Company, 1885.

Salmon, John. "Bellvue." *National Register of Historic Places Registration Form*. September 29, 1989. Accessed December 13, 2022. https://web.archive.org/web/20120926203837/http://www.dhr.virginia.gov/registers/Counties/Bedford/009-0003_Bellevue_1990_Final_Nomination.pdf.

"Samuel Peter Heintzelman (September 30, 1805–May 1, 1880)." Ohio Civil War Central. https://www.ohiocivilwarcentral.com/samuel-peter-heintzelman/.

Schultz, Duane. *The Dahlgren Affair: Terror and Conspiracy in the Civil War*. New York: W.W. Norton, 1998.

Sears, Stephen W. *Landscape Turned Red: The Battle of Antietam*. Boston: Ticknor & Fields, 1983.

Selenfriend, Steven, and Ted Myers. "The Iron Lady of Erie." American Society of Arms Collectors, Saratoga Springs, N.Y., *Bulletin* No. 79 (Fall 1998), chrome-extension://efaidnbmnnnibpcajpcglclefindmkaj/https://americansocietyofarmscollectors.

org/wp-content/uploads/2019/06/1998-B79-The-Iron-Lady-of-Erie.pdf.

Sheehy, Barry. "Conspiracy in Montreal 1864–1865: The Confederate Secret Service in Canada and the Lincoln Assassination." *North & South*, May–June 2019.

Sheehy, Barry. *Montreal, City of Secrets*. Montreal: Baraka Books, 2017.

Shepard, Frederick J. "The Johnson's Island Plot." *Publications of the Buffalo Historical Society* IX (1906).

Shepherd, Henry E. *Narrative of Prison Life at Baltimore and Johnson's Island Ohio*. Baltimore: Commercial Ptg. & Sts. Co., 1917. University of North Carolina, electronic edition, 1998. https://docsouth.unc.edu/fpn/shepherd/shepherd.html.

Shriver, Phillip B., and Donald J. Breen. *Ohio's Military Prisons in the Civil War*. Columbus: Ohio State University Press, 1964.

Singer, Jane. *The Confederate Dirty War*. Jefferson, NC: McFarland, 2005.

Slater, Margaret. *National Register of Historic Places Registration Form, George O'Bryan House, Nashville, Tenn.* (U.S. Department of the Interior, January 24, 1989), chrome-extension://efaidnbmnnnibpcajpcglclefindmkaj/https://npgallery.nps.gov/GetAsset/05921fa8-ac71-44e5-9f6f-0396ee375d11.

Slave Schedule, 1850 U.S. Federal Census, George B. Beall. Accessed July 24, 2022. https://search.ancestry.com/cgi-bin/sse.dll?_phsrc=nHH28&_phstart=successSource&usePUBJs=true&indiv=1&dbid=8055&gsfn=George&gsln=Beall&_83004003-n_xcl=f&msrpn__ftp=charles%20town,%20jefferson,%20west%20virginia,%20usa&msrpn=24681&_80100003=Beall&new=1&rank=1&uidh=6g2&redir=false&msT=1&gss=angs-d&pcat=3-5&fh=0&h=92811127&recoff=&ml_rpos=1&queryId=2ce962a6a1178b17ee00912efcafff3b.

Slave Schedule, 1860 U.S. Federal Census, John Yates Beall. Accessed July 25, 2022. https://www.ancestry.com/imageviewer/collections/7668/images/vam653_1392-0323?treeid=&personid=&hintid=341945742bdbfe1af2e31a51f439329c&usePUB=true&_phsrc=nHH36&_phstart=successSource&usePUBJs=true&pId=91145079.

Smith, Michael T. *The Enemy Within: Fears of Corruption in the Civil War North*. Charlottesville: University of Virginia Press, 2011.

Soodalter, Ron. "Murder with a Vengeance: John Yates Beall, John Wilkes Booth and the Killing of a President." Accessed October 21, 2021. https://www.historynet.com/murder-with-w-vengeance.htm.

Speer, Lonnie R. *Portals to Hell, Military Prisons of the Civil War*. Mechanicsburg, PA: Stackpole Books, 1997.

Speer, Victor, ed. *Memoirs of a Great Detective: Incidents in the Life of John Wilson Murray*. New York: The Baker & Taylor Co., 1904.

Spencer, Herbert Reynolds. USS *Michigan*. The Erie Book Store, 1966.

Squires, Melinda. "The Controversial Career of George Nicholas Sanders." M.A. thesis, Western Kentucky University, 2000. https://digitalcommons.wku.edu/theses/704/.

Stahr, Walter. *Stanton: Lincoln's War Secretary*. New York: Simon & Schuster, 2017.

Stakes, Edward T. *A True Account of His Suffering While a Prisoner of War—Fortieth Virginia Infantry*. Edited by Martin Stakes Lane. N.p.: Martin Stakes Lane, 2000.

Starr, Stephen Z. *Colonel Grenfell's Wars*. Baton Rouge: Louisiana State University Press, 1971.

Steers, Edward, Jr. *Blood on the Moon*. Lexington: University Press of Kentucky, 2001.

Stiles, Edward H. "General Fitz Henry Warren." *The Annals of Iowa* 6, no. 7, 3rd Series (October 1904).

Stone, Geoffrey R. *Perilous Times: Free Speech in Wartime*. New York: WW. Norton, 2004.

Stone, Richard G., Jr. "Jacob Thompson." NCPE-DEA. https://www.ncpedia.org/biography/thompson-jacob.

Strausbaugh, John. *City of Sedition: The History of New York City During the Civil War*. New York: Hachette, 2016.

Surdam, David G. "Traders or Traitors: Northern Cotton Trading During the Civil War." *Business and Economic History* 28, no. 2 (Winter 1999).

Sutherland, David A. "Wood, John Taylor." *Dictionary of Canadian Biography*, Vol. 13. University of Toronto/Université Laval, 2003. Accessed August 5, 2019. http://www.biographi.ca/en/bio/wood_john_taylor_13E.html.

Telegrams Received, Johnson's Island Prison (November 1863–October 1864). National Archives and Records Administration, Records of the Office of Commissary General. Record Group 249, File 311.

"Testimony as to Cause of Lincoln's Murder" *Confederate Veteran* 19 (July 1911).

Tidwell, William A., James O. Hall, and David Winfred Gaddy. *Come Retribution: The Confederate Secret Service and the Assassination of Abraham Lincoln*. Jackson: University Press of Mississippi, 1988.

Toomey, Daniel Carrol. "Where the Civil War Began." *Baltimore Magazine*, April 2011. https://www.baltimoremagazine.com/section/historypolitics/where-the-civil-war-began-2/.

Townsend, George Alfred. *The Life, Crime and Capture of John Wilkes Booth*. New York: Dick and Fitzgerald, 1865.

Trial of John Y. Beall as a Spy and Guerrillero, By Military Commission. New York: D. Appleton, 1865.

Tucker, Spencer C., ed. *American Civil War: The Definitive Encyclopedia and Document Collection*. Santa Barbara: ABC-CLIO, 2013

U.S. Department of the Navy. *Official Records of the Union and Confederate Navies in the War of the Rebellion*. Washington, D.C.: Government Printing Office, 1894–1927.

U.S. War Department. *The War of the Rebellion: A Compilation of the Official Records of the Union and Confederate Armies.* Washington, D.C.: Government Printing Office 1880–1901.

"The USS Michigan—the First Iron Ship of Her Age." Magic Masts and Sturdy Ships. https://magicmastsandsturdyships.weebly.com/the-uss-michigan---the-first-iron-ship-of-her-age.html.

Waugh, John C. *Re-Electing Lincoln.* Boston : Da Capo Press, 1997.

Weber, Jennifer L. *Copperheads: The Rise and Fall of Lincoln's Opponents in the North.* Oxford: Oxford University Press, 2006.

"Who Was Philo Parsons?" Digital Traveler. Accessed July 18, 2019. https://lemacks.com/2019/07/18/who-was-philo-parsons-of-brush-park-detroit-a-steamship-bearing-his-name-was-featured-in-the-civil-war/.

"Why Booth Killed President Lincoln." *Confederate Veteran* 9 (January 1901).

Wilkinson, J. *The Narrative of a Blockade-Runner.* New York: Sheldon & Company, 1877. https://archive.org/details/narrativeofblock0000wilk.

Will of George Beall. Accessed July 25, 2022. https://www.ancestry.com/discoveryui-content/view/532474:9087?tid .

Williams, W.W. *History of the Firelands, Comprising Huron and Erie Counties, Ohio.* Cleveland: Press Leader Printing Co., 1879.

Winks, Robin. *The Civil War Years: Canada and the United States.* Montreal: McGill-Queen's University Press, 1998.

Woodford, Frank B. *Father Abraham's Children: Michigan Episodes in the Civil War.* Detroit: Wayne State University Press, 1961, 1999.

Woolson, Constance. "The Wine Islands of Lake Erie." *Harper's Magazine* 47 (June 1873).

Yocum, Barbara. "Fort Jay: Historic Structure Report." Governors Island National Monument, National Parks of New York Harbor, National Park Service, 2005.

Zornow, William Frank. "Confederate Raiders on Lake Erie." *Inland Seas* 5, no. 1 (Spring 1949).

Newspapers

Baltimore Sun
Buffalo Commercial Advertiser
Chicago Tribune
Daily Commercial Register (Sandusky)
The Daily Dispatch (Richmond)
The Daily Ohio Statesman (Columbus)
Daily Press (Hampton Roads, VA)
The Fremont Journal (Ohio)
The New York Herald
The New York Times
Plain Dealer (Cleveland)
The Richmond Enquirer
The San Francisco Call
The Sentinel (Richmond)
The Tennessean (Nashville)
Virginian-Pilot (Hampton Roads, VA)
The World (New York)

Index

Numbers in *bold italics* indicate pages with illustrations

Alexander, Charles T. 105
Alford, Terry 144, 189–191
Alliance (schooner) 57–58
Alpha (steamer) 81
American Express Company 161
Amherstburg, Ontario (Canada West) *see* Malden, Ontario (Canada West)
Anderson, George S. 151–152, 154, 160–161, 164–165, 173–175
Annapolis, Md. 55, 102, 197
Antietam, Battle of (Md.) 32, 47
Appomattox, Va. 5, 82, 200
Ashbrook, John T. 160, 164
Ashley, Walter O. 109–110, 118–119, 121, 131, 173, 193
Atlanta, Ga. 97
Atwood, Sylvester 114, 119, 121, 129
Ayer, I. Winslow 126

Back River, Va. 56
Baker, William W. 54, 57–60, 164
Baltimore, Md. 40, 52, 60, 71–72, 82, 84, 110, 143–144, 147, 179–181
Banks, Nathaniel 22
Barnes, James Virgul 149
Barrett, James 88
Bates, James 152, 154–155, 157
Beall, John Yates *9*, 15, 21, 44, 49, 65, 75, 97, 101, 110, 125, 128, 145; Acting Master commission 43; and Booth, John Wilkes 3, 16, 144, 187–192; and Buffalo, N.Y. train raid 161–165; in Cascade, Iowa 26–27; on Chesapeake Bay 53–54, 56–60; clemency appeals after death sentence 181–183; Confederacy views 22–23, 166; and Davis, Jefferson 41–43; education 8; execution 184–186; family background 7–8; in Fort Columbus, N.Y. 5–9, 180; in Fort Lafayette, N.Y. 168; and Fort McHenry 60–61, 72, 82; and CSS *Georgian* 151–158; and Johnson's Island 38, 137; military service 15–17, 83–84; in Mulberry Street prison NYC 166–168; mutiny

of raiding team 128–129; with O'Bryan, Martha 22, 84; and *Philo Parsons* 114–120, 132–133; sentencing 179–181; and Thompson, Jacob 99, 113, 160; trial 171–178
Belle Island Prison (Va.) 63, 145
Benjamin, Judah 75, 94, 126, 140, 157, 198–199
Bingham, Robert 67–68
Black, Jeremiah 93
Blackburn, Luke P. 125, 142
Blair, Francis P. 181
blockade runners 34–35, 37, 51, 65, 78, 80, 142–143, 147, 195, 198
Bolles, John 171–175, 177–178
Booth, John Wilkes 35, 86; and John Yates Beall 3, 16, 144, 187–192; in Montreal 141–148, and quinine smuggling 147
Boteler, Alexander R. 172
Brady, James T. 172–177, 179
Brooke, John 55
Brotherhood of the Southern Cross, Order of 113, 159
Brown, Annie *see* Davis, Annie
Brown, John 3, 16, 191
Brown, John, Jr. 130–131
Brown Brothers 149
Browning, Orville H. 180–181
Bruce Mines, Ontario (Canada West) *156*, 157
Buckner, Simon B. 21
Buffalo, N.Y. 8, 42, 87, 98, 108, 112, 134, 136, 140, 151–155, *153*, 159, 161–166, *163*, 169, 178, 188, 190
Bullock, John J. 181
Burke, Martin 179
Burley, Bennet G. *55*, 145, 193–195; as actor in play 59; background 54–56; in Guelph 137, 152, 155–156; and *Philo Parsons* 110–111, 114, 118, 120–121, 129
Burnside, Ambrose 49–51, 74
Butler, Benjamin F. 82–83, 92, 98, 100–101, 127, 134, 138
Butternuts 46
Byrnes, Thomas F. 166

Calais, Maine 139
Camp Chase (Ohio) 12, 24–25, 86, 89
Camp Douglas (Ill.) 73, 88–89, 95, 97–98, 100, 134, 138
Camp Morton (Ind.) 85, 89
Campbell, Michael 117–118, 121, 129, 132–133
Cape Charles Light (Va.) 57
Carpenter, Horace 67–68
Carter, John C. 66, 98–99, 122–124, 127–128, 131–132, 154, 157, 195
Castle Thunder (Va.) 55, 63
Castleman, John B. 87, 92, 95–96, 98, 100–101, 138
Catawba Island, Ohio *14*, 130
Chesapeake Bay 32, 40, 42–43, *53*, 65, 82, 84, 99, 110, 145, 147, 151, 155, 164, 98; and Beall's privateering activities 52–54, 56, 60, 61
Chew, Margaret 26–27
Chew, Thomas 27
Chicago, Ill. 2, 8, 42, 66, 73, 109, 111–112, 125–127, 134, 138, 144, 155, 158–159; and Democratic Convention 88–101
Chicago Tribune 96
Chickanolee Reef (Ohio) 121, 132
Cincinnati Enquirer 28, 181
City Point, Va. 82–83
Civil War Military Draft Act 49
Clarke, Asia Booth 146
Clay, Clement 79–82, *80*, 85–87, 91, 98, 138, 140, 142, 187, 195
Cleary, William 80–81, 90–91
Cleveland, Ohio 8, 12–13, 42, 113, 134, 151, 153–155, *163*, 159, 201
Clifton, H.V. 147
Clifton House (N.Y.) 86, 91
Cole, Charles 98–99, 101, 111–13, 115, 118, 121–125, 127–128, 138, 160, 196, 201
Collingwood, Ontario (Canada West) 155, *156*, 157
Colored Troops, U.S. 56
Columbus, Ga. 84
Columbus, Ohio 12, 24–25, 34, 50, 74, 201, 134

Confederacy/Confederates in Canada 34–35, 38, 88, 93, 126, 141–142, 187, 190; and cotton trade 36, 47, 78, 149–150; and food shortages 69–70, 78, 149; and Great Britain 36–38, 47, 70, 136–137, 139; and plans for attacks on North 2, 8, 26, 42–43, 65–66, 68, 70–73, 75–76, 87, 91, 95–96, 98, 100–101, 108, 111, 113, 124–125, 134, 139, 151–153, 159–160; and plots against Lincoln 142–147, 182, 187; and Union prisoners 12, 30–32, 63, 82–83, 102

Confederate Commissioners 78–81, 85–87, 90, 94, 98–99, 108, 111, 125, 136–138, 140, 147, 151, 158–159, 172, 187; and Booth, John Wilkes 142, 145; and Niagara Falls Peace Conference 91–92, 94; and St. Albans raid 139–140

Confederate Secret Service 72, 83, 93, 143, 145, 147, 160, 162, 198

Confederate Volunteer Coast Guard 58

USS *Connecticut* 81

contrabands 56

Cooke, Jay 149

Cooke Brothers Bank 149

Copperheads 2, 27, 48, 50, 70–73, 75, 79, 86, 96, 101, 113, 126–127, 158, 170; and Chicago Democratic convention 89, 97, 100; geographical concentration 46, 75, 88; meaning of name 46; in Sandusky 112, 124, 196

cotton trade 35–36, 47, 78, 148; Montreal cotton sale negotiations 148–150

Dahlgren, Ulric 145–146

Daily Commercial Register (Sandusky) 13, 20, 24, 28–29, 120, 124

Daily Dispatch (Richmond) 69

Dana, Charles A. 171

Davis, Annie 112, 123, 138

Davis, Jefferson 36, 91, 145–146, 172, 175, 177; and anti-war sentiment in North 44, 70–71, 75, 77; and Beall, John Yates 41–43; and Confederate Commissioners 78–82, 86–87, 140; and Confederate Secret Service 72, and rebel raids in North 65, 68, 70, 72, 75–76

Day, H. 169

Dayton Journal 50

Democratic Convention of 1864 2, 88, 90, 92, 95–97, 100, 111, 125, 127

Denison, James 117, 132–133

Dennison, William 20, 26

Detroit, Mich. 12, 34, 42, 51, 68, 86, 88, 94, 96, 109–110, 113–114,

122–128, 131–134, 137, 155, *163*, 196

Detroit River 12, 34, 68, 86, 109, 114–115, *115*, 122, 128, 131–132, 137, 155, 196

Dix, John A. 134–36, 139–140, 162, 164, 185, 196; Beall trial 169–171, 175; post–Beall trial 179–183; and prisoner exchange cartel 31–33

Dix-Hill Cartel 30–32, 62–63, 71, 82–83; *see also* prisoner exchanges

Dooley, John 67

Douglas, Stephen A. 88, 180

Dragon Swamp 59

Drummond, Edward 28, 30, 32

Drummondtown, Va. 60, 61

Dubuque Herald (Iowa) 27, 49

Dunkirk, N.Y. *153*, 162, *163*, 174–175

Early, Jubal 89

Ellery, G.H. 149

Emancipation Proclamation 36, 45–47, 49, 56, 63

Emmons, Halmar H. 94

Enrollment Act 49

Erie, Pa. 42, 64–66, 99, 154, 159, 162, *163*

Evening Journal (Albany, N.Y.) 150

Fargo, William 149, 154

Farragut, David 92, 97

Federal Flotilla 52

Fighting Island, Mich. 132–133

Fisk, James "Diamond Jim" 149

Ford's Theater (D.C.) 147

Forney, John W. 181

Fort Columbus (N.Y.) 5, *6*, *7*, 12, 178, 180, 182, 184, 189, 191

Fort Donelson, Battle of (Tenn.) 21, 24–25, 31, 88

Fort McHenry (Md.) 52, 60, 72, 82, 99, 110, 167–168

Fort Monroe (Va.) 31–32, 52, 56–57, 82, 195

Fort Warren (N.Y.) 37, 51, 159

Fredericksburg, Battle of (Va.) 46, 49–50

Garfield, John A. 181

General Grant (steamer) 131

General Meigs (transport ship) 160

General Order No. 97 162

General Order No. 100 170

Genesee House (N.Y.) 161

Geneva Convention 170

CSS *Georgian* 152–157, 160–161, 175

Georgian Bay, Ontario (Canada West) 155, *156*, 157

Gettysburg, Battle of (Pa.) 62, 69, 72–73, 112, 159

Gibson, Elijah 67

Gould, Jay 149

Governors Island, N.Y. 5, *6*, *7*, 178, 180, 184, 189

Grant, Ulysses S. 21, 31, 63, 69, 70, 77, 88, 92, 150; 1864 spring campaign 82–84

Great Britain 2, 34, 36–38, 42, 47, 68, 70, 76, 90, 99, 135–137, 139, 148

Greek Fire 91, 108, 139, 160

Greeley, Horace 91–92

Gregg, Philander 19, 25

Guelph, Canada West (Ontario) 137, 152, 155–156, 193

"The Guerilla" (play) 59; *see also* Burley, Bennet G.

Haines, Henry 120, 132

Halifax, Nova Scotia 34, 65, 80–82, 98, 195

Halleck, Henry 103

Hamilton, William 120, 132

Hamilton, Ontario (Canada West) 34–35, 37, 161

Hampton, Va. 32

Hampton Roads, Va. 55, 82

Harrington, James T. 160, 164

Hay, John 91–92, 158

Hays, Edward 167–168, 173–174

Headley, John 151–152, 154, 160–162, 164

Heintzelman, Samuel P. 101, 134–136

Hemming, Charles C. 152–153, 160, 164

Hesseltine, William 82

Hill, Bennett J. 122–127, 155

Hill, Charles W. 103, 105–107, 123–124, 131, 135, 138

Hill, D.H. (Daniel Harvey) 31–32

Hines, Thomas H. 72–77, *73*, 79, 84–89, 87, 92, 125–126, 138, 144, 196–197; and Democratic Convention 89, 95–96, 100–101; and Lake Erie raid 111, 113; and Lincoln 86; and Vallandigham 88

Hinton, William 131

Hitchcock, Ethan Allen 83, 134–136

Hoffman, William 10, *11*, 26, 135, 197–198; and prison design 18–21, 24, 25 105–106; and prison overcrowding 107; and retaliatory actions 63–64, 102–104; and selection of Johnson's Island site 10, 12–15

Holcombe, James 81–82, 86–87, 91–92, 98, 142, 198

Holt, Forney 161, 164

Holt, Joseph 188

Hooker, Joseph J. 49

Horan, James D. 85

Howe, M.S. 169

Hukill, Frederick 117–118, 129

Hunter, Andrew 17

Hyams, Godfrey J. 125

Island Queen, steamer 10, 13–16, *15*, 24, 28, 119–121, 128–130, 132, 134–135, 137, 169, 173, 178, 193

Johnson, Clint 101
Johnson, Herschel V. 71
Johnson, Leonard B. 14–15, 63–64, 201
Johnson's Island 1–2, *14*–15, *19*, 24–26, 32, 38, 64, 74, 85, 89, 106, 109, 112, 118–119, 121, 123–124, 126, 128, 130–131, 134–136, 138, 143, 145, 152, 154–155, 157, 159–160, *163*, 169, 189, 195–196, 200–201; and baseball 70; and cold weather 68; and 1863 raid 65–66; and escapes 67–68, 107; and food rations 102–104; and hygiene problems 64, 105; and leadership 20, 103; and USS *Michigan* 64–66, 99; and overcrowding 62, 107; and plans for raid 38, 40–42, 71, 75, 97–99, 111, 122, 124–125; and prison design 18–21, 105; and prison photographer 30; and prisoner activities 28–30, 62–63; and prisoner organization 26, 112–113; and shootings 67

Kane, George P. 71, 143
Kansas-Nebraska Act 130
Kelley, Alfred 120
Kelleys Island, Ohio 13–14, 28, 114–115, 118–19, 121, 128, 131
Kennedy, Robert Cobb 107–108, 160, 164, 169
Kennesaw Mountain, Battle of (Tenn.) 92
Key, Francis Scott 60

Lafayette, Marquis de 169
Lake Balsam Ontario (Canada West) 137
Lake Champlain, Vt. 138
Lake Erie Islands 10, 12, *14*, 16, 109; *see also* Catawba Island; Johnson's Island; Kelleys Island; Middle Bass Island; North Bass Island; Put-in-Bay; South Bass Island
Lake Shore Railway 159–160, 162
Lane, G.M. 149
Langhorne, Maurice 125
Lee, Edwin Gray 41–43, 54, 198
Lee, Robert E. 5, 16, 29, 32, 41, 47, 49, 69–70, 72, 73, 77, 82–83, 150, 200
Lexington, Mich. 157
Libby Prison (Va.) 12, 63, 145
Lieber, Francis 170–171
Lieber Code 170–171; *see also* war crimes
Lincoln, Abraham 1–3, 45, 50–51, 70, 72, 77–78, 86–90, 94, 96, 125, 134, 136, 141, 146, 170, 172, 187–188, 192, 199; and anti-war sentiment 44, 46, 70–71; and Beall, John Yates 172, 180–183, 187–190, 192; and Booth, John Wilkes 141–147, 187, 189–192; and cotton sales 148–150; and

1864 election 8, 92–93, 158; and Emancipation Proclamation 45, 47, 56, 63; and Great Britain 36–38, 47, 140; and military draft 48–49, 93; and Niagara Falls Peace Conference 91–92; and prisoner exchanges 30–31, 63, 83; and war crimes 170–171
Lockwood, Henry H. 61
London Daily Telegraph 59, 143, 194–195
Lucas, Daniel 8, 22–23, 35, 40–41, 54, 121, 145, 172, 182, 190–191, 198
Lyons, Richard 66

Magle, George 130
Mahoney, Dennis A. 27, 49
malaria 41, 110, 146
Malden, Ontario (Canada West) 114, 116–117, 132, *153*, 155
Mallory, Stephen 42–43, 57, 83, 175
Marblehead Peninsula, Ohio *14*, 15, 121, 130
Marie Victoria, schooner 144
Markens, Isaac 182–183, 190
Martin, E.G. 123
Martin, Patrick C. 143–144
Martin, Robert M. 151–152, 154, 160–164, 175
Mason, James 37–38, 90
Mathews County, Va. 53, 57
Mathews Courthouse, Va. 53, 59, 84
Maxwell, John 55–56, 145
McClellan, George 8, 27, 29, 47; as Democratic presidential candidate 96–97, 158
McClure, James 9, 179, 180, 183–184, 192
McDonald, Roy 54
McFarland, Thomas 54, 58–59
McGuire, Edward 54, 59
McKennon, Archibald S. 113
McLean, Washington 181
Meade, George 83–84
Meigs, Montgomery C. 10, 12, 15, 18, 21, 25
USS *Merrimack see* CSS *Virginia*
USS *Michigan* 38, 42, 64–66, *65*, 98–99, 101, 151–152, 154, 157, 195; and Captain John C. Carter 98–99; description 64; and Johnson's Island raid 111–113, 116, 118, 121–124, 126–29, 131–132, 134–135, 137
Middle Bass Island, Ohio 13, *14*, 114, 118–121, 128–129, 131–132
military commissions 170
military draft 46, 48–49, 63, 70, 72, *93*, 142
Militia Act 48, 63
Monck, Lord Charles 66, 136, 155
USS *Monitor* 55
Montreal, Quebec (Canada East) 34, 65, 71, 80–81, 85–86, 93, 123, 138, 153; and Booth 141–145,

188, 190; and Confederates 35, 92, 126, 142, 144, 147, 158; and cotton sales 148–150, 154
Morgan, Edwin 150
Morgan, John Hunt 77, 79, 87, 89, 95, 98, 125, 138, 151, 160, 175, 197; Ohio raid and imprisonment 73–76
Morgan Thomas Gibbs 62
Morris, William Hopkins 169
Morse, Samuel 55
Mosby, John Singleton 53
Mudd, Samuel 144
Mulberry Street Police Station, N.Y. 165–166, 173–175
Murphey, Virgil 30, 106
Murphy, J.B. 107
Murray, Robert 184

New York City firebombing 108, 160, 165, 167, 170, 176
New York Daily News 90
New York Herald 142, 189
New York Times 5, 31, 172
Newport News, Va. 52, 56
Niagara Falls, N.Y. 34, 38, 66, 86, 91, 98, 117, 148, 152–*153*, *163*, 164–165, 173–174
Niagara Falls Peace Conference 91–92
Nichols, Dewitt C. 114, 116–118, 129, 132–133
Nichols, John W. 94
Norris, William 124
North Bass Island, Ohio 13, *14*, 114
Northwest Conspiracy 71–72, 75–77, 88–91, 95–97, 100–101, 126–127, 158
Nuremberg trials 171

O'Bierne, R.F. 169
O'Bryan, Martha 9, 22, 84, 189, 192, 198–199
Ogden, Richard D'Orsay 59
Ohio 130th Infantry Regiment 119
Ontario Bank, Montreal, Quebec (Canada East) 88, 143
Order of American Knights 70, 88, 127; *see also* Sons of Liberty
Orr, George W. 24, 120, 129, 132
Ould, Robert 83

Pacific (steamer) 155
Patterson, Edmund Dewitt 135
Peel, William 104
Pendleton, George P. 47
Perry, Oliver Hazard 14, 130
Petersburg, Va. 82, 92
Philo Parsons (steamer) 8, *110*, 114–122, 125, 127–134, 137, 157, 169, 173–174, 178, 193, 195; description 109; and role in raid 113
Piankatank River, Va. 57
Pierson, William S. 20, 25–26, 29, 64, 74, 103

Pinkerton, Alan 143
Port Colborne, Ontario (Canada West) 152–154, *153*, 160
Port Stanley, Ontario (Canada West) 155
Potter, John F. 35
prisoner exchanges 30–32, 62–63, 70–71, 82–83, 146; *see also* Dix-Hill Cartel
prisoners of war 5, 12, 18, 61, 63, 70, 72, 74, 79, 82–83, 89, 95–96, 102, 142, 145, 159, 168–170, 172, 197
privateering 26, 42–43, 52, 84, 99, 110, 154
provost marshals 48–49, 122, 124–127, 153, 155, 184–186
Pryor, Roger A. 171, 181–182
Put-in-Bay, Ohio *14*, 28, 114, 118, 120, 130, 132; *see also* South Bass Island

Queen, William 144
Queen's Hotel (Toronto) 35, 85, 93, 97, 188

CSS *Raleigh* 81
Raven (sailboat) 57–60, 104
Richmond, Va. 2, 12, 16, 27, 29, 32, 35–36, 40–41, 44, 49, 54–57, 59, 63–64, 68–69, 71–73, 75–77, 79, 82–86, 88, 91, 99, 110, 134, 138–139, 145–151, 158, 172–173, 189, 198–199
Richmond Enquirer 54, 58
Richmond House (Chicago) 100
Richmond Theater (Va.) 59
Richmond Whig 54, 57, 59
Ridgely, Andrew S. 180
Riley, John Slick 119, 189
Riley's Hotel (Hamilton, Ont.) 34–35
Risley, Hanson 149
Ritchie, Albert 9, 180–181, 183–184, 191–192
Robertson, Adam 137
Rock Island, Ill. 12, 95, 153, 198
Roe, Francis 157
Roebling, John 164
Rush-Bagot Treaty 38, 70, 99, 136–137, 140
Russell, Lord John 38
Rutland, W.P. 161, 164

St. Albans, Vt. 138–140, 142, 155, 162, 175
St. Catherines, N.Y. 66, 86, 88, 92
St. Lawrence Hall (Montreal) 35, 92, 141–144, 147–150, 154, 190
USS *San Jacinto* 37, 135
Sanders, George 86–*87*, 91, 142–143, 187–188, 199
Sandusky, Ohio 1, 10, 12–15, *14*, 18–21, 24, 28, 30, 64, 66, 68, 98–99, 103, 107, 109–116, 118–121, 123–125, 127, 129, 131–132, 134–135, 138, 152, *153*, 154, 159, 162, 196, 200–201

Sandwich, Ontario (Canada West) 110, 114–116, *115*, 132–133
Sarnia, Ontario (Canada West) 154–155, *156*
Seddon, James A. 75–76, 83, 89, 138–140
Sentinel (Richmond) 145
Seward, William 36, 66, 93–94, 136, 139–140, 153, 187, 189
Sheehy, Barry 35, 88, 92–93, 144, 147
Shepherd, Henry E. 68, 103–104
Sheridan, Phillip 83–84, 158, 160
Skinner, Alfred 117
Slidell, John 37–38, 90
Smith, G.B. 30
Smith, Sand 58–59
Smith, Thomas 58–59
Soldiers' Home (D.C.) 94, 146
Sons of Liberty 70, 75, 88–89, 92, 95–96, 100, 126–127; *see also* Order of American Knights
South Bass Island, Ohio 13–14, 114, 129–130, 132; *see also* Put-in-Bay
South Bend, Ind. 159
Speer, William 28
Spofford, Richard S. 181
Spotsylvania, Battle of (Va.) 83
Stakes, Edward Thomas 102
Stanton, Edwin M. 25, 31, 45, 48–49, 66, 93–94, 102–103, 127, 134–136, 145, 170–172, 187, 189
"Star Spangled Banner" 60
Stedman, George C. 54
Steele, George 113
Stevens, Thaddeus 92, 181
Stidger, Felix 127
Stockdale, J.L. 62, 68
Stuart, J.E.B. 83–84, 90
Swan (sailboat) 57–60
Sweet, Benjamin 101, 104, 127

Tallman, A.L. 184–186
Tangier Inlet, Va. 59
Terry, Henry D. 103, 144
Thistle (steamer) 78–81
Thomas, David H. 164–165, 173–174
USS *Thomas Freeborn* 58
Thompson, Jacob 79, 80–81, 85–89, 91–95, 108, 112–113, 125, 136, 138, 140, 142, 147, 159, 162, 172, 187, 198–200; background 78–79; and Beall, John Yates 99, 101, 113, 137, 158, 160, 172; Canada assignment 79–80; complaints about surveillance 126; and *Georgian* 151–153, 157; plans for attacks in North 89–90, 97–98, 111, 113; relations with other commissioners 87–89, 91–95
Tidwell, William 147
Tod, David 26, 74, 103
Toledo, Ohio 12–13, 48, 113, 119–120, 152–153, 159, 201

Toronto, Ontario (Canada West) 34–35, 80, 86, 93, 95, 97, 98–99, 107–108, 111–112, 125–126, 137–138, 152–153, 155–*156*, 160–161, 164, 172, 188, 193, 195–197, 199
RMS *Trent* 37–38
Trent Affair 37–38, 135
Trimble, Isaac 112, 159
Tucker, Beverley 149, 187

Vallandigham, Clement 44, *45*, 46–47, 90, 200; arrest 50–51; background 45; in Canada 88; at Democratic Convention 96–97, 100
Verrazano Narrows Bridge (N.Y.) 169
Vicksburg, Battle of (Miss.) 32, 69, 77–78, 146
CSS *Virginia* 55
Vorhees, Daniel W. 46

Wallace, George W. 169
Walsh, Charles 88, 95, 100–101
war crimes, law of 170, 178; *see also* Lieber Code
War of 1812 14, 36, 38, 42, 60, 70, 99, 130
Warren, Fitz Henry 169, 173, 177
Washington Sentinel (D.C.) 149
Waugh, John C. 89
Weber, Jenifer L. 48
Weed, Thurlow 93, 150
Weekly Tribune 91
Welland Canal 36, 86, 152, *153*
Welles, Gideon 52, 64–66, 99, 154, 157, 195
Wells Fargo 149, 154
West, William T. 19, 21, 25, 112
West House Hotel (Ohio) 19, 112, 123, 135
Weston, S.H. 184–186
Weston, William 173–174
Wheatly, Francis L. 180–181
Wigwam amphitheater (Chicago) 96–97
Wilderness, Battle of (Va.) 83
Wilkes, Charles 37–38
Wilkinson, John 65–66
Williams, Fenwick 136
Williams, Robert 21–22
Winder, John 56
Windsor, Ontario (Canada West) 34, 51, 86, 88, 113, *115*, 122, 125, 132–133, 136, 194, 197
Winks, Robin W. 70, 137
Wise, Henry 41
Wistar, Isaac J. 58–59
Wood, Benjamin 90–91
Wood, Fernando 90–91
Wood, John Taylor 53
Wright, David M. 180

yellow fever plot 125
Yellow Tavern, Battle of (Va.) 84
Yorktown, Va. 52, 58
Young, Bennett H. 138–142